A HOME DIVIDED

Contributors

MEAD CAIN
ELEANOR R. FAPOHUNDA
NANCY FOLBRE
SUSAN GREENHALGH
JANE GUYER
HOMA HOODFAR
JOAN P. MENCHER
MONICA MUNACHONGA
HANNA PAPANEK
PATRICIA R. PESSAR
MARTHA ROLDAN
CONSTANTINA SAFILIOS-ROTHSCHILD
LAUREL SCHWEDE

A HOME DIVIDED

Women and Income in the Third World

DAISY DWYER AND **JUDITH BRUCE**
Editors

Stanford University Press   1988
Stanford, California

A Home Divided: Women and Income in the Third World
is a project of The Population Council,
carried out with support from the Rockefeller Foundation
within the framework of the Council's program of research on
the roles and status of women.

Stanford University Press
Stanford, California
© 1988 by The Board of Trustees of the
Leland Stanford Junior University
Printed in the United States of America
CIP data are at the end of the book

Acknowledgments

This volume grew out of a seminar entitled "Women, Income, and Policy" held at the Population Council in March 1983 with support from the Ford and Rockefeller Foundations. That seminar, in turn, built upon an earlier seminar organized by Daisy Dwyer on "Women and Income Control in the Third World" held at Columbia University in October 1982. The volume editors wish to thank Patricia Engle, Susan Greenhalgh, Marianne Schmink, Mayra Buvinic, as well as other colleagues too numerous to mention for their comments on an early draft of the Introduction and support through the proess of shepherding the papers into final form in the book.

D.D.
J.B.

Contents

Contributors

DAISY DWYER has a Ph.D. in anthropology from Yale and a J.D. from Columbia. Her fields of specialization are the anthropology of comparative law, women's roles, and Middle Eastern societies. She has been an Assistant and Associate Professor of Anthropology at Columbia and has published numerous articles and several books, including *Images and Self Images: Male and Female in Morocco* (Columbia University Press), and, as editor, *Law and Islam in the Middle East* (Bergin and Garvey, forthcoming).

JUDITH BRUCE is a graduate of Harvard University in anthropology. She has worked extensively in all three regions of the developing world. As a Senior Associate at the Population Council, she coordinates a program of policy-oriented research and field projects related to women's productive and reproductive roles. Under this program numerous articles, case studies, and volumes of readings for use by development scholars and practitioners have been published.

MEAD CAIN is a Senior Associate at the Center for Policy Studies of the Population Council. His current research interests are the determinants and consequences of population change in developing countries, particularly those of South Asia.

ELEANOR R. FAPOHUNDA was formerly senior lecturer in the Department of Economics, University of Lagos, and currently is on the staff of the State University of New York at Farmingdale. She has written several articles on various aspects of African women's employment problems and recently contributed to *Women and the Industrial Development Decade in Africa,* published by the African Training and Research Center for Women of the United Nations Economic Commission for Africa.

NANCY FOLBRE, Associate Professor of Economics at the University of Massachusetts, has taught at Bowdoin College and the New School for Social Research. Her primary research interests lie in the area of household production and demographic decision-making, and she has done fieldwork in Mexico, Kenya, and Zimbabwe.

SUSAN GREENHALGH is an anthropologist at the Center for Policy Studies, the Population Council. Her research focuses on social and economic processes in Asia, particularly China. She has spent several years doing field research in Taiwan and plans to do research in the People's Republic of China in the near future. In addition to gender stratification, she has published articles on demographic aspects of income distribution, the definition of the income unit, China's one-child policy, and other issues.

JANE I. GUYER is Associate Professor of Anthropology at Boston University. She was born in Britain and took her undergraduate degree at the London School of Economics and Political Science. Her Ph.D. in social anthropology is from the University of Rochester, New York. Her dissertation research was conducted in Nigeria, and her subsequent field research was in Southern Cameroon. She has published a monograph, *Family and Farm in Southern Cameroon,* and articles on colonial economic history, African agriculture, and women in African rural economies.

HOMA HOODFAR received her B.A. in economics from Teheran University, her M.A. in sociology of development from Manchester University, and her Ph.D. in social anthropology from the University of Kent. Her fields of interest and expertise are the household economy and the household decision-making and priority-setting process. She has presented papers on her research in Egypt at international meetings, and one of her studies of health and hygiene among the poor in Cairo was published through the Population Council regional papers.

JOAN P. MENCHER is Professor of Anthropology at Lehman College of the City University of New York and teaches in the City University Graduate Program. Over the period 1958 to 1985 she spent more than ten years doing fieldwork in India, especially in Kerala and Tamil Nadu, where she has worked on a wide variety of research projects. Her current interests are in the area of women and agriculture and women and income-generating projects.

MONICA L. MUNACHONGA is lecturer in sociology at the University of Zambia. She has a B.A. in sociology from the University of Zambia, and both an M.A. and an M. Phil. in sociological studies from the University of Sussex. Her field research in Zambia has been concerned with changing patterns in the distribution of power between husbands and wives within urban households. From her M. Phil. research she has the forthcoming publication "Women and Development in Zambia," in J. L. Parpart,

A. Aidoo, and G. Nikoi, eds., *Women and Development in Africa,* to be published by the University of America.

HANNA PAPANEK is Co-Director of the United Nations University's "Comparative Study of Women's Work and Family Survival Strategies in South and Southeast Asia." She is also Senior Research Associate of the Center for Asian Development Studies at Boston University. She received her Ph.D. in Social Relations from Harvard University and has conducted research on the position of women in Pakistan, Bangladesh, India, and Indonesia. She has co-edited *Women and Development: Perspectives from South and Southeast Asia,* and is the author of many scholarly articles in books and journals.

PATRICIA R. PESSAR, an anthropologist, is currently the research director of Georgetown University's Center for Immigration Policy and Refugee Assistance. She has conducted major research in Brazil, the Dominican Republic, and the United States, and has published several articles on women and migration and on labor migration within the Americas.

MARTHA ROLDAN has a Ph.D. in sociology from the University of Leiden and is currently Professor of Sociology at the University of Buenos Aires, associate researcher at Flacso (Facultad Latinoamericana de Ciencias Sociales) in Buenos Aires, as well as an activist in the women's movement. She has completed extensive research in Argentina and Mexico on issues in labor studies, class formation, and gender subordination. Her publications include *Sidicatos y Protesta Social en la Argentina, 1969–1974* (CEDLA, The Netherlands).

CONSTANTINA SAFILIOS-ROTHSCHILD received a degree in agricultural engineering from the Agricultural College of Athens and a Ph.D. in rural sociology from Ohio State University. From 1980 to 1986 she was a Senior Associate at the Population Council. She has taught in both Europe and the United States, most recently as Professor of Human Development at Pennsylvania State University. She has conducted fieldwork in all three of the developing regions of the world. Based on this work, she has published numerous articles and books in the fields of development, with an emphasis on agriculture, comparative family sociology, and the roles of men and women in different societies.

LAUREL SCHWEDE is an anthropologist who has done fieldwork in Indonesia and a survey of technical assistance projects in Somalia for the United National Development Programme. Her dissertation for Cornell University, nearing completion, is entitled "Male- and Female-Headed Household Strategies of Labor Allocation and Decision-making in a Matrilineal, Islamic Society: The Minangkabau of West Sumatra, Indonesia."

A HOME DIVIDED

Introduction

JUDITH BRUCE AND DAISY DWYER

Purpose and Overview

This volume deals with inequality and negotiation among intimates within the household unit. We view the intrahousehold distributional process and its short-term and long-term consequences through the eyes of adult women, usually mothers and workers in marital diads. The intimates with whom these women covertly or overtly negotiate are primarily husbands, but depending upon the cultural setting they may be common-law partners, parents, in-laws, patriarchs of their own or other lineages, siblings, and children. As this volume's title denotes, the currency on which we focus most closely is income. Yet there are other valued but less negotiable currencies—the bearing of children, education and training, social networking, household-based production—that determine women's position in the family and wider society. This Introduction, and indeed most of the articles contained in this volume, view women as strategic actors—whether or not they are conscious of this role—in defending or expanding their own life prospects, and often, by extension, those of their children. The issue of perception is crucial throughout the volume. How women see themselves and value what they do may in part determine the outcomes they attain.

The women in this series of papers pursue personal goals, or simple survival, in the context of stronger forces: segmented and discriminatory labor markets for which they are ill prepared; powerful family systems that use them as instruments to patriarchal or kinship ends; discriminatory customs and laws surrounding divorce and widowhood; inheritance systems that deprive them outright of assets or undermine their economic rights; and norms that confine women's roles to production and the nurturing of dependents, sometimes at the cost of all else.

We learn that women's earned income and their ability to stretch this and other resources is vital to the survival of many households. We find that men's and women's economic contributions tend to be differentially valued by others and self, a circumstance that generally works to a woman's disadvantage. We see that just as men and women differ in their participation in labor markets, in their wage rates, and in their prospects when marriages dissolve through death or separation, men and women also frequently differ with respect to allocational priorities.

Seeking Appropriate Household Models

These observations suggest that various theories which treat the household as a unit, thereby ignoring the possibility of internal conflicts or positing a single overriding decision maker, must be reappraised. These constructs of household behavior—most prominently that of the New Household Economics (see Becker 1981)—are deficient, not only because they fail to acknowledge intrahousehold negotiation over assets and possibly severe inequalities within households, but because they tend to separate gender dynamics at the microeconomic level from the known external dimensions of gender differentiation and asset distribution. The empirical evidence in these chapters suggests that alternative visions of household dynamics may be more apt. For example, Nash (1953) and Manser and Brown (1979) promote the notion of a bargaining household in which members almost formally contend and exchange to gain their individual ends. This model has been revised and set in a poverty context by Sen (1985), who defines these households as experiencing "cooperative conflict." According to Sen's interpretation, individuals within the household contend, but in many cases cannot bargain in the precise sense of this word because individual utilities may overlap in some areas, because perceptions of self-interest and self-worth are indistinctly defined (an issue of extreme importance to women), and finally because in poor economies the ends to be attained are often fundamental elements of survival, not simply "utilities" such as satisfaction, pleasure, and so on (Sen 1985, paras. 21 to 27).

The propositions of Sen, Nash, and Manser and Brown seem reasonable, and certainly most people who are members of families have experienced differences of opinion over how money and other resources are spent. Why then has the unified household been such a consistently attractive formulation? The first powerful reason is the simplicity with which households as a unit, in contrast to individuals, may be integrated into economic decision making. Unified households are convenient policy tools. Located within wider social and economic institutions, they become manipulable economic entities. The New Household Economics approach acknowledges one central decisionmaker per household, and makes an implicit analogy between the household and the firm. As Folbre states in the last paper of this volume, according to this theory, the household is made to interface with a marketplace "deploy[ing] labor in response to differences between marginal production between home and market" (Folbre, p. 251).

A second point of resistance to conducting a search into the internal decision-making processes of households is skepticism that such potentially demanding research will bring with it explanatory powers far beyond those of the current model. What difference does the discovery of multiple decisionmakers with different agendas make if the outcome is still predicted by the unified household model? However, it appears that this is not always the case. Some authors (Dey 1983, Rogers 1983, Blumberg 1986) have documented unexpected and unproductive outcomes of development efforts likely best understood by taking into account the intrahousehold allocation process. What explains the agricultural production project which simultaneously raises household incomes, leads women to withdraw labor on their key cash crops, and results in declines in nutrition and other welfare indicators? Differences between households cannot explain these effects fully; internal gender relations over income may.

Finally, the assumption that households behave as economically rational units is not only analytically simpler to handle, but suits practical tastes as well. Policy makers, in both industrialized and developing countries, often prefer to direct resource flows and benefits to the household as a unit or to the nominal household head. They stand clear of the issue of internal distribution, possibly assuming it will prove difficult to develop mechanisms to deliver benefits to specific individuals within households. The household can be complicated to understand. Descriptions of household dynamics differ according to the person reporting them. Yet, standard survey methodologies do not assist us in accurately viewing the household and locating economic authority in it when adult males are mechanically identified as heads of household. These adult males, when present, are often exclusively interviewed about sources and overall levels of household income. Their welfare is too often taken as a proxy for the welfare of all household members.

Supporting the analytic and practical impetus to consolidate individuals into households is a strong psychological bias. The family, especially the marital relationship, is viewed as a sanctum protected from the conflicts that characterize virtually all other social institutions. This bias, however comforting, is also incorrect. Since men's and women's access to and control of resources differ systematically in the wider world—the external world of income relations—why would their personal economies be served by a common groundplan in the internal world of income relations? By reviewing some of the recent literature on adult men's and women's social and economic experience, we may see how utterly profound the distinction between the male and female spheres is, and therefore how unlikely it is that men's and women's needs and interests will fully accord within the intimacy of family and marriage.

Men's and Women's Contrasting Lives

Economic Contribution

In recent years, it has become important to establish what women contribute to familiy and society through household and market production.* Over the last thirty years, there has been a steady upward trend in the participation of women in the labor market in developing countries. Though still afflicted by the serious problems of underenumeration (Rec-, chini de Lattes and Wainerman 1981), the official rate of female labor participation in 1985 was 32 percent. A more important fact to consider is that the rate of growth of women's labor-force participation since 1950 has outstripped the rise in male workers by two to one (Joekes 1987). Apart from this, it has been established that women's compensated labor combined with household production renders them substantial and sometimes predominant economic contributors in all the developing regions of the world. This is true even in areas such as South Asia where cultural prescriptions mask women's productivity.† For example, it was recently estimated that Indian women contribute—exclusive of their services as housewives—36 percent of India's net domestic product (Mukerjee 1985).

Women's increased labor-force participation does not necessarily bring with it reductions in occupational segregation. In agricultural economies in the developing world, women tend to be concentrated in specific task areas that require long hours and very hard labor (transplanting rice, harvesting certain crops, post-harvest food preparation for market) (see Mencher, this volume). In formal labor structures, in both industrialized and developing countries, women are often confined to a limited range of fields. In a study of occupational assignment by gender and migration status in Thailand and Indonesia—two developing countries where women's economic participation is well accepted and visible—Smith (1981) found an extreme sex-specific allocation of occupation. Using a schedule of 38 occupational categories, he found significant female concentration among salespersons, cooks, maids, spinners, tailors, and teachers. In industrialized countries, it is well established that occupational segregation exists by race and sex. Even in Sweden, with its official ideology of greater gender equality, out of 270 occupational categories, more than 40 percent of women were in just five jobs: secretary, nurse's aide, sales worker, cleaner, and children's nurse (Sivard 1985).

*Beneria ed. (1982); Leacock ed. (1984); *Signs* (Summer 1979, Autumn 1979); Buvinic, Lycette, and McGreevy (1983); Boserup (1970); Agarwal (1981); Dixon (1978); Dixon (1982).

†Cain (1978); Abdullah and Zeidenstein (1981); Ahmad and Loufti (1982); Cain, Khanam, and Nahar (1979); Maher (1981).

Women subsidize economic progress in at least four ways: through their underemployment, their unemployment, their willingness to go in and out of the labor market, and their low wages. Women carry the gross share of part-time employment worldwide. In addition to the generally accepted observation that much of their productive work is uncompensated by wages, their hourly earnings in sectors like manufacturing compare unfavorably to men's. As reported in a survey of nine developing countries, women earned between 50 percent (South Korea) and 80 percent (Burma) of the wages of men who are comparably employed (Sivard 1985). A review of rural women's income conducted by the International Labor Organization reveals that women sometimes earned as little as one-third to one-fifth of the wages earned by men for work of equal or greater difficulty (Ahmad and Loufti 1982).

Allocation of Income

A central impetus to women's earning—attaining a better life for their children, which many may view as an extension of "good mothering" (Engle 1986)—may explain the allocational priorities they apply to their own income and other income that they control. Though this subject is difficult to research, a considerable body of information has built up on it in the last decade (Blumberg 1988). Kumar's study (1977) in Kerala, India, indicated that a child's nutritional level correlated positively with the size of the mother's income, food inputs from subsistence farming, and the quality of available family-based child care. Significantly, children's nutritional level did not increase in direct proportion to increases in paternal income. An expanding number of studies and project evaluations in Jamaica (Horton and Miller n.d.), St. Lucia (Knudsen and Yates 1981), Ghana (Tripp 1981), Kenya (Carloni 1987), Botswana (Carloni 1987), Sri Lanka (Benson and Emmert 1977), and another multi-village study in Guatemala (Blumberg 1986) strongly indicate a greater devotion of women's income than men's to everyday subsistence and nutrition.

Gender-based responsibilities are most explicit in Africa. In some societies, husbands are responsible for the provision of lodgings, children's tuition, and other educational costs. Providing income for food and clothing for children may vary as a male or female/male joint obligation. However, almost universally, women in Africa are viewed as ultimately responsible for fulfilling children's food needs (Nelson 1981). At issue is not simply the ways in which women's income is used, but the degree to which men and women differ in taking personal spending money from their earnings. Though the specifics of women's consumption responsibilities vary (in Africa and across the world), it is quite commonly found that gender ideologies support the notion that men have a right to personal spending money, which they are perceived to need or deserve, and that women's income is for collective purposes (Young 1987).

This building knowledge of the specific destinations of women's income was initially obscured by a larger debate about the possible losses to children's welfare of mothers working outside the home (Leslie 1987). This debate initially arose in industrialized countries, but it has been translated into the question succinctly posed by Engle (1986), "Can children's needs be met when their mothers work for cash income in Third World countries?" It should first be observed that many women have no choice about earning income. And research has begun to spell out in remarkable detail positive developmental impacts. Wilson (1981) noted that the children of "working" mothers have more adequate home diets at eighteen and thirty months than same-aged children of non-working mothers in a set of Guatemalan villages studied. Recent research by Engle (1987), also in Guatemala, confirmed the positive contribution of maternal earnings (of non-domestic workers) to the welfare of one- to two-year-olds, and noted that, "two-year-old children of working mothers were significantly heavier than non-workers' children" (Engle n.d., p. 2).

Fertility Decision Making

Although it sometimes appears that women's decisions about production and reproduction are fluidly linked, in fact women may be seeking a balance between two areas in which they have little freedom of choice: enhancing their access to income and implementing the preferences they may have about their own fertility. It has been argued that men consistently want more children than women because women bear a far greater burden for the production of children while men gain a disproportionate share of the benefits. The part of this argument most relevant to this volume is not women's right to choose the number of children they want (however desirable), but the way in which having or not having children fits into women's negotiations for survival.

Mason and Taj (1987) have illuminated this debate by laying out a set of four reasons why women may desire fewer children than men in traditional societies characterized by high fertility and mortality: (1) the risk of morbidity and mortality associated with pregnancy, birth, and lactation; (2) the social and economic costs of child rearing; (3) the lower likelihood that women will gain the benefits of children because of inheritance patterns and systematic sex bias; and (4) the assertion that high fertility may enhance men's position in part because it helps them maintain the dominance over women so preoccupied with many children. In reviewing the reasons why women may wish to have *more* children than men, Mason and Taj cite Cain (a contributor to this volume), whose work suggests that female fertility goals may exceed male goals—especially their desire for sons—as a hedge against their risk and insecurity in social systems that guarantee women's access to economic resources only through sons. It is further likely that many women view motherhood as conferring on them a valued social role, and much literature documents the utilitarian assistance that children provide mothers.

As both sets of reasons imply, the factors that men and women consider in defining preferences are likely to contrast, even when their preferred numbers agree. Women's unique role in childbearing and rearing, and the risks and benefits therein entailed, is possibly the most fundamental distinction between their experience and that of men.

Time Use

This leads us to a related topic. Fairly consistently, women in all parts of the world put in more work hours (paid and unpaid) than do men of the same age. Gender-differentiated time use occurs from early childhood through old age. Most critically, becoming a parent has a significant effect on women's time use and very little on men's. For certain developing societies, there are data which indicate that the addition of children reduces the already small amount of time a man spends in child care while typically erasing leisure and reducing the sleep time of women to a biological minimum (King and Evenson 1983). The tenacity of this gender-differentiated system of time use is most striking when one considers middle-class couples in industrialized countries where both spouses are full-time members of the work force, and where substitute child care during the parents' work hours can be purchased. Based on a study in the United States, Hill and Stafford (1980) conclude that "the overall impressions [are] that college-educated women make substantial re-allocations of time to direct child care . . . that they sacrifice personal free time and sleep to avoid an excessively large reduction in market hours. . . . [O]verall, the time use response of men to the presence of children in the household is minor" (p. 229).

Let us return for a moment to the New Household Economics model as depicted by Folbre. Under this theory, economically rational household units make decisions about fertility: "Decisions about family size are influenced by changes in the price of children due to increases in production costs such as education . . . or the increased cost of opportunity time devoted to child care" (Folbre, this volume, p. 251). These time-use data suggest that the decision making about these tradeoffs is not located in the household, but is rather the near-exclusive domain of the mother, who balances the conflict between market work and child care by reducing sleep and leisure.

Another aspect of these data worth pondering is the degree to which men and women do different things at different times of the day, and how few tasks are shared. If we analyzed individual time use at a distance, not knowing that the personalities under study were members of the same household and viewing time use like monetary investment as an economic choice, we would likely conclude that men and women belong to distinct social and economic groups, and sometimes would have difficulty regarding their behavior as cooperative or even linked. Does this segmentation of experience affect men's and women's perceptions of themselves, their partners, and the transactions between them? Devaki Jain (1985) suggests that it may. In *Tyranny of the Household,* she states that in poverty, "lives by necessity get acutely segregated both in space and in task, and to that extent, perceptions are limited to personal experience" (p. xiii). If this is so, then men and women of poor households have even less in the way of an overlapping agenda, and less opportunity to plan and live cooperatively than those in better-off households. Plausibly, the segmentation of household members' experience is one reason why poverty is likely to intensify age- and gender-based inequalities. Thus, the recent school of analysts exploring "household survival strategies" may find that what appears to be an adaptive, even finely tuned, balancing of household resources is actually the uneasy aggregate of individual survival strategies (Schmink 1984).

Perception

This leads us to the final subject this volume tentatively, and far from conclusively, explores: Do women see their dilemma, their disadvantage, and if so, do they consciously negotiate, bargain, or exchange to achieve ends? The literature already reviewed establishes widespread asset/income and social/institutional inequality between men and women. Yet the behaviors and feelings of the women portrayed in these chapters do not consistently reveal a discomfort with their lot. In some cases, women respond with apparently unconcerned acquiescence. In other cases, they openly conflict with partners and refuse to continue in the framework of the family. What role does self-esteem play in assisting women to mobilize external strengths (such as outside wages, the persuasion of kin, community opinion) to change their situation? Within Sen's (1985) cooperative conflict paradigm, "perception itself is one of the important *parameters* in the determination of intrafamily divisions and inequalities." If a woman undervalues herself, her bargaining position will be weaker, and she will be likely to accept inferior conditions. Outside earning provides both a psychological and practical leverage for her. It gives her (1) a better fallback position should negotiations break down (e.g., divorce); (2) an enhanced ability to deal with threats and indeed to use threats (e.g., leaving the house); and (3) a higher "perceived" contribution to the family economic position as perceived by her and others (see paras. 21 to 27).

The implication of this is that fundamental change for women cannot be based solely on increased earning. This resonates with the views of feminist theorists who have identified collective action as a primary step for women in achieving personal power and status in the public domain (Safilios-Rothschild 1982, Sanday 1974). Sanday's cross-cultural analysis of female status identified four indicators of high status, the most important of which—superseding female material control—is the existence of female solidarity groups. An empirical support for this analysis is the impressiveness of women's organizations in South Asia, specifically India and Bangladesh (Jain 1974, Sewa 1975, Chen 1984). Their achievements extend beyond enhancing the material prospects of the participants, to effecting changes in women's outlooks, increasing their freedom within the family unit, and enabling them to mobilize vital community resources, gaining access to literacy classes, a voice in community government, and so forth. Jain (1985) observes an *interplay* between the familial and extrafamilial: "The scene of women's advancement seems to be the household and . . . household's perception and evaluation of women's role, its hierarchy, its monetary and non-monetary sources of power" (p. 8). But key in changing the dynamics within the household are extrafamilial experiences which permit women an opportunity to see themselves differently, to become discomforted with their subordinated status, and empowered to confront and transform the aspects of family and income relations that oppress them. Women may need to become strengthened even beyond this point to effectively use direct and bilateral strategies of negotiation rather than less risky and often less effective unilateral or indirect means (Falbo and Peplau 1980). What remains to be detailed is how women transit to consciousness in their income relations with intimates, and what strategies they preferentially employ.

Volume Highlights

The contributors to this volume represent a range of perspectives and disciplines (economics, sociology, demography, and anthropology) that need to be brought to bear if we are to understand household arrangements and the potential role that the use of income plays in confirming or altering those arrangements. Though viewing gender and household dynamics through different disciplinary lenses, each author presents information about women's bargaining context. This entails defining (1) the broad cultural, socioeconomic, and production structures within which women function; (2) the prevailing intrahousehold framework of asset and income distribution; (3) the intimates with whom a woman must deal in pursuit of priorities that she holds for herself or her dependents; and (4) the outcome of the intrahousehold allocation process.

The papers are grouped by region, moving geographically through Asia, Africa, the Middle East, and Latin America, and moving in parallel fashion across family systems. The functional effects that family systems have on women's access to and control over resources are powerful in all parts of the world, but they are revealed especially clearly in the papers on Asia. At the extreme of female dependence, Cain describes women's range of choices in rural South Asia, as these occur in contrasting villages in Bangladesh and India. In Bangladesh in particular, women's access to income-earning opportunities is severely limited; their legal inheritance rights are generally forfeited, their chances of becoming widows (because of age differentials between spouses at marriage) are a near certainty; their risk of divorce is moderate though emotionally salient; and their control by patriarchal structures is extreme. These women must reproduce to survive. Sons are especially valuable: they are long-term risk insurance, and widows maintain a stake in their deceased husband's property largely through sons' productive activities and status.

The papers describing women in Taiwan, Indonesia, and India (including Cain's analysis of women's experience in selected Indian villages) indicate that these women fare somewhat better than their Bangladeshi sisters. In Taiwan, the powerful multigenerational patriarchal family concentrates power in older males who invest heavily in the income-earning power of their sons. In her paper, Greenhalgh recounts how Taiwanese parents create differential contracts with male and female children. Male children are bound by a longer and somewhat looser contract of obligation. They must achieve and earn over the long term to support and honor their aging parents. Females leave the family at marriage and so must repay their debt for nurturance and education before they are absorbed into their husbands' families. Greenhalgh contends that this system has operated in the presence of modern educational and employment opportunities to increase girls' educational attainment and their participation in formal wage labor, but that it has not resulted in an increasingly autonomous younger generation of females. Rather, she argues that the participation of young women in export-oriented production lines is a modernized version of an older family strategy that increases the value of sons' contributions to parents by using the income generated by their sisters to pay for and prolong the sons' education. Within the currently observed intergenerational contract, women's earning opportunities give them little new power and perhaps have served to subjugate them longer if not more severely.

Papanek and Schwede illuminate the mediating effects of the bilateral kinship system that characterizes parts of Indonesia. Their view is that the bilateral kinship system exerts less control over women than an extended unilateral family system, expands women's access to the labor market, permits and in some cases rewards two-earner families, and allows higher rates of divorce and remarriage than are commonly seen in Asia. By long-standing tradition, women are also the money managers of the family and men appear to turn over an unusually high proportion of their earnings to women. Women further participate to a notable extent in extrafamilial saving schemes, which benefit the household economy by aggregating sums of money for large expenditures in crisis while also giving women a means of controlling income outside the household.

Family systems are part of a broader scheme of constraints on women in Asia. Mencher, describing income levels and relations in landless families in Tamil Nadu and Kerala, focuses attention on women's limited access to sex-segregated rural labor markets. Her richest data demonstrate the percentages of male and female income devoted to the family and the degree to which these covary. She documents that in a variety of poor classes in fourteen different villages, women consistently devote a higher proportion of their income (nearly 100 percent) to family needs than do men. Men withhold some portion of their wages for personal use even when overall income is clearly inadequate. Mencher's data challenge the hypothesis that men's and women's income contributions are worked out cooperatively. And though it is sometimes alleged that men contribute more of their earnings when women are earning less, Mencher's data show that fluctuations in men's contributions to the household go in unexpected directions. Men tend to make higher contributions to the household budget in both relative and absolute terms when women are earning the most. Curiously, they do not usually increase their contributions in times of stress (when women are finding less work or have just given birth to a child). A man's income contribution to the household varies, in most cases, not with need in the family but with his own income. Most men subtract a constant amount of income for personal use. The consequences of this pattern are potentially serious in communities where infant mortality is high, where all families live very close to the edge of poverty, and where malnutrition is common. Mencher's final discussion also notes that planned new production techniques will bypass the poorest women and men and concentrate new technologies in the hands of a minority of men. Under present circumstances, any reduction in the income that women earn and devote to the family is liable to affect their survival.

Hoodfar's paper, the sole description of a Middle Eastern society, depicts life in a congested low-income neighborhood of Cairo. Male and female role ascriptions emerge as more powerful in this setting than kinship or religious structures in creating men's and women's differential modes of handling income. Hoodfar locates the power issues in a series of different income-pooling arrangements,* and she highlights the very different domains—spatial as well as economic—of men and women. Typically, men and women do not share income information. The man gives what he gives and the woman makes do. "Making do" or "stretching the wage" may require wives to change spending patterns, to deprive themselves or others of vital resources, or to earn some money on the side. What is striking in this paper is how much women "manage" without consulting their husbands, and how little men know of their wives' coping strategies. Hoodfar's observations resonate with those of Whitehead (1981), who describes how men in West Africa, absent from the home, remove themselves from the knowledge of the needs of children ("from the children's cries for food," as Whitehead dramatically puts it) as well as from community pressure to contribute more. The male world of coffee shops, movies, and work away from the neighborhood is also contrasted with the confined and impoverished environment of the women, who may not leave the small geographic territory of the district during their entire lives. Men's "outside" world can claim a sometimes substantial portion of their earnings and may loosen their personal and social contracts to provide materially and emotionally for their families. This description, when combined with what we know of the increasing migration of men, suggests an often forgotten dimension of male/female differentials—that of spatial separation, daily and long-term; men and women are literally moving in different worlds.

It is perhaps when approaching Africa that development scholars and practitioners see most distinctly the shortcomings of current theories of household dynamics. Africa's kinship structures, household forms of behavior, and decision-making patterns are astonishingly diverse and generally at variance with both Western and Asian patterns. Among the most striking features are the visibility of women in key economic activities, the explicitness of differential male and female income streams within the household, high fertility despite considerable marital instability, a lower marriage rate (observed in parts of the continent), and, in the traditional setting, the strength of natal or kinship ties over conjugal loyalties. The recognition of the high degree of separateness of male and female economic spheres, including women's dominance in subsistence agriculture, was one of the sparks to scholarly interest in women's roles in development. The poverty of sub-Saharan Africa, the famines, and the unique

*For detailed discussion and codification of income-pooling arrangements and their implications, see Young 1987 and Pahl 1983.

demographic dynamics of this continent have made it a priority region for bi- and multilateral assistance programs. A fuller understanding of women's roles, including women's authority over income and their production incentives, is essential if Africa's primary problems—food security and the highest fertility and child-mortality rates in the world—are to be resolved.

In her paper on Africa, Fapohunda uses African family patterns to advantage when examining the validity of key tenets of the New Household Economics, a theory rooted in Western concepts of household and family. She states, "Theoretically, the challenge to social scientists is . . . to consider the characteristics and functioning of heterogeneous, nonpooling domestic units, perhaps viewing the household with a unified budget as a special case" (Fapohunda, p. 153). She raises three important questions: "What are the economic benefits of income pooling and joint expenditure planning? What are the risks associated with such behavior for each spouse? How do these risks vary among socioeconomic environments and over time?" Fapohunda's findings demonstrate that the paradigm of a cooperatively executed household economy is not empirically valid in any of the three communities studied.

Guyer's paper explores some of the same theoretical ground. She critiques the research approaches to domestic budgeting with special emphasis on West Africa before analyzing her own data from the Cameroons. Whereas she notes that early studies (some almost 40 years old) had the advantage of conceptualizing intrahousehold relations particularly (sometimes almost wholly) through income behavior, most applied the concept of a single household expenditure plan. Although this analytic approach turned up differences between male-headed and female-headed households, the resulting analysis was limited in that it cast women's "unusual" behavior as earners and spenders purely in terms of their class positions rather than illuminating gender-specific economies. Guyer rights the balance, finding both class-related aspects in household spending and distinctive male and female economies within households. Male/female economic relations are portrayed as dynamic at both the community and the household levels. Women's earning opportunities are broadly linked to those of men—that is, when male occupational profiles and activities change, women's economic choices take advantage of or accommodate to these shifts. Over the long term, women are disadvantaged in their access to better-paying employment and modern productive techniques. As women's income falls relative to men's, or as the structural features of the general economy and society change (e.g., school fees rise, or the balance of income produced by cocoa sales versus food sales changes), women may seek to "renegotiate" the level and destination of their male partners' earnings.

Munachonga examines income allocation and control systems within changing marriage forms in the emerging middle classes of urban Zambia. Like Cain and Greenhalgh, she frames her analysis in terms of women's inheritance and property rights and women's formal and informal contracts with husbands and kin. Her descriptions of women's prospects in emerging urban Africa are quite pessimistic. There appears to be little observance of women's traditional rights in recently established ordinances and codes. Government policies affecting employment, education, income taxes, and housing reinforce and in some cases establish women's inferior status in the household. Although there are some new and uniquely African additions to these policies, Munachonga traces the history of the patterns from colonial times. Independence has brought educational policies that are nominally more equitable, yet decades of explicit discrimination against women's education must be overcome, and current curricula stress the domestic arts rather than job training for women. In Munachonga's description of urbanized Africa, it is suggested that the majority of women will seek status and security—however uncertain—through marriage. Even then, the working wife (managing a salary that reflects her gender more than her qualifications) finds that her traditional work obligations toward her husband have been reinterpreted in the urban context to mean that the husband owns her earnings. In reviewing differential financial arrangements, Munachonga finds "a continuum representing degrees of male control of money within the home." Traditional obligations to kin are factored into an equation that is reformulated in modern terms. For example, she recounts a story of one couple in her sample who called in representatives of each of their kin groups when either spouse bought a major household item "to explain who had bought and therefore owned the item" (Munachonga, this volume, p. 193). All this is necessary because current law does not provide women with property rights in case of divorce.

The three papers on Latin American societies describe the ways in which women's earning activities and women's own views of their income rights reflect rapidly changing, but still conflict-ridden, male/female relations. Safilios-Rothschild and Pessar explore shifts in household income relations in the context of significant policy-promoted economic changes: agrarian reform in Honduras, in the former case, and Dominican migration to the United States, in the latter. Safilios-Rothschild sees a missed opportunity to improve women's access to the country's chief resource, productive land, in a reformist environment that has extended direct rights in land to the men of farming couples but not to the women, and, that, while affirming the rights of female-headed households to land as a matter of policy, has denied them administratively. Her data have the special feature of allowing a comparison of men's and women's accounts of women's income. The majority of men underestimate their wives' economic contributions, a finding that should be of great interest to those who rely on a single informant for data on family income. Safilios-Rothschild sees a tendency to minimize women's contribution as part of a larger strategy of upholding the ideal of the male breadwinner, which in turn validates the broader system of sexual stratification. The greater these earnings are relative to the male's, the more likely they are to be underestimated. However, women themselves find it notoriously difficult to report their earnings accurately because of the irregularity of those earnings and the form they take; thus, to some degree, women collaborate in the obfuscation of female contributions.

Pessar reveals the intricacy of negotiations between spouses who have migrated from the Dominican Republic to the United States. The value of the new social context, which includes expanded earning opportunities for and an increased measure of monetary control by women, is clearly perceived by women, who are reluctant to return home in many cases. Among other indications of women's expanded power, Pessar documents a profound change in budgetary allocation patterns in Dominican households after migration. The conflict over this changing authority resulted in fourteen U.S. divorces among the 55 women in her sample. Women's new interests are to build their personal stake in the United States and to delay their return home, whereas husbands stress the importance of saving for that return and look forward to it with the elevated status of direct producer or owner of a business. Pessar's chapter calls into question the gender-blind models of migration that focus on household behavior and fail to inquire into the interplay of male and female interests that influence migration choices.

Roldan also addresses the theoretical limits of current household modeling, including neo-Marxist frameworks that have recently stressed household survival strategies and have assumed that "the family works to maximize its benefits to all, and each, of its members." She states, "My research on these topics follows from different theoretical premises. . . . Any analysis of distributional intrahousehold processes must be sensitive to the contradictory pressures exerted by the supportive and the oppressive elements involved in family interaction."

The women described by Pessar, Safilios-Rothschild, and Roldan, emerging out of different historical contexts, are a long way from their Asian sisters in the degree to which patriarchal systems envelop them. Yet they are also oppressed. Kinship pressures or parental support are weak elements in their economic framework. If they directly confront husbands over income, their way of life is threatened, but they do not face the literal loss of livelihood that divorce and widowhood can mean, for example, in Bangladesh. Rather, they are controlled by their lesser access to market activities, by their socialization into constricting norms of reproductive and nurturing behavior, and by male manifestations of disapproval that can include violence against them. There is an exit for these women, but it is at a great cost.

Pessar's women have found some leeway through migration abroad. Roldan's and Safilios-Rothschild's women are circumscribed in their attempts to negotiate greater authority for themselves by policy directives and economic structures that consistently give men the edge in earning and lay out few explicit responsibilities for men in supporting children. Roldan's women appease the men in their households for the moment, and use their earnings not as leverage but as a means to contain conflict by reducing the frequency with which they must ask for money or argue over expenditures. Roldan reports, "family interaction is fraught with friction." Forty of the 53 wives studied reported very frequent discussions and quarrels over shortages of money, wives' "faulty" administration (as husbands put it), children's discipline, and husbands' drinking, unfaithfulness, and jealousy. Violence was frequent, and surprisingly, 32 of the wives thought their marriage was a failure. Half of them had separated at one point or another in their married lives. Why did they return to their husbands? They mention several needs: economic protection for themselves and their children, social protection in a sexist society, and "a father's discipline to keep children straight" (Roldan, p. 245).

The situation of Roldan's and Safilios-Rothschild's women could be altered rapidly if women's access to labor markets was broadened, wages were made more equitable, and more explicit attention was given to women's property rights as heads of households and as productive partners in nominally male-headed households.

Folbre's paper is a theoretical summation. Should the empirical information offered in the preceding chapters fail in deconstructing the myth of the unified household, Folbre's analysis takes another route to convince the reader. She traces the persistence of unitary household constructs, as well as notions of altruism and cooperation within the family, through conventional economic theories that are diametrically opposed. She asks, "Why are both the neoclassical and the Marxian paradigms so silent on the issue of inequality within the home?" She identifies altruism within the family as an element of both the New Household Economics and evolved Marxist approaches and asserts that "it is entirely inconsistent to argue that individuals who are wholly selfish in the market (where there are no interdependent utilities) are wholly selfless within the family where they pursue the interests of the collectivity" (p. 252). Folbre's concern with the interplay of divergent male/female interests is unusual among economists. Indeed, Folbre's contribution is crucial here because it works its way through the economic literature to substantiate a revised link of theory to policy by observing that "the possibility that inequalities are partly a function of economic factors wreaks havoc with the traditional approach" (p. 256).

The Link to Policy

Understanding individual income streams within the household is analytically important for deciphering the determinants of economic change at both the upper and the lower ends of the economic spectrum. When monitoring the health and welfare of low-income groups, it becomes crucial for the policy maker to see the link between the earning and spending priorities of women and their roles as daily financial managers of the household and as primary guardians of the physical and social status of their children. Household authority patterns and norms may act to reduce the potential benefits to women of these economic opportunities by, for example, insisting that women take differential responsibility for children (and sometimes older dependents). There tends not to be a reciprocal pressure on men to contribute more to the family as their income increases; on the contrary, men may keep their bargaining edge by deciding what externally derived benefits are to be passed on to the household, and to what degree. Men serve as unacknowledged gatekeepers between the family and purportedly gender-blind new economic opportunities.

The forging of an appropriate theoretical link between macro-level policy and micro-level impacts (at the household and subhousehold level) could enlighten debates about development policy, such as the current controversy about the impact of economic readjustment (e.g., changes in debt structure and internal pricing policies) on the poor. The debate—in its most simplified form—engages the economists (generally working within a neoclassical framework with its presumptive unified household) and other social scientists who tend to be more sensitive to the interclass and intrahousehold distributional effects of economic policy. A third set of actors, also part of this debate, are the welfare planners who act principally through health and nutrition interventions.

These three groups diagnose and treat differently, but their models of the household are similar in assuming cooperation between the adult males and adult females. Economists help their households principally by increasing the earnings of the main breadwinner. It is assumed that income the male breadwinner earns from newly created employment opportunities will be distributed to his family. The degree to which this income will leak out for other purposes is not formally considered, nor is the degree of actual attachment of the economically benefited males to the needy females and children. The second group, the social theorists, more attuned to the distributional effects of macroeconomic policies, are alert to decreases in real wealth; they look for polarization within societies and the creation of new class disparities. Their sensitivity to increasing class differentiation and divisions within communities has often not been extended to a concern with what happens inside the household in times of stress. The third group, the health and welfare theorists and activists, have fewer resources and a good deal less in the way of policy instruments at their command; in effect, they take on "the women" as their agents. The invisible women of the economic theorists become the all-powerful mothers (within families and household units) of the health advocates. It is believed that these women, with more knowledge (but little more time or money), can heal, reconstitute, and fortify their children, although the underlying cause of much of the illness—inadequate nutrition owing to low incomes—cannot be dealt with at the level of health interventions.

One final point is worth noting when considering policy approaches: households are not permanent. By virtue of marrying men many years their senior, women in many settings face the near-certainty of widowhood and, in most cases, ensuing poverty. Women in many other societies face abandonment, extended separation, or divorce as a likely occurrence at some point in their lives. An already high, and in some settings rapidly increasing, proportion of women begin their families as pregnant adolescents without committed partners. Women's lifetime risks of being on their own are masked by survey classifications of family types that greatly underenumerate female-headed households (Buvinic, Youssef, and Von Elm 1978). Even according to the existing classification techniques and cross-sectional information, as many as one-third of the households in the world are woman-headed; in some communities, the recorded figure is as high as 50 percent.* An important missing piece of knowledge is how many women pass through a phase in their lives when they are the primary or sole economic support of young children.

The policy message of this volume may distill down to the proposition that individuals rather than households should be the recipients of economic outlays, whether those take the form of transfers or wage-earning opportunities, with women being more appropriate recipients when certain ends are desired. Cultural designation of some obligations as male or as female especially points to the appropriateness of directing allocations to

---

*Kossoudji and Mueller (1983), Massiah (1980), and Chaney, Simmons, and Staudt (1979) provide their own estimate of the incidence of female-headedness, and see the pattern as basic to roughly one-third to two-fifths of the world's rural households.

specific individuals. In cases where it can be determined that resources coming into the household are likely to be spent unproductively with regard to the well-being of target groups, allocations of aid might be directed to women outside the household. Women's cooperatives and women's informal savings unions can be regarded as possible mechanisms to protect income for use in meeting critical needs.

Policies that earmark individual recipients for aid rather than the household as a unit are not necessarily discordant with the goals of family maintenance or strengthening. In fact, insofar as male heads of household have been de facto "individual" recipients of development allocations, our proposal is not a radical departure. Moreover, the precise delineation of recipients may reinforce, in a positive sense, differentiation regarding areas of responsibility that indigenous households already make.

We hope the information in this volume will serve scholars and policy makers alike. We have seen that men and women are distinctive in their economic access, and similarly have distinct self-interest within the family. Male and female goals within nuclear and intergenerational households are typically pursued not through playing out cooperative plans, but rather through institutionalized inequalities. We argue for attention to these facts in pursuit of equality and economic progress. At the very least, the information in this volume suggests that to the many fault lines* along which social changes are monitored, the economic condition of male and female within the same household should be added.

* We gratefully acknowledge this phrasing as Hanna Papanek's and Laurel Schwede's in "Women Are Good with Money: Earning and Managing in an Indonesian City," this volume.

The Material Consequences of Reproductive Failure in Rural South Asia

An earlier paper described the pattern of family formation and dissolution in rural Bangladesh, the demographic sources of variation in the course of the life cycle, and their implications for the economic mobility of households (Cain 1978). Given the high-risk environment of Bangladesh, that paper suggested three ways in which economic mobility can be influenced by the course of the household life cycle, all of which revolve around the timely production of sons. The first is through the cumulative value of children's labor net of the costs that they engender. While children of both sexes begin work at young ages, the division of labor is such that boys are far more productive than girls. Thus the producer/consumer ratio depends as much on the sex of children as their ages, and households with a higher proportion of sons have better prospects for mobility. The second link to mobility is through sons as insurance against risk. Here the cumulative product of child labor is less important than the presence of sons during crises that threaten a household with property loss: a debilitating illness that strikes the household head, for example, or a natural disaster that destroys the crop. A son may help to avert property loss through distress sales by filling in for a sick father or permitting the diversification of income sources. A third link, a special case of the second, is distinguished because the crisis, or potential crisis, is occasioned by the death of the patriarch and thus the dissolution of the household. In the absence of a mature son, survivors are at substantial risk of economic decline during the transitional period, because of the insecurity of property rights and the appalling vulnerability of women in this society.

It was further argued that these links between demographic processes and economic mobility contribute to economic polarization in rural areas. Evidence was presented to suggest that fewer children of the poor survive to maturity and that those who do survive leave their parents' households at an earlier age. Other evidence shows that the poor exhibit lower fertility rates than the wealthy. Moreover, as indicated by the incidence of widowhood, poor adult males experience higher mortality than do the more wealthy. Consequently, the poor should face a higher risk of property loss and economic decline during intermittent periods of economic crisis and at the time of household dissolution. The poor are further disadvantaged because they accrue proportionally less child labor, the labor of their children is less productive, and they exert less control over their children.

The combination of a harsh physical and social environment and extreme economic dependence creates special hazards for women in Bangladesh (Cain, Khanam, and Nahar 1979). Under ideal demographic circumstances, a woman's progression through life is marked by the successive transfer of her dependency from one category of male to another: father, husband, and finally son. As a dependent member of a male-headed household, a woman's fortunes are determined by the forces that govern household mobility. This in itself is an unenviable situation: a woman has little control over decisions that most directly affect household welfare. An intelligent woman who marries a fool will usually suffer the fool's fate. Similarly, loss owing to the poor judgment or bad luck of a father or son is likely to be suffered by the daughter or widowed mother. And things can get worse quickly under less than ideal demographic circumstances: if a daughter is orphaned, if a wife is divorced or widowed at a young age, or if an older woman has no surviving son on whom to depend. As was illustrated by several case studies, under these circumstances women risk abrupt declines in economic welfare.

A subsequent paper examined the empirical pattern of economic mobility in detail and introduced data from several locations in rural India for comparative purposes (Cain 1981), focusing on the gain or loss of land assets by households between inheritance and the time of the survey. The analysis showed that overall mobility has been much greater in the Bangladesh sample; that the pattern of mobility in Bangladesh has resulted in increasing inequality in land distribution, while inequality has decreased in the Indian samples; and that those who began as small landowners in Bangladesh experienced a higher incidence of loss and a lower incidence of gain than large owners, while the opposite is true for India. Among the several factors contributing to the contrasting experience of the two settings are differences in the dependence and vulnerability of women. Despite similarities in kinship organization (patriarchal authority structure, patrilineal descent and inheritance, and patrilocal residence), women in the Indian localities are less dependent on men and less vulnerable in the absence of a male than women in rural Bangladesh. This is suggested by a comparison of the experience of women widowed at an early age or with no surviving mature son. Of 14 such women in the Bangladesh sample, 10 were left with some land at the time of their husbands' death and 4 were landless. Of the 10 who initially had land, all had subsequently sold or otherwise lost at least some of their land by the time of the interviews, and four had lost all through distress sales. Of the four who were initially landless, one became a beggar, and all were destitute. In the Indian villages, of 12 women widowed under similar circumstances 3 were landless at the time of their husbands' death and 9 were left with some land. Only one of these nine subsequently lost or sold land. The three landless widows have managed to subsist on their own, through wage work and operating small businesses.

This paper seeks to refine and test the mobility hypothesis. The focus is on the elderly, their means of support and quality of life, in selected areas of rural Bangladesh and India. Of particular interest are the material consequences of reproductive failure, defined as failure to produce a son who survives and is able and willing to assume responsibility for parents who are no longer able to care for themselves. Emphasis is given to the fate of elderly women; however, because of the dependent status of women in the region, this necessarily entails a consideration of the fate of elderly men also. Women's economic dependence links their fortunes to those of their husbands, for better or worse. Because wives are typically five to ten years younger than their husbands, however, women face a high probability of widowhood, and in this their dependence sets them apart: the consequences of reproductive failure for them are potentially much more severe. Data on the living arrangements of the elderly and on other aspects of their material well-being are drawn from fieldwork conducted in a village in Mymensingh District, Bangladesh (Char Gopalpur), from 1976 to 1978, several villages in Maharashtra and Andhra Pradesh, India, in 1980, and two villages in Raisen District, Madhya Pradesh, India, in 1983.*

Living Arrangements of the Elderly

The evolution of the typical household is similar in Bangladesh and the relevant areas of India. Residence patterns in both settings are patrilocal; when a daughter marries, she moves to her husband's home. After a son marries, he and his wife normally remain for a period as members of his parents' household. As other sons mature and marry, he may eventually establish a separate household adjacent to his parents' dwelling. In some cases, two or more married sons remain in a single large household together with their parents, until their parents die. More often, however, elderly parents live with one son, usually their youngest, the other sons maintaining separate, adjacent households.

* Descriptions of study designs, sample characteristics, and the setting of Char Gopalpur, the two villages in Andhra Pradesh, and four villages in Maharashtra are given in Cain (1981). The research in Madhya Pradesh, conducted in November 1983 in collaboration with the Economics Program of ICRISAT, focused on samples of 40 households from each of two villages in Raisen District. As in the case of the six other Indian villages, the samples were stratified according to size of landholding.

TABLE I

Distribution of Persons Age 60 or Older According to Living Arrangement

(percent)

Living arrangement	India (N = 114)	Bangladesh (N = 94)
With married son(s)	65%	62%
With unmarried mature son(s)[a]	11	16
No mature son:		
Married son(s) adjacent	4	13
Son(s) not adjacent[b]	7	6
With married daughter	6	2
Other[c]	6	1

[a] Aged 15 or older.
[b] Includes elderly people living alone, with a spouse, with sons less than age 15, and/or with unmarried daughters.
[c] For example, living with a brother's or a nephew's family.

When parents are fully dependent, all sons usually contribute to their support, even if they do not all live in the same household. There may be a larger allocation of family land to the son with whom the parent is actually living. Or where land is still cultivated jointly by all sons, the son with whom the parents are living will receive a larger portion of the agricultural product. Alternatively, each son might cultivate land independently and transfer a portion of his yield to his parents. Less frequently, an elderly parent circulates from son to son, taking meals for a period from each in turn.

Table I shows the distribution of elderly people according to living arrangement for the combined Indian sample (320 households) and Char Gopalpur, Bangladesh (343 households). The elderly are here defined as those whose reported age is 60 years or older. Living arrangements are classified according to whether or not a mature son lives with or adjacent to the elderly person. Those in the first category live in the same household with one or more married sons (they may have additional sons living in adjacent households). The second category includes those who live with one or more unmarried sons aged 15 or older (they too may have one or more married sons who live in separate, adjacent households). The third category includes elderly people who have neither a married nor a mature unmarried son living with them, but who do have one or more married sons living in adjacent households. People in these first three categories can be said to have achieved reproductive success: they have mature sons living with them, or in close proximity, upon whom they can depend.

The remaining three categories in Table I contain elderly people who have experienced reproductive failure—they do not live with or near a mature son—and whose living arrangements are, thus, abnormal. In the first group (no mature son and no son adjacent) are elderly people who live alone, with sons who are less than 15 years of age, or with unmarried daughters of any age. The next group includes those who live with a married daughter and her husband. Finally, a residual category includes persons who live with such other adult relatives as a brother, nephew, or uncle.

The majority of elderly people in both the Indian (65 percent) and Bangladesh (62 percent) samples live with one or more married sons. Overall, there is a marked correspondence between the distributions for India and Bangladesh, as one would expect given similar kinship and household formation systems. Altogether, 81 percent of the elderly in the Indian sample and 91 percent of the elderly in Char Gopalpur live either with or adjacent to a mature son.

There are differences between the two areas, however. A higher proportion of elderly parents in Bangladesh have sons living adjacent to rather than with them. This is reflected by a higher proportion of persons in the categories "no mature sons and married son(s) adjacent" (13 percent for Bangladesh and 4 percent for India) and "with unmarried mature son(s)," many of whom also have married sons living in adjacent households. While this difference might be interpreted as a reflecton of weaker ties between parents and children in Bangladesh than in India, it is in fact more a reflection of differences in settlement patterns and housing materials. In rural Bangladesh the settlement pattern is dispersed, while in the relevant areas of India the pattern is nuclear, with houses and huts clustered together. Thus, the relative cost of land for housing is lower in Bangladesh than in India. Moreover, building materials in Bangladesh are a good deal simpler and cheaper than in the sample areas of rural India. It is considerably less costly to form a new household in rural Bangladesh.

The significance of a household boundary separating elderly parents from sons varies a great deal between families. In a few cases, it signals serious disaffection between father and son. Often it reflects a simple preference for privacy and physical independence on the part of the elderly or the young, while intergenerational bonds of affection and obligation remain strong. In other cases, strains between the father or mother and the daughter-in-law precipitate the creation of an independent household, while relations between father or mother and son remain strong. It is important to note also that such boundaries are not immutable. Elderly couples are more likely than single widowed parents to live in separate households. When one spouse dies, the remaining parent is usually absorbed into a son's household.

More significant are differences in the proportion of elderly people living either with a married daughter or in other arrangements. In both India and Bangladesh these are second-best alternatives to the cultural norm of living with sons, and they are chosen only when the preferred arrangement is not possible: in almost all cases, that is, when elderly people have no surviving sons. As Table 1 suggests, these second-best arrangements are more viable in the Indian than in the Bangladeshi setting. The final two categories account for 12 percent of the elderly in the Indian sample, but only 3 percent in Char Gopalpur.

In the absence of one's own son, depending on a daughter, which, in effect, means depending on the daughter's husband, is precarious because in neither setting is there a strong, socially recognized obligation for a man to support his wife's parents. When he agrees to do so, it may be with considerable reluctance, and he accepts the responsibility through generosity rather than a sense of obligation. The quality of care, therefore, is likely to be inferior; and regardless of the adequacy of material support, an elderly person in this position is likely to experience emotional strain and unhappiness. A more satisfactory option, for those with property, is more akin to adoption. In this case, a daughter's marriage is arranged with an explicit understanding that her husband will move to her parents' residence and assume the duties of a natural son. But this is a contract that requires property to negotiate and sustain it. In the Bangladesh sample only two people aged 60 or over were living with a married daughter, both of them in the home of their son-in-law. In the Indian sample, of seven elderly people living with married daughters, only one lived in his own home.

Adopting a son is perceived to be another option for those with no son of their own, at least in the Indian villages. In fact, however, there are few such cases, and only one in which the adopted son is old enough to care for the elderly. In this case, a relatively wealthy widower in a Madhya Pradesh village adopted one of his sister's sons and now resides with him, his wife, and their children. There is one other case of adoption in the Indian sample, but the boy is only 13 years old. The Bangladesh sample contains only one instance of adoption. In this case, also, the boy was less than 15 at the time of the study and, in addition, the parents had natural sons of their own. In practice, there are few candidates for adoption, most of them offspring of brothers or sisters. The brother or sister must of course be willing to part with a son, a condition that is by no means automatically met. Adoption is thus a highly constrained option. It is the more so in Bangladesh, where the prevailing Islamic doctrine prohibits full adoption (Abdul-Rauf 1977:88–90).

Dependence on brothers as sources of support in old age, in the absence of sons, married daughters, and adopted sons, is a final option to be considered. An earlier analysis, drawing on data from many of the same samples, indicated that brothers demonstrated greater economic interdependence and cohesiveness in India than in Bangladesh (Cain 1982). In the Indian villages, for example, the incidence and average period of joint agricultural production among brothers whose father had died was much greater than in Char Gopalpur. Furthermore, in Char Gopalpur a large proportion of partners in land transactions—the great majority of which were distress sales—were brothers or other close patrilineal kin, suggesting that extended kin function poorly as a mutual support group or insurance cooperative. The distinction between India and Bangladesh in the closeness of brothers appears to apply also to support in old age. Among the elderly in Table 1 there are two old men, one a widower and one never married, living with brothers in the Indian sample, and none in Char Gopalpur. In interviews with adult males of all ages in the two Madhya Pradesh villages, the help of brothers was regularly mentioned, along with adoption and assistance from a daughter and her husband, as a potential source of old-age support. This was not a common expectation in Char Gopalpur.

These are the institutional or semi-institutional solutions, in the absence of sons, to the welfare needs of the elderly. All three alternatives are less readily available and less satisfactory in Bangladesh than in the Indian villages. Neither rural India nor Bangladesh maintains public or community-based institutions to provide for the needs of the elderly. The remaining varieties of living arrangements in Table 1, all of which are in the final residual category, include, for India, two widowed co-wives who live together; a widow living with her stepgrandson; a widow living with her widowed daughter, daughter's son, and his wife; and a widower living with his sister's daughter and her husband. There is only one person in this residual category for Bangladesh, a widower living with his father's sister's grandson. These exceptional arrangements in themselves have little significance; however, their prevalence in the Indian villages and rarity in Char Gopalpur indicate the systemic tolerance of such arrangements in the former setting and relative intolerance in the latter.

Material Consequences of Reproductive Failure

The distributions in Table 1 suggest that one consequence of reproductive failure is an early death. This is clearer in the case of Bangladesh. One can predict with some precision the proportion of people in a population who, given prevailing reproductive, mortality, and marriage regimes, can expect to have no surviving son at age 60 and older. For populations with demographic parameters similar to those pertaining in these parts of rural India and Bangladesh, this figure should be about 17 or 18 percent.* The

* This result, derived from a simulation model developed by John Bongaarts, assumes an age at first marriage (female) of 18, a TFR of 6.00, and an expectation of life at birth of 50 for females and 47 for males.

sample from India comes close: the proportion of elderly people in Table 1 with no surviving son is 16 percent. For Bangladesh, however, the proportion with no surviving son is only three percent. Assuming, as we can, that the difference is real rather than an artifact of small sample size, the only possible explanation for this deficit is that a disproportionate number of people in Bangladesh who are either childless or without living sons die before they reach age 60. More will be said about this pattern of differential mortality later.

Table 2 presents distributions of elderly people age 60 or older according to living arrangements, broken down by sex and economic status. Regarding differences by sex, recall that the age difference between once-married spouses is on average between five and ten years in these societies, the man being older than the woman. For any given age, therefore, women will be that much further along than men in the development of their families. This is reflected in Table 2: in both samples a greater proportion of women than men live with married sons, and a smaller proportion live with sons younger than 15 (the fourth category). In addition, a considerably higher proportion of women age 60 or older are currently unmarried. Seventy-three percent of women in the Indian sample are unmarried, compared to 37 percent of men, while in Char Gopalpur the figures are 67 and 11 percent, respectively. These sex differences in marital status reflect both the age difference between spouses and different rates of remarriage; the latter are considerably higher for men than for women, and considerably higher among Bangladeshi men than Indian men. As noted above, a single surviving parent is less likely than a surviving couple to maintain a separate household.

Differences by economic status are more striking. Economic status is here measured by ownership of arable land. For Bangladesh, the poor include the landless and those owning less than one-and-a-half acres. Similarly, in the Indian sample, the poor are either landless or owners of small amounts of land. In both samples, the rate of reproductive failure appears to be higher among the poor than the relatively wealthy. In Bangladesh, 96 percent of the relatively wealthy elderly live either with or adjacent to a mature son, compared to 81 percent of the poor. In India, the figures are 87 and 72 percent, respectively. As noted earlier, the poor are less likely to achieve reproductive success because they experience slightly lower fertility and their children are exposed to higher mortality risks. They are also disadvantaged because they lack the control over sons that comes with property ownership. In Table 2, the consequences of this disadvantage are more evident for Bangladesh, where only 42 percent of the poor live with married sons, compared to 74 percent of the relatively wealthy.

TABLE 2

Living Arrangements of Persons Age 60 or Older by Sex and Economic Status

(percent)

	India		Bangladesh		India		Bangladesh	
Living arrangement	Males (N = 62)	Females (N = 52)	Males (N = 61)	Females (N = 33)	Poor (N = 48)	Relatively wealthy (N = 66)	Poor (N = 36)	Relatively wealthy (N = 58)
With married son(s)	60%	71%	56%	73%	62%	67%	42%	74%
With unmarried mature son(s)	13	10	16	15	8	14	25	10
No mature son:								
Married son(s) adjacent	6	2	15	9	2	6	14	12
Son(s) not adjacent	10	4	10	—	12	3	14	2
With married daughter	5	8	2	3	10	3	3	2
Other	6	6	2	—	4	8	3	—

Table 2 offers further clues regarding the material consequences of reproductive failure and how these differ between Bangladesh and India. The mortality consequences (for parents) of reproductive failure should be less severe for the relatively wealthy than for the poor. Therefore, if there were no economic mobility over the course of the life cycle—that is, if there were no transitions between the categories of "poor" and "relatively wealthy"—one would expect, other things being equal, to find a higher proportion of elderly people with no surviving son among the relatively wealthy than among the poor. Furthermore, this proportion should approach the predicted level of 17 or 18 percent of those aged 60 or over. In fact, however, the reverse seems to be the case: the difference (deficit) between the observed and the predicted proportion of people with no surviving son is substantial among the relatively wealthy, and greater than among the poor. Thus, in Bangladesh, 2 percent of the relatively wealthy have no living son, compared to 6 percent of the poor, while in India the figures are 14 and 18 percent, respectively. This suggests, more strongly in the case of Bangladesh than India, that there are mobility consequences associated with reproductive failure, such that those who start off relatively wealthy and then experience reproductive failure suffer economic decline at a disproportionate rate. Table 2 also suggests that women bear the brunt of the mortality consequences of reproductive failure. This is clearer in the case of Bangladesh: a simple comparison of the number of men and women in this age group yields a sex ratio of 1.8 (men to women) for Char Gopalpur and 1.2 for the Indian sample.

Table 3 includes persons aged 50–59 in addition to those aged 60 and over and the samples are further disaggregated by sex and economic status. First, consider the ratios of men to women in Table 3 by age group and economic status:

| | India | | Bangladesh | |
Age	Poor	Relatively wealthy	Poor	Relatively wealthy
50–59	1.2	1.1	1.4	1.1
60+	1.5	1.0	2.6	1.5

This pattern suggests that poor elderly women are at greatest risk of excess mortality. In the Indian sample, a substantial deficit of women relative to men is apparent only among the poor aged 60 or older. In Char Gopalpur, a deficit of women is also noticeable in the younger age group of the poor, and among the relatively wealthy aged 60 or older.

A comparison of persons aged 50–59 with those aged 60 or older permits a fuller description of how living arrangements evolve. I focus initially on males. The critical category in Table 3 is that containing males

TABLE 3

Living Arrangements of the Elderly by Sex, Class, and Age

(percent)

INDIA

Living arrangement	Males				Females			
	Poor		Relatively wealthy		Poor		Relatively wealthy	
	50–59 (N = 42)	60+ (N = 29)	50–59 (N = 41)	60+ (N = 33)	50–59 (N = 34)	60+ (N = 19)	50–59 (N = 38)	60+ (N = 33)
With married son(s)	38%	62%	63%	58%	56%	63%	55%	76%
With unmarried mature son(s)	29	10	24	15	24	5	24	12
No mature son:								
Married son(s) adjacent	2	3	5	9	6	—	11	3
Son(s) not adjacent	29	14	7	6	9	11	5	—
With married daughter	—	7	—	3	6	16	3	3
Other	2	3	—	9	—	5	3	6

BANGLADESH

Living arrangement	Males				Females			
	Poor		Relatively wealthy		Poor		Relatively wealthy	
	50–59 (N = 28)	60+ (N = 26)	50–59 (N = 20)	60+ (N = 35)	50–59 (N = 20)	60+ (N = 10)	50–59 (N = 14)	60+ (N = 23)
With married son(s)	—	35%	45%	71%	50%	60%	74%	78%
With unmarried mature son(s)	39%	23	40	11	15	30	—	9
No mature son:								
Married son(s) adjacent	7	15	5	14	10	10	21	9
Son(s) not adjacent	54	19	10	3	15	—	—	—
With married daughter	—	4	—	—	10	—	5	4
Other	—	4	—	—	—	—	—	—

who, by ages 50 to 59, have no mature son living with or adjacent to them. Men in this category are already in an unenviable position relative to others in their cohort who have a married son living with or close to them, and their prospects for the future are not good. By this age their physical powers have begun to decline and their susceptibility to illness has increased; thus, their need for a son on whom to depend is greater. They find themselves in this position because they have been in childless marital unions or in unions that produced no sons, their sons have died, or their sons were of a high birth order. (An additional possibility is that they have mature sons who live elsewhere. I found no such cases among males 50–59; however, among men aged 60 or older, there was one instance in Char Gopalpur and two in the Indian villages.)

As men in this group age, they face several possibilities. Those with no surviving son must look for alternative arrangements or else continue living alone or with unmarried daughters. As we saw earlier, very few men in Bangladesh succeed in finding an alternative. (In India the chances are better.) Those who have sons younger than 15 will, depending on the age of their eldest son, remain in the same category for a considerable period or "graduate" to one of the more desirable living arrangements. In the Bangladesh sample of males aged 50–59 with no mature son and no son living adjacent, 6 have no son and 11 have one or more sons younger than 15. Of the latter, the age of the eldest son ranges from 2 to 12. Those who have no son may be considered the most vulnerable; however, with the prospect of increasing debility, those with young sons are not in a much better position and those whose sons are younger than 10 may, in fact, be worse off because of the added burden of dependency that young sons represent. Another outcome for males in this category is, therefore, an early death. The survival prospects for their wives and young children are also not good.

The inference drawn from Table 2 regarding the mobility consequences of reproductive failure seems to be substantiated by a comparison of the distributions of poor and relatively wealthy males in Table 3, particularly for the age group 50–59. All face roughly the same probabilities with respect to childlessness and the sex composition and ordering of births. The survival chances of children of wealthier parents should be better than those of the poor, but not to the extent implied by the distributions in the table—for Bangladesh, a fivefold difference in the proportion with no mature son and no son adjacent between the poor (54 percent) and the relatively wealthy (10 percent). A similar, although smaller, difference is evident for the Indian sample (29 and 7 percent, respectively). The numbers underlying the cells of Table 3 are rather small and thus allow only tentative conclusions; however, the differences are consistent with the hypothesis that reproductive failure greatly increases the probability of economic loss. The evidence is stronger for Bangladesh because the difference in distributions by economic status is more pronounced, and the proportion of poor males in the relevant category for Bangladesh (54) is almost twice that of India (29).*

To explore further the mobility hypothesis, I attempted to reconstruct the economic histories of each of the individuals in the Bangladesh sample who live neither with nor adjacent to a mature son. This category contains 26 people aged 50 or older, 3 women and 23 men. Two of the women are married to men in the same category, and thus there are 24 unique histories. The mobility profiles are shown in Table 4. The information available for constructing these profiles was not equally good or complete for all cases. In the course of fieldwork in Char Gopalpur, a sample of approximately one-third of all households was singled out for intensive study. For individuals from this sample there are detailed records of land asset gain and loss from the time of inheritance to the date of the survey. For those not in this sample it was possible, in most cases, to determine whether they had experienced net gain or loss. For example, in a number of cases persons not in the intensively studied sample had a brother who was in it. Determining the amount of their inheritance was straightforward. Current land ownership information was gathered for all households; therefore, net change in assets could be estimated with precision. In other cases it was possible to establish only that some loss had occurred, without being able to pin down the exact amount. There is, in fact, only one case (number 16) about which I can say nothing regarding net change in assets between inheritance and the time of the study.

Twenty-one of the 23 individuals (91 percent) for whom I have information have either lost land assets or registered no change. The majority have lost assets, and of those whose position did not change, almost all were landless or practically landless to begin with. Furthermore, the majority of those who lost assets had lost everything and by 1976 were landless. Recalling that the category "relatively wealthy" includes households with one-and-a-half acres or more, one can see that four cases (numbers 2, 4, 9, and 11) shifted from relatively wealthy to poor in the period between inheritance and 1976. Others for whom I do not have information on amount of land inherited may also have made this transition, but I cannot be certain. What is clear, however, is that the experience

---

*Also, in the case of India, the possibility that sampling variability may be partly responsible for the interclass difference is suggested by an apparent inconsistency between the younger and older cohorts of the less poor group: that is, the younger cohort has a smaller proportion in the last three categories of living arrangement (7) than the older cohort (18), whereas it should be the reverse.

TABLE 4

Economic Mobility Profiles of Persons Aged 50 or Older Who Live Neither with nor Adjacent to a Mature Son, Char Gopalpur, Bangladesh

Case no.	Arable land inherited[a]	Land owned in 1976	Net change	Comment
1	?	0	−	
2	20	1	−	
3	?	0	−	
4	16	8	−	
5	11	4	−	
6	?	0	−	
7	6	0	−	
8	12	0	−	Dead by 1980 at age 56
9	18	0	−	
10	1	0	−	
11	28	0	−	
12	114	86	−	
13	?	0	−	Widow
14	0	0	0	Dead by 1980 at age 55
15	0	0	0	Dead by 1980 at age 60
16	?	14	?	Leases all land to others
17	?	0	0 or −	
18	?	0	0 or −	
19	?	0	0 or −	
20	?	0	0 or −	
21	?	1	0 or −	
22	?	0.5	0 or −	
23	?	32	+	
24	17	49	+	Sold some land in recent years

[a] Units of land are tenths of an acre.

of this subgroup of elderly people with respect to economic mobility is extraordinarily bad. Compare their record with that of a representative sample of 114 households from the same village: 39 percent gained assets between inheritance and the date of the study, 45 percent lost, and 16 percent registered no change (Cain 1981:446).

The frequency of land transactions in the Indian villages was much lower than in Char Gopalpur, and the proportion of all sales that could be classified as distress sales was also much smaller (Cain 1981). Of all sample households in three of the Indian villages, only 18 percent experienced a decline in their land asset position. The great majority of those who lost land were relatively well off, and they disposed of land for reasons demonstrably unrelated to reproductive failure. This is not to say that the material consequences of reproductive failure are negligible in these Indian settings; however, they are not reflected in changes in land owned and are certainly less severe than in Bangladesh.

During a visit to Char Gopalpur in 1980, I learned of the death of the three individuals noted in Table 4.* All three were landless at the time of their death, and two had never owned land. One cannot attribute their deaths directly to the fact that they did not have mature sons to depend on during the periods of illness immediately preceding their deaths, but this lack surely affected their chances of survival. Life is harsh for all villagers, and mortality risks are high for all regardless of reproductive histories. Life is harsher and mortality risks are higher for the poor: work, when it is available, is physically demanding; diets at the best of times are poor; shelter, clothing, and medical care are inadequate; and drinking water is contaminated and the environment is otherwise unhealthy. Seen through Western eyes, practically all adults look older than their years. The added difficulty for those in Table 4 without land is that if they get sick and are unable to work, there is no one in their households who can replace them as the family provider. Their children are too young and their wives, no matter how willing, are excluded from most kinds of wage work and other forms of economic activity by the strictures of purdah, the prevailing division of labor, and extreme labor market segregation. Therefore, illness brings a loss of income, which, in turn, may exacerbate the illness and hasten death.

There is only one woman in Table 4, a widow aged 52 in 1976, with nine daughters, four of whom were still unmarried and living at home. The woman lives a marginal existence, earning some income by processing paddy, selling rice, and working in others' households. She receives occasional assistance from a son-in-law and from neighbors. She inherited some land from her husband, which has since been sold. The reason there are so few women in this category, either divorced or widowed, is simply that it is an economically untenable living arrangement—they cannot (and do not) survive. The widows of the three men in Table 4 who died must find another adult male on whom to depend or they too will probably die. Alternatives are scarce in Bangladesh; thus, as indicated by the distribution of elderly females in Tables 2 and 3 and the very high sex ratios at older ages, a great many women in this position die before they reach age 50.

All but one of the men in Table 4 were married at the time of the study, and it is important to remember that their wives have shared any economic loss that they have experienced. The only difference between men and their wives is that wives experience the loss at a younger age. With respect to economic mobility, the consequences of reproductive failure for widows with property are worse than for men. Judging from the experi-

*Others may have died by 1980. I visited only one-third of the village households.

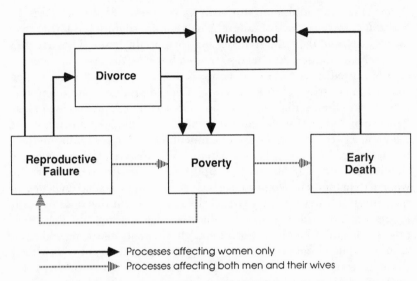

Processes affecting women only
Processes affecting both men and their wives

FIGURE I. The Consequences of Reproductive Failure

ence of widows in Char Gopalpur as reported in the beginning of this chapter, property loss for them is a certainty and their transition to poverty can be very abrupt.

A more immediate potential consequence of reproductive failure, also with adverse economic implications for women, is divorce. In Char Gopalpur, if a marriage is childless it will often be terminated by divorce. (Less commonly, a man will take additional wives.) Regardless of which partner is infertile or who initiates the divorce, a woman's "value" as a potential spouse is severely eroded as a consequence, and if she remarries it will most likely be to someone who is less desirable (for instance, poorer or older) than her first spouse. Furthermore, this process delays the start of childbearing (assuming that the woman is fertile) and thus lessens a woman's chances of achieving reproductive success. Divorce may also be initiated by a man if a union produces daughters but no sons. A sterile man or one who fathers only daughters can thus "damage" several women. One man in Table 4 has been married six times, for example, and another five times. A number of others have been married twice. One can contrast this to the situation in the Indian villages, where repeated divorce and remarriage in such circumstances is tolerated less and thus is less frequent.

The material consequences of reproductive failure in Bangladesh are summarized in Figure 1. The solid lines in the figure pertain to both men and women; the broken lines indicate processes that involve women alone.

Poverty increases adult mortality risks for both sexes. It also increases the probability of reproductive failure. The poor are slightly less fertile than the wealthy, and their children face higher mortality risks. They are thus less likely to produce a son who survives. However, the primary determinant of reproductive failure or success is not economic status but, rather, chance. Those who are unlucky enough not to produce a surviving son, regardless of their initial economic position, face a high probability of loss. Absence of a mature son at later ages increases a couple's vulnerability to economic crises. Through impoverishment, reproductive failure induces heavier mortality among aging parents. The material consequences of childlessness or of failure to bear and raise a son are more severe for women than for men. Women have little choice but to depend on males for their survival. Infertility may trigger divorce, an event that automatically lowers the value of a woman in the marriage market and delays the process of family building. For unions that remain intact, reproductive failure, through impoverishment, increases the probability of widowhood. A young widow with no mature son faces the prospect of further rapid economic decline and very high mortality risks.

The vicious circle portrayed in Figure 1 is less pronounced in the areas of rural India that I have considered. Women there are less vulnerable than in rural Bangladesh, and thus the adverse consequences of divorce and widowhood, although present, are less severe. In general, the environment of risk in the Indian settings is more benign, and better means of adjusting to risk have evolved. Therefore, reproductive failure does not so automatically lead to the distress sale of assets and economic decline. For those elderly persons with no mature sons, there exist alternative living arrangements, which, although less desirable than the cultural ideal, are at least economically viable. The apparent contrast between Bangladesh and India may in part be a function of my criterion of economic mobility— gain or loss of land assets. More sensitive criteria and analysis are likely to diminish the contrast. Nevertheless, in view of the evidence on mortality and mobility differentials, it seems clear that the material consequences of reproductive failure are worse in rural Bangladesh than in rural India.

Conclusion

In the heyday of modernization theory, the predominance of nuclear households in such societies as India and Bangladesh was interpreted, quite incorrectly, as evidence of erosion of the "traditional" joint family and a shift toward the "modern" nuclear form. Although modernization theory, with its image of social change proceeding from traditional to modern Western institutional forms, is no longer widely accepted, social scientists remain poised in anticipation of dramatic change in family structure in developing societies. We await the demise of the joint family system, reversal of intergenerational wealth flows, collapse of patriarchal authority structures, and an end to gerontocracy. At present, there is a tendency to infer such change from the fertility declines that are taking place in many developing countries. Fundamental change in family structure may indeed be occurring; however, it is important to emphasize that we owe our anticipation and inferences largely to untested theory rather than to empirical observation. Hajnal's work on household formation systems provides a counterpoint to those who assume that basic change in family institutions is either at hand or inevitable (Hajnal 1982). His work suggests that one can, instead, anticipate the dogged persistence of such systems through time.

Residential patterns of the elderly are products of particular systems of household formation. The patterns for rural India and Bangladesh are wholly consistent with the joint household formation system as defined by Hajnal. As such, they give evidence of the persistence of the joint family system in these areas, the associated authority structure (with elderly males at the apex), and the associated family-based approach to welfare provision. On the basis of my fieldwork, I see no reason to predict any appreciable change in this situation. Thus, I fully expect elderly people to continue to rely on their sons as needed, and I cannot foresee the timely evolution of an alternative welfare system that would diminish the importance of sons in this capacity. One need only assume that people's reproductive behavior is attuned to such welfare concerns (an assumption that has some empirical support) to see that this state of affairs has important potential consequences for the future course of fertility in the region. In particular, it can be shown that the pursuit of individual security goals will continue to produce fertility rates that are well above replacement levels (see Cain 1983, 1985).

No matter how convincing I may find this argument, there is precious little credible research that can be brought to bear in support of it. The meager amount of existing research has, in fact, yielded conflicting claims regarding the fate of the elderly and the responsiveness of their children in times of need, ranging from the position taken in this paper to the flat assertion that children are practically useless to aging parents (see Nugent 1985 for a review). Carol and Michael Vlassoff, proponents of the latter view, would have us believe, for example, that the rural elderly work until they drop and that children are either unreliable or, because of the suddenness of death among the elderly, unnecessary as caretakers (Vlassoff and

Vlassoff 1980). Whatever the merits of their analysis, and there are problems with it (Datta and Nugent 1984), the wide range of published assertions on this matter, the scarcity of valid empirical work, and the potential policy importance of a link with reproductive behavior together provide a strong rationale for further research on the elderly.

Intergenerational Contracts:
Familial Roots of Sexual
Stratification in Taiwan

SUSAN GREENHALGH

In recent years researchers examining the origins of women's subordination have recognized the close relation between women's productive
roles outside the household and their reproductive roles within the household (for example, Green 1983; Hartmann 1976; Lim 1983; for related
theoretical developments see Eisenstein 1979; Young, Wolkowitz, and
McCullagh 1984).* In this production-reproduction perspective, the roots
of women's secondary status can be traced to the interaction of capitalist
economic institutions with patriarchal family institutions. However, the
fundamental source of women's subordination is the patriarchal family:
long before capitalism came on the scene, patriarchy was already creating
mechanisms to control women and their labor.† By comparison, capitalism is a "latecomer" (Hartmann 1976:138), merely building on, and in
some cases intensifying, entrenched systems of gender inequality.

Traditional Confucian China evolved one of the most patriarchal family systems that has ever existed. Despite the remarkable advances of
Chinese societies in promoting the rights of women, if the arguments of
Hartmann and others are correct, we should expect that the historical
residue of an elaborate set of patriarchal institutions has presented for-
midable obstacles to efforts to reduce gender inequality.

This paper explores changes in women's status in Taiwan. The focus is
on the way the traditional system of sexual stratification was perpetuated

* My research was supported by a Fulbright-Hays Fellowship, and by grants from the
American Association of University Women and the Wenner-Gren Foundation for Anthropological Research. I am also indebted to Charles Keely, James Trussell, Edwin
Winckler, Arthur Wolf, and Margery Wolf for their detailed and thoughtful comments on
an earlier draft of the paper.

† Patriarchy is used in the general sense to mean a sociosexual system in which males
possess superior power and economic privilege. The issue of the sources of women's
subordination is the focus of a major debate among liberal, radical, and socialist feminists.
In this chapter I do not attempt to resolve this debate. Rather, my aim is to elucidate some of
the relevant features of the Chinese case that might help to firm up and flesh out comparative theory. Space limitations preclude discussion of related issues such as the feminist
critique of family and household and the role of class in gender differentiation.

and even intensified with the rapid development of the economy after the Second World War.* My work supports the hypothesis that the roots of women's subordination lie first and foremost in the family system. Although both the economic environment and the family exacerbated gender differences, the capitalist environment only provided the resources that the family system used to reproduce and strengthen traditional hierarchies.

Because the role of the family was central, my primary concern here is with the way the family acted to shape gender differentials. From a life cycle perspective, it is clear that gender differentials are created not in adulthood, but much earlier, during childhood and adolescence. It is during these years, when children are still jurally dependent, or without rights, that the economic basis for structured inequalities between men and women is laid. To see the economic roots of sexual differentiation in Chinese society, we need to look at parents' use of different types of intergenerational "contracts," or expectations about mutual obligations, in raising their sons and daughters. In the Taiwan case I will argue that differences between sons and daughters in obligations to their parents, and in the terms of fulfillment of these obligations, gave rise to systematic differences between the sexes in socioeconomic resources and personal autonomy. The pivot of this process, by which daughters lost autonomy and resources relative to sons, was the education of daughters. By educating their daughters, parents increased their daughters' obligations to them and, in turn, increased the resources available for investing in their sons.

At present our knowledge of trends in sexual inequality in postwar Taiwan is decidedly imperfect. Aggregate data on education, occupation, and the like tell only part of the story, for they contain incomplete measures of some resources (in particular, education); they tell us nothing about who controls the use of the resources; and, most important, they conceal processes of sexual stratification that occur within families over time. To see the roots of sexual inequality, we need longitudinal, family-level data that include detailed histories of all the sons and daughters who were raised in each family. In the absence of a large data set of this sort, I will rely primarily on my own data from a small sample in northern

---

* My use of the term "sexual stratification" requires some explanation. Feminist writers distinguish sharply between sex, a biological fact, and gender, a social and cultural construction. I use the term sexual stratification because the categories of people who are stratified are the two sexes. What I mean, strictly speaking, is stratification along lines of gender. Stratification has a dual meaning of an increase in inequality over time, and the existence of structured inequalities at a given point in time. The former is implied in the title of the paper.

Taiwan, and supplement it with evidence collected by other researchers elsewhere on the island.

Women in the Family

Two features of the traditional family system, in my view, have played the key roles in mediating changes in women's status in postwar Taiwan: the basic familial institutions, descent line and *chia*, and the intergenerational "contracts" that guided relations between parents and children.

In traditional China, the descent line and the *chia* were two distinct but crosscutting familial institutions.* The descent line was the group that held corporate property transmitted by inheritance. Almost exclusively a male group, the line included living males, their ancestors, and their descendants. Women were "attached" to their fathers' and later their husbands' lines, but in general they became full-fledged members of a descent line only after they died, when they became ancestors in their sons' lines (Sung 1975:194-95).

Whereas the line was a transhistorical unit of males concerned with inheritance and succession, the *chia* was a contemporaneous unit of males and females concerned with the tasks of livelihood: production, reproduction, and consumption. Women belonged to their fathers' *chia* before marriage and their husbands' *chia* after marriage. The *chia* controlled a separate body of resources, the "acquired resources," which included the tangible and liquid assets acquired by family members during the lifetime of the family (see Sung 1975:217). While daughters, who were not members of the descent line, had no rights to the inherited property,† as temporary members of the *chia* they did have rights to a small share of the acquired property, which they usually received in the form of a dowry. The great bulk of the acquired property was owned by the *chia* as a whole. However, it was also possible for individuals who earned money to invest their personal funds in private property. The right to own large-scale private property was restricted to sons; unmarried daughters did not have this right.

Since my primary concern is with processes of stratification that occur

---

*Here traditional China refers to China during the Ch'ing, the last imperial dynasty, which ruled the mainland until 1911 and Taiwan until 1895. This discussion of familial institutions draws heavily on the work of Lung-sheng Sung and Arthur P. Wolf. My own data on property rights and division support the *chia*/line distinction.

† Despite legal provisions giving daughters a share in their father's property at division, this right is routinely signed away at marriage (Cohen 1976:83; Chuang 1983:46-47; Hu 1983:109, 168-69).

within the *chia*, I will look more closely at the position of sons and daughters within this institution, departing from existing treatments of Chinese family organization and proposing new ways of analyzing sex and generational hierarchies.*

Relations between parents and children can usefully be thought of as sets of contracts or understandings about expected flows of material and nonmaterial goods (for a similar approach, see Ben-Porath 1980). The contents of these contracts have conventionally been analyzed from a jural perspective, which views them as exchanges of rights and duties, or obligations and counterobligations, by different family members (see the work of such anthropologists as Cohen 1976; Freedman 1979; and A. Wolf and Huang 1980). At birth, children in Taiwan were jural dependents who had no rights within the family. Their parents had complete jural authority over them and could dispose of them as they pleased. As they matured, their rights gradually came to be recognized, and at marriage they became jural adults with acknowledged rights in their natal families (for sons) or their families of marriage (for daughters) (Cohen 1976: 72–73).†

Seen through Chinese eyes, the most important exchanges were these: parents gave their daughters their bodies ("the gift of life"), support before marriage, help in finding a spouse, and a small share of the *chia* property in the form of a dowry at the time of marriage. Sons received the first three things as well as training for productive work (daughters were taught reproductive skills such as housework), and roughly equal shares of the *chia* and line properties at family division.

Although parental gifts such as education came to be embodied in the children, because they were provided by the parents they were seen as fundamentally belonging to the parents rather than the children. As long as the parents were alive, children who belonged to the *chia* (that is, all children except married out daughters) could not dispose of these resources as they wished, but had to use them in ways their parents approved. Parents could not avoid investing their resources in their children, but they could treat the investment as a loan that had to be repaid by the fulfillment of a number of obligations. These obligations included obedience (filiality) and large contributions to the family economy. Sons were also obliged to support the parents in their old age.

* My interpretation is based largely on data from the first half of this century, but it is consistent with the data that are available from earlier periods. (See, for example, Fei 1939; Fei and Chang 1945; B. Gallin 1966; Levy 1971; Smith 1970; M. Wolf 1972; Yang 1945).

† Although adult offspring (in particular, sons) could bargain over the contents of intergenerational exchanges, they acquired the right to bargain long after the basic terms of the contracts had been established. For this reason my analysis emphasizes the role of the parents in defining the terms of the contracts.

While the jural perspective has revealed the contents and the exchange nature of parent-child resource flows, it has told us little about the timing and nothing about the precise levels of flows between different family members. Yet it is precisely these aspects of the exchanges that must be comprehended if we are to understand changes in sex stratification in this society.

Following the anthropologist Sahlins, we can distinguish three ideal forms of exchange: balanced, generalized, and negative (in Sahlins' terms these are forms of reciprocity; see Sahlins 1972:191–96). In balanced exchange one thing is exchanged for another of equivalent value with little delay. Generalized exchange describes transactions that, while apparently altruistic, in fact generate a counterobligation. In this case, however, the repayment need not be equivalent in value and may occur at a much later time. This is the kind of exchange that several scholars have suggested characterizes all family relations (Becker 1981:172–99; Ben-Porath 1980; Sahlins 1972:196–204). In family exchanges, "there is generally no explicit balancing of the exchange in terms of a unit of account. . . . Instead, large outstanding balances are tolerated; . . . when and how these balances are liquidated remains open" (Ben-Porath, 1980:3). Finally, there is negative exchange, which is not exchange at all, for in it all the resources flow in one direction. In addition to Sahlins' distinctions, we can also distinguish between high-flow and low-flow contracts, which depend on the share of total family resources that is exchanged between the parties to the contract.

Within the Chinese family contracts were not uniform, but varied systematically by sex. Contracts between parents and sons were higher-flow contracts that approximated generalized exchange, while contracts between parents and daughters were lower-flow contracts that fit more closely the balanced model.* While there was no free lunch for either sons or daughters, daughters received a smaller portion and had to repay it in more equivalent amounts over a shorter time. Sons got a larger share of *chia* resources and could repay it in unspecified amounts over relatively long periods of time. Thus, the relatively altruistic generalized exchange, which many have seen as characterizing all intrafamilial relations, here characterized only relations between parents and sons; parents were much more "selfish" in their treatment of daughters.

The differences between sons' and daughters' contracts were rooted in the different membership statuses and functions of males and females in the basic familial units. Different statuses gave rise to different durations of membership and thus different lifetimes of parent-child contracts. Sons

---

* Parent-child contracts also varied by the sex of the parent. Because of space limitations I cannot elaborate on these differences here.

were long-term members of the family whose contracts were, from the parents' perspective at least, for life. Daughters were temporary members whose contracts lasted only until their marriage, usually from 15 to 20 years.

The different lifetimes of the two contracts provided the economic basis for favoring sons over daughters in levels of investment and terms of repayment. Because parents' long-term well-being depended crucially on their sons, parents invested as much as they could in their sons' upbringing, providing schooling, apprentice training, and the like. This investment served a dual purpose, both increasing the son's ability to provide for his parents in the future and ensuring his adherence to the contract by increasing his debt to them. Because parents had to secure their sons' loyalty, they could not be too "mean-spirited" (hsiao-ch'i) in demanding immediate and equivalent repayment for the cost of their training and marriage. Nor did they have to be, for sons had decades in which to repay these debts. Especially when economic opportunities were brighter elsewhere, parents might allow sons a bit of freedom to leave and find a more promising line of work, even if it meant temporary loss of labor or income to the family. This strategy served the parents well in the long run; if the sons were successful, they would expand the family's assets and thus improve their ability to provide for their parents after the family divided. These considerations lay behind the use of relatively generalized contracts in raising sons.

Daughters faced a very different parental calculus. As short-term members of the chia, daughters were unlikely to contribute much to its economy. As a result, parents did not "waste" resources in schooling them, but restricted their education to on-the-job training in the "feminine" tasks of housework, child care, and home-based productive work. With only a few years to repay the debt for their upbringing and marriage, daughters were expected to begin repayment early. Thus, while their brothers had spare time for play until they were 16 or so, girls started assuming responsibility for family chores at 5 or 6, and continued to spend much of their time on housework until their marriage. Yet even this contribution was not seen as sufficient repayment for the costs of their subsistence and marriage. In the traditional environment daughters simply had no way to balance the account. From an economic point of view, daughters truly were "goods on which one loses," "water spilled on the ground," and all the other epithets by which they were commonly known.

Intergenerational contracts varied somewhat by class (see, for example, Levy 1971 : 75–93). However, in the nonelite majority that I consider here (peasants, workers, shopkeepers, and the like), there was an essential uniformity in the differential treatment of sons and daughters. In the sections that follow we shall see how these differences were later maintained and built on by parents. First, however, we need to look briefly at the global and national context in which these processes occurred.

Development and Change:
The Global and National Context

Following the Second World War, the environment in which Taiwan's families operated was shaped by the policies of their government as it adapted to and attempted to take advantage of changes in global political and economic systems. Although this is not the place to explore these power relationships or their policy consequences (see Winckler and Greenhalgh 1988; S. Ho 1978), we do need briefly to chart their course and their influence on opportunity structures in three key areas: education, occupation, and wages.

From the beginning, the government gave high priority to education, providing opportunities for boys and girls alike. Well aware of the links between education and development, in 1953 the government made six years of primary education free and compulsory, and in 1968–69 it added three more years of free schooling at the junior middle school level.

The expansion of educational opportunities was reflected in a phenomenal increase in school attendance at every level. Though girls initially lagged behind boys, especially in the upper levels, the gap between the sexes narrowed rapidly, so that by the early 1980's the ratio of girl to boy graduates was .97 at the junior high level and .85 at the senior high level, while the ratio of female to male entrants was .93 at the university level (Ministry of Education 1983). These figures confirm what most people on the island believe—that sex discrimination in the educational system is relatively mild, and appears mostly in subtle forms.

Since my primary concern is with sex differentials in work outside the family context, I ignore the important changes that have occurred in agriculture and focus on changes in manufacturing, the industry that has grown the most rapidly in the postwar period. The roots of Taiwan's manufacturing explosion are part of a global story that is now well known (Ozawa 1979; on the impact of global processes on women, see Nash and Fernandez-Kelly 1983). Briefly, in the 1950's and early 1960's rising production costs in the industrialized countries set off a search for new production sites with abundant supplies of low-cost, unskilled labor. Meanwhile, in Taiwan, import substitution policies were running up against a narrow market, causing a slowdown in industrial growth and intensifying the problem of surplus labor in agriculture. A solution to both problems was found in Taiwan's switch to export-oriented industrialization based on foreign investment and exploitation of the largely untapped reserve of educated, unskilled female labor.

This switch was engineered by the government, which acted as a broker in getting the factories to Taiwan and the women, who were eager for the income, to the factories. In the economic sphere, it began around 1958 to create one of the most attractive investment climates in the world; in 1965 it opened the first export processing zone; and in the years that followed it continued to update and improve its policies to accord with changes in the domestic and global economies (for details, see Galenson 1979b; S. Ho 1978; Lin 1973). In the cultural sphere, the government's messages in newspapers, television, and textbooks reinforced traditional views that the good woman was a good wife and mother (thus, outside work was a temporary phase in her life cycle); that the purpose of education was to make better mothers (hence it did not matter if it did not lead to a good job); that women were supplementary earners in the family (and therefore did not need high wages); and so forth.

While these efforts attracted a healthy number of foreign companies, more important numerically were the local firms, which, multiplying furiously, sought to outdo their global competitors in the race to lower labor costs and increase exports. As the strategy grew increasingly successful, the island's prosperity came to depend on its continued high level of exports, which in turn depended on a continued supply of low-wage female labor. Even in the 1970's and early 1980's, when import quotas and competition from lower-wage countries led the government to promote capital- and technology-intensive industries, the bulk of Taiwan's exports continued to be made up of labor-intensive goods produced primarily by women (in particular, textile products, electrical machinery, and miscellaneous manufactures).* These basic facts of the modern world system—that for late developers, competitiveness depends on cheap labor and that women provide the largest body of cheap labor—have fundamentally shaped the opportunities open to women in Taiwan.

These developments in the global economy brought an explosion of job opportunities for women and a massive entry of women into the labor

*In 1981, for example, 66 percent of exports were in these three industries. In the mid-1970's women made up 72 percent of the labor force in textile products, 55 percent in electrical machinery, and 63 percent in miscellaneous manufacturing (calculated from Council for Economic Planning and Development 1982:204–5 and Directorate-General of Budget, Accounting and Statistics 1977:60–71). In 1984 the great majority of new jobs in manufacturing (about 85 percent) were for unskilled workers, and the great majority of these jobs (about 87 percent) were for women (*Free China Journal*, 24 June and 8 July 1984).

force. While the proportion of men in the labor force declined slightly, between 1956 and 1966 the proportion of women 15 and older (12 and older in 1956) who were working (both inside and outside the family context) rose from 20 to 34 percent; in the late 1960's and early 1970's it increased to 40 percent, and it has remained slightly below that level since. Much of the increase in the paid female work force has been among unmarried women. In 1982, for example, 58 percent of paid women employees had never married (DGBAS 1982:102–3).

While the number of jobs for women increased very rapidly, the number of industries open to them remained limited. The greatest number of new jobs, of course, were in manufacturing. However, the boom in manufacturing set off a spurt of development throughout the economy that opened up other opportunities in commerce and in social and personal services. In 1982 these three industries absorbed about 91 percent of the female labor force outside agriculture (DGBAS 1982:8–9). Job opportunities for men were more broadly distributed across the industrial spectrum. In addition to the three industries that absorbed most of the women workers, as well as 71 percent of the men in 1982, there were new opportunities for men in construction, in transport, and in communication (DGBAS 1982:8–9; for historical trends, see Liu 1983).

Working women also faced occupational segregation and limited access to the most prestigious and lucrative jobs. The great bulk of the opportunities were in production work, with clerical jobs coming in a distant second. Access to professional jobs remained limited to about 7 percent of working women (most of whom were primary school teachers), while administrative, managerial, and employer positions were closed to all but a handful of women (Census Office 1976; DGBAS 1982; Taiwan Provincial Labor Force Survey and Research Institute, various years). Among women in nonagricultural, nonmilitary jobs, fully 12 percent were employed in the most common occupation; among men, the comparable figure was 7 percent (Census Office, 1976). Thus, the overall picture is one of moderate occupational concentration and relatively limited access to high-status and high-paying jobs.

Income opportunities also favored men. The real earnings of women workers increased slowly in the 1950's, declined in the mid-1960's, and then rose rapidly (Liu 1983). In most industries, however, the increase in female wages did not keep up with the increase in male wages. In manufacturing, which contained almost half the paid female labor force, the ratio of female to male wages fell from .83 in the early 1950's to .51 in the early 1960's, climbed to about .62 in the early 1970's, and remained at about that level into the early 1980's (DGBAS 1982; Galenson 1979a). In commerce, which contained one-fifth of the paid female labor force, the wage ratio remained steady at about .69 in the period 1966–80. In other services, which absorbed another fifth, the wage ratio declined from .72 in 1966–70 to .63 in 1976–80. Although income opportunities for women improved absolutely, over most of this 30-year period they worsened relative to the earning opportunities of men.

Such an environment did not provide many incentives to parents to discard their traditional bias against daughters. Although educational opportunities were relatively neutral as to sex, opportunities in employment and income were heavily biased in favor of males. In the next section we will see how parents who faced this environment took up these new opportunities, fitting them into traditional strategies in ways that advanced their own interests to the detriment of their daughters'.

Parents as Agents of Sexual Stratification

In capsule form my argument is as follows: in perhaps the majority of families sexual stratification increased in the postwar period.* These families saw growing differences between sons and daughters in personal autonomy or freedom from parental control and in possession of socioeconomic resources.

The key agents of this process were not the state or the multinationals, but the parents themselves. For Taiwanese parents, who grew up in an era of slow economic change and modest improvements in living standards, the postwar period brought a veritable explosion of opportunities to improve their lives. Correctly perceiving that their future well-being depended on their sons—after all, their daughters would marry out—these parents responded by using these opportunities to improve their sons' resources in order ultimately to improve their own long-run mobility and security.

Their key tools were the intergenerational contracts that had been used by Chinese parents since traditional times. These contracts proved particularly useful because they allowed parents to treat sons and daughters differently. While offering their sons the relatively costly form of generalized exchange, with high levels of investment and easy repayment terms, parents could displace some of the costs onto their daughters by giving them less generous contracts stipulating balanced exchange with lower levels of investment and more rigid, quid-pro-quo terms of repayment.

*This argument applies to all families whose resources were limited and had to be carefully allocated. Thus it applies to all but the tiny elite of large industrialists; data not included here suggest that patterns of sexual stratification were different in this class. The argument may apply to migrants from the Chinese mainland, but it is designed specifically to explain sex differentiation within the indigenous population (the "Taiwanese"), who constitute about 85 percent of the total.

Put baldly, parents' key strategy was to take more from daughters so as to give more to sons and thus get more for themselves. They were able to take more from their daughters by investing a bit more in their education; since in these contracts parental investments had to be repaid, increased investments generated increased debts. Whereas traditionally, daughters could repay their parents only by helping around the house—and even then there remained an unpaid balance—now daughters could repay their debts—and repay them fully—by working outside the home and remitting their wages to their parents. I suggest that parents were willing to increase their investments in their daughters' education in large part because they expected, if only subconsciously, that they could extract increased returns from them. This was true not so much for primary school, which was necessary for basic literacy—a prerequisite for all functioning members of society and all girls who wished to make reasonable matches—as for postprimary school, which was increasingly necessary to obtain a factory and particularly an office job (see, for example, Diamond 1969:36–39).

While remittances were the predominant form of repayment for educational and other investments, they were by no means the only form. Indeed, there was a bundle of "goods" parents could receive in return for their investments. These included relatively material benefits, such as assistance in finding jobs and housing for other family members; sociopolitical advantages that could accrue to parents making advantageous marriages for their daughters; and more purely status returns, such as those that came from providing a daughter with a large dowry or marrying a daughter into a high-status family. The form of repayment a daughter made depended largely on her position in the sibling set. The majority of daughters, and all oldest daughters, repaid their investments primarily in the form of remittances, which could be used to help educate their siblings. However, things were likely to be different for daughters with no younger siblings and no older siblings still in school, especially if their parents were wealthy enough to support themselves at their desired standard of living. Because parents did not need money from these daughters, they were less interested in monetary returns than in the sociopolitical and status returns that would come from making good matches for their daughters and sending them off into marriage with large, showy dowries.

Although the form of repayment was somewhat flexible, the necessity of repayment was not. Parents enforced this expectation by socializing their daughters to believe that they themselves were worthless, and that literally everything they had—their bodies, their upbringing, their schooling—belonged to their parents and had to be paid for.

If taking more from daughters held pitfalls, giving more to sons was fraught with greater perils. By enabling their sons to obtain a better education and occupation than they themselves had had, parents would lose control and power over them; they thus risked losing their sons' loyalty and promise of support in their old age. Such a risk, however, was offset by a potential advantage in increasing the resources available to sons. Traditionally, the most successful families were wealthy families that had diversified their economies and assigned a different son to manage each part of the estate (Chow 1966; P. Ho 1962; Meskill 1979). The evidence available suggests that in these families sons were allowed to accumulate tangible private property that was not part of the family estate (Ebrey 1984:103–6; on Taiwan, see Meskill 1979:245). In short, the heads of these families bought their sons' loyalty by allowing them to enjoy a modicum of independence and personal wealth.

For contemporary Taiwanese families, this tradition—which remained part of the cultural repertoire—suggested that by investing in their sons' education and giving them freedom to develop their own careers, parents would not necessarily jeopardize their sons' loyalty, and might in fact help to secure it. If successful, such a strategy would doubly benefit the parents in their sunset years: first, by making sons wealthier, it would delay family division, and thus reduce the period of dependence on sons' largesse; second, it would guarantee prosperity in old age, for well-to-do sons lose face if they are miserly in supporting their parents. Thus the strategy involved risk, but the risk was offset by potential benefits. In any event, parents did not have much choice, for the option of keeping their sons in agriculture was being rapidly eliminated by massive structural change in the economy.

The results of this strategy of using daughters to elevate sons were twofold. First, it increased the gap between sons and daughters in their degree of personal autonomy. While parents gave their sons increasing freedom to develop the knowledge, skills, and contacts that would enhance their future earning potential, they sought to increase their control over their daughters. As their investments in their daughters rose, the time available to the daughters to repay their debts shrank (although the age at marriage rose, the age at graduation rose faster).* Parents therefore applied increasing pressure to ensure that the debts were repaid by seeking

---

*In the prewar period girls who did not attend school began to take responsibility for household tasks at about age 6 and married between 17.6 (cohort born 1891–95) and 18.9 years of age (1916–20 cohort) (data from northern Taiwan, calculated from A. Wolf and Huang 1980:135). By 1982 the mean age at first marriage had risen to 24.2, while the average age at graduation had risen to 15.8 (among women aged 20–24) (calculated from Ministry of Interior 1983). Thus, the time available for repaying debts to parents shrank from about 12 years to 8.4. In the sample we examine below, the number of years available to daughters to repay their debts fell from 10.3 in the cohort born in 1940–45 to 9.0 in the 1946–49 cohort, and 8.3 in the 1950–53 cohort (N = 72).

control in such areas as job selection, residence, and remittance of income. For most daughters the most important area was the last one: abundant evidence suggests that parents sought control in other areas primarily to ensure control over their daughters' wages (see especially Kung 1983). For youngest daughters with economically secure parents and no siblings in school, however, parental control over residence and job selection was designed primarily to increase control over their entry into the marriage market. By guiding their daughters' entry into this market, parents could improve their chances of contracting a marriage that offered sociopolitical and status benefits for themselves. The result was a growing gap between the sexes in subjection to parental domination.

The second result was increased inequality between sons and daughters in access to strategic socioeconomic resources—education, a good occupation, income, and property. While there were educational differences between sons and daughters in the traditional period, they were held down by the limits on educational opportunities. In the postwar period the expansion of opportunities led to a sharp rise in educational inequality, as parents deliberately took their daughters out of school early so they might earn the money that would keep their brothers in school longer. Equipped with more training—and favored by a pro-male environment—sons were able to obtain higher-status jobs, earn higher incomes, and save part of these incomes to invest in personal property. In short, educational differences set off a spiral of economic differences so that by the time of their marriages sons and daughters were separated by a substantial economic gulf.

The linchpin of the process by which parents engineered growing inequalities among their children was the education of daughters. By educating their daughters, parents increased their daughters' debts to them and, in turn, increased the resources available for investment in their sons. The system developed smoothly because education and remittances fit easily into existing patterns of intergenerational investment and repayment. Indeed, the exchange of remittances for education was already well established for sons; its extension to daughters entailed only minor adjustments to the system. Furthermore, these changes were not only palatable to but actively sought by the daughters themselves. In their view, education was the key to personal mobility—bringing both a better job and a better husband—while work outside the home brought a novel chance to gain some personal autonomy and see a bit of the world. Thus, modest improvements in their own resources, coupled with the knowledge that ultimately their status would depend on their husbands' resources and not their own, worked to mask the fact that their brothers were advancing at their expense.

In order to see how these parental strategies developed, we now turn to a body of data that allows us to examine sex differences among children in the same families. These data come from a longitudinal study of families in northern Taiwan conducted in 1978–80. Collected in a series of intensive interviews, the data cover the socioeconomic strategies used by all members of 80 families during the 25-year-period 1954–78 (methods of data collection and analysis are detailed in Greenhalgh 1982).

To reduce some of the variability expected in so small a sample, I limited the sample to native Taiwanese families whose economic heads were born between 1915 and 1935. The sample is not representative of the population as a whole, but can be thought of as a kind of multi-cohort sample whose parental generation passed through the full period of Taiwan's postwar development together.

The children I studied were born between the late 1930's and mid-1960's. Because their parents belong to a limited number of age groups, among the children age tends to be related to sibling position; children born in the earlier years of the study period fall at the beginning of the sibling set, while those born near the end fall at the end of the sibling set. This bias in the sample creates certain difficulties for the empirical analysis because some of the investments, notably education, vary by sibling position. These problems will be dealt with below by controlling for sibling position.

The families are about equally distributed among three communities: a cluster of villages in Sanchih township, the small city of Tanshui, and the metropolitan center of Taipei. The sample includes a range of socioeconomic groups typical of the bulk of the population: temporary workers, including landless agricultural laborers and peddlers (N = 18); farm groups, including tenants, owner-cultivators, and landlords transformed into owner-cultivators by the 1953 land reform (N = 36); regular workers, including full-time employees, mostly factory workers (N = 12); and shopkeepers, or owners of retail and wholesale stores (N = 14). (Families are classified by group membership at the beginning of the period of observation, i.e., late 1940s/early 1950s.) While interclass differences are not unimportant, in most of what follows I suppress this information because the number of cases is too small to permit generalizations. In most areas we will discuss, parental strategies turned out to be relatively uniform across classes, varying not in kind but only in degree.

Educational Investments in Children

Education has been identified as the pivot of the process of growing sexual inequality. If the argument set out above is correct, we should find a growing sex gap in education, as parents increase their investments in most of their daughters' educations just enough to get them a good-paying job but not beyond a level they could repay before they married, while increasing their investments in their sons' educations as much as they could on the assumption that the higher the investment the higher the long-run return.* Systematic discrimination against daughters in the provision of education has been reported from many parts of the island (see, for example, Diamond 1979; B. Gallin 1966; R. Gallin 1984; Hu 1983; Robins and Cheng 1977; M. Wolf 1972). For quantitative and longitudinal data, however, we will have to turn to the study of the northern region (Greenhalgh 1982).

Trends in the absolute levels of education received by sons and daughters in the northern sample are shown in Table 1. To see change over time, I have grouped sons and daughters into three cohorts, those born in the periods 1940–50, 1951–55, and 1956–63. (These data cannot be used to assess trends in gender inequality because the three cohorts represent older, middle, and younger siblings, and sibling position is closely related to education; relative levels are estimated below.) Data on formal schooling (shown in Panel A) suggest that parents' investments in their daughters grew rapidly between the 1940's and 1970's, but in most groups and cohorts remained lower than investments in their sons. For all groups together, the number of years of schooling obtained by daughters increased from 6.7 in the 1940–50 cohort to 9.4 in the 1956–63 cohort, while the amount of schooling received by their brothers increased from 9.2 to 9.8 years. The high level of schooling obtained by sons in the first cohort is not a real phenomenon, but reflects the large number of first sons in wealthy families in that cohort. Here and below, great care should be taken in generalizing the findings from this small sample to the population as a whole.

Schooling, of course, is but one component of education. Equally im-

---

* Although there is no evidence that parents consciously calculated the value of their expenditures on daughters and then demanded an equivalent amount in return, evidence of other sorts suggests that such calculations may be made subconsciously. The treatment of marriage expenses provides the best illustration of the utilitarian, quid pro quo approach taken to expenditures and returns on daughters. In both traditional and contemporary China the betrothal gift (engagement money sent by the groom's family to the bride's) has been described as compensation for the money invested in raising a girl (Croll 1981 : 50–54; A. Wolf and Huang 1980:270). In Japanese-period Taiwan, Wolf has calculated that the average engagement gift did in fact constitute an approximate compensation for the cost of bringing up a young girl (A. Wolf and Huang 1980: 270). Despite government protestations, the custom has persisted through mainland China and Taiwan, giving rise to new forms of bargaining over a bride's value as the social and economic resources of girls change (see, for example, Croll 1981 : 50–54; Hu 1983 : 129–53).

TABLE I

*Years of Total Education Obtained by Sons and Daughters
in Different Socioeconomic Groups*

A. SCHOOLING ALONE

	Cohort (year born)					
	1940–50		1951–55		1956–63	
	Sons	Daugh.	Sons	Daugh.	Sons	Daugh.
Socioeconomic group	Yrs. (N)	Yrs. (N)	Yrs. (N)	Yrs. (N)	Yrs. (N)	Yrs. (N)
Temporary workers	6.0 (8)	4.2 (11)	6.7 (13)	5.4 (5)	7.8 (13)	8.7 (16)
Regular workers	9.6 (7)	6.9 (7)	8.8 (12)	9.0 (6)	10.6 (10)	10.1 (7)
Farmers	7.5 (24)	6.7 (30)	9.0 (29)	9.1 (23)	9.7 (38)	9.0 (29)
Shopkeepers	12.9 (17)	10.1 (8)	12.0 (15)	13.3 (15)	13.8 (6)	12.4 (5)
All groups	9.2 (56)	6.7 (56)	8.7 (59)	10.0 (49)	9.8 (67)	9.4 (57)

B. SCHOOLING PLUS APPRENTICESHIPS

	Cohort (year born)					
	1940–50		1951–55		1956–63	
	Sons	Daugh.	Sons	Daugh.	Sons	Daugh.
Socioeconomic group	Yrs.	Yrs.	Yrs.	Yrs.	Yrs.	Yrs.
Temporary workers	6.8	4.5	7.6	6.0	9.5	8.7
Regular workers	10.4	6.9	10.3	9.0	10.9	10.3
Farmers	7.9	6.9	9.9	9.2	10.5	9.1
Shopkeepers	13.1	10.1	12.0	13.3	13.8	12.4
All groups	9.6	6.9	9.6	10.1	10.6	9.4

NOTE: Includes sons and daughters who had finished school or were in their final year of school in 1976.

portant is on-the-job training that prepares the individual for a specific
job. In contemporary Taiwan, as in traditional China (Burgess 1928), on-
the-job training is formalized in a system of apprenticeships that generally
last three years. Apprenticeships, which remain little studied and absent
from the official education statistics, play a critical role in sex stratification;
while such training is available to boys in virtually all blue-collar jobs, it is
available to girls in only a few, mostly service-sector jobs (as seamstresses
or beauticians, for example). The magnitude of the sex gap in opportunities for such training can be gauged from my sample, in which 25 percent
of the sons (N = 182) but only 4 percent of the daughters (N = 162)
received apprentice training.

An important additional measure of human capital, then, is the total
number of years spent in school and apprenticeships. The figures shown in
Panel B of Table I show even more clearly than the figures on schooling
the effect of parents' investment calculus, operating in a male-oriented
environment, on educational attainment. According to this calculus, some
schooling for daughters is essential preparation for a job (unskilled factory

jobs generally require a junior-high-school degree), but an apprenticeship is a luxury that would drastically shorten the period of repayment and, in the worst possible case, eliminate it altogether. Since parents cannot be sure when their daughters will marry, they opt for immediate returns on their investments, and send their daughters into the work force without specialized skills. Thus we find that for girls the amount of education was virtually identical with the amount of schooling. For boys, however, the educational level increased from 9.6 years in the first cohort, .4 years more than schooling, to 10.6 years in the last cohort, almost one year more than schooling.

While there have been marked improvements in the absolute educational levels of both sons and daughters, the data presented above cannot be used to infer changes in the relative educational positions of the two sexes because they are affected by differences in sibling position. Before attempting to measure the actual sex gap in education, we need to see how sibling position affects educational attainment.

Among parents with limited resources, a major strategy for raising the educational level of their sons is to educate their daughters a little, send them out to work, and then use their incomes to pay for higher education for their sons. Studies of young women workers suggest that a substantial number are working for the explicit purpose of supporting their siblings', especially their brothers', schooling (Arrigo 1980; Diamond 1979; R. Gallin 1984; Huang 1984; Kung 1983). If this strategy has worked, we should find a direct relationship between the number of sisters a boy has and the amount of schooling he obtains.

The data from northern Taiwan suggest that the strategy has been nothing less than a smashing success; see Table 2. In the lower 80 percent

TABLE 2

Effect of Number of Sisters on Schooling of Brothers

No. of sisters	Bottom 80 pct. of families in 1954		All families	
	Years of schooling	No. of brothers	Years of schooling	No. of brothers
0	6.8	11	7.9	13
1	8.0	41	8.6	46
2	8.3	49	8.8	54
3	9.6	49	9.7	54
4 and over	11.4	8	11.3	12
Average	8.7	158	9.1	179

N O T E: Sample includes brothers who had finished school or were in their final year of school in 1978. It excludes one highly atypical wealthy family with four sons and no daughters. This family brings years of schooling for sons with no sisters to 9.7.

of families (defined by income position in 1954), as the number of sisters increased from none to four or more, the number of years of schooling obtained by their brothers increased from 6.8 to 11.4. For all families together the relationship is similar but slightly less dramatic.

If widely used, such a strategy can be expected to produce a pattern of variation by sibling position such that, among same-sex siblings, the older the child, the lower the level of education. While this pattern should be found among both boys and girls, it should be more pronounced among girls. This is because the education received by girls is determined in large part by the needs of other family members. Oldest daughters are often expected to sacrifice for all their younger siblings and leave school at a very early age. Younger daughters with no younger siblings not only have no one to sacrifice for, but may have older siblings in the labor force, enabling them to stay in school much longer. The result should be a marked increase in education with increase in sibling order.

While the education of daughters is allowed to vary by sibling position, the education of sons is considered so important that even when their sisters are too young to work, parents will go to great lengths, even restricting consumption, to enable sons at the beginning of the birth order to get some schooling. My interviews suggest that most parents attempt to equalize educational opportunities for their sons. However, some parents who have limited resources prefer to concentrate their investments, allocating the bulk of their educational investments to one son, often the first son, and channeling the other sons into technical careers via apprenticeships. The education of sons, then, is determined both by the number of sisters they have, and by their parents' preference for equalizing or concentrating educational investments. Thus, we should expect an increase in education with sibling order, offset to some degree by strategies of concentrating or equalizing investments.

Data on sibling position and schooling are shown in Table 3. To control for the secular increase in schooling that occurred during this time, we examine differences between same-sex siblings within the same cohort (a procedure that greatly limits the size of the sample). Educational differences among sons are shown in Panel A. Comparison of first and second sons reveals that first sons received less schooling than second sons in the first cohort, but more schooling in the later cohorts. The major reason eldest sons in the first cohort obtained less schooling than their younger brothers would seem to be that most of these sons had no older sisters to help finance their education. Among all first sons in the first cohort, those with no older sister received 1.2 years less schooling than those with an older sister (8.0 compared to 9.2 years, N = 25 and 10 respectively; data not shown in table). The educational advantage of first sons in the later

TABLE 3

Sibling Position and Amount of Schooling

A. Sons

Cohort	Families with first and second sons in same cohort		Families with second and third or higher sons in same cohort	
	First son	Second son	Second son	Third or higher son
1940–50	7.8 (14)[a]	9.4 (14)	13.5 (6)	13.1 (7)
1951–55	11.1 (8)	9.5 (8)	n.a.	n.a.
1956–63	10.7 (7)	9.3 (7)	8.3 (4)	8.3 (4)

B. Daughters

Cohort	Families with first and second daughters in same cohort		Families with second and third or higher daughters in same cohort	
	First daughter	Second daughter	Second daughter	Third or higher daughter
1940–50	6.4 (17)	7.4 (17)	7.5 (2)	9.0 (2)
1951–55	12.0 (5)	12.0 (5)	13.0 (4)	13.0 (4)
1956–63	9.0 (6)	9.5 (6)	9.0 (4)	10.6 (5)

[a] Numbers in parentheses are sample sizes.

two cohorts suggests the strength of parental strategies of concentrating investments in their eldest sons. The comparison of second with third or higher sons shows negligible differences in schooling, suggesting parental attempts to equalize educational investments among second and later-born sons.

Data on daughters, shown in Panel B of Table 3, indicate a much stronger relation between sibling position and level of schooling. In two of the three cohorts, first daughters obtained less schooling than second daughters, and second daughters received less schooling than third and higher-order daughters. The special position of the youngest daughter with no younger siblings cannot be seen from this table, but it is revealed in data on third and higher-order daughters in the third cohort (in which the youngest daughters are most numerous). Among that group of daughters, the average schooling of daughters with younger siblings is 8.9 years (N = 12), while the schooling of daughters without younger siblings is 10.1 years (N = 8). In sum, these data show substantial differences in schooling by sibling position, especially among daughters.

The degree of success parents had in restricting the schooling of their daughters to extend the schooling of their sons suggests that there were systematic differences between the sexes in the amount of education obtained. Yet we still do not know the size of these differences and whether they grew or shrank over time. To examine these issues we need to eliminate the effects of sibling position and control for the large variations

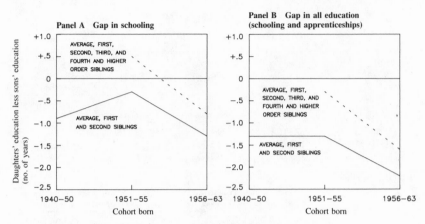

FIGURE I. Educational Gap Between Sons and Daughters

in the proportion of the store-owner group, whose educational levels were well above average (see Table 2).

Figure 1 shows changes in the gender gap in schooling and education after controlling for these two factors. To control for the variations in the share of the store-owner group, I have simply eliminated the children of that group from the sample. To smooth out variations in the number of children in each sibling position, I have computed two measures of the average educational levels of children in each position. These measures assume that each cohort contains equal numbers of siblings of each birth order. One measure is an average of the group averages for first, second, third, and fourth and higher-order same-sex siblings. Because the first cohort contains very few higher-order siblings, this measure can only be computed for the second and third cohorts. A second measure is the average of the group averages for first and second same-sex siblings. Because it is based on only two siblings, this measure provides a less complete picture of trends in gender inequality. However, it is useful because it can be computed for all three cohorts.

Panel A of Figure 1 shows changes in the gender gap in schooling. This gap is measured as the number of years obtained by daughters minus the number of years obtained by sons. Comparison of first and second sons and daughters (unbroken line) shows a modest decline followed by a large increase in the sex gap in schooling. In the first cohort, daughters received .9 year less schooling than their brothers. In the second cohort they obtained .3 year less, while in the last cohort daughters got 1.3 years less schooling than sons. Comparison of sons and daughters of all sibling positions (broken line) shows a 1.3-year increase in the gender gap in schooling between the second and third cohorts. (The reason daughters in the middle cohort received .5 years more schooling than their brothers is likely to be that when this cohort was entering the labor force the bulk of the jobs open to women required some education, while there were many jobs for men that required no schooling.)

Trends in the gender gap in education (schooling plus apprenticeships) are explored in Panel B. Both measures show unambiguous increases in sexual inequality over time. Among first and second siblings (unbroken line), the gap increased from 1.3 years in the first and second cohorts to 2.2 years in the third cohort. Among children of all sibling positions (broken line), the gap between daughters and sons increased from .3 year in the second cohort to 1.6 years in the third cohort.

In sum, the data in Figure 1 support the hypothesis that parental strategies worked to increase sexual stratification in schooling and education in the generation born between the early 1940's and the mid-1960's. The difference between the size of the two gaps—.8 years in schooling and 1.6 years in education (among all siblings in the youngest cohort)—suggests that while daughters were only slightly discriminated against in formal schooling, they were greatly disadvantaged in the acquisition of specialized skills. As the economy shifted from labor-intensive to more technology-intensive forms of production, it is likely that this growing inequality in training provided the basis for growing inequality in access to skilled jobs and high incomes.

Parental Control over Returns on Investments

Chinese children are educated on the assumption that after they graduate, they will work and contribute to the family economy. In this section, I consider the degree of autonomy a young worker has in deciding where to live and how much money to send home.

Young people living at home are subject to their parents' authority in a wide range of areas. Perhaps most important to the parents, unmarried children living at home are expected to participate in the common economy, contributing their labor and most of their earnings (usually 60 to 100 percent) to the family (Arrigo 1980; Cohen 1976; Diamond 1979). Parents can also monitor their children's friendships and heterosexual activities, greatly influencing their children's, especially their daughters', marriage prospects. Those living outside the parental household—in a dorm or, less frequently, an apartment—are scarcely autonomous. But they nonetheless gain a measure of freedom in decisions as to precisely how much to remit, and in areas such as food, clothing, entertainment, and friendships (Kung 1983). Thus we can use data on where workers live—inside or outside the parental household—as a measure of the amount of control they exercise over their labor and income, and over some areas of their personal lives.

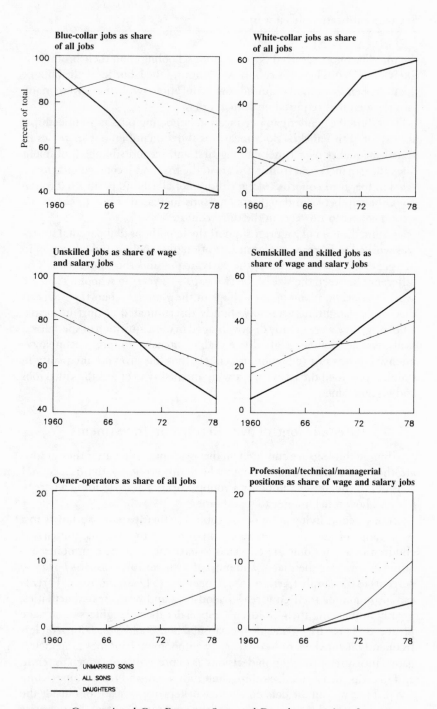

FIGURE 2. Occupational Gap Between Sons and Daughters, 1960–78

Evidence gathered by other researchers supports the hypothesis that parents seek to keep girls at home while boys are allowed or even encouraged to move out if they can find a better job elsewhere (M. Wolf 1972:87–98; Wu 1976). Although the desire to have daughters live at home is frequently explained in terms of preserving their reputation and thus marriageability, a closer look suggests that for most daughters, parents' more fundamental concern is control over their labor and, even more important, their income (Arrigo 1980; Kung 1983; Wu 1976). By keeping daughters at home, parents can both ensure that their investments are repaid and influence their daughters' entry into marriage. If successful, such a dual strategy should give rise to a growing gender gap in residential autonomy.

Trends in residence of working sons and daughters in northern Taiwan are displayed in Figure 2. These curves contain striking support for our hypothesis. Between 1960 and 1978 the share of working daughters living outside the parental household fell 25 percentage points, from 63 to 38. At the same time the share of all sons living outside rose by 24 points, from 29 to 53. Some of this rise was associated with the marriage of sons and the formation of new households by their nuclear units. However, the rise in outside residence among unmarried sons was also high, and almost as marked as that found for all sons.

Although we may never be able to disentangle all the causes of these changes, it would be grossly oversimplifying to suggest that they are due solely to changing levels of parental control. Changes in the economic environment also played a critical role. For example, the decline in outside residence of daughters partly reflects changes in the economy that enabled parents to increase their control over their working daughters. In 1960, outside residence was high largely because the majority of jobs then available to daughters were distant from the parental home (for example, dishwashers or factory workers) or required workers to live at the place of employment (such as maids). Parents who wanted their daughters to work were essentially forced to allow them to live outside the home. In the 1960's and 1970's, as opportunities for women in industry and services expanded and spread from urban to rural areas, parents were able to increase their control over their daughters by ensuring that they took jobs that enabled them to live at home, where they would have to turn over most of their wages.

The second area of autonomy is income control. Assuming that working sons and daughters would prefer to keep all their earnings for themselves, we can use the amount they remit to their parents as an indicator of the level of obligation they have to their parents or, put another way, the amount of control their parents exercise over them.

My hypothesis here is similar to those outlined earlier. Because daughters' intergenerational contracts were of shorter duration and more balanced than sons' contracts, at any given time we would expect working daughters to remit higher portions of their income than their brothers. More important, over time, the gap in the portion remitted should increase, as parents seek to control the returns on increased investments in their daughters while making smaller claims on the returns from their sons, enabling them to use their earnings to advance their careers. Finally, we should note that in this sample, the share of income remitted by both sexes is likely to fall over time because workers in later years tend to be younger siblings, whose repayments are less likely to take the form of material goods.

Unfortunately, reliable remittance data are difficult to collect. Remittance levels often vary from month to month and may include in-kind goods that informants neglect to report. In addition to these problems, my data are also likely to suffer from recall problems, especially for the earlier years. Thus the data presented below should be treated with considerable caution.

Data on remittances from sons and daughters working full-time and living outside the parental household are shown in Figure 3. Because married sons are allowed to keep most of their earnings to support their small families, this figure includes only data on unmarried sons and unmarried daughters. In general, the data contain relatively weak support for the hypotheses. Panel A shows changes in the percentage of total income remitted. In all years daughters were more filial than sons, remitting slightly more of their income to their parents. Panel B shows the sex gap in remittances, measured both as the ratio of daughters' to sons' remittances (as a share of income) and as the difference in the percentage of income remitted by daughters and sons. Both measures show little change in inequality between 1966 and 1972, followed by a small increase in inequality between 1972 and 1978. During the later period the ratio of daughters' to sons' remittances grew from 1.09 to 1.45, while the gap between the shares remitted increased from 3 to 8 percentage points.

As expected, the share of earnings remitted declined slightly over time, especially after 1972. The main reason for the decline in remittances, especially of daughters, was the decline in the number of younger siblings these daughters were expected to help support. Between 1960 and 1978 the average number of school-age or preschool-age siblings in these working women's families fell from 3.3 to 1.2. The argument that daughters' obligations to parents did not decline over time but only changed form is supported by data from individual years, which show that, in all years, daughters with one or no dependent siblings remitted only one-quarter to one-half as much as daughters with two or more dependent siblings.

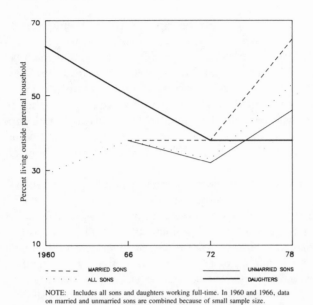

NOTE: Includes all sons and daughters working full-time. In 1960 and 1966, data on married and unmarried sons are combined because of small sample size.

FIGURE 3. Residence of Working Sons and Daughters, 1960–78

In all, the changes were in the right direction, but their size was disappointing. I suspect this is due to data deficiencies, but until better data are available it is impossible to say for sure. Perhaps more important than the question of the amount of income received from workers living outside is the broader issue of the total amount of income appropriated from all working sons and daughters. If we enlarged the sample to include working children living at home, the gender gap in income control would certainly increase, because the proportion of working daughters living at home rose, while that of sons fell (see Figure 2).

Differential Access to Socioeconomic Resources

In this section I observe the impact of differential investment in education on access to strategic socioeconomic resources. My first hypothesis concerns sex stratification in occupation. Here I consider both occupational status, the social or "face" value of different jobs, and the economic rewards sons and daughters receive from working at different jobs. It was argued above that, in the context of a male-biased environment, growing sex differences in level of education and in freedom to experiment with different jobs would lead to growing differences in the types of occupations sons and daughters would be able to obtain. This hypothesis refers primarily to occupational differentiation between unmarried sons and daughters. Married sons can be expected to have better jobs (and higher incomes, more property, and so on) because they are generally older and have more work experience. Nevertheless, in this and the following sections I include data on married sons because their careers show not only the effect of greater age and experience, but also the impact of the boost they received from their sisters, who financed their higher skill levels. Thus the hypothesis can be amended to predict moderate gaps between unmarried daughters and their unmarried brothers, and wider gaps between unmarried daughters and their married brothers or all brothers together.

This hypothesis is explored in Figure 4 and Table 4. As in China historically, in Taiwan today there is a marked status gap between those who work with their heads and those who work with their hands. From this point of view, the position of women appears to have improved dramatically. Between 1960 and 1978 the share of working women in blue-collar jobs dropped from 94 to 41 percent, while the share in white-collar jobs leaped from 6 to 59 percent (see Figure 4). Among their unmarried brothers, the proportion of blue-collar workers declined only slightly, from 83 to 75 percent, while the share of white-collar workers increased only from 17 to 19 percent.

The women themselves perceive this move from factory to office as a big step upward (Kung 1983). And indeed, by their scale of values it is, for the jobs they have left are among the lowest-status jobs in the society (maid is ranked 91st out of 94 jobs, female factory worker is 79th, bus attendant is 80th; see Wen and Chang 1979). Nevertheless, long acquaintance with the

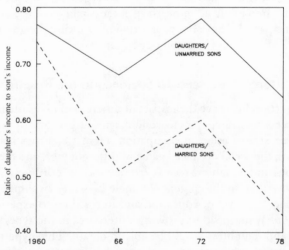

FIGURE 4. Income Gap Between Sons and Daughters, 1960–78

TABLE 4

Occupations of Sons and Daughters, 1960–78

Occupation	Daughters				Unmarried Sons				All Sons			
	1960	1966	1972	1978	1960	1966	1972	1978	1960	1966	1972	1978
EMPLOYEE												
Blue-Collar, unskilled												
Agricultural laborer		1			3	6	5	4	3	6	8	8
Maid	5	5	1	1								
Construction worker						4	4	13		5	8	22
Dishwasher, janitor	4					1	2	2		1	2	3
Waitress, waiter		1	1	4		1	1			1	1	1
Factory worker	5	13	17	16	1	7	12	18	2	7	15	20
Bus attendant			1									
Dancer			1	1								
Blue-Collar, semiskilled												
Nurse		1	1									
Cook, tailor							1	3			1	4
Skilled production worker						5	6	9		5	6	11
Driver (bus, taxi, truck)					1	2	2	1	1	2	3	5
White-Collar, less skilled												
Office helper	1	2	3	1		1	3	1		1	3	2
Store clerk		1	4	3	1	1			1	1		
Clerical worker	1	2	4	14			2	5			2	7
Accountant		2	10	11								
Salesperson		2		1	1			1		1	1	1
White-Collar, skilled and managerial												
Teacher, researcher			1	2				3		1	1	5
Skilled technician								2			1	4
Assistant manager							1	1		1	2	2
OWNER-OPERATOR												
Store owner-operator							1	3			1	6
Factory owner-operator								1			1	5
No information		2	2	2			1				1	
Total number of workers	16	30	48	56	6	29	41	67	7	32	57	106

island suggests that society at large does not consider this shift a sign of marked improvement in women's status. A look at the nature of the white-collar jobs women held suggests why (see Table 4): of the 32 women who held such jobs in 1978, 25 were in clerical or "accountant" positions (a euphemism for someone who works with numbers; essentially a book-keeper), 3 were store clerks, and 2 were teachers. On a scale of 1 to 94 the clerical/accountant positions were ranked 53d to 58th, while store clerk was ranked an even lower 73d. Teaching was much more prestigious, ranking 16th (at the primary level), just above airplane pilot and economist.

When we turn to the top of the status ladder we find unambiguous gaps that increasingly favored men. Among men, the proportion of entrepreneurs—those owning or co-owning a store, factory, or other business—grew from none in 1960 to 6 percent among unmarried men and to 10 percent among all men in 1978 (Figure 4). The proportion of owner-operators among women remained zero throughout the period.

An equally large gap appeared in the proportion of professional, technical, and managerial workers. Among men, the proportion of such workers among all employees rose from none in 1960 to 10 percent for unmarried men and 12 percent for all men in 1978. Among their sisters, this proportion increased from zero to only 4 percent.

What the data suggest is that at the bottom of the occupational ladder—in unskilled and blue-collar jobs—the position of women relative to that of men improved throughout the 1960's and 1970's. However, although women moved up from the bottom, they remained on the lower half of the ladder. At the top of the ladder—in entrepreneurial and professional/managerial positions—a process of sex stratification favoring men began to occur in the mid-1960's. As more of these positions became available in the 1970's, they were taken almost exclusively by men, so that by the end of the decade there was a large gender gap in access to highly valued jobs.

As the sex gap in education and occupation increases, we expect to see growing stratification in income; while sons receiving higher, skill-intensive education monopolize the high-status, high-income occupations, daughters, obtaining lower, skill-deficient education, remain at the bottom of the occupational ladder or move up to middling-status, less well paid jobs.

Estimates of the income of full-time workers confirm this expectation.* Figure 5 charts the ratio of female to male earnings per worker for the years 1960–78. In these two decades the income of daughters fell from over three-quarters to less than two-thirds of that of unmarried sons (unbroken line). Their income position relative to married sons declined even more drastically, from three-quarters to two-fifths (broken line). The rapid rise in married sons' income can be attributed both to their growing age and work experience and to the head start their sisters gave them before they entered the labor force. The rise in unmarried sons' income, on the other hand, is due largely to the boost supplied by their sisters.

In traditional China a small portion of the privately owned tangible property was owned by individuals. Although daughters were not allowed

---

*Income was estimated by a complex procedure that involved matching detailed information provided by informants on jobs, assets, and the like with aggregate data on the amount of income earned in each type of job or enterprise in each of the selected years. Although the income estimates are subject to limitations, the reconstruction procedures are internally consistent and provide a relatively reliable picture of changes within the sample over time. Detailed explanations of these procedures can be found in Greenhalgh 1982b.

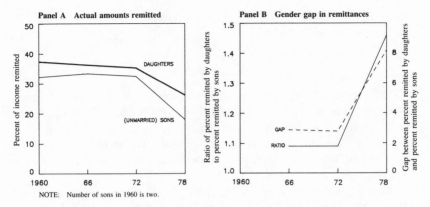

FIGURE 5. Remittances of Working Sons and Daughters Living Outside the Parental Household, 1960–78

to own large-scale private property, the property gap between sons and daughters was probably small, for the purchase of property by sons was strongly frowned upon, and few sons were wealthy enough to buy it anyway.

In postwar Taiwan sons not only have acquired the means to purchase property, they have been increasingly encouraged to do so, for parents see the personal prosperity of their sons as the most certain route to their own economic security (see B. Gallin and R. Gallin 1982). At the same time, daughters have been systematically deprived of the means to buy property. Nor have they had the right to buy it. Daughters could buy consumer durables for their dowries (and even those might be claimed by their parents; see Kung 1983:118), but not tangible assets such as a store or factory. In view of these trends, we would expect inequality to increase between the sexes, as sons use their growing incomes to acquire property while daughters remain propertyless.

And indeed, this is what the data show. In the whole period of study I uncovered no cases of unmarried daughters buying tangible assets such as a house or a shop. Beginning in the late 1960's, however, a small but growing number of their brothers started to acquire immovable property that was theirs alone. Between 1968 and 1978, eight sons (two single, six married) used their personal funds to buy houses, while six more (three single, three married) used their savings to purchase productive assets ranging from a plastics factory to an audio shop. Even at the end of the period, in 1978, the number of private properties owned by sons was tiny on a per capita basis—only one in 13 unmarried sons and one in 4 or 5 married sons who were working full-time owned some large-scale private property. Nevertheless, this incipient change supports the hypothesis that the trend is toward greater inequality between the sexes in access to strategic economic resources.

Conclusion

Taken together these data lend considerable weight to my hypothesis. Although some of the measures are coarse and the sample is small, the overall picture suggests that parents have systematically discriminated against their daughters and favored their sons and, in the process, may have created a growing sex gap in personal autonomy and resource ownership.

I have argued that the key strategy by which parents engineered this gap was the provision of education to their daughters under the terms of a traditional, low-investment balanced contract. Because this strategy brought substantial benefits to these daughters, they failed to see its exploitative nature. Yet a closer look at the conditions underlying its provision reveals that, for these postwar daughters, the acquisition of education was not an unmitigated good, but hid a catch-22. It was the key to their personal mobility, necessary for both occupational and material success. At the same time, however, it was the tool of their subordination, for its receipt entailed heavy obligations to those who provided it.

Caught in this net of obligations, unmarried daughters had few holes through which to escape. One group of daughters, however, did have an option. Working daughters who lived away from their parents could use a portion of their earnings to pay for their own higher education. Indeed, ethnographies are filled with cases of such daughters who, often acting against their parents' wishes, used their own funds to pay for high school or training in specialized skills (Arrigo 1980; Kung 1983).

While these struggles over higher education have gone unnoticed, they are potentially significant, for they may contain the seeds of change. Although, in the parents' view, unmarried daughters' earnings all belonged to them, daughters who had received small educational investments and had remitted money for several years could claim with some justification that their debt had been repaid, and at least some of their earnings were theirs to keep (for an illustration of this kind of reasoning, see Salaff 1981:123-76). Justified even by the terms of their parents' contracts, these daughters' use of their own money to enhance their own resources marks a potentially important change in the age-old pattern of virtually complete parental control over unmarried daughters.

In the area of feminist theory, this study provides new evidence that during periods of rapid capitalist development women may make great absolute strides while at the same time losing ground relative to men.

With respect to the causes of women's subordinate or even deteriorating position, the Taiwan data support the formulation of Hartmann (1976), Green (1983), and others that the low status of women is rooted in patriarchal family systems, and that the decline in women's status stems from the interaction of these patriarchal institutions with capitalist institutions. The Taiwan case richly illustrates the interlocking nature of these processes. Industrial capitalism (shorthand for all aspects of the economic environment) and the state provided new means (education and jobs) for parents to use old tools (sex-differentiated intergenerational contracts) to recreate and exacerbate old hierarchies (sexual inequality). Capitalism in turn took advantage of the sexual hierarchies the family created, using women's greater docility, lower skill levels, temporary labor force status, and the like to offer them dead-end, low-paying jobs. These discriminatory features of the labor market in turn reinforced women's subordinate status in the family, and provided the justification for parents to continue treating their daughters as tools for the advancement of others. While both capitalism and patriarchy were important, interlocking and reinforcing each other, capitalism was not responsible for creating these sexual hierarchies; it simply used the gender differences that it found, differences that have marked Chinese society for centuries. In this sense the patriarchal family was the more fundamental cause of the increase in sexual stratification we have observed in the postwar period.

This study also contributes to our understanding of the way precapitalist gender systems are perpetuated under capitalist development. The most compelling analysis of this process, in my view, is that presented by Hartmann (1976). She argues that the emergence of capitalism profoundly threatened men's position of dominance, both by destroying old institutions that supported it and by creating new institutions, such as a labor market, that removed women and children from patriarchal control and gave them independent means of support. Threatened by this loss of control, men—ordinary men, most men—took active if unconscious steps to maintain their gender-based power. Mechanisms by which they maintained power included reviving precapitalist techniques of control; continuing the assignment of all reproductive tasks to women; and restricting women's access to high-paying jobs (see also Green 1983). In identifying the class of individuals responsible, Hartmann underscores the fact that social systems do not merely persist; rather, they are actively perpetuated by individuals whose interests lie in their continuation and who have the resources and mechanisms necessary to do so.

While Hartmann's work provides a useful starting point, the Taiwan material suggests that her discussion of the agents and the mechanisms by which systems of gender inequality are perpetuated needs to be elabo-

rated. On Taiwan, the mechanisms by which men (and women) perpetuated sexual stratification included the education of their daughters, a
process that is usually associated with the advancement of women's position (see especially Boserup 1970). The agents who perpetuated the system
were not only men, who stood to benefit most, but also married women,
who stood to benefit in the later phases of their life cycle. Because the
interests of women were tied to their male-dominated families, and because the achievement of a modicum of security and power in old age
came through the careful use of their daughters to advance the fortunes
and secure the loyalties of their sons, married women were actively involved in perpetuating and intensifying the system of sexual stratification.
In examining how patriarchal systems are perpetuated, then, we must
consider not only sexual hierarchies, but also generational hierarchies
through which mothers actively discriminate against their daughters.
Generational hierarches are embedded within sexual hierarchies, creating
a set of nested patriarchal systems—husband/wife, family, school, firm,
society—that simultaneously deflect feminist consciousness and allow
parents to reproduce the system generation after generation.

Women Are Good with Money: Earning and Managing in an Indonesian City

HANNA PAPANEK AND LAUREL SCHWEDE

Women in many parts of Indonesia play an unusually central role in their household and wider economies. Large numbers of women are active in earning money through formal employment or a wide range of informal income-generating activities.* They are also believed to be good money handlers and play an important role in household financial management. A prevailing attitude among the Javanese is that women have thrift and foresight in money handling that men generally lack (H. Geertz 1961) and that women are more likely to put family interests and the desires of children first (Jay 1969): "The wife is the custodian of all the family cash . . . and has a decisive voice in any expenditure or borrowing of capital. She exercises undisputed control over daily expenditures" (p. 61). According to Manderson (1983:14), most studies of Indonesia stress women's control over finances and authority within the home. These active economic roles of Indonesian women both within and outside the household contrast sharply with the restricted economic roles of women in other predominantly Muslim societies in western and southern Asia.

In this paper, we provide both a general overview of the structural and demographic conditions shaping women's lives and a detailed look at urban lower-middle- and middle-class women, based on a study of 146

*The study of Jakarta women was carried out in 1972–74 by a team of Indonesian and American researchers affiliated with the Faculty of Social Science of the University of Indonesia and headed by T. Omas Ihromi, Hanna Papanek, and Mely G. Tan. Support for the study came from a grant by the Interdisciplinary Communications Program of the Smithsonian Institution to the Faculty of Social Science. The efforts of a large and hard-working research team were made possible by the friendly understanding of the women of Jakarta who invited researchers into their homes to talk about family life and family planning. In 1976, a special analysis of the household expenditure data was completed by Leila Budiman and Atika Makarim. More recent data for our analysis of the Indonesian national context came primarily from the 1980 population census. Rizal Ramli's assistance in this analysis is gratefully acknowledged. We are especially indebted to Dr. Mayling Oey and Dr. Pudjiwati Sajogyo for making recent papers available to us. We also thank Gustav F. Papanek for comments on sections of this essay and Martin Wulfe for helpful suggestions on statistical analysis of the survey data. The reanalysis of survey data was partially supported by a grant from the United Nations University, Tokyo.

Jakarta women carried out in 1972–74. Occasional comparisons are provided with other Asian societies, especially those with large Muslim populations, where women's access to labor markets is much more limited and the patriarchal family more dominant.

Returning to the findings of an earlier study poses important theoretical and methodological problems. It is a straightforward task to relate women's patterns of earning, managing, and saving money with the social, economic, and demographic correlates of these patterns. It is harder to reinterpret these linkages in the light of concepts, such as that of "strategies," developed in the intervening decade—always providing that the researcher wants to stick closely to the empirical base. Few of the Indonesian women in our study made explicit statements about life plans or career options, although many of them clearly had an overall sense of how many children they wanted to have and why.

The concepts of individual and household strategies used throughout this paper, therefore, are defined on the basis of inferences from observed behavior as well as explicit statements. As we show in this paper, these Indonesian women appear to play out both personal and household strategies that, at key points, seem to be complementary. We cannot tell on the basis of our interviews whether this was intentional and whether the women themselves were conscious of underlying patterns or overarching strategies in their lives. No doubt some were. People with sufficiently broad options to choose among various strategies are clearly in a different position in their societies from people living on the edge of poverty or constrained by powerlessness. In considering findings about women's strategies these differences must be kept in mind; from the perspective of policymakers and activists, these distinctions are crucial.

Structural and Demographic Factors Affecting Women's Economic Options

The Structure of Earning Opportunities

The Indonesian labor market has a much broader range of options available to women than is typical of other Asian nations with large Muslim populations. Not only is the economically active proportion of women higher than in many other countries of the region, but the distribution of economically active women covers a wider range of occupations. According to the 1980 Indonesian population census, one-third of women (aged ten and over) were counted as "economically active"; this category excludes housewives but includes those looking for work (Biro Pusat Statistik 1982b: Table 31.8, p. 107). This stands in striking contrast to the situation in Bangladesh, an ecologically similar nation with a majority Muslim population: only 4 percent of females were counted as economically active in the 1974 census (Alamgir 1981 : 172).

Women without formal schooling face hardship anywhere in the world when their customary source of income dries up—whether it be from a job or subsistence agriculture, as an employee or as an "unpaid family worker." The range of options available to such women differs sharply from one society to another. For these women as well, Indonesian society presents more earning opportunities than Bangladesh, particularly in market trade, where women have long played important roles in both urban and rural areas (Dewey 1962; Jellinek 1976, 1978; Panjaitan 1977; Chapman 1984). According to the 1980 population census, women now outnumber men as traders in rural Java, particularly among the ethnic Javanese. Supporting the crucial importance of trade as an alternative earning opportunity for women, Oey (1985) concludes that this expansion is a response to declining earning opportunities for women in rural manufacturing and agriculture.

The comparison between Indonesia and Bangladesh can be illustrated by figures drawn from the 1974 census of Bangladesh and the 1980 population census in Indonesia. In the much smaller female labor force of Bangladesh, a negligible proportion of women (1.3 percent) worked in sales; in Indonesia, nearly one-fifth (18.7 percent) of a much larger female labor force did so. Nearly three-fourths (72.5 percent) of economically active women in Bangladesh were engaged in agriculture; this was true for only half (52.4 percent) of economically active women in Indonesia (Biro Pusat Statistik 1982b: Table 36.8, p. 146; Alamgir 1981 : 176).

The distinction is equally clear in the single most significant sector, rice agriculture. In many parts of South and Southeast Asia, rice agriculture is considered particularly appropriate for women workers. Some tasks, such as transplanting and harvesting with the finger-knife (*ani-ani*), are considered female specialties in Indonesia, although there are regional and class variations in the degree of female preponderance (Stoler 1975; Hart 1978, 1986; United Nations Development Program 1980; Sajogyo 1983). Yet in Bangladesh, women do not participate in any aspects of rice cultivation, although their work is crucial in the primary processing of this crop, carried out within the house compound. Women are specifically excluded from rice agriculture in at least some parts of Bangladesh but are sometimes allowed to harvest other crops for much lower wages than men (Cain 1980).

In market trade the difference is equally striking. In marked contrast to Indonesia, women in Bangladesh may be forbidden to go to markets even as buyers in rural areas (Bertocci 1970, Islam 1982), and their participation as sellers is extremely rare. Participation in market trade violates the norms of sex segregation because of women's possible contacts with unrelated males.

Differences are less marked between Indonesia and Bangladesh with respect to urban occupations dependent on formal education. Although the total numbers are much smaller in Bangladesh because of the much smaller female labor force, comparable proportions of the female labor force are in professional and technical occupations (3.2 percent in Indonesia and 2.6 percent in Bangladesh). As we note in the next section, class and socioeconomic status determine women's educational participation to a larger degree than is true for men (see also Papanek 1985). Participants in professional and technical occupations tend to be from middle- and upperclass backgrounds, especially if they are female. These occupations rarely function as viable options for poor women in need of earning opportunities. Other education-dependent occupations, requiring more moderate levels of schooling, represent increasingly important opportunities for urban women. Class backgrounds may again enter the picture, however, because of the network connections often required in urban Indonesia to get education-dependent jobs.

Employment, Education, and Class

Formal education is a critical factor in women's options and family strategies of survival and social mobility. Linkages between formal schooling and employment options are an important issue in all countries, but they pose particular problems where educational participation remains tied to class background and household income. In Indonesia, female participation in formal education compares favorably with that in other countries in the region. Female enrollments are nearly as high as those of males at the primary level. At the secondary level, Indonesian females participate in higher proportions than is true for many other countries in the region, particularly those with large Muslim populations (*World Development Report 1984*: Table 25, pp. 266–67). In recent decades, the rate of increase in overall female educational participation has surpassed that of males, but it has not led to a corresponding increase in female labor force participation (Oey 1979).

Nearly half the enumerated female labor force in Indonesia (43.5 percent) consists of women without formal schooling, according to the 1980 population census. These women are most likely to belong to poor households where men, women, and children must all contribute to income. Given the difficulties of enumerating all economic activities by women, the actual economic significance of the work done by uneducated women for household survival is probably even greater than these figures indicate.

Uneducated women also form a large proportion of the total female population (38 percent). The fact that they are slightly overrepresented in the enumerated labor force suggests the great economic significance of this group in the overall Indonesian employment situation. One of the most serious issues confronting the country is the need to provide continuing employment opportunities for women whose schooling is rudimentary and whose employment opportunities are therefore limited.

Among moderately educated women, the need for additional income may be less pressing than for poor, uneducated women. At the same time, they are usually not sufficiently educated to enter the prestigious professions that might enhance family status and add significantly to household income. Census figures bear this out: only one-fifth of women with a junior high school education are counted as economically active, compared to one-third of the uneducated women. Alternative activities that contribute to household income without constituting formal employment are quite frequent in this sector of the female population (see below). In addition, "family status production" activities, which are not immediately remunerated, may be a rational choice for moderately educated women. Family status production activities include unpaid assistance to family members who are earning in cash or kind, support and assistance to children in their schoolwork, family status politics in the community, and ritual activities, such as *slametan* feasts among the Javanese (Papanek 1979c).

Highly educated women constitute only a minute fraction of the female population (0.3 percent), but the majority of these women (61 percent) are in the enumerated labor force. Although these women's household incomes may be high, family aspirations are also rising and women's earned incomes are often seen as necessary to support new consumption habits. Furthermore, the substantial investments made in higher education are considered to justify labor force participation at the end of schooling. Most highly educated women are also highly motivated to be professionally active and seek the intellectual, social, and financial rewards of their work.

As already noted, the Indonesian situation is distinctive. The range of opportunities open to women is much wider in Indonesia than in many countries in South Asia. Moreover, in comparison with countries like India, Bangladesh, Pakistan, and Egypt, fewer traditional earning opportunities seem to have disappeared; in these countries, declines in traditional work have led to sharp drops in the labor force participation of illiterate or unschooled women (Papanek 1985). Societies within the South and Southeast Asian region differ sharply with respect to the kinds of work considered acceptable for women of a particular class and status. While the typical woman worker in Indonesia—as in these other countries—is still likely to be poor, poorly educated, and probably working in agriculture, Indonesian women's earning strategies appear to be particularly flexible—perhaps a consequence of the less sex-segregated social system, and a further reflection of the broader range of available earning options. During the postindependence periods of economic stress, middle- and upper-middle-class women in urban Indonesia earned money through a variety of informal activities without losing status. Activities such as catering meals, sewing clothes, teaching children, selling eggs and home-grown vegetables, and brokering sales of real estate, jewelry, or costly batiks were common even among the wives of cabinet ministers in the late 1960's. As husbands' incomes have risen, some of the less lucrative of these activities have been abandoned; perhaps family status was adversely affected, or perhaps active involvement in the "wives' associations" required more time.

The diversity of these informal activities appears to be greater in Indonesia than in other countries of the region, supporting the general observation that women are closely involved in both earning and spending household income. The availability of a wide variety of earning options reinforces women's continued involvement in the financial affairs and strategies of their households. Equally important, as we discuss in the next section, the prevalence of divorce and remarriage in many sectors of their society may influence Indonesian women as individuals to retain control over skills and assets.

Employment, Age, and Marital Status

The pattern of labor force participation among Indonesian women is strikingly different from that in other nations of southern and western Asia. The most distinctive aspects of the Indonesian pattern are the high levels of labor force involvement among older women and among women who are widowed or divorced and have not remarried.

The age profile of the female labor force in Indonesia is very different from that of the male. According to the three most recent population censuses (1961, 1971, 1980), female participation rates peak in the age group 45–54. The age profile is bimodal, however, and a somewhat lower peak occurs among 15–19-year-olds. By contrast, male rates are highest in the groups between 25 and 44 years of age, dropping off at those points where female participation rates are highest.

Divorce and widowhood are major elements in the picture. According to 1980 census figures (Biro Pusat Statistik 1982a), the percentage of widows who have not remarried rises steeply after age 40, whereas the proportion of divorced women who have not remarried rises very slowly but then remains stable. For example, among women 45–49, 17 percent were widowed and 6 percent were divorced; for women 55–59, the proportion of widows was 34 percent, that of divorced women slightly over 6 percent; more than half of all women 60–69 are widowed. In all age groups and in both rural and urban areas, labor force participation rates are highest among women classified as *janda*, which connotes "unpartnered" and refers to both widowed and divorced women. In recent years the category *janda* has been broken down into widowed (*cerai mati*) and divorced (*cerai hidup*), but it remains difficult to differentiate earlier findings. In other words, although labor force participation rates are lower for females than for males, a large proportion of Indonesian women in the enumerated labor force are working to support themselves and often others on their own earnings. The large numbers of older women and of women not currently married in the labor force suggest first, that these women must depend on their own earnings, and second, that there is some room for them in the labor force. In many nearby countries, this is not always the case.

Unpartnered women may also intensify their work in informal production or redeploy family labor to meet family needs. In comparing the family economic strategies and decision-making patterns of no-longer-partnered women with those of their married counterparts in the large Indonesian matrilineal society of the Minangkabau, one of us found that divorced, widowed, and abandoned women were much more involved than married women in dryland crop cultivation. They were also much more likely to have grown children living and working in other areas of Indonesia and sending remittances home to supplement the family budget (Schwede, forthcoming).

These labor force characteristics reflect significant aspects of social organization that are particularly relevant to our analysis. First, with respect to kinship and residence patterns, many (not all) Indonesian ethnic groups tend toward relatively small nuclear households. In several ethnic groups, including the Javanese, bilateral kinship patterns mean that newly married couples can live apart from both sets of parents and remain relatively independent of them. This stands in sharp contrast to the extended patrilineal households that remain common—at least as an ideal—in China, Bangladesh, Pakistan, and parts of India. This affects women's strategies, as there are few or no other adult women to help with either earning or childcare. In case of desertion, death, or divorce (initiated by either the husband or the wife), a woman is forced to rely on her own resources unless she can persuade relatives to help.

Second, patterns of marriage formation and dissolution in the society as a whole affect the strategies of individual women in relation to household income and expenditure. In addition to trying to maintain adequate levels of income for the household through their own earning activities, Indonesian women are also trying to keep expenditures low. If they think they are facing an uncertain future, they will do better to retain control over both income and expenditure. That is not to say that individual Indonesian women are constantly fearful of being divorced—although we found in our study that many worried about the possibility—but that they live in a social environment where divorce and remarriage are not uncommon. Under the circumstances, being prepared for the possibility of marital dissolution and the formation of a new family is highly rational.

Indeed, Indonesia has reported very high rates of both divorce and remarriage for the Muslim population for decades, although these rates have recently declined. For instance, in 1955, 1.3 million registered marriages (*nikah*) and 760,000 registered divorces (*talak*) were reported—a ratio of 58 percent, or nearly three divorces registered for every five marriages. Throughout the 1960's, *talak/nikah* ratios were still very high, especially on Java (55 percent in West Java, 53 percent in East Java, 47 percent in Central Java). One reason for higher rates of divorce during this period may have been widespread poverty and civil unrest, which caused individuals to migrate in search of employment (Papanek, Ihromi, and Rahardjo 1974). By the 1980's, divorces had declined; for Java as a whole, the *talak/nikah* ratio was reported to have dropped to 19 percent (Biro Pusat Statistik 1982a).

Large-scale population surveys from the 1970's support the high registration figures for divorce and provide evidence of the strong propensity of women to remarry. The Indonesian Fertility-Mortality Survey of 1973 reported that between one-third and one-half of Javanese women had been married more than once. Women married more than once were particularly prevalent in West Java (38 percent of urban women over 35 and 43 percent of rural women) and only slightly less so in other parts of Java (UI/FELD 1973, East Java volume, p. 27). According to the same survey, about four-fifths of divorced women and just under half of widowed women under age 50 in urban West Java remarried within five years of the cessation of their previous marriages (Kusuma 1976:87). Remarriage rates would be expected to decline in the older age cohorts owing to a decreasing pool of available men.

Surveys including other parts of Indonesia as well as Java support these findings. Calculations made from a subsample of the wider Indonesian Fertility-Mortality Survey (covering Java, Sumatra, Sulawesi, and Bali) indicate that 26 percent of urban women and 30 percent of rural women in the 45–49 age cohort had been married more than once. About one-fifth of both the rural and urban women in this subsample had been married twice and one-tenth had been married three or more times (calculated from Kusuma 1976:82–84).

These are remarkably high rates of marriage dissolution and remarriage, comparable to the highest rates reported for some Western industrialized countries. It is often assumed that the high rates of divorce in Indonesia and Malaysia can be attributed to the relative ease with which Muslim men can pronounce unilateral divorce, although this practice has now been somewhat circumscribed by recent Indonesian laws. However, several other nations with large Muslim populations show much lower divorce rates. According to Lev, the Indonesian divorce rate up to the early 1970's was "anywhere from two to five or more times that of several Middle Eastern countries, though about the same or even less than that of Malaya" (Lev 1972:141). In Indonesia, it also appears to be easier than in some other Muslim countries for women to initiate divorce. Lev (1972) found judges relatively sympathetic to women's requests for divorce. Nakamura studied divorce records for one area of Central Java for the 1964–1971 period and found roughly equal numbers of husbands and wives seeking the dissolution of a marriage. The most frequently cited reason was "neglecting marital obligations," including the failure of men to support their wives (Nakamura 1983:67–74).

There is no direct evidence to support the conclusion that Indonesian women are likely to seek divorce because of their access to earning opportunities and control over household expenditures; the reverse is more likely. High remarriage rates indicate that both women and men prefer the married state. There are no studies in which divorced women were asked about the role that economic opportunities played in their decision to divorce. Observations and labor force statistics already cited above suggest that many poor women enter the labor force precisely because they have been divorced or abandoned by husbands who could not or would not support them. This is often the case with rural women who work in domestic service in large cities.

Data from Pakistan indicate the extent of the difference between Indonesia and another Asian nation with a large Muslim population that follows similar (but not identical) personal law. According to the 1975 Pakistan Fertility Survey, over 95 percent of women in all age groups between 15 and 49 had been married only once. Among women aged 45–49, only 8.8 percent were found to have been married twice and almost none more often than that (Alam and Karim 1986:89). In the total sample, only 4 perent had married twice and hardly any had married three times. In spite of the well-known prescriptions in Islam that favor the remarriage of widows, only about half (52.4 percent) of Pakistani women whose first marriages had been dissolved had remarried. Women under 40 had much better chances of remarrying than older ones; 60 percent of the younger women had remarried but only 45 percent of those over 40 had done so (ibid).

In Bangladesh, another South Asian nation with a large proportion of Muslims and an ideal of patrilineally extended residence, remarriage rates for women were also low. In the 45–49 age group, just 11.5 percent of rural Bangladeshi women had been married two or more times. Only 5.3 percent of the urban women in this age cohort had had more than one marriage (Ahmed and Chaudhury 1981).

Table 1 shows the striking contrast of Indonesia with Pakistan and Bangladesh in regard to divorce and remarriage. About 30 percent of Indonesian women are in their second (or higher-order) marriage before they are 50; this is true for less than 12 percent of urban and rural women in Pakistan and Bangladesh.

The implications for women's strategies are clear. In Pakistan and Bangladesh, where almost all women remain in their first marriages throughout their lifetimes, it is reasonable to invest one's energies in the maintenance of household well-being and solidarity. Most women, regardless of socioeconomic status or class, are dependent on the household for economic survival and social status. Women have few alternatives to investing their energies in the household as a work unit. Employment opportunities remain limited because of continuing sex segregation in the labor market. Women face continuing (and sometimes increasing) constraints on their rights before courts of law and administrative bodies. Both economically and socially, most women are dependent on men throughout their lifetimes.

In Indonesia, on the other hand, women's strategies that emphasize individual control over household expenditures and continued involvement in income-earning activities make a great deal of sense. Where divorce and remarriage are frequent, even if individual women do not expect them in their own lives, it is reasonable to develop strategies that emphasize a division of responsibilities between women and men. There is a clear complementarity between women's personal and household strategies. Contributing to the financial support of their families by earning incomes and managing household expenditures and savings gives Indonesian women considerable leverage in devising and fulfilling household strategies to meet the demands of changing economic circumstances. A woman's active role in earning income and managing household finances thus benefits her family, but it is also of long-term benefit to her personally. She develops the skills and resources to support herself and family members in the event of divorce or widowhood. In addition, many

TABLE I
Number of Marriages of Rural and Urban Women Aged 45–49
in Indonesia, Pakistan, and Bangladesh

(percent)

	Indonesia		Pakistan		Bangladesh	
	1	2 or more	1	2 or more	1	2 or more
Urban	74%	26%	n.a.	n.a.	95%	5%
Rural	70%	30%	n.a.	n.a.	88%	12%
Urban and rural	71%	29%	91%	9%	n.a.	n.a.

SOURCES: For Indonesia, calculated from Kusuma 1976: 82–84; for Pakistan, Alam and Karim 1986: 89; for Bangladesh, Ahmed and Chaudhury 1981: 97.

women clearly derive personal satisfaction from the independence and income that their economic activities bring them. In a social setting where women's social and economic participation is well accepted, rather than associated with poverty and stress, the positive aspects of women's work and earning are very important.

The Research Project:
Jakarta Women and Family Life

In the larger context of these trends and variations, a 1972–74 study of lower-middle- and middle-class women in Jakarta provides details about the lives of a particular sector of the urban population. A team of researchers affiliated with the Faculty of Social Science of the University of Indonesia conducted depth interviews with 146 married women (ranging in age from 20 to 50) who were living with their husbands and at least one child in stable neighborhoods in Indonesia's capital city. By design, one-third of the women selected were employed in one of five typical "women's occupations" requiring moderate levels of education. The women belonged to a variety of ethnic groups and religious affiliations typical of urban Jakarta. The sample was not stratified by ethnicity or religion or class, largely because the relevant aggregate data were not available, but it did cover a typical range of population characteristics. Although literacy had not been a factor in sample selection, it turned out that all the women had been at least to primary school and none was illiterate. We deliberately excluded highly educated professional women because, in the generations studied, such women usually came from the upper-middle or upper classes.

Although the class from which our respondents were drawn is numerically small compared to the vast rural majority of the population, its values and experiences play a disproportionately large role, as one might expect in a highly centralized state. Jakarta itself is a magnet for migrants of all classes and the locus of political decisions. Many of the nation's administrators and decision makers come from a background not very different from that of our respondents. Either deliberately or unconsciously, the aspirations and lifestyles of the middle class affect the goals of the nation as a whole.

Women of the socioeconomic groups from which our sample was drawn also play important roles in voluntary associations. Women's groups directly affiliated with the bureaucracy—the so-called "wives' associations"—play an increasingly visible role in implementing government policies at the local level. Women's voluntary associations, most of which have been in existence since early in the century, have had a declining impact, in part because they cannot compete for women's limited time with the official groups, in which participation is compulsory (Papanek 1979a, 1983, Sullivan 1983, Soewondo 1984).

The interviews covered women's educational, employment, residence, and pregnancy histories, as well as a wide range of attitude questions. Previous publications on this study include Papanek, Ihromi, and Rahardjo (1974); Papanek et al. (1976); Rahardjo et al. (1980); and Papanek (1979a, 1979b, 1983). In this essay, we examine women's patterns of earning, managing, and saving money, explore their sociodemographic correlates, and discuss the implications for women's personal and household strategies.

The Jakarta women's earning, managing, and saving strategies were deeply affected by uncertainty in their own lives resulting from political and economic turmoil. They vividly remembered the severe inflation of the 1950's and 1960's and the civil unrest and widespread violence of the mid-1960's, as well as earlier periods of localized civil war in several regions of the archipelago. Older women recalled the colonial period, the deprivations of the Japanese occupation during the Second World War, and the fight for independence from the Dutch in the late 1940's that had shaped their childhoods and disrupted their schooling.

Between 1966 and 1972, there had been steady improvements in the economy: inflation had declined and real wages had risen, often quite steeply. In the fall of 1973, during the field interviews, bad harvests and a worldwide increase in rice prices had led to a resumption of inflation. Economic problems were on everyone's mind. The perception of renewed problems was probably also exacerbated by rising aspirations. Newly available consumer goods and the proliferation of modern media of communication had greatly stimulated the aspirations of the lower-middle and middle classes. For many members of the middle class, upward social mobility and more costly consumption patterns were beginning to be possible. The women interviewed in the 1970's knew that their contributions to income and expenditure management were needed by their families. They expected to pitch in, to do whatever was necessary to achieve the goals they and their families wanted to attain.

Earning Cash Incomes: Formal Employment and Informal Activities

The study was designed to compare women who held regular jobs with those who described themselves as housewives (*ibu rumah tangga*). We sampled five typical "women's occupations" accessible to women with moderate levels of formal schooling. In Indonesia, the jobs of secretaries, typists, pharmacists, teachers, and trained midwives (*bidan*) working in private firms or government had been open to women for several decades and were considered acceptable, even desirable, for women of lower-middle and middle-class status, although not for the upper-class elite. Had their lives taken a slightly different turn—had schooling not been disrupted, say, or had they chosen a different husband—some of the women in our study who were not in such a job might well have chosen one.

In the coding of interview transcripts, we distinguished among the women's self-descriptions as housewife, working for an employer, or self-employed. We also separated out work activities according to their regularity and their timing in women's life cycles (for example, before marriage, since marriage but not now, at present). There are obvious difficulties in classifying many of the informal activities through which these women earned incomes. For instance, women who carried out brokerage activities from a home base might engage in more or less regular, or more or less remunerative, activities at different times, depending on economic need and available opportunities. Generally, we classified as self-employment those activities carried out regularly and for significant income, particularly in a location other than the home; women's self-definitions also played a major role. The activities from which respondents earned cash incomes included food catering to homes and offices, running small shops or food stalls in or near the home, operating beauty shops and tailoring enterprises on home premises, and commission selling and brokerage of land, jewelry, household equipment, batik, and so on. Some women taught lessons to children, usually in music or a foreign language; others did occasional secretarial work or typing.

Fully two-thirds of the women (97 of 146) reported that they were currently earning regular or irregular cash incomes, as shown in Table 2, either from a job or through a variety of other activities, regardless of their

TABLE 2

Reported Type of Work by Current Earning Status

| | Earning now? | | | | | |
| | No | | Yes | | Totals | |
Type of work	No.	Pct.	No.	Pct.	No.	Pct.
1. Housewife or retired	49	100.0%	27	27.8%	76	52.1%
2. Self-employed	0	–	15	15.5%	15	10.3%
3. Employed by private employer	0	–	35	36.0%	35	23.9%
4. Employed by government	0	–	20	20.6%	20	13.7%
Total	49	100.0%	97	99.9%	146	100.0%

self-descriptions. Of these 97 women, 56.6 percent were employed by either a private employer or the government, while 15.5 percent were self-employed and the remaining 27.8 percent were housewives who were earning irregularly. If the latter two categories are combined, it is seen that 43 percent of the women currently earning money were doing so on their own terms, not those of an employer. Earning money without the involvement of an outside agency controlling either the timing or location of their work gave these women flexibility in juggling their responsibilities as wives, mothers, and income-generators. Some respondents also engaged in informal activities in addition to regular employment.

More than one third (27 of 76) of the women who identified themselves as housewives were nonetheless economically active. This shows that in Indonesia, and probably in many other areas, surveys and censuses that rely on stated occupations and whether or not a person holds a job in the formal sector to determine who is economically active would seriously underestimate the economic productivity of women classified as housewives.

In our analysis of the Jakarta survey, we distinguished two dichotomies of income generation. The first contrasted those who were regularly employed (categories 2 through 4 in Table 2) with the nonemployed, that is, the self-described housewives (category 1). The second dichotomy compared those who were earning any money through either formal or informal activities (categories 2 through 4 as well as the 27 housewives earning irregular incomes) with the 49 other housewives in category 1 who were not earning any income at the time of the survey. We then examined the degrees of association of both groupings (employed / not employed and earning / not earning) with selected sociodemographic variables. We found some striking differences between employed and nonemployed women, but very few significant relationships between earning / not earning and other variables. It appears that while holding a job outside the home (whether working for herself or another employer) is related to some distinctive features of a woman's life, simply earning money is not. In the next section, we will focus primarily on the comparison of employed and nonemployed.

Sociodemographic Correlates of Employment. Some very clear differences emerged between women who held paid jobs outside the home and those who did not. Education is among the most noteworthy: 68 percent of currently employed women had completed high school or university, whereas only 38 percent of the nonemployed had done so. This distinction involves an interesting generational difference: among current jobholders, equal proportions of younger and older respondents were highly educated, while among those not currently employed, more of the younger women (under 35) were highly educated than was true for the older group. In other words, the educational pathway to employment has been important to women currently holding the types of jobs sampled regardless of age, but the higher levels of education achieved by some of the younger women have not (or not yet) impelled them into the labor force. For lower-middle- and middle-class women, educational qualifications are likely to be necessary for the kinds of jobs acceptable to their aspirations. But they are not sufficient conditions for labor force entry, at least for some women at this point in their lives.

Another distinctive feature of the Indonesian pattern is that currently employed women were more likely to come from outside the city of Jakarta, while those not currently holding jobs were more often born in the city. Moreover, the women who had migrated to Jakarta tended to be better educated: fewer than half of the Jakarta-born women had completed high school or university, whereas 67 percent of those born in provincial capitals and 53 percent of those from rural areas had done so.

The typical employed women in this sample, then, came to Jakarta from another part of the country. Among women who were long-term residents of Jakarta, both education and employment were less prevalent in the same age groups than among the migrants. These conclusions support the more general observation that upward social mobility is associated with migration to the capital city—particularly in poor, largely agricultural nations with a small middle class. What distinguishes the Indonesian case from many others is the active participation of women in both higher education and employment in connection with moving to the capital city. In more highly sex-segregated nations, such as Bangladesh, the common pattern appears to be that female education and education-dependent employment *follow* a family's move to urban areas. The generation gap between educated men and women, in which investment in female education is a sign rather than a contributing cause of upward social mobility, seems to be less typical in Indonesia. This supports the more general observation of women's active involvement in Indonesian social and economic life along a broad front.

The majority of our respondents had done regular paid work at some time in their lives: 65 percent of the 146 women had either been self-employed or had worked for an employer on a regular basis, even if they were not doing so at the time of the interview. Many of the women also came from families in which mothers had actively earned or had even fully supported the household. Of the 71 mothers of respondents on whom we have information, 65 percent had engaged in full-time earning. In over a quarter of these households, mothers were the sole support of the family after men had died or divorced them or because the men were unemployed.

Some of our findings relating to women's age and life-cycle position are unexpected. Most important, the data presented in Table 3 show that women are significantly more likely to be working for an employer if there are preschool children at home; women without preschool children at home are more likely to be self-employed or not currently earning. This directly contradicts the conventional assumption that the time pressures of child care keep women out of the labor force. The great majority of the women in our sample who were working for employers did so outside the home. Moreover, the sample as a whole consisted of lower-middle- and middle-class women, not the very poor with extremely pressing economic needs. What, then, explains this apparent contradiction?

The contradiction is all the more striking because these women had been married long enough for family strategies about work and money to be well established. The respondents' mean age was 36.9 years and mean age at marriage to the present husband was 21.8 years, so the typical respondent had been in her present marriage for ten years or more. Although currently employed women and self-described housewives differed sharply in terms of their age at marriage (74 percent of the employed had married at 22 or later and only 43 percent of others had done so), neither group of women had delayed childbearing very long after marriage. Among all respondents, 94 percent had had a first pregnancy within the first two years of marriage. This confirms the widespread preference, stated repeatedly in the interviews, to start childbearing as soon as possible after marriage—*lebih baik punya anak dulu* (best to have a child first). We found no evidence that these women wanted to delay childbearing for the sake of career advancement or felt they had to be financially secure before starting a family. In fact, starting a family and earning an income to

TABLE 3
Wives' Earning Activities and Presence of Preschool Children in Home

| | Preschool children present? | | | | | |
| | No | | Yes | | Totals | |
Earning activity	No.	Pct.	No.	Pct.	No.	Pct.
Not currently earning	26	34.7%	23	32.4%	49	33.6%
Earning, not from employer	33	44.0%	13	18.3%	46	31.5%
Earning, from employer	16	21.3%	35	49.3%	51	34.9%
Total	75	100.0%	71	100.0%	146	100.0%

NOTE: chi square = 15.86008; chi square p = 0.0004; gamma = 0.28571.

support it were clearly complementary rather than antithetical choices. Some respondents even commented that one reason that they were so eager to earn an income was to be able to afford more children, since they felt strongly that a large family was more desirable than a small one. These sentiments were expressed in the early years of a strong nationwide government-sponsored family planning program; attitudes may have changed during the intervening decade. The prosperity in which some members of the middle class participated as a result of rising oil prices may also have affected attitudes and practices concerning family size. However, our findings are consistent with the conclusions of some demographers during the same period that Indonesian middle-class families had higher fertility than the poor (Hull and Hull, 1977).

Given the preference for having children as soon as possible after marriage, sample households with preschoolers were often those of younger couples who were usually not well established financially. Women who had held jobs before marriage preferred to keep them, since it is difficult to get one's job back after an extended absence.

In short, women's employment and household financial strategies were to some extent determined by the couple's position in the life cycle, reflected in household composition and adult earnings. Rising aspirations, linked to upward social mobility and changing consumption patterns in these families, help to explain the apparent contradiction: women continued to earn cash incomes even when home responsibilities were especially heavy.

Reasons for Earning, Reasons for Stopping. Currently employed women and those not currently employed differed markedly in the reasons they gave for ever taking a paid job outside the home. Financial reasons were clearly more important to women not currently employed: 68 percent of them mentioned these as a primary reason for holding a job, but only

42 percent of those actually employed did so. Employed women were more likely to stress the importance of using their education and living up to their social responsibilities; these factors were rarely mentioned by women not holding a job.

Husbands' attitudes toward their wives' employment outside the home were considered particularly important by our respondents. Among women not currently in a job, 16 percent reported that their husbands would not approve of their employment; to our surprise, a few women who did hold jobs also reported that their husbands disapproved. The most common attitude among husbands, reported by 37 percent of employed women and 42 percent of those not holding jobs, was one of conditional approval: husbands did not object to their wives having a job, provided it did not interfere with what were considered the women's obligations as wives and mothers. In the lower-middle and middle class, these obligations are clearly quite separate from earning an income. Men's major family responsibility is to earn a livelihood to support women and children. Among the very poor, women must earn along with men and children if all are to survive. In this sense, the husbands' provisional acceptance of their wives' jobs in our sample illustrates both class and gender differences regarding women's work and earning activities.

The respondents' expectations for their daughters' future were also affected by husbands' attitudes. While 85 percent of the women felt it would be a good thing for their daughters to do some kind of paid work before marriage, most said the daughter's husband should have a decisive say in the matter after marriage. Employed women emphasized this point especially strongly, perhaps on the basis of their own experience.

Findings on both questions support the conclusion that, at least among these lower-middle- and middle-class families, women's earning activities are a secondary consideration and that maternal and wifely obligations come first. These matters also play a role in decisions to stop earning activities. By the early 1970's, some women of this class had already stopped some of their earlier earning activities. Families were more confident that they could rely on the steady earnings of husbands as inflation began to be brought under control. Moonlighting was still very common among men but seemed to be declining among women. Many women retained what little capital investment they had made in such items as beauty-shop equipment and sewing machines but were using them less actively. The informal activities by which many women had been earning could as readily be discontinued as they could be restarted. Jobs, on the other hand, were (and are) harder to come by and more difficult to reclaim once a woman had left a position. This accounts in part for women's propensity to stay in a job, especially a permanent one, in spite of heavy home responsibilities while children are young.

To summarize, we found that women working outside the home at the time of the survey tended to be more highly educated, to originate from places outside Jakarta, to have married later, and to have young children at home. Just under half of the women with preschool children were working for an employer, the great majority outside the home. They had less flexibility in their work schedules than the one-fifth of the women with young children who were earning money through self-employment or informal activities. Starting a family and simultaneously earning an income to help support it were complementary rather than antithetical choices for these women. While informal earning activities could readily be slowed or stopped, with the possibility of later resumption, formal jobs usually could not be reclaimed. Rising aspirations and changing consumption patterns may also have played a role in the employed women's decisions to continue working in a formal job at a time in their life cycle when maternal and wifely responsibilities were especially heavy.

Managing Household Expenditures

Respondents were asked to describe the household arrangements for deciding about money matters. Replies were coded in terms of categories developed after all interviews were completed, to minimize the influence of stereotypes. The results nevertheless confirm the Indonesian stereotype of women as preeminent money managers. Only 5 out of 146 husbands were reported to be sole financial decision makers; see Table 4. Wives were primary money managers in 70 percent of all households, including 24 families in which they decided both large and small financial matters. An interviewer described such an arrangement:

Respondent arranges all household matters because the husband is in the office the whole day. She keeps the husband's salary because he deposits it with her every payday. In case there is overtime pay, he reports it to her. She thinks he is honest in this. The husband never keeps any money and never buys anything. (Wife is a 28-year-old Javanese who has never had any kind of job; husband works in a bank; household of ten persons including five children and two servants.)

In another case, the wife described her husband as being "like a king at home"—she managed all the household finances and gave him pocket money.

In the most common case (categories 2 and 3, 54 percent of sample), wives made most of the recurrent money decisions but consulted husbands

TABLE 4

Wives' Perception of Financial Decision Making

Budgeting patterns	No.	Pct.
WIVES DOMINANT		
1. Wife decides all money matters, including large expenditures	24	16.4%
2. Wife decides all money matters, consults husband on big expenses	77	52.7%
3. Wife decides all money matters, consults husband and other household members	2	1.4%
Subtotal	103	70.5%
JOINT DECISIONS		
4. Husband and wife discuss important money matters but responsibility and fixed amounts allocated to each for specific expenditures	25	17.1%
5. Husband and wife have "separate purses" and there is no overlap of responsibility	4	2.7%
Subtotal	29	19.8%
HUSBANDS DOMINANT		
6. Husband decides all money matters including daily expenditures	5	3.4%
7. Husband decides all major money matters but leaves daily expenditure decisions to wife	4	2.7%
Subtotal	9	6.1%
OTHER PATTERNS	5	3.4%
Total	146	100.0%

or other family members on major matters. For example, in a household where the wife was not currently earning, the interviewer reported:

She handles every decision of daily household expenses alone by herself, but concerning unusual matters, she asks her husband's opinion and they together make the decision. For example, replacing household furniture, making house repairs . . . but for her husband's car, she herself took the decision. (School-age children in this household own chickens and sell eggs for pocket money; above-average level of household expenditure; husband is former government employee now in private business. Respondent supports a nephew in university and contributes to her mother-in-law's living costs.)

A carefully negotiated pattern of joint decision making was less common than wife-dominant arrangements. In 17 percent of the cases, husbands and wives had separate spheres of responsibility with set amounts allocated in advance to each. They consulted each other on major matters.

Since the wife-dominant pattern was so pronounced throughout the sample, none of the major variables was useful in explaining particular choices of financial arrangements. It made no difference whether wives were or were not currently earning: wife-dominant patterns were reported by 76 percent of women currently earning (either from a job or informal activities) and by 73 percent of women not currently earning.

Divergent arrangements were likely to result from individual preferences and particular circumstances rather than from some general characteristic like education or ethnicity.

Would a different picture have emerged had we asked the husbands about their perceptions of family financial arrangements? Probably not. Indonesian culture stresses modesty rather than assertiveness as a desirable attribute, especially for women, and it is unlikely that these respondents overstated their responsibility and authority. It is clear that handling money is a woman's responsibility—at least at home and perhaps also in traditional trade.

In public life, on the other hand, women are accorded no special hiring preferences in financial institutions or the bureaucracy. They do not play major roles in banks, government budget agencies, or national planning departments. It is law, not accountancy, that has attracted female professionals since colonial times. Not economics but languages and psychology are the academic disciplines considered most suitable for women and those in which they are said to have a "natural advantage" over men. In short, while women's skills in handling money are clearly valued and widely acknowledged, they are also restricted to the household arena. Women's control over household income does not translate into authority or power on a wider stage.

Arisan Saving Strategies

Three-fourths of the women in the study belonged to one or more *arisan*, informal groups formed for the limited purpose of saving a specific sum of money over a predetermined period of time. *Arisan* members meet regularly to pay an agreed-upon amount into a common pot. Each member wins the entire amount once during the cycle of an *arisan*. The financial significance of *arisan* lies in making a lump sum available within a limited time. The sociability of most *arisan* groups provides the encouragement that members need to persevere toward their savings goal; once the commitment to the group has been made, it would be shameful to stop. Although a few *arisan* among our respondents did not require actual meetings but only regular contributions, most provided the combined benefit of saving and sociability. The combination of these two factors, both very important in Indonesian society, accounts for the popularity of these evanescent institutions among women, men, children, and couples in a wide variety of social settings.

When an *arisan* is formed, members decide jointly on the length of the cycle (usually one year) and the number of meetings (usually one per month), since these determine the size of the group. Prospective members agree on the size of the contribution and the method for winning the common pool, typically drawing lots among those present. The uncertainty of winning assures regular attendance at meetings, especially if the *arisan* is combined with other types of group meetings. But alternative methods are often chosen, indicating the highly flexible and pragmatic character of *arisan* organization. Sometimes all members agree to save for the purchase of the same item; this may enable them to arrange for a quantity discount. *Arisan* meetings may also be the occasion for other informal economic transactions, including buying and selling items, making brokerage arrangements, and exchanging information.

A recurrent problem for *arisan* savings methods is that members who "pull" (*tarik*) the common pool early in the cycle benefit in comparison with those who receive their lump sum later on, especially when interest rates are high. We heard of no method to compensate late winners, but were told repeatedly that respondents nevertheless preferred saving through an *arisan* to making frequent small deposits in a bank. Social pressures among known persons prevent early winners from dropping out.

Arisan are not limited to women but may be particularly common among them. In the 1960's, the anthropologist Clifford Geertz noted *arisan* groups among men; he urged that such groups be used to stimulate the development of indigenous entrepreneurship (C. Geertz 1962). More recently, the existence of "rotating credit associations" (ibid) has been documented among women in many different societies around the world (March and Taqqu 1982); occasionally, these groups are an important strategy of savings, economic growth, and empowerment. We are not aware of any recent systematic studies of the role of *arisan* among women in Indonesia, although they continue to be important at both the personal and associational level (see Sullivan 1983).

The 108 women in our sample who belonged to at least one *arisan* reported a total of 262 current memberships, with some women belonging to as many as eight *arisan* simultaneously. Given the considerable control that our respondents exercised over household financial management, we see *arisan* savings as part of a larger pattern of stretching limited resources as far as possible. Groups may be formed among friends, neighbors, coworkers, or members of an extended kin group, club, or association. Our respondents belonged predominantly to *arisan* formed among friends or work colleagues (149 memberships, 57 percent of total); there were also 75 neighborhood *arisan* (29 percent) and 38 kin-group *arisan* (14 percent). In short, *arisan* are ad hoc social institutions that depend for their effectiveness on preexisting social bonds that form the basis of mutual trust. These bonds assure regular attendance and dependable payments into the common pool and prevent default and misappropriation. We heard of no *arisan* group formed among strangers.

TABLE 5

Reported Use of Arisan Savings by Members

(percent)

Use	Pct.
Daily expenditures	24.3%
Children's education	6.1%
Household equipment, car, motorcycle	16.5%
Land, house, similar investment	2.6%
Jewelry or similar investment	14.8%
Savings	34.8%
Pilgrimage (*hajj*)	0.9%
Total	100%

Three-quarters of the women who belonged to *arisan* reported success in reaching a particular goal; only one-fourth plowed their winnings back into the daily household budget. As Table 5 shows, most savings were intended for the acquisition of capital assets: land, house, car, motorcycle, household equipment, jewelry. Only one of these categories—jewelry—could be said to be for the woman's personal use and benefit. One-third of the women reported banking their winnings, but we lack information about whether these sums went into individual or family accounts. However, given the women's overall role in financial management, it is safe to assume that they had considerable discretion in setting up accounts and managing them. Less frequent uses of *arisan* winnings included saving for children's education and the pilgrimage (*hajj*); these were long-term investments in human capital.

The source of the funds being saved through *arisan*-like groups is an important issue because of the possibility of achieving a redirection of control over expenditures. In societies where household funds come primarily from male earnings and women have little say in decisions, women may achieve increased control by saving small amounts out of household allowances, either accumulating them through a savings group or maintaining a secret hoard. But many Indonesian women already have considerable control over household budgets and expenditure decisions. Our respondents were saving mainly for capital goods that would benefit the whole household (including, of course, themselves) rather than any particular individuals. In this case, *arisan* savings are part of a larger household financial strategy rather than a means of increasing women's personal control.

On the other hand, our data also show that *arisan* memberships were more common among employed women and that employed women tended to stress purely economic reasons for belonging. Among the employed women, 86 percent belonged to at least one *arisan* but only 67 percent of the others did so. Many respondents in both groups mentioned that the mix of sociability and financial gain made membership attractive, but 25 percent of employed women, compared to 6 percent of others, stressed purely economic reasons. As we lack information about the ultimate sources of *arisan* contributions, we cannot judge whether this reflects more economic worries or easier access to funds among employed women.

The real significance of *arisan* in this particular sector of Indonesian society is best understood in terms of the overall income and expenditure patterns of households. At the time of the study, lower-middle- and middle-class urban households depended on a complex combination of funds from several different sources to meet their regular expenses. This required careful management and stringent control of expenditures. Many of the husbands of respondents worked in lower-middle- and middle-level occupations where typical monthly salaries were about Rupiah (Rp) 20,000 (U.S. $48); similar amounts might be earned by the self-employed. In addition to their salaries, government employees (and some in the private sector) had substantial perquisites, including monthly rice allocations, support for housing, transportation, and medical care. But even including these side benefits, the regular salaries earned by husbands in their primary jobs covered only about one-third to one-half of actual monthly household expenses. The rest was typically covered by second or third jobs, casual incomes, and the formal and informal earnings of women. Unfortunately, at the time of our interviews, government regulations had just been issued intended to limit moonlighting in second or third jobs among government employees. Most of our respondents (even if their husbands or they themselves were not in government employment) therefore refused to talk about second jobs or to divulge incomes. Many of the women, however, freely discussed household expenditures, although a detailed discussion of household expenditures is outside the scope of this paper. To give only one example: typical daily food costs for a moderately sized household of six persons, common in the sample, came to Rp 1,000 ($2.40); thus, food expenses alone would total Rp 30,000 per month. Other significant expenses included housing, transportation, medical costs, and school fees for children.

A substantial amount accumulated through regular contributions to an *arisan* pool could play an important role in the household financial strategy because it made a lump sum available for a larger purchase. A reliable technique for accumulating meaningful lump sums is particularly important in circumstances where women face multiple pressures to spend small sums for many different needs. To clarify this point, typical *arisan* winnings must be compared with typical monthly earnings and also with typical household expenditures. For example, the minimum contribution to a monthly *arisan* was around Rp 2,000 ($4.80); this was equivalent to twice the daily food budget for the typical six-member household in our sample and could be scraped together fairly easily in one month. Among our respondents, 57 percent contributed Rp 2,000 to the first *arisan* they mentioned; another 20 percent contributed Rp 2,000–5,000; and nearly one-fourth of the women made monthly deposits of more than Rp 5,000 into their first *arisan*. The yearly lump sum obtained from a typical twelve-month *arisan*, therefore, ranged from Rp 24,000 to 60,000—substantial savings in households where an employed earner's monthly salary might be no more than Rp 20,000. By participating in a single *arisan*, a woman might accumulate in a year the equivalent of one to three monthly salary payments. Since many women belonged to several *arisan*, the total amounts accumulated by this method could be substantial.

Women commented on the importance of *arisan* in their household savings strategies. For example, *arisan* were helpful in protecting small sums against casual requests by men and children because all family members could understand how shameful it would be not to make one's promised contribution at the next meeting. Some women said that husbands who might object to what they considered women's excessive socializing were mollified by the economic gains that *arisan* membership brought with it. As noted, *arisan* meetings also provided occasions for other gainful transactions. More important than these comments, however, was the objective fact of widespread *arisan* membership among our respondents. It was a strategy of saving that obviously worked for these women, perhaps because it was flexible enough to meet changing needs and was fully controlled by group members.

Conclusion

Gender differences are key factors in the allocational processes of all societies, at all levels of social organization. They constitute one of the great fault lines of social groups—the lines of division along which resources, power, and authority are allocated to group members. Gender differences do not stand alone as social fault lines; they derive their real meaning only from their specific social placement. Gender differences within a particular class, ethnic group, age cohort, or racial or religious unit are the real bases of differential allocations. Gender relations—the interactions between women and men—also take place within the same specific contexts. Processes of accumulation and distribution of resources within households reflect the subtleties of negotiation and bargaining among members, but they do so in a concrete form that can be observed and sometimes measured by nonparticipants. Participants may not be

conscious of engaging in a process of negotiation—the concept of strategies is rarely used by people talking about their actions—but the accumulation and allocation of concrete resources are often the focal points of
negotiation.

From this perspective, both the national Indonesian data and selected
findings from the Jakarta study yield a distinctive picture of gender differences and gender relations within a specific sociocultural setting. This
distinctiveness emerges more clearly in comparisons with somewhat similar societies, some of which have been presented here.

A variety of historical, structural, cultural, and demographic factors
affected the economic roles and strategies available to the women in our
sample. Major sociopolitical changes and widely fluctuating economic
conditions during their lifetimes produced a shifting matrix of economic
opportunities. The women did what was necessary to cope with severe
economic stress and pull their families through bad patches while still
trying to get ahead. With a wide range of earning opportunities available,
these Indonesian women had more options than women in other parts of
Asia, especially where sex segregation is still stringent. Economic activity
of some form is an ever-present possibility for Indonesian women at all
levels of educational preparation and social status, even if actual participation rates differ among these levels. Cultural values concerning women's
economic acumen and trustworthiness in putting family interests before
their own desires underlie and reinforce women's central roles in household financial management and decision making. Finally, the high frequency of marriage dissolution and the visible prevalence of no-longer-
married women in the labor force make women aware of the possibility
that they might become responsible for their own support and that of
others at some time in their lives.

The most telling characteristic of women's relations to household resources drawn from our observations is the degree of independent judgment and independent action that women exercise. There appears to be a
division of responsibility among household members that reflects mutual
trust and delegation of authority rather than hierarchical differences
among women and men. This represents a major difference—albeit one
drawn in overly general terms—between the patterns of gender relations
in Indonesia and those in such Asian societies as India, Pakistan, and
Bangladesh, where gender relations are far more hierarchical.

Although we have referred only briefly to the structural characteristics
of households in this paper, these are fundamental to the pattern of gender
relations. Where households are small and relatively independent from
larger kin units—as in many ethnic groups in Indonesia—and where
divorce and remarriage mean that a person can belong to several marital

households in the course of a lifetime, it is very likely that survival skills and concrete resources inhere in the individual rather than in the household. Negotiation among household members rather than unilateral action is likely under circumstances where individuals exercise more control over skills and assets.

On the other hand, where households are composed of several generations—or even where this is only the unattained cultural ideal—it is much more likely that individual action is constrained by the limits set by specific social roles. For example, in the extended patrilineal households still common, either as ideal or in practice, in China, Pakistan, Bangladesh, and parts of India, there may be several marital couples and their children living under the same patrilineal roof. Often, some or all of the members of these larger households depend for their livelihood on commonly owned land or other assets, such as a family trade. Even where circumstances do not permit the formation of large extended households, it is very probable that the specific social roles of household members still reflect earlier cultural ideals in terms of a gender and age hierarchy. As a result, the codes of conduct of particular individuals may be highly differentiated within a single household—that is, the behavior of daughters is very different from that of daughters-in-law, that of widows unlike that of currently married women. These highly differentiated roles limit the options of individuals so that fewer skills and resources can be acquired and controlled. Although this is changing as a result of education and acquisition of new job skills, individuals remain more closely controlled by the family hierarchy in South Asia and negotiation is often more difficult.

Several salient features of the Indonesian situation reflect these broad differences. We have noted the high incidence of divorce and remarriage in Indonesian society as a whole, in order to indicate the context in which women's relations to accumulation and distribution take place. This is not a new pattern, but some changes have occurred in it over time for reasons that are still unclear. But it would clearly be false to argue that divorce is frequent *because* women and men have independent financial responsibilities. It would be equally false to argue that women struggle for financial control *because* they fear unilateral divorce. It makes more sense to argue that the cultural values and social arrangements of Indonesian societies (plural) generally encourage individual actions, whether in family formation or financial activity, consistent with a division of responsibilities among participants. This division of responsibilities is based on a subtle but continuous process of negotiation among individuals within groups as well as among groups within the society. At both levels, negotiations often fail, especially in the case of groups with widely divergent access to resources. This interpretation should not be misread to refer to an egalitarian society, which Indonesia clearly is not, but only to a particular mode of social interaction.

In this sense, it becomes important to conceptualize the bargaining power of women (although this term was never openly used among Indonesians with whom we worked or whom we studied), because the process of subtle negotiation is such an important constant in social relations. To put it briefly, Indonesian women have a strong bargaining position within their households and their social groups because they have some control over the acquisition and use of individual skills and resources. In comparison with women in societies where households are hierarchical, embodying the ideal of age and gender distinctions in specific role constraints, Indonesian women are less bound by hierarchical constraints and somewhat freer to make independent, responsible decisions.

Women's Work and Poverty: Women's Contribution to Household Maintenance in South India

JOAN P. MENCHER

This paper looks at men's and women's contributions to household maintenance in two regions of South India, Kerala and Tamil Nadu. It focuses on landless agricultural laborers in a number of villages in several districts of both states, making use of data collected between 1979 and 1982.* An article in *Mazingira* (the United Nations Environmental Programme journal) in 1980 contained a short note about a new kind of "no-till" farming that has come to the dry zones of Sri Lanka, in which all the work in rice cultivation is done by the farmer—of course, a male farmer (Wijewardene 1980). The use of a small amount of herbicide and a roller-injecting planter greatly reduces labor requirements. The conditions described for Sri Lanka are not much different from those found in many parts of Tamil Nadu. While there is no objection to reducing drudgery for people, this paper challenges two assumptions made in the *Mazingira* article: that every farmer is necessarily a man working on his own or rented land; and that it is desirable to eliminate transplanting and weeding under all circumstances, even before alternative employment has been found for women.

At a conference on women and rice cultivation in 1982 at the International Rice Research Institute, descriptions were presented of other labor-saving innovations, such as herbicides (to eliminate weeding), hand-operated transplanting equipment (which would reduce the number of women needed to transplant by a factor of six), and very simple harvesting equipment. These are all well beyond the demonstration stage. It is possible that these innovations will come soon to Tamil Nadu and Kerala.

*The data presented here were collected as part of a study on women and rice cultivation in which the author has been engaged since 1979, in collaboration with Dr. K. Saradamoni of the Indian Statistical Institute, New Delhi (with funding from the Smithsonian Institution, the Indian Council of Social Science Research, and the Research Foundation of the City University of New York). Some additional data are derived from a study of the socioeconomic effects of the green revolution in Kerala, carried out in 1975–76 by the author and Dr. P. G. K. Panikar of the Centre for Development Studies, Trivandrum, with funding from the Indian Council of Social Science Research, the Guggenheim Foundation, and the Wenner Gren Foundation. (See Panikar 1983.)

Such changes, blind to gender dynamics in income processes and to the class structure of the society, have the potential to do profound damage to large numbers of households.

The data for this paper are drawn from a larger study that attempted to document the involvement of women in the different stages of rice production and in the processing of paddy. The larger project was intended to be helpful both to the women themselves and to policymakers formulating plans and decisions relating to women's work and wages (Mencher and Saradamoni 1982b: A149). In collecting the data on women's earnings and contributions to household maintenance, I was motivated by earlier informal observations that women's earnings play an important part in family maintenance and survival, and that in some of the households women appear to take household maintenance more seriously than men do. Women, especially those who have young children or grandchildren or aged or ailing household members, are less likely than men to spend their earnings on themselves, and more likely to give everything to the household. Normatively, it is clear that the culture places a greater responsibility on women for the reproduction of the work force.

The culture also makes some conflicting demands of males, expecting them to spend at least some of their earnings (or even their wives' earnings) on such role-maintaining activities as sitting in teashops, eating food and drinking toddy or *arrack* (distilled liquor) with friends, and wearing a clean white shirt on special occasions. A woman would feel guilty if she used household money for such things. A good woman is defined as one who sacrifices everything for her family, especially for her children. Women do spend small amounts of their earnings on betel chewing. Otherwise, mothers or those who support elderly parents tend to spend money on themselves only when absolutely necessary, for example, in work situations where food is not provided by their employers.

Unmarried girls sometimes try to save something from their earnings to buy jewelry as an investment in the future, that is, to bring with them when they marry. When not working, women spend most of their time with their children (either at home, or visiting someone else), except when the child is in school. Thus, if a child is ill or hungry, the mother is more likely than the father to know about it. As noted elsewhere, even women who are active in union activities sometimes take work that pays below the minimum wage if there is nothing else available, especially if they have had to stay at home for a few days listening to the cries of hungry children (Mencher 1978).

These observations, as well as a number of others, have led me to examine the following closely related types of information: the relationship between the amount earned and the amount contributed for household maintenance by our main informant, her husband, and other working members of the household; the maximum and minimum earnings and contributions per adult for the total sample, as well as the ratio of all male contributions to all female contributions in each village; and the difference in the ratio of husband's to wife's contributions in months when wives are able to earn and contribute more, and in lean months when less work is available.

The Rice-Producing Regions

One of the features of intensive paddy cultivation is that rice is capable of supporting much larger populations than any other grain. The population per square kilometer ranges from 1,013 in rural parts of Alleppey District in Kerala to 203 in Tirunelveli District in Tamil Nadu, compared with an India-wide average of 148 in 1971. In most rice-growing areas of India this has led to highly stratified societies in which the owners of the land, who normally belong to the higher castes, rent it to tenants; even owners belonging to the so-called agricultural castes often leave most of the labor-intensive tasks to hired laborers, apart from plowing and preparing the land for cultivation. In Kerala and Tamil Nadu, since at least the ninth century, the most onerous tasks of paddy cultivation (sowing, transplanting, weeding, harvesting, threshing, and winnowing) have been done primarily by people who had at best only limited rights to the land, and often no rights at all.

Tamil Nadu and Kerala have high proportions of Harijans, or members of scheduled castes (formerly known as Untouchables), as well as Christians and Muslims converted from these castes. In India as a whole, the percentage of scheduled castes in the population correlates fairly closely with the extent of irrigated wetland, as well as with paddy cultivation in general (Mencher 1974). The main exceptions to this are the southern part of Kerala and Kanya Kumari District in Tamil Nadu, where one finds many Christian laborers (mostly converts from Untouchable castes), and the northern part of Kerala, especially Malappuram District, where many of the laborers are Muslims (again, often converts from low-ranking castes).

Traditionally, most of the agricultural laborers belonged to the scheduled castes. However, in more recent times poorer members of traditional landowning castes have taken to this kind of work. In many instances, the incomes of the poorest caste-Hindu families are lower than those of Untouchable or scheduled-caste families, because women from the higher-caste households often refuse (or are unable) to do certain kinds of work that are considered fit only for low-caste women—primarily the messy and delicate work of transplanting and the more arduous work of harvesting, both of which also require considerable training and expose the women to various health risks.

Women's Work and Men's Work

Many writers, such as Boserup (1970), have noted the important role of women in intensive rice cultivation, which they observe has been less responsive than other forms of agriculture to intensification by mechanization (1970:34–35). Whether because tasks such as transplanting and weeding were too arduous, or because the paddy harvest required a large number of people, the introduction of animal-drawn plows did not displace women in the rice-producing regions of southern and eastern India as it did in the wheat-growing regions of the north. In India, even where a relatively large surplus labor population of underemployed and unemployed males exists, women have continued to play a large part in rice production. Indeed, my 1975–76 research in one of the Palghat villages (included in the present project) demonstrated that landowners on the average used women for 417 hours per acre of wetland per crop season, whereas they used males for only 106 hours per acre.

The utilization of women varies from region to region and from season to season in a given region, depending on a number of factors, including the availability of alternative employment for males and certain local customs. For example, in two villages in Alleppey District of Kerala studied in 1975–77, women constituted 69 percent of total employment in one village and 81 percent in the other (Panikar 1983:70).

Hired labor, both male and female, accounts for a major share of the total labor input in India's rice-producing regions. In the study I carried out with Panikar it was found to exceed 90 percent in the four villages studied (Panikar 1983). In Chingleput District of Tamil Nadu, where I collected intensive materials over a 15-year period (see Mencher 1978a: 203), even among the small holdings where the percentage of hired labor is lower, it never fell below 87 percent for plowing and 81 percent for transplanting and weeding. This holds true even for many low-caste, Untouchable, and Christian households, where in addition to working on their own land, members also do wage work for others. In some instances, the reasons for the use of hired labor have to do with agronomic or social practices; for example, the expectation that a piece of land will be completely transplanted in the course of a single day (or even a half-day) often requires hired female laborers to work alongside the household females (Mencher 1978b: 358–61). In South India, the majority of the female labor in the paddy fields is hired labor.

TABLE I

Annual Household and per Capita Income

(rupees)

State and village	Total income			Per capita income		
	Mean	Standard deviation[b]	Median	Mean	Standard deviation[b]	Median
KERALA						
Cannanore-1	3263[a]	1464	3411	754	378	733
Palghat-2	3313	1526	3193	666	313	645
Malappuram-1	2579	1452	2350	531	560	406
Trichur-2	2186	1123	2114	464	259	429
Alleppey-1	1741	816	1693	322	146	321
Alleppey-2	1342[a]	362	1409	262	80	254
Trivandrum-1	3054[a]	1531	3308	684	370	482
Trivandrum-2	3635[a]	1616	4148	807	368	777
TAMIL NADU						
South Arcot-1	3063	1218	2805	636	289	580
South Arcot-2	2032	1236	1744	436	297	400
Thanjavur-2	2639	1365	2572	554	264	557
Madurai-1	2083	843	1897	562	278	532
Tirunelveli-1	2927	1529	2586	848	376	774
Kanya Kumari-2	1837	1064	1719	410	181	364

NOTE: In the villages studied earlier, data were collected on household contributions only, and not on total earnings. At the time of the study, $1 = approximately Rs. 10.

[a] The mean for total household income is higher than the median except in four villages where there are more large households with more working people.

[b] There is a wide range within the class of landless agricultural laborers in each village, as well as between villages, which is the reason for noting the standard deviation.

Rosenzweig and Schultz (1982) have pointed out a significant positive correlation in rural India between normal levels of rainfall in a district and the employment of women: the more rainfall, the more rice; the more rice, the more women are employed. Others (Bardhan 1974, Miller 1981) have pointed out that the economic value of female children (and thus apparently the value placed on their survival in infancy) is generally much higher in the rice regions of the south than in the north or northwest.

The households considered in this paper all live close to the edge of poverty. Table 1 presents data on the average household income for some of the villages in the sample, as well as the average per capita income. There is a considerable difference in income between as well as within the villages. Even in those villages with the highest average household incomes, the large majority of the households are living well below the poverty level (defined in the sixth five-year document as approximately $10 per capita per month at 1979–80 prices).

The sexual division of labor varies from region to region as well as from state to state. However, in all the villages weeding and putting in the transplanted seedlings is considered female work, just as plowing is male work. Harvesting is primarily female work in northern Kerala, shared work in central and most of southern Kerala and northern and central Tamil Nadu, and primarily male work in the extreme south of both states (the area that was under the Travancore Maharaja before 1800). Other tasks also vary considerably. The reasons for these differences in task allocation are complex and difficult to ascertain. Wherever a task is done by women it is considered easy, and where it is done by males it is considered difficult (see Mencher 1984).

The work these women do is not only arduous and tiring, it also poses health risks. Their feet are often in mud, and they must work in pouring rain as well as in hot sun. They are subject to a wide variety of diseases caused by worms and protozoa, as well as various respiratory ailments. Many women told me that they often made their children walk on their backs at night after a day's transplanting, in order to give them enough relief from pain so that they could go back and work the next day.

Women clean the stables and wash, feed, and milk animals, but work involving the use of animal power is the province of males. Thus, males alone have advantageous access to draft power. In much of Kerala, where threshing is only done manually, women do all the threshing, beating the straw for hours on end. In Tamil Nadu, where threshing is often carried out with bullocks walking in a circle around a pile of paddy, it is men's work. This is justified by the argument that only men have the strength to control animals; it is also true, however, that driving the bullocks involves less expenditure of energy than hand threshing. When threshing was done manually in Tamil Nadu, women helped the men by bending to pick up the bundles and handing them to the men to beat against a stone. Interestingly, in Tamil Nadu it is said that women are not strong enough to beat the bundles, but Kerala women manage to do it.

Even though we are able to report certain general tendencies, variability should be emphasized, since differences were found even between villages in the same district. The differences found involve the amount of work available in rice cultivation; differentials in wage rates; the sexual division of labor in agriculture; the local pattern of labor migration (for example, whether the village women migrate to other villages, or female or male migrant workers come to their villages and take work away from them); cropping patterns; forms of land tenure; the caste composition of the village, including landowners as well as laborers; differences in the type and extent of nonagricultural employment available to household males and females; differences in ways of recruiting labor; the availability of other sources of income within the household, such as cows or chickens whose products can be sold; the presence or absence of outside revenue in the village (particularly earnings sent by migrants to the Middle East); and the uneven impact of modernization. Thus, a village with two or three large landlords who control the labor market might have vastly different labor requirements and wage rates from a nearby village with a predominance of smaller landowners, despite the existence of a legally sanctioned minimum wage for each agricultural operation.

For example, in the village labeled South Arcot-1 both males and females from nearby nonirrigated villages (which are dependent on rain and pump-sets) come to the sample village to transplant and to harvest. But the women from the sample village are only occasionally able to get work in the other villages. The reason given for this is that the sample village is irrigated by the Cauvery/Caleroon system, which creates short periods of heavy demand for labor when the water is released for the fields and transplanting suddenly starts. In the nonirrigated villages work is staggered throughout the year, with fewer sharp fluctuations in labor demand and thus little need for imported labor, except occasionally during the peanut harvest.

In the Muslim-dominated part of Kerala, vast changes have occurred since the late 1950's, when I first worked in the region. At that time most laborers were tied by traditional semifeudal obligations to particular landowners, and most of the land was owned by wealthy Hindu landlords and cultivated by tenants with the help of tied laborers. The cost of labor was quite low, and alternative employment was much more limited than it is today. Recently, many males from Malappuram have obtained employment in a small nearby factory, and many others (particularly Muslims), especially those with a little education or a skill such as tailoring or construction, have managed to get jobs in the Middle East. The resulting influx of money to some households has brought far-reaching changes in the division of labor, wage rates, and social values. For example, many men are now involved in construction work, from working in sawmills to building houses, which is much better paid than agriculture.

Males in this village tend to avoid agricultural labor other than preparing the land for cultivation, which includes plowing and carrying the harvested sheaves. The latter task was formerly carried out by both men and women as part of the harvesting operation. When Middle East money flowing into the village made better-paying work available, men turned away from harvesting work. The women responded by refusing to carry the harvested sheaves back to the landowners' household compounds, thus obliging the landowners to hire men not yet engaged in construction work to carry the sheaves at a wage comparable to what they were paid for other kinds of work.

Although the influx of Middle East money definitely improves the

economics of individual households, it may also be contributing to lower-
ing women's status, or at least imposing new constraints on them. In
another village in this region, while compiling the list of households for
the sample, I found many poor, landless Muslim households in which the
women were no longer working in the fields, although most of them had
done so previously (and probably still needed the income desperately). A
new notion of male prestige had led some men to feel uncomfortable about
allowing their wives to work in the fields, even though their particular
families may not yet have benefited from the flow of Middle East money.

In Malappuram-1, meanwhile, many women have continued to work
for low wages even when their menfolk's wages are high. Intensive interviews with agricultural laborers make it clear that these women feel
deeply that without their work the family would be unable to manage. We
also noted in this village that many of the landless laborers' households
now appear to have cows or female water buffaloes, whose care is largely
in the hands of women. The addition of an animal to the household can
significantly add to its income.

Sources of Household Income

Total household income seems to be fairly closely related to the number
of working people in the household, which usually correlates with the
number of adult household members. Households with more earners are
better protected against sudden reversals in income resulting from shifts in
labor markets for both men and women, changes in the climate or environment (such as changes in levels of rainfall, or loss of access to forests
through changes in government regulations), and natural events such as
childbirth or death.

There seems to be considerable variation in the percentage contribution
that a woman can expect from her unmarried sons and daughters. On the
whole, unmarried daughters tend to give most of what they earn to the
household, although they may save some money for their marriages.
Occasionally, they buy cheap bangles or other ornaments, which do not
make a significant dent in their incomes. Unmarried sons tend to give a
higher proportion of their wages to the household than do husbands or
other males. This may be because of the proverbial power of the mother
over her son. It is perhaps also because a son is likely to be more aware of
the mother's distress about the family's poverty and of her struggles to feed
everyone.

Of 48 landless and marginal landowning households in Malappuram-1,
in 18 households the husband is either absent (owing to death, divorce, or
desertion) or too ill to earn much. In many instances the woman has a son
or brother who is contributing to the household. Although we lack statis-

tical evidence, it is striking that this is the only village in which we have found so many landless and marginal households of divorced women. It is possible that the increased prosperity of some men may be leading them to feel freer to abandon their first wives. The increased impoverishment of many women is especially striking in the case of women who do not have children old enough to earn significantly.

At the same time, however, in looking at our data for total household income, it is clear that the poorest households are those in which there are no earning males (with the rare exceptions of households headed by men who spend all their income on their own pursuits and give nothing to the family). Yet it does not necessarily make sense to treat female-headed households as a separate category with respect to income, since a widow with working daughters or sons might not be any worse off financially than a woman with a husband; on the other hand, the poorest households include not only those of widows or divorced women, but also elderly couples living alone, or women with sick and/or aged husbands who have no children of working age.

Determinants of Women's Income

The most important influence on a woman's income is the number of days' work she can get (see Mencher 1985a, 1985b for detailed dicussions of this point). This is influenced by: (1) whether or not a village is in a monocrop region, that is, by the availability of work on alternative crops or in agriculture-related or forestry-related crafts (such as working with coconut leaves or collecting firewood, honey, or leaves); (2) the extent to which female laborers in a given village go to nearby, or even slightly distant, places seeking agricultural work; (3) agronomic practices in the region, such as the extent of herbicide use and broadcast sowing versus transplanting; (4) the availability of nonagricultural work for women when there is no agricultural work, such as making *gur* (raw sugar) from palm sap, carrying headloads, handicraft work, and so on; (5) questions of prestige and training (in certain areas, some kinds of work have come to be associated with Harijans or Muslims: for example, in Malappuram-1 Muslims converted from Untouchable castes transplant, but other Muslim women do not know how—or refuse—to transplant since it is considered the work of Untouchables; similarly, in South Arcot-2, Hindu caste women do not know how to transplant or harvest); (6) the reluctance of women to learn to do certain tasks that they were not trained for when they were young. While this lack of training depends in part on caste, it can also be the result of childhood illness, or being a petted only child or an only girl, or living in a somewhat better-off household.

Other factors that affect the level of a woman's income reflect certain

TABLE 2A

Earnings (E) Versus Contributions (C) to Household Maintenance, Females and Males

	Informant		Ratio C/E	Husband		Ratio C/E	Ratio of wife's to husband's earnings	Ratio of wife's to husband's contributions
	E	C		E	C			
KERALA								
Cannanore-1	1138	962	0.85	1954	1249	0.64	0.58	0.77
Palghat-1	–	854	–	–	645	–	–	1.31
Palghat-2	1065	990	0.93	2039	1406	0.69	0.52	0.70
Malappuram-1	435	421	0.97	1219	1020	0.84	0.36	0.41
Trichur-1	–	467	–	–	377	–	–	1.24
Trichur-2	786	688	0.88	1787	1294	0.72	0.44	0.53
Alleppey-1	752	691	0.92	748	569	0.76	1.01	1.21
Alleppey-2	530	438	0.83	743	541	0.73	0.71	0.81
Trivandrum-1	1027	938	0.91	2214	943	0.43	0.46	0.99
Trivandrum-2	1420	1209	0.85	2235	1141	0.51	0.64	1.06
TAMIL NADU								
Chingleput-1	–	301	–	–	155	–	–	1.94
Chingleput-2	–	265	–	–	216	–	–	1.23
South Arcot-1	699	693	0.99	1449	1226	0.85	0.48	0.57
South Arcot-2	587	566	0.96	935	667	0.71	0.63	0.85
Thanjavur-1	–	468	–	–	490	–	–	0.96
Thanjavur-2	759	756	1.00	1247	901	0.72	0.61	0.84
Tirunelveli-1	1173	1099	0.94	1653	1478	0.91	0.71	0.74
Madurai-1	564	556	0.99	1240	938	0.76	0.45	0.59
Kanya Kumari-1	–	369	–	–	365	–	–	1.01
Kanya Kumari-2	599	570	0.95	1297	808	0.62	0.46	0.71

NOTE: Districts within each state are listed from north to south. In six villages data on earnings were not collected.

socially aggregated disabilities. Women's health status, already poor overall, is made worse by the nature of their work. The health problems observed during the course of the study year include certain types of seasonal illnesses that women are more prone to get, such as splitting heels from standing in the water and mud all day transplanting; severe arthritic pains, which are more common among women than men; age-related illnesses; and problems from the stress of recent pregnancy or childbirth. The frequent illnesses some women report may be related to levels of calcium in their diets inadequate to replace that lost through pregnancy and lactation* (see Mencher and Saradamoni 1982b: A161–64).

*Calcium is provided both by the leaf and the lime (calcium carbonate) eaten with the areca nut, which itself provides a small amount of calcium. Since people in these areas get vitamin D from sunlight, they are probably able to utilize this calcium effectively. How much calcium is actually provided by betel chewing is controversial. These women cannot afford milk products, except an occasional small amount in tea. (They do occasionally eat fish bones.)

Gender-Differentiated Contributions
of Income to the Household

An earlier paper (Mencher and Saradamoni 1982b) showed that in six of the villages female income is as important to the household maintenance as male income; it constitutes a significant proportion of total household income, especially in landless and marginal landowning agricultural laborer households. In these households, which have little or nothing to spare, female income cannot be regarded as supplementary. The data gathered from all the villages continues to support this. It is clear from Table 4 that regardless of how much a woman earns, she gives a fairly high percentage to her household, always a much higher percentage than that given by her husband or other male household members. In those villages where females contribute a comparatively low percentage of their income, there is usually an explanation. For example, women who have to work very far from home are obliged to buy food near the workplace. The extent to which this occurs is partly related to the distance between home

TABLE 2B

Maximum and Minimum Contributions to Household Maintenance,
All Females and All Males

	All females		All males		Ratio of contributions, all males to all females
	Maximum	Minimum	Maximum	Minimum	
KERALA					
Cannanore-1	1924	500	2935	211	1 : 0.79
Palghat-1	1394	361	2799	113	1 : 1.29
Palghat-2	1606	104	3029	115	1 : 0.62
Malappuram-1	1333	101	3517	45	1 : 0.25
Trichur-1	1585	313	790	56	1 : 1.20
Trichur-2	1323	309	2824	380	1 : 0.56
Alleppey-1	1181	14	1072	49	1 : 1.30
Alleppey-2	600	211	970	137	1 : 0.77
Trivandrum-1	1371	370	1518	544	1 : 0.97
Trivandrum-2	1797	480	2165	317	1 : 1.16
TAMIL NADU					
Chingleput-1	1223	140	614	27	1 : 1.20
Chingleput-2	368	100	540	36	1 : 0.86
South Arcot-1	1040	164	1885	225	1 : 0.52
South Arcot-2	907	61	1330	41	1 : 0.71
Thanjavur-1	816	801	616	127	1 : 1.20
Thanjavur-2	1510	80	1544	263	1 : 0.80
Tirunelveli-1	1997	428	4651	289	1 : 0.63
Madurai-1	1072	184	1716	135	1 : 0.60
Kanya Kumari-1	577	204	1463	174	1 : 0.85
Kanya Kumari-2	891	156	1681	399	1 : 0.61

TABLE 3A

*Average Contributions to Household Maintenance by Income Level
of Main Female Informant, Selected Villages, Kerala State*

Income level of main female informant	Informant		Husband		Other females (where present)		Other males (where present)	
	Pct.	Rs.	Pct.	Rs.	Pct.	Rs.	Pct.	Rs.
Cannanore-1								
Rs. 1200+ (N = 4)	87%	1305	56%	1467	–	–	–	–
Rs. 900–1199 (N = 7)	84%	880	70%	973	82%	1594 (N = 2)	75%	999 (N = 3)
Rs. 600–899 (N = 2)	88%	778	67%	1775	87%	1743 (N = 1)	–	–
No earning husband (N = 11)	83%	924	–	–	82%	863 (N = 5)	64%	1395 (N = 7)
Palghat-2								
Rs. 1200+ (N = 9)	95%	1273	68%	1226	96%	404 (N = 2)	59%	1561 (N = 2)
Rs. 900–1199 (N = 6)	95%	1038	68%	1624	76%	400 (N = 3)	–	–
Rs. 600–899 (N = 2)	96%	796	78%	1427	–	–	–	–
Rs. 400–599 (N = 1)	80%	406	63%	2240	–	–	–	–
No earning husband (N = 8)	89%	993	–	–	83%	394 (N = 5)	65%	1420 (N = 4)
Malappuram-1								
Rs. 400+ (N = 9)	98%	622	84%	970	93%	129 (N = 7)	68%	675 (N = 2)
Rs. 143–361 (N = 9)	95%	196	85%	1426	97%	77 (N = 7)	80%	1061 (N = 10)
No earning husband (N = 9)	95%	273	–	–	96%	399 (N = 6)	78%	1061 (N = 13)
Trichur-2								
Rs. 1200+ (N = 4)	86%	1100	69%	1402	82%	619 (N = 2)	69%	377 (N = 1)
Rs. 900–1199 (N = 1)	89%	867	70%	1926	–	–	–	–
Rs. 600–899 (N = 4)	86%	446	70%	1156	–	–	–	–
Rs. 400–599 (N = 6)	91%	319	67%	1456	75%	259 (N = 1)	–	–
No earning husband (N = 7)	91%	714	–	–	82%	507 (N = 1)	67%	1344 (N = 2)

TABLE 3A—continued

Income level of main female informant	Informant		Husband		Other females (where present)		Other males (where present)	
	Pct.	Rs.	Pct.	Rs.	Pct.	Rs.	Pct.	Rs.
Alleppey-2								
Over Rs. 500 (N = 16)	82%	490	74%	552	84%	372 (N = 7)	56%	462 (N = 1)
Rs. 200–499 (N = 8)	86%	358	74%	579	79%	366 (N = 2)	72%	661 (N = 2)
No earning husband (N = 8)	80%	388	–	–	85%	293 (N = 7)	67%	709 (N = 2)

NOTE: The income categories used to subdivide the data vary because of the considerable differences among villages in such variables as basic wage rates and the number of days of employment available. The category "No earning husband" includes widows, women with elderly or infirm husbands, as well as abandoned and divorced women. Some of these women have adult children who make substantial contributions to the households.

and workplace, and partly to the disappearance of the traditional practice of employers providing food for workers.

The need to purchase food away from home is an important factor in Trivandrum-1 and Trivandrum-2, where the ratio of the female contribution to earnings is lower than average (though still higher than that of their working husbands). This accords with the description given by Gulati (1981) for agricultural laborers in this district, who often have to buy food from shops. In Alleppey-2, the other village with low female contributions, women have to travel considerable distances in search of work, and must pay bus and ferry charges out of their earnings, along with having to buy food. In addition, women often have to buy food on credit when they have no work, or when they have not been paid. (It is common in the Alleppey region for landlords to give workers IOU's to be redeemed at harvest time.) When the women do get paid, they have to pay back their debts to shopowners, both in cash and in kind. What they brought home (or what was reported as a contribution to the household) often excluded the amount given to the shopkeeper. Yet even in Alleppey, women's contributions run to 80 percent of their income, whereas male contributions average about 70 percent (see Table 2A). Throughout Tamil Nadu the amount that the women contribute to their households varies from 95 to 99 percent. Apart from *pan*, the women buy very little for themselves from what they earn.

As can be seen from Table 2B, the ratio of absolute amounts contributed by women and by men varies from 1.20 in the eastern delta of Thanjavur and in one of the Chingleput villages to 0.56 in Trichur-2 and 0.25 in the exceptional case of Malappuram-1. (In Trichur-2 as in Malap-

TABLE 3B

Average Contributions to Household Maintenance by Income Level
of Main Female Informant, Selected Villages, Tamil Nadu State

Income level of main female informant	Informant		Husband		Other females (where present)		Other males (where present)	
	Pct.	Rs.	Pct.	Rs.	Pct.	Rs.	Pct.	Rs.
South Arcot-2								
Rs. 550+ (N = 8)	100%	758	81%	885	–	–	85%	463 (N = 3)
Rs. 200–450 (N = 4)	100%	369	82%	485	100%	213 (N = 2)	68%	851 (N = 1)
No earning husband (N = 3)	99%	580	–	–	92%	758	87%	353 (N = 4)
Thanjavur-2								
Rs. 1000+ (N = 7)	99%	1247	70%	1042	99%	899 (N = 4)	75%	852 (N = 2)
Rs. 700–999 (N = 7)	98%	854	81%	807	94%	525 (N = 3)	80%	913 (N = 2)
Rs. 500–699 (N = 7)	98%	574	75%	784	97%	520 (N = 2)	74%	1039 (N = 2)
Rs. 100–300 (N = 3)	97%	204	64%	1030	–	–	91%	1526 (N = 2)
No earning husband (N = 5)	100%	450	–	–	100%	232 (N = 2)	95%	1674 (N = 3)
Tirunelveli-1								
Rs. 1200+ (N = 11)	99%	1541	93%	2127	97%	225 (N = 3)	97%	1283 (N = 2)
Rs. 900–1199 (N = 8)	99%	998	89%	1217	98%	1896 (N = 1)	100%	40 (N = 1)
Rs. 600–899 (N = 5)	98%	701	84%	803	97%	695 (N = 1)	–	–
No earning husband (N = 5)	99%	799	–	–	100%	550 (N = 1)	96%	3213 (N = 1)
Madurai-1								
Rs. 800+ (N = 3)	99%	966	78%	1238	100%	144 (N = 1)	95%	603 (N = 2)
Rs. 600–799 (N = 7)	98%	664	73%	949	95%	452 (N = 2)	–	–
Rs. 450–599 (N = 4)	98%	543	73%	751	–	–	–	–

TABLE 3B—*continued*

Income level of main female informant	Informant		Husband		Other females (where present)		Other males (where present)	
	Pct.	Rs.	Pct.	Rs.	Pct.	Rs.	Pct.	Rs.
Rs. 300–449 (N = 9)	98%	360	77%	972	97%	514 (N = 2)	52%	68 (N = 1)
Less than 300 (N = 2)	100%	266	80%	664	96%	700 (N = 1)	–	–
No earning husband (N = 6)	98%	620	–	–	97%	619 (N = 4)	77%	1159 (N = 4)
Kanya Kumari-2 Rs. 600–799 (N = 6)	95%	658	61%	582	89%	431 (N = 3)	–	–
Rs. 450–599 (N = 5)	95%	506	57%	982	99%	510 (N = 1)	–	–
Rs. 300–449 (N = 3)	98%	381	72%	1237	90%	73 (N = 1)	86%	189 (N = 1)
No earning husband (N = 16)	95%	578	–	–	76%	451 (N = 8)	54%	850 (N = 9)

puram-1, most of the work reported for males is nonagricultural work, such as masonry, woodwork, and loading.)

A number of factors seem to affect this variability, including the actual wage rates. In some villages there is a greater disparity in the wage rate between males and females. In Chingleput-1 both males and females have been paid the same rate for harvesting since 1979, whereas in Chingleput-2 there is still a difference in the rates paid for essentially the same work. Accordingly, in Chingleput-1 the ratio of male to female contributions to household maintenance is 1 : 1.20, whereas in Chingleput-2, where the rate for women is lower, it comes to 1 : .86.

Although the amounts contributed by males are sometimes greater than the female contributions in absolute terms, the proportion of male contributions to male earnings is always much lower than that of females; see Tables 3A and 3B. Even in Malappuram-1, most of the women give almost all of what they earn to their households. Thus, in the small subsample (9 households) of women with husbands who earn over Rs. 400 per year from agricultural work, while the women's income is only 55 percent of that of the men, their contribution to the households comes to 70 percent of that of the men. The income of women who earn less than

Rs. 400 is sometimes only a small fraction of that brought in by the men, yet they view their contribution as essential.

Implications of Differences in Male and Female Contributions to the Household Budget

Conventional development theory and practice assume that if men's wages are increased, all the household members will automatically be better off. However, our data make it clear that the issue is a great deal more complicated. This is especially apparent when we examine household well-being in terms of the well-being of individual members.

Our data indicate that women contribute proportionately more of their income to the household and withhold less for personal use than men. Even in the months when both earn little, men continue to give a lower proportion of what they earn. When a man is earning more, he can keep a certain amount of money for his personal use and still contribute a higher proportion of his income to the household. Thus, in South Arcot-2 in January, when both husbands and wives earn the most, men give an average of 85 percent of what they earn to the household, while in April, when their wives' incomes are at the lowest point, the men's contributions average 71 percent of their earnings; see Table 4. Since this is only an average, many men in fact give quite a bit less. A man's personal expenses might be slightly curtailed in April when there is not enough money to feed his family adequately, but it is also easy for him to ignore the problem and to meet his friends as usual at the tea or toddy shop.

If men's spending patterns were established more in line with families' needs and lives, men would not withhold a larger proportion of their income at times of greater need. However, men are not at home as often as women. For a woman there is no such escape, because of her own self-image as well as society's view of her role and the demands of her children (Whitehead 1981).

I have spoken to groups of male and female laborers in several villages about the fact that men withhold more income for their personal use than do women. The men always agreed that this was the case, and that it was the normal and natural way of the world. As one man put it, "It is part of being a man." Village women in general accept this, and even though some resent it (especially those whose husbands spend excessively on themselves), they do not expect it to change. Those few women whose husbands spend less on themselves, for whatever reason, always pointed this out. Often the reason for this was that the husband had some illness that made it difficult for him to drink or eat in public eating places, although one does occasionally find even healthy men giving everything to

TABLE 4
Average Monthly Contributions to the Household in Six Sample Villages

	Average contributions in a month when wives' contributions were at a minimum				Average contributions in a month when wives' contributions were at a maximum			
	Wife		Husband		Wife		Husband	
	Rs.	Pct.	Rs.	Pct.	Rs.	Pct.	Rs.	Pct.
KERALA								
Palghat-2	26	93%	110	71%	221	99%	116	75%
Alleppey-1	4	80	10	66	123	83	82	73
Trivandrum-1	22	71	100	53	168	89	142	79
TAMIL NADU								
South Arcot-1	9	100	63	85	146	100	185	86
South Arcot-2	35	99	46	71	90	99	90	85
Thanjavur-2	20	100	19	76	16	100	146	76

NOTE: This table is based on a subsample of households with only husband and wife working. The percentages represent contributions as a percent of total earnings.

their families. Yet the majority held back money for status-maintaining activities and saw nothing wrong with doing so.

For better-off families this is not a crucial matter, but for most of the households being discussed here, which are living close to the margin of survival, this can have serious consequences, especially in times of crisis. As the earlier discussion of women's health indicates, childbearing withdraws the women, at least briefly, from field work. How soon a woman goes back to work depends primarily on the availability of someone else to look after the baby and the distance she has to travel to work. The need for the women's daily income is so great that associations of very low-income, self-employed women, such as the Self-Employed Women's Association of Ahmedabad, have provided a form of insurance for themselves that gives them some payment for the days just after childbirth, because they know that the family food intake depends in part on a woman's income.

Informal discussions and observational data from this study indicate that women who are unable to work soon after childbirth because there is no one to care for the baby, and who depend on their own and their husband's income, are forced to cut back at the very time when their needs and those of the baby are likely to be the greatest. There is no indication that men increase the proportion of their income contribution at this time, since they do not increase it when their wives' earnings fall for other reasons. When a baby happens to be born at a time in the agricultural cycle when there is work only for women and none for men, the family faces an even greater crisis. Childbirth often forces a household to go into debt, borrowing against the woman's anticipated future income, since the husband's current contribution is often not enough to sustain the household. If at that time a woman has any gold jewelry left from her marriage, it may be pawned.

Though our data cannot be used to trace a direct link between women's loss of income at the time of birth, lowered food consumption, and maternal and child morbidity or mortality, some observations about the sample population suggest that such a relationship should be examined. All of these households live close to the margin in terms of food availability. Any major loss of income through childbirth, illness, or other causes could have serious consequences. How close to the margin they live is documented by some observations in one of the Tamil villages. In a small subsample of households, arm circumference measurements were taken of children under the age of 5. Among the 26 landless and marginal households for which measurements were taken, we found children in six households who were clearly in the danger zone with circumferences less than 80 percent of standard, which means that their body weights were less than 70 percent of the weight standard (Voluntary Health Association of India 1981). In one household, both a 4-year-old and a 1-year-old had severe deficits. In another case we found one of two 2-year-old twin girls in the severe danger zone. In the other four households, two of the children in the danger zone were still nursing, which means that the mother was probably producing insufficient milk. While the children in the remaining 20 households were not noticeably malnourished, any major loss of income could have had serious consequences.

Income Control

To what extent do women retain control over what they earn? How much freedom do they have in this matter? Table 5 indicates the number and percentage of women who report that they hand over their income to their husbands. Except in two villages, less than half the women report doing so.* My own interview data, while not quantitative, also suggest strongly that many of the women do retain control over their earnings. Indeed, in many households it is the wife who handles the family's fi-

---

*The senior investigators for Tamil Nadu recently expressed suspicions about the responses from Tirunelveli-1, since in this village an outside male administered the senior interview, and even he expressed some qualms about the responses. (In all other cases the interview was done by an outside female, one of our female village assistants, or, in one case, a male village assistant.) Both Palghat-1 and Tirunelveli-1 are better off than the average village, but there are other better-off villages where women retain their earnings. I find myself suspicious also of the data from Palghat-1 on the basis of my own informal work there in 1975–76, when I lived in the village for about four months and visited many of the landless laborer households.

TABLE 5

*Women Who Hand over Their Earnings
to Their Husband*

	Yes		No	
	No.	Pct.	No.	Pct.
KERALA				
Palghat-1	1	8%	11	92%
Palghat-2	26	70	11	30
Malappuram-1	13	31	29	69
Trichur-1	11	40	18	60
Trichur-2	15	48	16	52
Alleppey-1	8	17	38	83
Alleppey-2	7	22	25	78
Trivandrum-1	6	23	20	77
Trivandrum-2	3	15	42	85
TAMIL NADU				
Chingleput-1	5	23	17	77
Chingleput-2	6	29	15	71
South Arcot-1	8	17	38	83
South Arcot-2	13	27	36	73
Thanjavur-2	6	21	22	79
Tirunelveli-1	31	84	6	16
Madurai-1	1	3	36	97
Kanya Kumari-1	18	41	26	59

NOTE: The number of cases varies considerably from village to village for two reasons: (1) some cases were not included because they were irrelevant, for example, households without a husband; and (2) in some villages the question was not asked of all the informants, thus the data are missing.

nances; the men hand over their earnings to their wives to manage (after deducting their own personal expenses). If, however, the husband asks for money for his personal use on days when he did not get work, the wife is generally not free to refuse, regardless of what he wants the money for. To refuse might lead to a beating.

A few examples may illustrate. An informant in a Tamil Nadu village said that her husband asks for money for expenses when he does not go to work, and beats her if she refuses. Her husband was not particularly hard-working; she complained that he earns only enough for his *pan* and liquor, and for the children's clothing. In another Tamil village one of the husbands not only takes money from his wife, but also borrows from his neighbors, obliging her to repay them from her wages. Another husband had pawned his wife's jewelry without her permission. (In that household both the informant and her husband hand over their earnings to the informant's mother-in-law, who is in charge of buying daily provisions and medicines. The husband used his wife's jewelry to get money for himself beyond his daily allowances.)

On other aspects of financial autonomy the data are more mixed. When we asked women if they could buy a sari for themselves without asking their husbands, many said yes. Many others said that they would first tell their husbands and then go and buy the sari, and still others stated that they would require their husband's permission. In eight villages where we coded the response (for those households where it was relevant, that is, where there was a husband, and where there was no elder member who might actually have more of a say than either husband or wife), more than half the woman said they needed permission. But it is unclear whether this was merely a pro forma way of showing respect, or if they really were required to obey their husbands in matters of personal purchases from their own earnings. This would require greater probing than was done in this project. Some said the husband would make the purchase, but it is also clear that there were matters involved other than control over finances, such as whether there was a sari shop in the village, whether prices were lower elsewhere, or whether people selling saris come to the village. (While women are generally free to move about within the village, purchases outside the village are mostly made by males.)

As noted above, men's control over women's income can extend to the ability to create debt for women and indirectly take their personal property. In one Muslim-dominated village in Kerala, several women reported that they gave all of their jewelry to their husbands when asked for it. Afterward, when their husbands abandoned them, they felt it was a mistake. One woman commented, "Then he loved me and my children, but now he doesn't take care of them at all. He is a drunkard. He no longer forces me to give him money since he married another woman three years ago and now he gets money from her."

While the above responses are by no means typical, they do make clear that in at least some households, the woman must contribute to her husband's personal expenses on top of financing the maintenance and reproduction of the household. There are certainly many households where a respectable proportion of the husband's earnings go to the family, and where he is very concerned about their well-being. On the other hand, there are households where, for one reason or another, the husband's contribution is very low, and the woman is the main provider. We found at least one such case in each village sample.

In general, when the husband handles the finances, he also has the responsibility of bringing home food. When the woman handles them, she either purchases the food herself or sends a child to make the purchases. Both women and men pay for clothes for schoolchildren, although it appears to be more commonly the responsibility of the husband. The proportion of fathers who do this varies by village, and we cannot tell from our large-scale data which factors make the greatest difference. In general, there is a fair amount of variation among villages and among states, but an evaluation of this variation requires more intensive data.

Conclusions

Any examination of female laborers forces the investigator to take into account the wider political, social, and economic implications of economic development. As childbearers and child-rearers, women are concerned with precisely those human questions that development planners tend to exclude. This greater concern is reflected in the different ways in which men's and women's incomes are spent. This paper has focused on women in landless agricultural laborer households. The data presented strongly indicate that a very high percentage of the income earned by females goes to household maintenance, whereas a lower percentage of male income is comparably spent. In absolute terms, the amount given by females varies considerably within as well as between villages, but in most cases, when a woman is able to work, the amount earned and thus available for contribution tends to be sizable. In many of the households where women earn less, the difference is not made up by the men's contributions and the net effect is simply greater poverty for the household as a whole.

At this point we can state categorically from our study area that eliminating female work, even if it means some improvement in male employment, would have a very negative effect, not only on the females themselves, but also on the families they support. In assessing production and employment policies, a distinction needs to be made between those labor-saving technologies that increase production by reducing women's drudgery and those that eliminate crucial work opportunities for women. As noted in the beginning of this paper, important policy decisions that could effect the earning power of women in Tamil Nadu and Kerala are likely to come up in the next five or ten years. The decisions taken will critically affect household maintenance—and even survival—among agricultural laborers.

Household Budgeting and
Financial Management in a
Lower-Income Cairo Neighborhood

HOMA HOODFAR

M any social scientists, particularly social policymakers and development planners, treat households and families as homogenous units
where individuals have equal access to household resources.* This "ideal
model," based on the ideology of family in Western Europe and the
United States, ignores the structural differences that operate through
cultural practices and ideological principles, such as gender and age hierarchies, as well as more complex interpersonal issues. It thus prevents us
from examining the social relations that discriminate against vulnerable
categories such as women and children. The cross-cultural studies in this
volume, on the other hand, build a more realistic picture of household
interaction, and they illuminate the diversity and dynamism of the family
in its historical and cultural contexts.

Such cross-cultural studies shed light on the variety of interwoven
factors that underlie the position of women within the family, the labor
market, and the society as a whole. At the theoretical level, they help us to
understand and conceptualize the basis of power within a conjugal relationship. Only by conceptualizing power, identifying its basis, and measuring it can we develop a relevant methodology.†

Many have argued that the "housewifization" of women and their
separation from social production that occurred as a result of industrialization have had adverse effects on them (Oakley 1974). Advocates of
this thesis argue that the wife's power relative to the husband increases

*This paper is based on a broader research project that was partly funded by the Ford
Foundation, to which I am most grateful. I wish to thank Cynthia Myntti, Barbara
Ibrahim, and Frederic C. Shorter for their constant moral and intellectual support during
my field research. I am also indebted to Nanneke Redclift, Cynthia Nelson, and Jan Pahl,
who read and made valuable comments on the first draft of the paper.

†Measuring power, particularly power within any interpersonal relationship, where
there are often strong and dynamic interactions between the complex emotional attachments and the actual and potential material basis of the relationship, is a very difficult task.
At their present stage, social science concepts and methodologies are not equipped to
perform this task adequately. However, the recognition of the need for and attempts to
develop appropriate tools are the major road to progress in this respect (see McDonald 1980).

when she is a wage earner (Oppong 1981; Bahr 1974), and they therefore favor the economic activity of women and their full introduction into the labor market (Engels 1972; Leacock 1978; Sandy 1974).

However, existing studies reveal data that contradict such a position. The power of wives vis-à-vis their husbands may decrease when they earn incomes of their own; some husbands then keep more of their earnings for personal expenditure while the women's earnings go to pay for collective family needs (Maher 1981; Whitehead 1981; Pahl 1982). These findings support the argument that the economic activities of women provide the basis for even more exploitation, privatization, oppression, and appropriation of their labor (Malinowski 1963; Shorter 1978). It is clear that there is no universal answer to the question, and any broad generalization will only obscure the realities.

The present case study of a complex urban society suggests that it is not the economic or noneconomic participation of women per se that guarantees their higher status and position. What appears to be important is the balance of their total recognized and valued contribution to their immediate social group (in this case, the family unit) and the wider society.* Inherent in the question of recognition are the ideology of gender role and the sexual division of labor, the social organization of work, and the extent to which male and female are dependent on each other for their survival in a given society. The nature of this interdependence appears to have a profound effect on the power relations between husband and wife.

Much of the research and discussion has failed to consider the context and conditions in which women's economic participation takes place. Women's participation should be examined in terms of factors that may affect the balance of power between husband and wife. These factors include cultural beliefs and practices as well as the way in which changes and development are taking place. For example, ideological differences between different societies, such as whether men or women (or both) are responsible for providing for the family, affect the way women's economic contribution is viewed. Segregation of the sexes, which often places constraints on women's physical movement, lessens the possibility of women

*What determines the level of recognition and value given to the contribution of women (or any other social group or individual) is the economic structure and cultural practices of a given society. The recognition and attribution of a certain value to the women's contribution have at least three distinct levels which are closely linked and are in continuous dynamic interaction: the recognition of the value of the contribution by the contributor (the women themselves); the recognition of the value of the contribution by the immediate social group (the family unit); the recognition of the value of the contribution by the wider society. These issues have been discussed more fully elsewhere (Hoodfar 1986), but in this paper, I have attempted to demonstrate the impact of power relations on the day-to-day marital life and vice versa.

being involved in income-earning activities. In the more industrialized societies, should women initiate alternative earning strategies, their menfolk often retain control of women's income. Similarly, many societies require the approval of the husband or male guardian for a woman to engage in any economic activity. It is often the case that a woman's contribution to the household income pool encourages her husband to withhold more of his money for personal expenses. Finally, social change and development—even when identical—may affect sex-role ideologies differently in different societies. For example, while the concept of "man the breadwinner" has introduced a new approach to sex-role stereotyping in many African communities, it has reinforced the traditional ideology in Muslim societies. Consequently, Muslim women's need or desire to work for pay is viewed as secondary by both the state and the household, and very little is done to equip women with earning skills or opportunities.

The controversial debate on the status of women, and its correlation with the extent of their economic participation, has also raised questions about the sources and legitimacy of political power within the conjugal unit. This important factor has often been overlooked, partly because of its complexity. It asks such problematic questions as: What are the bases underlying the legitimacy of power within the conjugal bond? Will these bases change, and how will the power relationship be affected by these changes? Can we make the generalization that the modern social system is detrimental to the position of women? If not, why not?

For the sake of clarity I define power in terms of (1) actual decision-making authority over scarce material resources and (2) control of and access to knowledge of household resources. Although the possibility that children and other members of the kinship network will have power should be taken into account, here I am concerned only with the relationship between husband and wife.

The Research Sample

My study was carried out during 1983–84 in a lower-income neighborhood in Cairo. The neighborhood had developed during the last 20 years, and its population consisted primarily of first- or second-generation migrants. Some had left rural areas to settle permanently in Cairo; others, usually of a younger generation, had been born in densely populated parts of old Cairo and had found it difficult to find accommodation in their own neighborhoods when they began to set up their own independent households.

The study sample consisted of 50 families, for 33 of which I have a complete set of detailed data. For the sake of comparability two house-

TABLE I

*Education of the Male and Female Heads
of the 31 Sample Households*

Education level	Male	Female
Illiterate	6	18
Partially literate	7	2
Primary school	11	7
More than primary school	4	2
High school diploma and above	3	2

holds are not included here: one was a single-parent household, and the other consisted of a mother and son, in which the son was simultaneously head of another household in the sample. Of these 31 sample households, 6 consisted of two or three members, 14 had four or five members, 6 had six or seven members, and 5 had eight or more.

Most women in the neighborhood were totally illiterate, while most men, although they did not have much formal education, had learned to read or write, often through their jobs or friends at the workplace.

Most families lived in small, two-room apartments without a kitchen. The small corridor between the rooms, or sometimes a small balcony, was used for cooking. All households had electricity, but most did not have running water even though it had been introduced to the area some time ago. Twenty-nine households considered better housing and more space their most pressing needs, but none hoped to attain it in the near future because of the rising cost of housing in Cairo.

Most working men spent very little time at home; they often left early in the morning after drinking a cup of tea and returned at night to sleep. Some men had two jobs and therefore little free time; others spent their free time with friends at tea houses in the neighborhood or elsewhere in the city. Men believe that home is the women's place, and men who spend more time at home are openly teased and said to be "womanlike." At the same time, most women did not want their husbands around—segregation ideology would curtail the coming and going of female friends, and children would feel they had to be quiet.

Most men did not eat at home regularly. Only three men ate three meals a day at home, ten were home for dinner only, four had one meal a week at home, and 14 ate at home "very rarely" (less than once a week).

Both males and females were engaged in a wide range of occupations. Eleven of the women considered themselves working women, and ten of 31 women had independent incomes. Four of these worked for the government in blue- or white-collar jobs. Twenty women declared themselves housewives only, but many of them raised chickens. Some of the women occasionally traded in staple foods such as sugar, rice, eggs, or meat, but not on a scale that contributed an important amount to the family income.

Women also helped their husbands or brothers in their businesses, but they did not receive regular income (except for housekeeping money) and thus did not consider themselves working women. Women who declared themselves housewives but also worked drew prestige from bringing extra resources into the household. Several women formerly worked as maids or shopkeepers, but did not have cash-earning activities at the time of the study. Some women had more than one economic activity. Table 2 shows the different kinds of occupations. Four of the men worked overtime regularly, and ten had a permanent second job (these 14 men were all government employees). Several men in the sample and many of the adult men in the neighborhood had spent some years as migrant workers in the Arabian Gulf countries. Gulf workers (overwhelmingly male but with increasing female participation) visit their families once a year or so and send money home more often.

According to cultural practices and Islamic ideology, Egyptian men are responsible for providing for the family. Most women argue that this is natural—it is what God has arranged and should not be questioned. This social belief is likewise hardly ever openly or directly questioned by men. In a patriarchal society where the ideology of sexual segregation and the division of labor is very strong, a man cannot question his responsibilities without relegating himself to the ranks of women. On the other hand, the engagement of women in cash-earning activities is accepted and expected if the family is relatively poor or if the women are involved with the family business. Nowadays, white-collar jobs and government employment are being accepted more easily. Women's labor in the family business is usually unpaid.

Most women considered that life today requires that they too should take some kind of employment to help their husbands fulfill their financial responsibilities to the household. Their life-style had changed and men had to buy many goods and services that women previously provided, and basic necessities were becoming increasingly expensive. However, it was rare for a woman to consider continuing her employment after she had all the things she thought she needed, or if her husband provided all the things she needed.* These findings correspond with those of Hammam (1979) and Macleod (1984). Many women, especially older women, ex-

---

*Women defined their needs according to what durable household goods, housing, clothes, and jewelry were considered necessities of a good life in the neighborhood. But in the face of the improvement of their material life, they continuously redefined their needs at a higher level.

TABLE 2

Occupations of Males and Females

Males	
White-collar worker	5
Blue-collar worker	17
Labor in small business	6
Unskilled casual worker	1
Semi-skilled and unskilled migrant	2
Females	
Housewife	20
White-collar worker	2
Blue-collar worker	2
Small-scale trader	5
Maid	2

pressed sympathy and pity for their husbands and for men in general because life was becoming more expensive and the burden of their responsibilities was greater. On the other hand, they occasionally commented ironically that, in the past, women had had to work far too hard, so now it was the men's turn. They gave me examples of how hard the peasant women worked; most believed that women in cities did much less. For this reason they preferred to marry in town or to have their husbands come and live in the city. This is not to say that all women were pleased with their situations; many husbands did not provide for their families, either because they could not gain employment or because they did not want to pay. But women considered this a matter of luck. They often talked of unlucky women whose husbands were selfish or unable to provide for the family. At times of family crisis the example of these husbands was often used by other wives to make it easier for them to resign themselves to their situations.

Financial Arrangements

In contrast with prevailing practices in many other societies, financial arrangements were discussed openly among these women, and they knew how other households arranged their money matters. Prices, the family's daily expenditure, and budgeting for the day, week, or month were popular subjects.

Whenever women congregated, whether in the street or in someone's home, it was usual to hear complaints about their financial problems with their husbands. Many women in the neighborhood had no information about how much their husbands earned or spent on themselves. (Other researchers have reported similar cases in different societies; see Pahl 1980;

Gorer 1971.) Their talk had a number of common themes, such as how life had changed and men had changed, too. In the old days the family had come first for men, but not anymore. Now it was important for a woman to have money of her own. (It was mostly younger women who complained of their husbands.)

At this level women were very supportive and sympathetic and encouraged one another to talk, either by talking about their own similar problem and how they were all in the same boat, or simply by siding with them. Occasionally they advised one another on how to manipulate their husbands. The very careful and detailed advice given in this connection was based on the intimate knowledge they had of one another's family and personal lives. However, once the talks—and at times tears—were over, they said, "*Alhadoullelah* [praise be to God], at least I have my children," or "he is not as bad as [someone with a worse reputation]," and they tried to count the positive things they possessed, such as children or health. If the person complaining did not comment on these blessings, she was often reminded of them by the other women.

It was not unusual for women to remind other women that to complain of their lot was to complain of God's will, and that was a sin. Acceptance of one's luck made life easier and bearable. Everyone lived the life that was written for her, and there was nothing that one could do. After one of these gatherings a middle-aged woman commented, "Women's lives are always difficult whether they are among the rich or among the poor. That is why we prefer sons. It is for this reason that God has placed the power of divorce in the hands of men and not women; otherwise, there would be no families left!" Religion and the wisdom of religious law were often used to justify a woman's situation or as reasons to resign herself to it. There was little searching for alternatives outside the accepted norms.

Patterns of Financial Arrangements

Studies of household financial arrangements in other communities have suggested that the origins of the region's cultural practices, the family cycle, the age of the couple, the nature of the subsistence activity of the male and female heads of households, and the level of aggregate income all have profound effects (Gonzalez 1984; Roldan 1982; Pahl 1980, 1982). However, each factor may weigh quite differently in each community, particularly when we are concerned with complex and fast-changing urban communities of developing nations.

The financial arrangements of the sample households varied; some women had total control of cash and family expenditure, while others were in the opposite situation. In explaining the different methods of budgeting, women often referred to the traditions of the regional origins of the household. Most women who had married men from cultures or traditions different from their own reported that their families had discussed the financial arrangements before the marriage. In most cases, however, at some point in the history of the household some modification had taken place.

My data suggest a remarkable degree of flexibility; consistent patterns or customs do not seem to have been continued or transformed. For example, people of Upper Egypt (Saidies) traditionally favor male control of financial matters, particularly cash transactions relating to the household. It is up to the husband to decide which of his wife's needs, and those of their children and the household in general, are to be met. Some male Saidie informants expressed the view that women should never touch money, even if they wear kilos of gold. Furthermore, a woman is never to ask for any information about her husband's income; she is supposed to know only what he is willing to tell her.

Although some of the Saidies in my sample had retained their customs, the majority had modified their ways. Those who had retained their customs were older couples who had recently migrated to the neighborhood; the husbands spent more time nearby. In the more modern households, the males spent much of their time at their workplace away from the neighborhood. Some of these husbands explained that while they agreed with the traditional ways, life had changed, and while they were away all day or even all year (a reference to the many husbands who migrate to the Gulf countries, sometimes for several years, while their families are left behind in Cairo), it was virtually impossible for the families to observe their old customs. It is important to note that women openly welcomed the change.

In contrast to the upper Egyptians, women of the Delta participate in public life. It is acceptable for them to take up varieties of traditional occupations in the public sphere, such as selling vegetables in the *suq* (local market), particularly in the residential areas. Women are also expected to play some role in household management, including financial matters. This role varies from being in total control of all cash and income—including that of her husband and children living at home—to receiving a daily allowance for vegetables and the family's day-to-day needs. No matter how limited a Delta woman's role, in virtually every case it is larger than that of her Saidie counterpart.

The results of my study suggest that the male's economic activity had the greatest influence on the way a household organized its financial matters. In most cases the frequency of payment of housekeeping money was affected primarily by the husband's income pattern (whether he was

paid monthly, weekly, or daily). The extent of the woman's involvement in
expenditure and disposal of family income was profoundly affected by the
amount of time her husband spent at the workplace, the distance between
home and workplace, and the opportunities for shopping available at the
workplace.

Other researchers have suggested that age and domestic cycle play an
important role in the arrangement of family matters (Roldan 1982). However, these factors had little significance in this Cairo neighborhood. Similarly, the occupation of the earning women seemed to have no discernible
effect on the financial strategies they adopted (the exceptions are those
families in which the husbands did not contribute financially). However,
the nature of women's occupations did have a significant effect on the
extent to which they undertook shopping tasks.

Aggregate family income did not appear to be related to any particular
patterns of financial arrangement. For example, the common fund system
was practiced by the richest and the poorest families. However, as the
income or, more precisely, the family consumption increases, women
show more tolerance of men's personal expenses, even when these are high
relative to the level of family consumption. Distinguishing between the
aggregate income and that portion which is spent on communal consumption is important, because it was rare for a man to allocate all his income to
a household pool, particularly when the total income met the family's basic
needs.

On the other hand, the flow of information between husband and wife
about income and available resources seemed to play a more decisive role
than cash flow, for in most cases the income only just covered the basic,
immediate needs. Their concern was therefore budgeting rather than
access to and control of cash.

Other models—for example, where husband and wife shop together,
the wife choosing what to purchase while the husband pays—were inappropriate to poor districts of Cairo, where cultural practices and economic
possibilities preclude such a procedure. Only on rare occasions, such as
when traveling, do men and women go out together. Furthermore, life-
style, preference for fresh foodstuffs, lack of storage space and refrigera-
tors, periodic shortages of some goods in the market, and unavailability of
large sums of money make shopping a daily or even more frequent task.
Where the women receive no household allowance, they have no say in
family expenditures. Women can directly intervene in or exercise control
of family expenditure only insofar as there is excess income to control.

The wide range of financial arrangements in the neighborhood and
their pronounced differences from those of other communities studied
make it difficult to use existing categories suggested by other studies. First,
the various financial arrangements seem to range along a spectrum, and

therefore the differences between them are more a matter of degree than of kind. Second, some models are based on the particular weight attached to such factors as aggregate family income, family cycle, and the like, which do not carry the same significance in my study. Finally, some of the common and recurring models are inappropriate for both cultural and practical reasons. Nevertheless, I attempt below to classify the data in such a way as to be useful for comparative studies of this kind.

Patterns of Budgeting

The budgeting and financial arrangements can be divided into six categories: woman as financial manager (5 households); woman as family banker (6 households); woman receiving full housekeeping allowance (6 households); woman receiving partial housekeeping allowance (7 households); man as financial manager (4 households); "guest" husband (3 households).

Woman as Financial Manager

In this type of arrangement men hand over the whole of their income to their wives, and the wives have to meet all the family's needs, such as rent, school fees, food, clothing, and presents. Men ask for their personal expenses, which normally include cigarettes, tea, and food (most men do not eat at home). Sometimes men hand over all their regular income from their first and second jobs, but keep for their personal expenses whatever they earn from overtime and odd jobs. In these cases women undertake all the shopping, including the purchase of the men's clothing.

Five households had adopted this pattern. Two of them reported that they adopted the method the day they got married (at first men helped with the shopping, but as their jobs required more hours, they left everything to their wives). The other three households were extended families at the start of their marriages. In one the mother-in-law died two years after the marriage, and the daughter-in-law, who was 18 years old at the time, immediately took over her responsibilities. In the two other households the families had formerly lived in the village, where the mothers-in-law controlled the resources, but once they moved to the city the wives were expected to become the financial managers. In these cases the sons were still expected to contribute to the parents' household. The daughters-in-law saw this as important, and had never asked how much the sons gave to their mothers. In the words of one young informant:

It is his money and that is his responsibility. I shall never ask him how much he earns or how much he pays to his parents. [Everybody knew the basic income, but since overtime, odd jobs, and government bonuses are not regular, total income varies from month to month]. They are his responsibility just like we are. He should help them as much as they request. But his parents too have an understanding that his income is limited, and life in the city is expensive. You see, I really do not know how much he earns, but I know he is careful with money and does not spend a lot on himself, only on cigarettes and tea, and sometimes he goes to tea houses, but not much. He does not go to cinemas, restaurants, or cafe bars.

The other household was in a similar position, and that wife's ideas confirmed this informant's. Both women told me that if their situation changed and they went back to the village their mothers-in-law would resume financial responsibilities because they are senior to them. In households with school-age children this was unlikely to happen, but households with very young children did sometimes return to the village and live as an extended family in the absence of their husbands.* One of the young women in this group had gone back to the village to live with her mother-in-law while her husband worked in the Gulf. She did not raise any objection, and saw it as temporary. She told me that of course she would prefer to live in Cairo with him, but the situation was more difficult for him than for her. She explained that he might migrate again if he got a good contract and they could improve their financial situation.

All women in the sample except one preferred being the financial manager even though it meant more responsibility for them. Women took pride in the fact that their husbands trusted them with money, and they often explained that they had won their husband's trust by being a good wife. "From the beginning, my husband saw that I was saving money and not spending it on myself or for my relatives, but rather I preferred to buy things for our home and for our children. It is for this reason that now he does not bother to ask me what I do with the money." Invariably they gave examples of other women who were incompetent money managers or who spent all the money on themselves and therefore could not be trusted by their husbands. However, some saw these women as lucky, clever, and capable of controlling their men. Younger and more urbanized men regarded these husbands as stupid and peasantlike (*fallah*) and teased them quite openly, especially if they were young. All five households where women served as financial managers were from the Delta regions, where women have traditionally played a greater role in the public domain.

The relationship between husband and wife in these families was one of mutual respect and understanding. They spoke respectfully of each other,

*Changing schools in very densely populated areas of Cairo, and even elsewhere in Egypt, is in fact not possible, although there is no legal barrier. When young men migrate to the Gulf for a year or two, their wives and young children usually go to live with either his or her parents. Once the children have reached school age, however, the household cannot move.

and the wives made sure their husbands' demands and comforts were met for the short time they spent at home. Children too were respectful of their parents, and if they contributed money to the household, they often paid it directly to their mother. On the whole, the intrafamily relationship in these households was closest to the ideal model described at the start of this paper.

Woman as Family Banker

These six women might have had only a partial or conditional right to control the family income, but they had full access to detailed financial information, and full physical access to the money itself. The husbands left the money with their wives and demanded it as their needs arose. Some, but not all, of these husbands were responsible for all shopping. Some women had a monthly or daily housekeeping allowance, which generally included money for vegetables, bread, children's pocket money, and small daily incidental expenses; the rest of the shopping and decisionmaking was done by the husband.

The major difference between this group and the first was that these women had physical access to the money but they did not have unilateral authority to spend it. Usually the husband did the major shopping or allocated money for major items. The wife might participate in the decision-making process to some degree, but this often went unrecognized by both of them.

Women often took their husband's trust as a gesture of good will. They recognized that their husbands could secretly spend money on themselves, but none felt her husband did so or put himself before the family. Although these women acknowledged that they had less decision-making power than women in the first category, their relationships with their husbands were often complementary and respectful. Finally, those wives who considered economic matters the major problem area did not blame their husbands. Their criticism was instead directed against inflation and Egypt's economic situation in general.

Full Housekeeping Allowance

The six women in this category received monthly, weekly, or daily allowances and were responsible for all normal family expenses (usually with the exception of medicine). Husbands might occasionally bring home some extra food or clothing, but this was seen as a present. These women often had little knowledge of their husbands' income, and in the cases where the husband was present or lived with the family, there were continual problems and arguments over money.

In two of the households the husbands were not present; one worked in a different town and came home every two weeks, and the other was a migrant to the Gulf who visited the family once a year, but sent his wife a monthly check. It is interesting to note that despite these women's total lack of information about their husbands' income, they did not complain about financial matters. They were sure that they received a fair allowance. They both told me that their husbands saved money and bought things for the house, and both believed that it was more difficult for their husbands to be away and live without them, but that because they were good men they did it for their families.

Discussing the effects of the husband's absence on the wife and children, Badia, whose husband visits them every two weeks, said: "This is better for us, since if he was here all the time, and with the children making all the noise and the neighbors coming and going, things would get on his nerves and problems would develop. When he worked in Cairo we had arguments all the time. But since he started to work outside Cairo we have less problems and generally we seem to be happier with one another."

In two of the households women had incomes of their own, and although they were very critical of their husbands, they had stopped arguing with them and concentrated instead on making ends meet with their own earnings. They both said that their husbands contributed only enough for food (supplying a simple diet) and the rent; clothes, medicine, household utensils, private tutors for children, and other daily expenses had to be paid for out of their own pockets. Their complaints invariably ended with: "You see how he spends his money. He eats chicken and kabab for lunch and dinner; we do not see meat more than once a week. He spends the rest of his time in cafes and cinemas, while we cannot leave the neighborhood from year to year."

Another bitter wife (the only Christian in the sample) worked in the family's small shop; her husband gave her only housekeeping money. She accused him of mismanaging their finances. She wanted to control the shop, since it had been her idea to open it, and she had saved and borrowed money and had found and rented the shop herself. She was also the one who traveled to upper Egypt and the free trade zones of the Delta to buy goods, and she worked from morning until 3 P.M. in the shop. However, her husband absolutely refused to leave her in charge of the financial management of the business. She told me: "If you take into account the time I spend in the shop and the way he pays me such a small amount of housekeeping money, then you can see why I am not happy with him. We are poor and my children have to suffer because he is stupid with money and too selfish and wants to control everything." He did pay some money to his own family, but she did not raise any objection to that. Rather, she gave examples of his mistakes and short memory.

With the exception of the households where the husbands were away, this group unanimously saw disputes over money as their major problem. Some added that this was because men were selfish and put themselves before the family.

Partial Housekeeping Allowance

In seven households the wives received a fixed daily, weekly, or monthly allowance for vegetables and some other small items, while the husbands were responsible for all other expenditures, such as meat, schooling, and rent. These wives might or might not have knowledge of their husbands' income, but all of them regarded this method as acceptable as it saved them from standing in long queues at government shops while providing them with a fixed income and some latitude to spend it.

All women in this group told me that as long as they bought what they were supposed to, their husbands did not ask them to account for their allowances. Some entered into savings clubs with their friends and neighbors with or without their husbands' knowledge.* With their savings they bought small items for the house; older women bought clothing for their daughters, paid their children's educational fees, or bought presents for their friends and relatives that their husbands would not pay for. Occasionally they bought some gold, not only because it is prestigious, but also because they viewed it as a long-term investment.

The degree to which women expressed satisfaction with this method of budgeting depended very much on how they evaluated their husbands' household contribution relative to his earnings or to what they estimated he spent on himself. This method was usually adopted by younger couples, yet there were also older couples where the husband had previously been the financial manager but after a turning point—such as his migration or accepting a second job—had delegated some of his responsibilities to his wife. Five of the women in this category had been married ten years or less, and their family origins were in upper Egypt or the Delta provinces. However, they had all either been born in Cairo or had migrated there as children. The other two households consisted of older couples who had been married more than 25 years.

---

*The savings club, *jamaaia*, is an old tradition that is still widely practiced by Egyptians, particularly urban lower-class women. A group of women under the supervision of one person joins together and contributes an equal amount on a daily, weekly, or monthly basis. Each round is given to one member, and this continues until everybody has received one round of money.

Man as Financial Manager

In four families men were financial managers and bought everything except vegetables. Usually—but not always—they left a small sum of money with their wives for bread and vegetables, but this was neither a fixed amount nor on a fixed schedule. It might be given every day, every few days, or every week. These wives were expected to demand what they needed for the kitchen, children, house, and themselves, and the husbands would try to provide them with it. In cases where the husbands' economic activities made them easily accessible (if they worked in the neighborhood), then the wives could demand money and goods whenever the need arose.

This method was unpopular with younger couples, even those from upper Egypt where traditionally men controlled all financial transactions. Only one couple in this category was young. This can be explained by the new job conditions imposed by the labor market; traveling from the workplace and residential areas to shop is hard, costly, and time-consuming. The difficulties involved in shopping in Cairo have encouraged more men to share this responsibility with their wives.

The relationship between these husbands and wives was one of respect, although the women often expressed a desire for more decision-making power in shopping, and often advised their daughters or sisters to encourage their husbands to give them more money and responsibility, at least for part of the expenses. They did not want to change their own practices now because, as they explained to me, shopping is an art (*fan*) that must be practiced for years. If they changed their family system now the family would lose a lot. These wives could not tell me how much they would need to manage their households relatively well, nor did they know how much per month, week, or day their husbands spent. The only exception was the young household. That wife told me: "He likes himself too much and his needs and comforts come first. I know it is his money, but we are his responsibility. You can see how much he spends on his suit, jeans, and shirt, and he goes to the cafes and not to the teahouses; he goes to the cinema regularly, and worst of all he goes to the bar with his friends to get drunk. You see, if I was not living with my five children in this tiny room, I would not complain, but life is difficult."

"Guest" Husband

In some of the houses where women had incomes of their own the husbands refused to contribute at all, or else they contributed irregularly. In two households the husbands paid rent only, and occasionally brought some meat or sweet as a present to their wives. They might also pay for medicine or clothing, or buy a durable item for the house, but this was inconsistent.

In one household the husband paid the rent and had bought a cheap washing machine (his only large purchase during their two years of marriage). Whenever he and his wife had an argument about money he mentioned that he had bought the washing machine. The wife's wages were spent on food and other daily expenses and, as she put it, she had nothing to show for it. She was particularly bitter because her husband asked her for detailed information about her earnings and how much she spent, but he never revealed anything about his income and spending.

Another wife in this group had worked since she was eight years old, and had bought all the furniture that is considered necessary to start a good life in the community. She had moved to an apartment that her husband had rented, and she had left her job to be a housewife. She had thought that being a housewife was a luxury that being married offered her, particularly since she already had all the things she considered necessary prior to her wedding. But her husband refused to pay for anything except rent, and came home demanding food. After months of bitter arguments she demanded a divorce. He refused to grant it unless she paid him 2,000 pounds, more, she said, than she could raise in ten years. She dropped the idea of divorce and sought a job. She no longer demanded any money for household expenses; she continued to cook for him and he continued to pay the rent. She said, "At least now I do not get any headaches."

In a third household the husband had migrated ten years before, leaving behind his wife and two children. He visited them every year or year and a half and brought them presents. Occasionally he sent home some money, but it was neither a fixed amount nor regular. The wife managed day-to-day on her income, and used his money in times of crisis. She told me that of course she was angry and thought she had been cheated, but she thanked God that she had an income and did not have to beg from other people.

These three women wished they could give up their jobs and stay at home. One was expecting her second baby in June 1984 and was eagerly looking forward to the birth because it meant she would have to stay home for two years, since there was no one else to care for her children. She had applied for unpaid leave at her job, and was hoping that this would force her husband to act more responsibly toward the family. If it did not work she would have to resume work and find another solution. When I asked if she would stay at home permanently if her husband asked her to, she readily agreed, but added that "young men today choose to marry working women because life is so expensive and they want to have a home and wife and also to continue the fun they had before the marriage, such as going to the cinema, cafes, and bars and buying expensive clothes." She concluded that husbands would never ask their wives to give up their jobs.*

Another working wife offered a detailed account of her husband's refusal to pay for household expenses as soon as she acquired an income of her own. They argued, and she even demanded a divorce, until he finally accepted his responsibilities and made arrangements to pay for fixed items, food, medicine, part of the rent and gas bills, and some clothing. She said that in this way she had saved part of her income to buy household equipment.

What Happens to Women's Wages, and How Women Feel About Having an Income

Although all the women in my sample held men financially responsible for the household, all the nonearning women except one said they would prefer to have an income of their own. Without exception they said that a woman who worked must spend her wages on her family; a few also mentioned spending money on themselves. When asked to provide examples of the kinds of spending a woman should do, they all mentioned items of communal consumption such as washing machines, dishes, children's clothing, beds, and the like. In reply to my comment that men might also be responsible for these things, they said that if a woman does not use her income to purchase these sorts of items, then why should her husband allow her to go to work? A man would allow his wife to work only if he wanted her to help out.

All wage-earning women said that they were working because they wanted to improve their homes. Some said life was too expensive for one person to manage, especially since no man is willing to contribute all his income to the family. These women worked to buy things for their homes and clothes for their children and themselves. Many of the husbands implied that if they felt that their wives were spending too much of their incomes on themselves and not enough on their families, they would prevent them from working. All the wives were very conscious of this fact.

No working woman had to hand over her income to her husband. Two households had a common fund; in three households the men refused to contribute on any regular and substantial basis (these three husbands had

*All the married women in my sample (except the one Christian) believed that it is the Islamic right of a husband to keep his wife at home if he wishes to do so. A few made it conditional by adding that if a husband provides his wife with all she needs, then it is his right to keep her at home.

deliberately chosen to marry working women). There was no marked difference between the amount of money spent on food in the families of wage-earning and non-wage-earning women, although the latter group may have had a more varied diet and may have cooked on a more regular basis. All working women were very conscious of their domestic responsibilities and the possible criticism by others of neglect in this regard. They often had a rigorous routine for most of their tasks, a routine that they rarely if ever neglected, and they made an effort to keep their children clean and well fed, especially the younger ones.

In the families where husbands contributed regularly, the women often spent their incomes on household durables and on clothes for themselves and their children. Men are unwilling to invest in household goods unless there are clear advantages for them. For example, men are more willing to invest in a television or a cassette recorder than a gas cooker. The most visible difference between families where women had and did not have independent incomes was in how women and children were clothed. In most families the men were dressed much better than their wives, especially those men who did not wear the traditional *gallobia*. But where women had an income they spent it on clothing for themselves and their children. Women were also more willing than men to pay for their children's education and private lessons. Household members were very aware of each individual's contribution, and often mentioned that a major item like a television or a refrigerator was in one person's name because he or she had paid for it. Women themselves were outspoken about the things they had bought for the family. Traditionally, the bride brings some household goods to her husband's home. A list of these items is prepared by her parents and kin, and the bride and groom sign the list. At the time of divorce and separation he is legally obliged to return these items to her. Any items acquired during the marriage belong to the husband unless the wife has the purchase slip in her name, but since the man is usually the one who actually makes the purchase, even though his wife may have earned the money, the slip is usually in his name.

To summarize, in households in which women were financial managers or had independent incomes, they tried to save for household durable goods and schooling expenses. These were given priority immediately after the basic needs of food and clothes. Allocation for a better diet or better clothes came after the household's consumer goods were supplied. It is important to note that nearly every family recognized its most pressing need as better housing, but because of accelerating housing prices they had little hope of improving their situation.

Although most working wives resented the way their husbands spent a disproportionate amount of their income on themselves, they generally had fewer arguments than wives who did not work. They explained this by saying that, after all, when there was an argument he would leave the home and spend time with his friends and return only to go to bed; she would stay at home and get upset and the children would suffer. They often ended their reasoning by saying "Allah Karima" (God is giving) or "Kul eshshi nasib" (everything is according to one's faith). They were thankful that they had their own incomes to spend on their children, and they pitied those women who did not have husbands who were "good" and who did not have incomes of their own. Every woman said that having an income made her more of an equal partner in the eyes of her husband. Yet only one woman said that she would never give up her job— even when she had everything, or even if it meant choosing between her marriage and her job.

Women whose husbands either did not contribute at all or contributed very little to the household pool were asked why they married and why they continued with their marriage union. They explained that a woman's primary desire was to be independent of her parents and to have a home of her own and children. But most women did not earn enough to pay for a home of their own, and even if they did, a woman can never set up a home by herself; the community would not accept her. An unmarried woman must always be a part of her parents' household and give her money to them and work for them; she might also be part of a brother's household, but no sister-in-law would welcome her. And they were explicit that a grown woman in her parents' house was a servant. Furthermore, there is a social stigma attached to an unmarried or divorced woman. Even if a woman surmounted these obstacles, she needs to have children, which is impossible outside marriage. Most Egyptians, particularly women, are not childless by choice, and people without children are deeply pitied. Women often referred to their children, saying "just so-and-so is my world and is what I want."

Both women and men saw financial issues as an important source of family conflict. Ten households reported that money was a constant source of fights and bitterness. Nine of these women had no knowledge of their husbands' income and felt that their husbands spent a disproportionate amount of their income on themselves.

In order to explain the relative predominance of the full-allowance system among these ten households, we need to examine the conditions under which this system developed. Apart from the two migrants' house-holds, which will probably not remain in this category when the husbands return, the rest had adopted this method because the husband did not want to be involved in shopping. Although none of these husbands had a second job, and some even had permission to do shopping at their workplace, their refusal to participate in shopping was mainly a reflection of their lack of interest in family life in general. The allowances were so low it was often difficult for the wives to meet basic needs. The husbands were reluctant to increase allowances in the face of inflation and the increased demands of the children, even when their own incomes increased considerably. In contrast, family consumption in the partial-allowance system remained more or less balanced; husbands continued to buy items as prices rose. In addition, husbands who shop now and then buy extra items, particularly if they eat at home.

Another source of conflict was differences of opinion over the husband's income. Many women said that their husbands' incomes belonged to the family, or that the money belonged to the men since they earned it, but they were wholly responsible for supporting the family. Men, on the other hand, felt that the money was theirs and that they were responsible for food, clothes, and rent. The more traditional men, especially the older men, like their wives did not differentiate between family money and personal money. Most wage-earning women, although clearly distinguishing between their money and their husbands' money, said that they would spend theirs on the home to try to make a better life.

None of the women had any pocket money for personal expenses. Indeed, many of them could not distinguish between personal and family consumption. For example, two women after careful thought said that sometimes they would buy 5 piasters (3 cents) of *lib* (watermelon seeds), which they ate with their children; some working women considered their bus fare to work and their clothes to be personal expenses.

The Effects of Modernization and Social Change on the Marital Relationship

The data revealed that although changes and developments in urban life and the social system have made women more dependent on men, men have become more independent from women.

The majority of the husbands in the ten families with continuous conflict were from the younger group, and they were also those who had been born in Cairo or had moved there when they were very young. Most of these husbands had higher levels of education. I label them nontraditional since they chose to wear suits or jeans and were often very well dressed. They expressed distaste for traditional Egyptian food, and often preferred to buy hamburgers or grilled chicken for lunch. They went to cafes rather than to tea houses, and their leisure time was spent at the cinema and clubs, or at bars where they drank beer. They dissassociated themselves from the neighborhood, and often made fun of the traditional

way of life. They often worked in the modern sector, particularly in
services, or were in contact with it through their work. Their occupations
included working as a driver for a foreign company, a barber in a hotel, a
worker in a beer company, a tax officer, and a train driver. In short, they
had adopted the modern value system.

There were exceptions to this generalization, including one of the
poorest households in my sample. That husband was unemployed for a
good part of each month, and they had to rely on the little income the wife
earned from selling vegetables in the market. The other exception was a
businessman married to two wives and known in the neighborhood as
mean (*bakhial*) and selfish (*Bahabo nafsou aoai*).

The modern way of life together with the modern value system have
made these men far less dependent on their wives—they do not eat at
home; they send much of their clothing to the launderette because they
claim their wives would ruin it if they washed it. Since they spend very
little time at home or in the neighborhood, they see little reason to spend
much of their income at home. Also, since they have little respect for the
neighborhood, women cannot organize community pressure to make
their husbands conform and pay more money. These women are dis-
armed, and they feel it very strongly.

It is the norm in this neighborhood for households to have a television
set, a gas cooker, and electrical appliances, and there has been an active
policy of promoting the use of convenience and ready-made foods.* Many
goods and services that were previously fully provided by women are now
bought for cash. This situation has discouraged the exercise of women's
traditional skills without replacing them with new ones. The general
condition of the labor market, together with the traditional ideology and
sexual segregation, have made it difficult for women, particularly those of
the lower social strata who have no capital or saleable skill, to gain access to
cash income. Where they do have access, it is through badly rewarded
activities in the informal economy, such as trading vegetables in a local
market. Consequently, their hopes and desires are all invested in being
lucky enough to find a "good" husband on whom they can depend.

All these factors have made men relatively independent of their wom-
enfolk. They spend most of their time away from home, and they eat out.
Their new urban socialization has opened up new forms of leisure activity
to them, such as cinemas, bars, clubs, restaurants, and sports, which are
being promoted and sold to them through the conscious and unconscious
efforts of the media. Both the old and new ideology of man the breadwin-

---

*The booming Egyptian economy has encouraged the purchase of durable household
goods, but they are mostly simple and Egyptian-made. They rarely reduce women's labor
by any meaningful amount.

ner have made it possible and justifiable for the state and individual households to give men more opportunities to gain marketable skills and earn higher salaries. But they have very little incentive to spend their incomes, which after all are still severely limited, on their families when they are continuously encouraged through various means to spend their incomes on themselves, especially as men derive only limited material benefits from their families.

Conclusion

My research has confirmed the suggestion of other researchers that since men and women are socialized differently in most societies, they tend to have divergent priorities in expenditure and disposal of cash. Hence, the control of cash flow and disposal has been recognized as the element that most affects both the welfare of household members and the power relationship between husbands and wives.

There is no particular relationship between the stage in the domestic cycle, the age of the couple, or the household's aggregate income and the degree of women's power and financial control. By contrast, the nature of the husband's occupation—whether it took him away from home for many long hours—and the traditions of the couple's regional culture were strongly related to patterns of financial management. However, cultural traditions were not strictly observed. Role changes in response to a family's crisis, such as male migration, and changes in the economic activities of both husbands and wives are common. If a woman gained power and responsibility in a crisis situation, it was possible that she would retain them wholly or partially after the crisis was over.

The accepted norm in Egypt is that men are financially responsible for the family. Since nearly two-thirds of the women in the sample households were non-wage-earning or earned very little, the data was categorized in terms of husbands' financial contributions to the households. The patterns of financial arrangement ranged from total control by women to total control by men. Full or partial control, as well as the right to exercise some power over how the family income was spent, was desired by all women, but access to financial information was the key to whether there was frequent strife. This is because such knowledge militates against excessive personal expenditure by the husband. In nearly all the households that had constant arguments over money, the wives had no knowledge of their husbands' incomes. These included households with guest husbands who refused to contribute financially as well as the majority of full-allowance households, in which the allowance was often calculated to allow a minimal level of existence. The male heads of these households tended to be the younger husbands who were more urbanized and had more formal education. They considered themselves modern, and rejected the traditional value system.

Women did not and in fact often could not distinguish between their personal needs and those of the family. Those who had independent incomes or control over the family income gave priority to communal expenditure and to their children. Men's personal expenditure was recognized and accepted by both sexes, and women's complaints were directed not at the men's expenses per se, but rather at the amount spent in relation to total household income.

The modern way of life together with the modern value system and increasing consumerism have changed the balance of power between husband and wife. Men have emerged as less dependent on their wives since they can now buy most of the services previously provided by their wives. They spend little time at home or in the neighborhood. Therefore, there is little reason for them to spend much of their income at home and on the family.

On the other hand, women have become more dependent on their husbands, who are the major cash earners. The new social changes have failed to provide corresponding cash-earning opportunities for women of the lower social strata, who are handicapped by widespread illiteracy coupled with a lack of formal education, saleable skills, and any sizeable capital. Other important constraints are the crippling cultural practices and values that allow a woman to engage in independent cash-earning activities only if her husband fails to provide for the family. This failure is so socially discrediting for both the husband and the wife that only the most desperate family will admit it. In addition, the social necessity of obtaining the husband or male guardian's permission to work for an income, together with sex segregation, keep women in a disadvantaged position.

The changing socioeconomic conditions in urban Egypt have intensified the inequalities between lower-income husbands and wives. Consequently, while the economy is booming, the most vulnerable groups are not beneficiaries. All the women in my sample, although readily accepting the ideology of man the breadwinner, thought it necessary under the existing social order for a woman to have an income of her own to help provide a better life for her children and herself and to make her more of an equal partner in the eyes of her husband.

The Nonpooling Household:
A Challenge to Theory

ELEANOR R. FAPOHUNDA

Economists have delineated a theoretical framework commonly called "the New Home Economics" to explain micro-level household behavior (see Becker 1981). This framework has been used to explain such related phenomena as declining marriage rates, decreasing fertility trends, and increasing female labor-force participation. Although the model was originally used to explain empirical trends in industrialized economies, the basic model, with modifications, has been used more recently to explain family behavior in developing countries (see, for example, Rosenzweig and Evenson 1977; *Philippine Economic Journal* 1978).

In the model, households are utility-maximizing units motivated by stable, uniform preferences but constrained by pooled economic resources. Implicitly, the households consist of monogamous nuclear units.* The model also assumes that household tastes are historically stable and do not vary significantly by income, subculture, or society. Given stable household preferences, changes in household economic-demographic behavior are responses to family income and price variations. Furthermore, as the model assumes common preferences, it does not explicitly consider the internal household distribution of goods and services.

Earlier economic explanations of domestic consumption behavior focused on rational individuals as the basic units of analysis. These economic agents maximized their personal satisfactions by consuming market produced goods subject to price and income constraints. In contrast, the New Home Economics model views the basic unit—the homogeneous household—as maximizing its satisfactions from a more limited number of abstract commodities such as good health or child services. These basic commodities, or "z" goods, cannot be directly purchased in the marketplace, but are produced within households by using purchased goods, house members' time, and domestic capital equipment.

As unified production units, households are guided by the economic

---

*Although Becker does consider polygyny in his theory of marriage, he and other theorists have not explicitly considered how polygyny would affect consumption or investment behavior (1981:38–65).

principles of allocative efficiency in producing "z" goods. Basic commodities vary in terms of the relative proportions of market goods and household members' time necessary for their production. The prices of these abstract commodities are not market prices, but rather implicit prices representing the marginal costs of production to the household. Therefore, even though the market prices of goods might be constant, the price of a particular "z" good varies among households owing to differing proportions of purchased inputs and varying implicit time costs. A household's consumption of a "z" good depends on its income level and the implicit prices of basic commodities.

Theoretically, two key assumptions are required before the New Home Economics model can treat households as homogeneous units. First, household preferences must be the same or, in the terminology of the economist, households must have joint utility functions. Second, household members' economic resources must be pooled.

Theoretical Joint Household Utility Function

Becker argues that the presence of one altruistic household member who controls significant economic resources and makes compensatory transfers to other members is sufficient to explain the existence of a joint household utility function (1976: 284–85). Essentially, the altruist's happiness or satisfaction depends on both his personal consumption and that of other household members. Therefore, at times he is willing to reduce his own consumption to increase others' consumption opportunities. He transfers enough resources so that he receives the same marginal satisfaction from his personal and beneficiaries' consumption. The altruist's behavior is not constrained by his personal income, but rather by what Becker calls his social income; that is, his personal income in conjunction with his beneficiaries' income.

A beneficiary, perhaps an egoist, would do nothing to reduce the altruist's personal consumption or income, fearing that such behavior could lead to a larger fall in his own consumption due to diminished transfers. Thus the altruist's utility function theoretically becomes the joint household utility function, and his social income operationally constitutes pooled household resources.

Such an analysis implicitly assumes that the altruist's intrafamily transfers do not involve any risks for the beneficiaries. Yet in situations of rapid socioeconomic change, the continued creditability of the altruist may become an issue as the probability of marital disruptions rises or as the economy becomes more commercialized.

Moreover, altruism is a behavior that is socially encouraged to promote the cohesive and efficient functioning of social groups. The location of altruistic behavior varies in different economies, often reflecting differences in the organization of production. For example, in an economy based on the extended family system, altruistic behavior is more likely to be socially encouraged among kin rather than within the conjugal pair.

The existence of a household altruist assumes away all domestic conflicts concerning the intrahousehold distribution of costs and benefits, and, in the extreme, obliterates the possibility of intrafamily exploitation. Some critics have actually argued that the existence of a joint utility function may depend on the existence of a household dictator who controls economic resources and provides minimum incentives for compliance (Manser and Brown: 3). (Such a description may be more accurate in the male-dominated societies of much of the Third World.) It follows, by implication, that although individual preferences may be stable, the household utility function changes as the relative bargaining position of household members by gender and age varies in response to changing socioeconomic conditions.

Income Pooling Theory

Conceptually, there is a continuum of possible income-pooling arrangements within households. At one extreme, income pooling involves a generalized combining of income and assets for an unspecified time period. At the other extreme, pooling may entail merging limited economic resources for specific expenditures within a limited time frame. Clearly, the New Home Economics model assumes that generalized pooling is normative. By assuming generalized pooling and a joint household utility function, the model conceives of the household as a unified consumption and investment unit.

The underlying assumption of generalized income pooling represents, in reality, a continuation of an earlier tradition in the economics literature. In the single-person household of traditional theory, an individual sought to maximize his utility from the consumption of purchased goods subject to an income constraint. The socioeconomic characteristics of households were subsumed in the ceteris paribus (other things being equal) assumptions of the model, or were thought to be related to income (Ferber 1966: 126). Economists, concerned with how individual consumption of market goods varied quantitatively with changes in the level of income and market prices, developed concepts of income and price elasticities.*

*Income elasticity is defined as the percentage change in quantity demanded divided by the percentage change in income. Price elasticity is calculated as the percentage change in quantity divided by the percentage change in price.

However, actual empirical budget studies in Western industrialized economies investigated multiperson households but presumed a pooling of family income. In many cases, the family units investigated were dependent on the income of a single earner, the husband. Two recent studies have investigated dual-income households in the United States but have continued to assume pooled incomes (Stober 1977; Stober and Weinberg 1977).

Similarly, economists studying consumption or savings behavior in developing economies have also assumed pooled household income (see, for example, Kelley and Williamson 1968; Gupta 1974). Cross-sectional budget studies that estimate elasticities of specific commodities or predict future consumption patterns are difficult to undertake in developing countries, as many commodities are produced within households, and family incomes include payments in kind or substantial extended family transfers. Two Nigerian studies have tried to deal with these problems in different ways, while assuming pooled household resources and common budgets (Adejumobi 1970; Adamu 1970). Such studies have also implicitly assumed a shared consumption level among family members.

Despite the problematic character of the model's assumptions, the usefulness of the New Home Economics model depends, according to an instrumentalist approach, on its ability to generate successful predictions with significant policy implications (Boland 1979:509). However, its theoretical construction may limit the scope of researchers' empirical questions, limit their methodological choices, and cause them to overlook divergent or unexplained information (Kuhn 1969).

The fundamental issue is whether the New Home Economics' theoretical concepts render important socioeconomic processes, particularly in a cross-cultural context, invisible. Recently, some social scientists have argued that the interaction of family members needs to be explicitly taken into account in order to understand cross-cultural consumption and investment behavior (Lewis 1977; Oppong 1981; Guyer 1979). This paper examines this issue by considering the applicability of the New Home Economics model to the domestic consumption and investment behavior of the Yoruba of southern Nigeria. It argues that a collective or homogeneous household model is insufficient.

Some social scientists have argued that West African conjugal units are gradually approaching the organizational and functional characteristics of the Western homogeneous family because of modernization (Oppong 1981). By implication, the explanatory and predictive capacities of the New Home Economics model should improve as West Africans have increasing contact with Western education or society. Yet this paper suggests that Yoruba conjugal units, although evolving, are not changing in a one-directional manner. Specifically, the more highly educated and wealthier conjugal units do not exhibit innovative consumption or investment behavior more consistent with the New Home Economics model.

The discussion is based on a 1980 sample survey of 226 monogamous and polygynous Yoruba conjugal units living in the present Nigerian capital of Lagos.* This metropolis, the center of most rapid socioeconomic change in Nigeria, is populated primarily by Yorubas. The sample was subdivided into three strata—traditional, low-income migrant, and elite families—in order to compare the domestic behavior of conjugal units with varying degrees of contact with Western society and education. For this purpose, households were selected in three sections of the city. Traditional families living in compounds were chosen from Northwest Lagos Island (called in the Yoruba language *Isale-Eko*); low-income migrant families were interviewed in Shomolu; elite families were drawn from Surulere. Suitable statistical tests showed that the neighborhoods varied significantly in terms of husband's and wife's average monthly income, spouse's educational background, and spouse's migratory status. In the original sample equal numbers of households in each locality were to be interviewed by university undergraduates. This sampling distribution is not representative of the city as a whole, but would indicate covariation in behavior and explanatory variables. Information was solicited separately from each coresident spouse in the household.

Characteristics of Yoruba Financial Management and Domestic Consumption Behavior

Financial Management Practices

Generally, spouses in the data set had limited knowledge of each other's financial affairs. Approximately 80 percent of the wives did not know their husband's income, and 65 percent acknowledged ignorance about their spouse's expenditure behavior. Almost 78 percent reported that they did not pool their incomes or jointly plan expenditures with their husbands; see Table 1.

The 84 traditional Yoruba wives had extremely limited knowledge of their husband's financial resources. Approximately 91 percent lacked knowledge of their husband's income and 88 percent reported that they did not know how their husbands dispensed their funds. Almost 90 per-

*The research on which this paper is based was undertaken as part of a doctoral dissertation supervised by Professor Michael P. Todaro and funded by the Compton Foundation, Inc., of New York.

TABLE I

Wives' Description of Family Financial Behavior by Neighborhood

	NW Lagos Island		Shomolu		Surulere		Total sample	
	No.	Pct.	No.	Pct.	No.	Pct.	No.	Pct.
Wife knows husband's income	8	9.5%	7	10.1%	34	39.1%	49	20.4%
Wife does not know husband's income	76	90.5%	62	89.9%	53	60.9%	191	79.6%
Wife knows husband's expenditures	10	11.9%	29	42.0%	46	52.9%	85	35.4%
Wife does not know husband's expenditures	74	88.1%	40	58.0%	41	47.1%	155	64.6%
Wife pools income and jointly plans expenditures	9	10.7%	27	39.1%	18	20.7%	54	22.5%
Wife does not pool income and jointly plans expenditures	75	89.3%	42	60.9%	69	79.3%	186	77.5%

cent of the Northwest Lagos Island wives reported that they did not pool their income or jointly plan expenditures with their spouses.

In order to derive a more encompassing and quantitatively measurable definition of joint household financial management, responses from four questions were used to form the basis of a "pooling index." (As approximately 19 percent of the conjugal units were polygynous, it seemed appropriate to use wives's responses to these questions.) The purpose of this index was to measure the extent and variation of unified family financial management among the three classifications of Yoruba conjugal units. The four questions were:

1. Do you know how much money your husband earns a month?
2. Do you know how your husband spends his money?
3. If you know how your husband spends his money, do you and your husband pool your incomes and jointly plan your household expenditures?
4. Do you own any of the following properties with your spouse?
    a. farmland?
    b. house?
    c. car?
    d. stock certificates? *

*Traditionally, houses and land were the usual forms of assets. As part of an indigenization program in the 1970's, foreign corporations operating in Nigeria were forced to sell a percentage of their capital shares to nationals.

The first two questions were included because household resources pooling in some cases may be de facto in the sense that one person, knowing his or her spouse's income and discretionary expenditures, plans his or her own expenditures accordingly to fulfill household needs. The responses were assigned numerical scores which, when tabulated, were used as a rough indicator of the extent of household resource pooling. Possible scores varied from zero to 8; recorded scores ranged from zero to 6.

The majority of the conjugal units were not practicing any form of joint financial management; see Table 2. Over 52 percent of the 240 conjugal relationships had a pooling score of zero.* If conjugal relationships characterized by extremely limited resource pooling—in other words, having an index score of 1—are included, then over 76 percent can be classified as primarily non–resource pooling.†

The proportion of zero-pooling conjugal relationships varied significantly by neighborhood. Approximately 76 percent of the Northwest Lagos Island wives reported a completely non-resource-pooling relationship with their spouses, compared to 44 percent of the Shomolu and 37 percent of the Surulere wives.‡ Moreover, 94.1 percent of Northwest Lagos Island conjugal relationships had pooling index scores that did not exceed 1, compared to 67 percent of both the Shomolu and Surulere marital unions. Traditional Yoruba family financial management behavior can therefore be characterized as a conjugal relationship having a pooling index equal to or less than 1. Generally, traditional Yoruba spouses lack knowledge of each other's economic resources, and do not have joint budgets or commonly held assets.

Innovative family financial management behavior was extremely limited. Approximately 24 percent of the conjugal units had pooling index scores of 2 or above. Only 7 percent had scores of 3 or higher. Significantly, none of the Northwest Lagos Island conjugal units was in this category. Indications of innovative financial management behavior do not imply the

*It should be remembered that the pooling index is based on wives' responses. There were 240 wives interviewed in the 226 conjugal units.

†One reason for combining these two categories is that variations in the answers of one of the composite items may not be entirely due to actual differences in family behavior but rather to an exogenous variable. Although the vast majority of wives did not know their husbands' income, there was a statistically significant relationship between residence and wives' knowledge. Less than 10 percent of the Northwest Lagos Island wives knew their spouses' income, compared to 39 percent of the Surulere wives. However, this proportional variation may not be due entirely to a greater discussion among elite families about finances; rather, it may reflect the fact that a greater percentage of Surulere spouses work for government agencies with public salary and grade structures.

‡The proportion of "zero-pooling" conjugal relationships in Northwest Lagos Island was significantly greater than that of Shomolu or Surulere at the 1 percent level.

TABLE 2

Pooling Index by Neighborhood, Based on Wives' Responses

Index value	NW Lagos Island		Shomolu		Surulere		Total sample	
	No.	Pct.	No.	Pct.	No.	Pct.	No.	Pct.
0	64	76.2%	30	43.5%	32	36.8%	126	52.5%
1	15	17.9%	16	23.2%	26	29.9%	57	23.8%
2	5	6.0%	15	21.7%	21	24.1%	41	17.1%
3	–	–	4	5.8%	6	6.9%	10	4.2%
4+	–	–	4	5.8%	2	2.2%	6	2.5%

NOTE: $x^2 = 36.94$ with 8 degrees of freedom; significant at the 1 percent level.

emergence of the financially integrated household, but rather a limited movement along a nonpooling-pooling household continuum.

Traditional economic theory has suggested that a rational pooling of household resources leads to economies of scale and, thereby, to increased family consumption. But several West African studies have suggested that a wife's decision not to pool her resources is a rational decision to avert risks or to invest in indigenous insurance (see Lewis 1977; Karanja-Diejomoah 1978; Oppong 1981). Economic autonomy permits a wife to invest in extended family relationships and social networks, thereby improving her bargaining position in her ongoing marital relationship. Such social relationships provide a measure of insurance in case of marital disruption. Economic independence also lessens the risk of asset loss under traditional inheritance or from potential polygynous practices. Moreover, personal financial secrecy limits to a degree the ability of a husband, motivated by extended family obligations or extramarital commitments, to pass household financial responsibilities on to his wife.

Domestic Consumption Behavior

The concepts of a homogeneous household model are insufficient to predict or explain patterns of Yoruba domestic consumption. Such concepts relate patterns of consumption expenditure to pooled income, implicit or explicit prices, and time use, but not to gender.

In the context of a nonpooling household, a gender-specific expenditure shall be defined as one for which one spouse contributes more than half the cost of the item. A group of gender-specific expenditures is the basis for discerning a pattern of divided conjugal financial responsibilities. A pattern of divided responsibilities implies that although spouses jointly contribute to the unit's financial well-being, they do so in a fairly restricted, well-defined, and socially recognized manner. In other words, husbands and wives have separate allocative priorities.

To develop a pattern of divided responsibilities, wives were asked to specify what proportion of various expenditures their husbands paid for. Four general categories of expenditures were investigated: household consumer durables (furniture); investments in human capital (children's school fees and medical expenses); personal items (individual spouse's clothing); children's personal items (clothing).* Rent, consumer durables, children's school fees, and children's medical expenses were decidedly male-specific expenditures. For example, more than 80 percent of the wives in the three neighborhoods claimed that their husbands paid for more than half of all furniture expenditures. On the other hand, wives paid for their own and their children's personal items, such as clothing. Only 37 percent reported that their husbands paid for more than half of their children's clothing expenditures. An even smaller amount, 17 percent, stated that their husbands paid for more than half of their own personal clothing expenditures. But 85 percent of the women did report that their husband's clothing expenditures were primarily his financial responsibility, see Table 3.

Patterns of gender-specific expenditures were similar among the three neighborhoods, suggesting that the wealthier, more educated families do not exhibit consumption behavior more consistent with the New Home Economics model. Table 4 illustrates that among traditional Northwest Lagos Island families, as well as among Shomolu and Surulere families, more than 80 percent of the husbands were primarily responsible for furniture expenditures. Overall, there was not a statistically significant relationship between neighborhood and family furniture behavior. Knowledge of neighborhood did not increase by any percentage the ability to predict the husband's proportional contribution (the asymmetric lambda was 0.0 with furniture the dependent variable).

Similarly, children's clothing was consistently a female-specific expenditure. Over 50 percent of the wives in each neighborhood reported that their spouses contributed half or less of the children's clothing expenditures. Again, there was no significant statistical relationship between neighborhood and family expenditure behavior; see Table 5.

But, significantly, Table 6 shows that the most educated women con-

*An unsuccessful attempt was made to obtain information on food expenditures by gender. A questionnaire approach to obtaining such information was found to be unsatisfactory as there are three different methods of food financing among the Lagos households: the housekeeping-money method, in which the husband gives his wife a monthly sum of money which she at her own discretion adds to and allocates; the soup-pot method, in which every other day or on demand the husband gives a sum of money to buy ingredients for a common pot of soup; and the bulk-purchase method, usually used in polygynous families, in which the husband supplies foodstuffs in bulk and never gives money to the wives to make direct purchases.

tribute the largest proportion to children's clothing expenditures. It appears that wives of the more educated or westernized conjugal units are not modifying traditional expenditure behavior, but are maintaining the customary pattern of economic independence and are actually accentuating traditional gender-specific expenditure patterns.

The existence of gender-specific expenditures and patterns of divided conjugal financial responsibilities implies that Yoruba households do not have joint utility functions or a family altruist. A family member is likely to use an additional unit of income to fulfill his socially expected obligations, not to increase the general living standard of other family members (Jones 1982:11).

Yoruba household consumption patterns reflect the proportional contribution of each gender to total expenditure, and not simply the level of pooled income (Guyer 1979:6). Altered household consumption patterns would, therefore, result from changes in men's and women's personal

TABLE 3

Husband's Proportional Contribution to Specific Family Expenditures,
Based on Wives' Responses

Expenditure item	Half or less		More than half		Item not purchased	
	No.	Pct.	No.	Pct.	No.	Pct.
Rent	5	2.1%	170	70.8%	65	27.1%
Husband's clothing	32	13.3%	205	85.4%	3	1.3%
Furniture	22	9.2%	209	87.1%	9	3.8%
Radio	17	7.1%	193	80.4%	30	12.5%
Refrigerator	14	5.8%	165	68.8%	61	25.4%
School fees	34	14.2%	141	58.8%	65	27.1%
Children's medical expenses	65	27.1%	150	62.5%	25	10.4%
Children's clothing	149	62.1%	89	37.1%	2	0.8%
Wife's clothing	199	82.9%	40	16.7%	1	0.4%

TABLE 4

Husband's Proportional Contribution to Furniture Expenditures
by Neighborhood, Based on Wives' Responses

Proportional contribution	NW Lagos Island		Shomolu		Surulere		Total sample	
	No.	Pct.	No.	Pct.	No.	Pct.	No.	Pct.
Half or less	9	10.7%	3	4.3%	10	11.5%	22	9.2%
More than half	70	83.3%	63	91.3%	76	87.4%	209	87.1%
Item not purchased	5	6.0%	3	4.3%	1	1.1%	9	3.8%

NOTE: $x^2 = 5.48$ with 4 degrees of freedom; not significant at the 5 percent level.

TABLE 5

*Husband's Proportional Contribution to Children's Clothing Expenditures
by Neighborhood, Based on Wives' Responses*

Proportional contribution	NW Lagos Island		Shomolu		Surulere		Total sample	
	No.	Pct.	No.	Pct.	No.	Pct.	No.	Pct.
Half or less	44	52.4%	46	66.7%	58	67.8%	149	62.1%
More than half	38	45.2%	23	33.3%	28	32.2%	89	37.1%
Item not purchased	2	2.4%	–	–	–	–	2	0.8%

NOTE: x^2 = 8.01 with 4 degrees of freedom; not significant at the 5 percent level.

TABLE 6

*Husband's Proportional Contribution to Children's Clothing Expenditures
by Wife's Educational Background, Based on Wives' Responses*

	Wife's educational background										
Proportional contribution	None		Some primary		Completed primary		Secondary		University		Total sample	
	No.	Pct.	No.	Pct.	No.	Pct.	No.	Pct.	No.	Pct.	No.	Pct.
Nothing	5	11.1%	2	16.7%	8	7.4%	6	14.6%	7	23.3%	28	11.9%
Less than half	6	13.3%	1	8.3%	18	16.7%	4	9.8%	7	23.3%	36	15.3%
Half	10	22.2%	4	33.3%	43	39.8%	17	41.5%	8	26.7%	82	34.7%
More than half	18	40.0%	3	25.0%	26	24.1%	11	26.8%	7	23.3%	65	27.5%
Everything	6	13.3%	1	8.3%	13	12.0%	3	7.3%	1	3.3%	24	10.2%
Item not purchased	–	–	1	8.3%	–	–	–	–	–	–	1	0.4%

access to income, or renegotiated responsibility for expenditures by gender, assuming constant gender-specific incomes.

The Theoretical Challenge of
the Nonpooling Household

A homogeneous household paradigm is clearly insufficient to predict or explain empirical Yoruba financial management or consumption behavior. Theoretically, the challenge to social scientists is, therefore, to consider the characteristics and functioning of heterogeneous, nonpooling domestic units, perhaps viewing the household with a unified budget as a special case.

In developing such an approach the emphasis should be placed on the individual as an economic actor within a household and confronted with a world of risk and uncertainty. The first stage of such a development might entail a consideration of the preconditions that encourage the formation of income-pooling households with unified budgets. Three questions would be important: What are the economic benefits of income pooling and joint expenditure planning?; What are the risks associated with such behavior for each spouse?; How do these risks vary among socioeconomic environments and over time?

The second stage might be to develop further the theoretical implications of nonpooling households on the micro level. For example, if income is not pooled, what determines expenditure patterns by gender? Do these patterns persist over time and among various socioeconomic groups? What are the implications of such expenditure behavior for related domestic activities such as fertility behavior? How do domestic power relationships or external factors such as drought and migration influence expenditure patterns or gender-specific investment behavior?

A theoretical recognition of nonpooling households with gender-specific expenditure patterns also has important implications for the development of appropriate public and private social policies in Third World countries, particularly in such areas as land reform, taxation, agricultural extension, and collective bargaining agreements. Policies based on inappropriate household paradigms may fail to achieve project targets, result in distorted goals, or increase social inequities by gender (see, for example, Fapohunda 1988).

Dynamic Approaches to Domestic Budgeting: Cases and Methods from Africa

During the 1970's the concern with making women visible in social research developed into a broader concern with theoretical orientations. The study of domestic groups has been redirected by three related changes: the revival of concern with historical processes, the concentration on interpersonal relationships rather than formal group structures, and the growth of feminist theory. Several reviews of households encourage systematic documentation of changing patterns of interaction at the micro level and their relationship to political and economic change at the macro level (Edholm, Harris, and Young 1977; Yanagisako 1979; Guyer 1981; Sanjek 1982). For Africa, the dialectic of this interaction is thought to be crucial, because domestic organization has not followed patterns of change that are familiar from elsewhere, and neither have the major social processes of differentiation (see Muntemba 1980; Williams 1981).

Such a research agenda is problematic because the data are limited with which to trace subtle and cumulative changes in a sphere as intimate as domestic relations. The question of "how" is critical. Committed to "the art of the soluble" (Medawar 1967), at least one historical anthropologist has turned to a better-documented area of the world (Netting 1981). In Africa, we are faced with the paradox that although African ethnography has provoked much of the theoretical debate about domestic groups and wider social structures (Meillassoux 1981; Goody 1976), the data with which to explore issues of historical change in African domestic relations are particularly thin. In addition, the problem of the invisibility of women in many of the older studies becomes acute if one calls into question methodologies based on the undifferentiated household.

It is here that budget studies can be important. Budget surveys have been carried out in Africa for about 40 years, and constitute a rich resource on household methodology. Since the beginning, the methods of data collection and interpretation have been considered problematic, so that long before the growth of a feminist theoretical orientation one finds discussions about documenting and interpreting women's independent activities. Innovations were made, but they centered almost exclusively on the documentation of income, with only descriptive attention to the divi-

sion of responsibilities for expenditures. This goes only partway toward a
dynamic approach to domestic relations in which the central concern is to
document changing control of the flow of resources. The first part of this
paper reviews budget methodologies in Africa, with particular attention
to the way in which households and their internal relationships have been
conceptualized. In spite of these problems, when the information collected
in household budget surveys is placed historically and ethnographically, it
is critical for the reconstruction of domestic economies. The second part of
this paper analyzes a set of women's budgets collected in rural Southern
Cameroon and interprets them in both short-run processual and long-run
historical terms, relying heavily on budget surveys done over a twenty-
five-year period. The conclusion reconsiders the problems of studying
domestic relations with a temporal orientation to changing flows rather
than with a spatial orientation to units and their composition.*

Wages and Incomes, Prices and Expenditures

Family budget studies were developed in Europe as a means of assessing the social and economic implications of the wage structure. A major
purpose was to document absolute levels of living at the bottom of the
wage scale as a basis for social commentary and reform. The wage-price-
welfare concern dominated family budget methodology. In both Booth's
(1889) and Rowntree's (1902) classic studies, the sample was chosen from
sober-living working-class households, that is, family units dependent on
the single wage of an employed man; in the living conditions of this kind
of unit one could see the effect of wage levels most clearly. The study of
expenditures from this single wage was also used to examine Engel's
observation that the proportion of income devoted to food rises as income
declines (known as Engel's Law—see Houthakker 1957). As a result,
Rowntree showed that the earnings of a significant proportion of the
regularly employed working class were insufficient to meet the basic
necessities of life for a worker and his family. The study of families with a
single wage and budget supporting a group of dependents was a strategy
for bringing the wage-price relationship into sharp relief, not a sociological statement about internal family structure. In fact, Rowntree
pointed out that while the men earned the wage, on the whole the women
managed the family expenditure.

*My fieldwork in Cameroon, 1975–76, was financed by a grant from the National
Institute of Mental Health, and sponsored by the National Advanced School of Agriculture, Yaoundé. (Since this paper was written, the field data on budgets have been discussed
more extensively in Guyer 1984). The author has benefited greatly from comments by
members of the conference, Daisy Dwyer, and the Boston Household Study Group.

Similar concerns with short-run description and prediction animated attempts to document household welfare in the colonies in the postwar period. These included analyses of wage levels following the widespread labor unrest of the late 1930's and of effective demand as a result of the expansion of international trade in consumer goods, as well as the construction of consumer price indexes that were valid as a basis for local wage and price policy. The employment of Africans in the civil service was increasing, and urban populations were growing, so a larger and more politically vocal category of people was affected by the wage-price relationship.

In the urban areas budget methodology followed European practice very closely in the beginning. Studies carried out in Nairobi in 1950 and in Accra in 1953 were limited to households with wage-earning heads, "because these families are the ones principally affected by price changes" (Gold Coast 1957: 2), and because the colonial government needed a basis from which to interpret the implications of the minimum wage (Kenya 1951). In the Kenyan study the sample was further restricted to eliminate people known to be earning outside income, for example, from beer sales. The restrictions were even greater in the Accra study, which limited the size and composition of the family unit, the number of income earners in the family, and the range of wage incomes. Remittances were also excluded from consideration.

The role of women in domestic economies was not quantified separately, although the interpretation of the Kenyan study included some speculation that the extraordinarily high expenditure on food might be due to the purchase of prepared meals, "because of lack of facilities for cooking, absence of wife in the Native Land Unit or merely male laziness" (Kenya 1951: 16). Women entered into the study in the traditional European role of stretching the wage. Even so, it was apparent that such a classic issue as the proportion of the wage spent on food could not be interpreted without attention to internal household structure. However, what seems in retrospect an unjustified assumption of internally undifferentiated household structure was not a simple function of gender or culture blindness; it was also due to taking the wage as the central focus.

Concentration on income, as distinguished from wages, altered the frame of inquiry. Neither accuracy in data collection nor confidence in interpretation could be approached without attention to two cross-cutting divisions within domestic economies—the division into commodity and noncommodity sectors, and the division into male and female sectors.

Most early income studies noted that women earned cash on a regular basis. The study by Fortes, Steel, and Ady of Ashanti in 1945–46 showed that out of 246 women interviewed in one town, only 22 claimed to be nonearners, and these were mainly the wives of clerks and teachers (1948: 163). As McCall (1961) pointed out later, women were expected to earn a cash income and take responsibility for certain expenses. In the rural areas it was also obvious that income included not only the earnings of different family members, but their home production as well.

Critiques of budget methodology for urban as well as rural areas addressed the problem of arriving at an accurate measurement for household income, seen increasingly as a complex composite of different kinds of goods deriving from the efforts of several members of the domestic group. In what amounted to a point-by-point demolition of conclusions reached about Engel's Law and its application to Ghana, Lawson pointed out the misleading nature of assumptions from a wage economy, for example, that there is no source of income other than the wage, and that there is no seasonality to incomes. If women also earn, and if families are split between rural and urban economies, "the differences between them [income and expenditure] may be so variable, variable between seasons, between rural and urban strata, and between members of the same extended family, that the real economic indicators may be concealed" (1962: 39). Further, the assumption that urban consumption is necessarily paid for entirely in cash is incorrect because of a significant level of self-provisioning.

Lawson attacked the assumptions underlying the income data as invalidating the conclusions about expenditure. However, she did not attack the concept of a single-household expenditure plan. The conceptualization of intrahousehold relationships was centered on income. Some of the problems with limiting the issue at this point are apparent in studies undertaken later.

Two budget studies done in Ghana in the 1960's addressed the importance of women's incomes and documented the high proportion of female-headed households. But they did not carry over the gender-specific analysis into the section on expenditure (Dutta Roy and Mabey 1968; Golding 1962). Male and female incomes were collected, but the analysis of consumption was done in terms of household units classified according to the occupation of the household head. As a result, the differences in patterns of expenditure are difficult to interpret. In the rural sample of Dutta Roy and Mabey's study, the poorest category of households consisted of those headed by "petty traders." The patterns of expenditure in these households reflected a very low level of self-provision in food compared to farmers, and a consequently high proportion of cash spent on purchased food. However, almost the entire category of "petty trader" consists of female-headed households, so that it is unclear whether the spending patterns are more reflective of class position in the classic sense, or of the particular activities of women as earners and spenders. One would need to compare this group with other categories of the female population, married and unmarried, to see whether it represented a specifically female personal economy that may be embedded in, or detached from, a larger family context. Questions of this sort demand attention not only to the sources of income and the directions in which it is spent, but to control of its flows.

At a practical level, the importance of documenting individual resource control had been faced much earlier. In setting up a methodology for surveying village economies in Central Africa, Deane noted the importance of interviewing every individual since a married couple might have imprecise knowledge of each other's income and expenditure (1949: 47–48). The authors of some rural surveys of the 1950's were explicit about the limitations of their data on women's incomes. Activities "of the kind which [earn] small but quick returns" (Lawson 1972: 96), like much of the work that women do, pose difficult problems for accurate documentation. As Binet put it, "they say they don't remember anything" (1956: 14). One of the few studies that succeeded in generating information about women's cash incomes, transfers, and patterns of expenditure was Galletti, Baldwin, and Dina's (1956) survey of Nigerian cocoa farmers.

However, ethnographic research suggested that the problem was not just a practical one; institutional bases existed for women's resource control. Fortes, Steel, and Ady, for example, analyzed the rights of Ashanti women in their natal lineages, which accorded them security of property ownership and the right to a home, independently of their marital status. They placed the collection and interpretation of family budgets in this social structural context: "The collection and analysis of family budgets hinges on the delimitation of the domestic group and requires an understanding of its structure" (1948: 165).

The analytical problem then becomes very difficult. The reluctance to abandon the notion of a unitary spending pattern, while accepting the possibility of independent and complementary earning, is related to the problem of defining a household at all. Once a domestic unit has been defined as "all persons living under the same roof and sharing common provisions of housekeeping" (Dutta Roy and Mabey 1968: 14), one cannot pursue the possibility of autonomous spending patterns.

The methodologies developed in French research reflect a considerably greater awareness of the problem of defining units of study in order to capture the various centers of decision making. Studies done in the 1950's routinely distinguish between *l'exploitation* (the enterprise) and the consumption unit (for example, Binet 1956). Some further refinements were also made. For example, in a large-scale survey of rural budgets done in

Cameroon in 1964–65, the budgetary unit was distinguished from the subsistence unit and from the income-earning unit (Winter 1970: 64). These distinctions were developed primarily to deal with polygynous arrangements, where different kinds of decisions are typically made at different levels of internal segmentation. Here particular kinds of autonomy were recognized for expenditure as well as for income earning, but the problem of the interaction among these groups was still conceptualized in terms of relations among constituent units. Gender is the most obvious characteristic of these mediating relationships, and should be faced directly.

In her overview of the West African farming household, Hill (1975) comments on the relative autonomy of men's and women's incomes and expenditures. She particularly notes that women's investments, far from complementing their husbands' or being incorporated into a general household decision, may be geared toward setting up an insurance against divorce. Akan women may set up cocoa farms for this purpose (1975: 131), and Hausa women purchase small livestock that are "safe from seizure by husbands" (1972: 317). Where women retain rights in their natal kin groups after marriage, they often invest in these groups as well as in their current domestic groups. Expenditure and investment by women, according to their own plans and within their own constraints, clearly affect patterns of production and consumption within the domestic enterprise as a whole.

The implication for conceptualizing household structure in terms of internal segmentation into constituent groups is that the lower-level units are not, in fact, entirely enclosed within the larger unit; they are linked to external units as well. The assumption that the domestic group is a tightly functional unity of the kind put forward in Becker's recent theoretical work (1981) is untenable, even at the straightforwardly descriptive level. It matters who gains control of the output because men and women have different spending preferences, not necessarily because they hold different values but because they are in structurally different situations.

On the other hand, it is equally untenable to claim that male and female expenditure patterns do not interrelate at all. Having examined the constraints and flexibilities in women's economic rights, Kaberry nevertheless concludes that "any attempt to discuss it [women's part] without any reference to that of members of the opposite sex, who are their copartners and dependents, would be meaningless" (1952: 152). Hill makes a similar statement: "The varying responsibilities and functions of the heads of farming households are best examined in relation to those of their wives" (1975: 121).

The definitional problems, phrased in either-or terms, defy resolution.

On methodological grounds alone a strong case could be made for treating both income and expenditure as individually controlled, leaving the specific structures and levels of transfer as an empirical question. But this also constitutes a more powerful set of assumptions when the theoretical focus is shifted from structures to processes of change. Male and female, commodity and noncommodity sectors have interrelated in different ways over the past century. The noncommodity sector has always been both a source of accumulation and a buffer for fluctuations in the commodity economy. Family forms of insurance and support, which often depend crucially on female resources, have been counted on to pick up some of the costs of economic changes. Boserup (1970) presents a stark view that the male-female relationship is a major point of articulation of commodity and noncommodity relations. But the model is too simple; it is not applicable to all areas of Africa, and it has certainly not been static. Women have shifted their activities into the market in response to changing constraints and possibilities. In the process both men and women have redefined their rights and obligations toward one another and their wider social networks. When it comes to tracing the implications of patterns of "household" income and expenditure, neither production nor welfare can be understood without attention to the shifting interrelationship of gender-specific decisions.

In this endeavor it is obviously women's activities, incomes, and expenditure patterns that constitute the relatively unexplored territory. The following analysis of women's budgets in two farming villages in southern Cameroon explores the different dimensions of autonomy and complementarity in their ethnographic and historical contexts.

Women's Budgets among the Beti

Like many African systems, the Beti domestic economy has been deeply divided ideologically between men's and women's spheres as far back in time as can be reconstructed (Laburthe-Tolra 1981), but the organizational form of domestic relations has changed since colonization.* In the precolonial period patrilineal descent ideology and local group leadership by polygynous headmen formed the framework for a segmentary social order. Men were hunters, warriors, craftsmen, housebuilders, and clearers of the forest. Women were primarily cultivators and childbearers. At

*Fieldwork was done during 1975 and 1976 in two villages of the Eton subgroup of the Beti. The villages were chosen to represent two different positions on the food-marketing networks; one is on a major paved road, the other on a road that was very poor at the time of the fieldwork, although the two are equidistant from the capital city. Many other villages are more remote from market networks.

present the Beti live in villages that were administratively organized and relocated during the colonial period, and that now consist of one or more groups of patrikinsmen and their wives.

Each man has a house, and a kitchen for his wife. Such a household has no specific name in the Beti language; the indigenous terms refer to structures that no longer exist. In the past, a man's house (*abaa*) belonging to a polygynous headman, and its associated women's houses (*menda*, sing. *nda*) belonging to his wives, made up a village (*dzal*, or *tan* in the Eton dialect). *Dzal* is now used to refer to a village or a hamlet, but not to the *abaa-nda* complex of the restricted family.

The group that now lives together in a single house and kitchen complex has an average size of 5.3 persons. The majority of households have a single resident man and either one or two resident adult women, only one of whom is his wife. The rate of polygynous marriage is low, partly due to the influence of the Catholic church. Of the 136 married men in the two villages studied, only 16 (12 percent) were polygynously married. The marriage rate is also low. Currently married women accounted for only 47 percent of adult women (age 16 and over) in one village and 61 percent in the other.

The ethnographic present represented by census and budget studies provides a profile of current domestic relations. This is outlined in the first sections of the budget analysis. The later sections concentrate on variation, fluctuation, and change along those parameters that theory and local history suggest to be critical in determining the response of internal and external forces to one another. Briefly, these comprise two sets of conditions: those that influence the market involvement of women's enterprise, and those that influence men's and women's access to each other's resources. Before moving on, let me give a contextual description of what this means.

In the post–World War II period the dominant division in the rural economy has been between the female farming of food for family consumption and the male farming of cocoa for sale. Women have maintained subsistence food supply to a remarkable degree. In 1964 about 80 percent of the value of food and drink consumed by rural households was home-produced (SEDES 1964–65: 56), which contrasts dramatically with the extent of food purchases among certain other African peoples (see Galletti, Baldwin, and Dina 1956; Raynaut 1977). However, women's possibilities for earning a cash income, which were very limited in the 1950's, have expanded considerably because of the post-independence growth of the urban market for food in Yaoundé, the capital. At the same time, cocoa prices have been stagnant. The last twenty years, therefore, have been characterized by differential changes in men's and women's cash-earning capacities, although there has been little alteration in the ideology or practice of rural self-subsistence on the basis of women's food farming. There was little purchase of staple foods throughout the study period in 1975–76. In the 1964 budget study the value of home-produced food was calculated at about 45 percent of household real income (SEDES 1964–65).

Such quantitative precision is impossible with respect to the marital relationship, which is the primary framework for claims by men and women on each other's resources. However, there is a clear decline in the marriage rate, leaving many women to make a living outside the marital bond. In the past marriage was universal for adult women, and widows were inherited. Since the abolition of widow inheritance after World War II, it has become rare for a widow past menopause to establish a new marital economy. During the same period bridewealth has been inflated, and marriage for young women is often postponed until after the birth of children. The two trends together mean that an increasing proportion of adult women do not gain access to resources through the culturally dominant ideology of the marital relationship, but through the less specific system of rights associated with kinship. Understanding the implications of the increasing market involvement of women's farming and a declining marriage rate depends on studying the budget data with these processes in mind.

The budget data were collected on a limited sample for a limited time, but close attention was paid to their potential for illuminating dynamics. Daily income and expenditure budgets were collected from 26 women in two villages for two months of the year: July, a peak harvest period in the women's agricultural year, and November, the cocoa harvest period for men. The women were selected from larger samples studied in an ethnography of the farming system. The budget study was started only after several months of work in the villages, so that although the sample was in no way randomly chosen, it does not reflect any consistent bias of which I am aware. The sample includes women from the late teens to very advanced ages, of different marital statuses, married to husbands with a range of current incomes.

Women's Budgets in the Family Context

Table 1 shows that women's disposable cash incomes come from two main sources: they earn money on their own from the sale of farm products, processing, or trade, and they receive transfers from other people, most of whom are current or past residents in their domestic units.

Several observations are important. Women's income from their own enterprise is somewhat greater than their receipts from direct cash trans-

TABLE I

Women's Average Monthly Cash Income, 1975–76

Income source	Amount (CFA)	Pct. of total income
Own earnings		
Sales of own produce	1,724	38%
Trade, processing	531	12%
Cocoa work	305	7%
Subtotal	2,560	57%
Transfers		
Husband	1,292	29%
Other men	308	6%
Women	370	8%
Subtotal	1,970	43%
Total	4,530	100%

NOTE: There were 26 women in the sample; 1,000 francs CFA = approximately $5.00.

TABLE 2

Women's Average Monthly Cash Expenses, 1975–76

Expenses	Amount (CFA)	Pct. of total expenses
Food and minor household	3,341	74%
Personal transport	718	16%
Clothes (own and children's)	433	10%
Total	4,492	100%

NOTE: The slight difference between income and expenditure in Tables 1 and 2 is probably accounted for by gifts of cash to others, a category that was less well covered for expenses than for income.

fers. Half the money that passes through women's hands is generated from food sales, processing, or trade, and another 7 percent from work on the cocoa harvest. The absolute amount of their self-generated income, if generalized over the year, would give a cash return approximately one-third as great as the average cocoa farmer's income.* If one extrapolates

*Average cocoa incomes have been calculated from the records of the cooperative that, in one of the villages, had monopolized cocoa marketing for the three previous years. The mean income for the 58 farmers who had been cooperative members in all three years was 89,966 CFA. As a proxy for men's income generally this figure has two problems: it overestimates income, since some men are not cocoa farmers and, for those who are, about 15 percent of their gross income is overhead; and it underestimates income, since some men earn additional money from palm-wine tapping and tomato cultivation. Estimating women's annual incomes from two-month budgets is not valid, but it does give some idea of the quantum differences between men's and women's cash incomes.

from the real income estimates made in earlier studies, the women's food economy probably produces, in kind and in cash, about half of total real income in the rural areas, with quite limited labor input from men.

Cash transfers come mainly from men, two-thirds of them from husbands. Some of these contributions are accompanied by instructions about their use, and some are given in kind. A husband may give his wife money to buy a certain ingredient for the diet, or for a child's medicine or school supplies. Occasionally he may make a food purchase himself. Such cases, and the odd case where a husband regularly buys items that in other families are the responsibility of the wife, I have counted as transfers. Other male contributors are mainly consanguine kin, with several of the unmarried women reporting gifts from lovers. Receipts from other women come primarily from mothers or daughters.

The expenditures covered by this income are summarized in Table 2. The women's budgets are clearly dominated by supplements to the family food supply in the form of meat, salt, and oil, and household needs such as kerosene and soap. These account for 74 percent of cash expenses. By contrast, men's expenditure patterns are dominated by housing, school fees, and bridewealth. The approximate one-fourth of their cash income that men give to women accounts for only about one-third of the household's total expenditure on food. The balance is accounted for by women's own cash incomes. That is, of total cash expenses for food and routine household supplies, women contribute two-thirds and men one-third. This leaves women with one-quarter of their personal incomes for other purposes, while men are left with about three-quarters.

In addition to these amounts, most women save 500 CFA per month in a savings fund. Sometimes husbands help to make the contributions, but even if they do not, women feel pressure to give them a significant proportion of the receipts. For some couples the spending of this money is cooperative, since its dispensation—for bridewealth or school fees—has been planned and relates to their children. Examples of other uses are: a woman whose husband earned very little devoted her savings to improving her own kitchen; a childless woman devoted a large sum to the naming of a child in her natal family, rather than giving the money to her husband; an elderly, childless widow gave the entire amount to her brother for his children's school fees.

The shifting or sharing of new responsibilities as women's cash incomes creep up relative to men's takes place over these larger sums as well as over the day-to-day basics of life. A great deal about men's and women's decision making can be illuminated through study of the source of contributions to credit associations, the size of the purse, and the uses to which it is put.

Married and Unmarried Women

One way of estimating the effect of marriage on a woman's budget, and the aggregated effect of declining marriage rates, is to compare the personal economies of married and unmarried women. The sample includes 17 wives and 9 unmarried women (4 single women, 2 separated women, and 3 widows). The wives had an average of 2.7 dependent and coresident children, while the currently unmarried had 1.1. Table 3 summarizes the income data.

Unmarried women have larger self-generated incomes than married women, although their total incomes are smaller. All women provide their own staple foods from the farm, regardless of marital status. Rights to the use of land can be activated through kinship ties as well as through marriage, although in the former instance security of tenure is somewhat lower. With respect to cash, unmarried women average 80 percent of the disposable income of married women. They make up for the lack of transfers from a husband, which accounts for 40 percent of married women's cash, by earning more from farming and trade. Their own activities bring them 25 percent more money than the independent work of married women. In addition, unmarried women get considerably more support from other men than do married women.

Expenditures reveal the smaller amounts of disposable cash income controlled by unmarried women, but also underscore that the proportion devoted to the major items is very similar; see Table 4. Thus, while unmarried women are poorer than married women, in per capita terms they cover the basic expenses of life for themselves and their children at

TABLE 3

Average Monthly Cash Income of Married and Unmarried Women

Income source	Married women		Unmarried women	
	Amount (CFA)	Percent	Amount (CFA)	Percent
Own earnings				
Sales of own produce	1,692	35%	1,782	45%
Trade, processing	349	7%	875	23%
Cocoa work	316	6%	296	8%
Subtotal	2,357	48%	2,953	76%
Transfers				
Husbands	1,977	40%	–	–
Other men	129	3%	645	17%
Women	415	9%	285	7%
Subtotal	2,521	52%	930	24%
Total	4,878	100%	3,883	100%

TABLE 4

Average Monthly Cash Expenses of Married and Unmarried Women

	Married women		Unmarried women	
Expenses	Amount (CFA)	Percent	Amount (CFA)	Percent
Food and minor household	3,843	76%	2,393	71%
Personal transport	723	14%	710	21%
Clothes	512	10%	285	8%
Total	5,708	100%	3,388	100%

similar standards and in similar ways. The greater proportion of unmarried women's expenditure devoted to transport reflects their greater freedom of movement, which is also reflected in their greater income from trade.

These figures relate only to current income and expenses. The real poverty of unmarried women lies less in the basic expense of providing food than in the difficulties of raising the relatively large sums of money needed to pay major medical costs, bridewealth for sons, and children's school fees. In the ideology and former practice of kinship the male guardian of an unmarried women was responsible for her children, but men's willingness to meet these responsibilities is diminishing as the costs rise. To meet major expenses from their own income sources, some unmarried women allocate more time to trade than to farming. However, it is difficult for a woman to earn as much as a male cocoa farmer, that is, to substitute for the contribution of a man to the domestic economy.

The feeding and basic provisioning of a family appear, therefore, to be relatively protected from the vicissitudes of access to a man's cash income. Seasonal analysis shows, however, that what may be true on the personal level for individual women cannot be extended to collective welfare.

The Seasonal Cycle

Lawson (1962) observed that in southern Ghana women earned and spent their income in small, regular amounts, while men's activities tended to be intermittent. If the spheres were autonomous, the cycles might interact very little. If they were functionally responsive to each other they might tend to fluctuate inversely so that total combined income remained fairly steady. The comparison of Beti married and unmarried women's budgets suggests that, at the level of day-to-day provisioning of a domestic group, the female sector is relatively detachable. The data on seasonality shown in Table 5 suggest, however, that the female sector as a

TABLE 5

Women's Average Cash Income in July and November

	Amount (CFA)		Percent	
Income source	July	November	July	November
Own earnings				
Sales of own produce	1,280	2,167	39%	37%
Resale	238	825	7%	14%
Cocoa work	–	611	–	11%
Subtotal	1,518	3,603	46%	62%
Transfers				
Husband	1,032	1,533	32%	27%
Other men	379	237	12%	4%
Women	345	394	10%	7%
Subtotal	1,756	2,164	54%	38%
Total	3,274	5,767	100%	100%

whole is dependent on the viability of the male occupations. The seasonal trend in women's incomes and expenses reflects the cycle in the male agricultural economy; women's incomes are higher in November, when men have cash from cocoa sales, than they are in July. Women's cash receipts are 75 percent higher in November than in July; this is accounted for, not by gifts and transfers from men to women, but by additional money earned by the women themselves through market activities. The absolute amounts men give to women are higher in November, but the proportional contribution to women's funds is not. Women's own earnings from sales, trade, and remunerated work are more than twice as high in November as in July. Women take advantage of the increased demand in the local economy to earn extra money. Some is gained through the increased economic relations with outsiders, and some through tapping the cocoa incomes of local men. During the cocoa season new occupations emerge: distillation of alcohol; trade in wine, beer, and cigarettes; preparation and sale of cooked food; sewing; and work on the cocoa harvest itself. Women explicitly discuss and assess the various means of tapping men's incomes at this time of year. In general, the pressure for women to find ways into the incomes of their menfolk is greater in more remote villages than in areas where outside alternatives present themselves. But in neither case do women rely on intrafamilial transfers. They look for a variety of ways to redistribute male income, and their success depends on the general state of the male economy.

In times of depression in the cocoa sector women's cash incomes do not remain insulated. The purchased food supply suffers, since women use their higher November incomes largely to enrich their diet. In spite of the higher level of cash income in November, women use almost exactly

75 percent of their total expenditure for food and minor household supplies in both months.

In summary, the welfare of the women's economy taken as a whole is positively responsive to levels of income in the male economy, but less through transfers into a collective pooled income than through the transactions of exchange and the market.

But again, the generalization that male and female incomes rise and fall together may apply to the population collectively over the seasonal cycle, but it does not apply to categories of the population across income strata. The issue of how women's incomes and expenditure patterns vary with the incomes of their husbands is particularly difficult to address, and interpretations have to be inconclusive, because the stratification of village populations is still fluid, and no one is wealthy.

Wealth Differences and Developmental Cycles

The data do not lend themselves to any systematic correlations between women's cash incomes and their husbands' wealth, or between incomes and the developmental cycle. However, a series of brief cases illustrates the considerable variability. At present it is impossible to judge the significance of this kind of differentiation.

The two women with the highest disposable incomes were in totally different situations. One was the wife of a salaried employee who commuted to town. She was in her early thirties, with four children. Seventy-nine percent of her cash came from her husband, but she still took in sewing and sold produce from her farm and fed the family. The other woman was in her mid-twenties, unmarried, with two children. She had a small food farm of her own but was also fed from her mother's farm. Only a token amount of her income came from men; the rest came from the sale of tomatoes and other agricultural produce (33 percent), the purchase and resale of local agricultural goods (53 percent), and work on the cocoa harvest (13 percent). The first woman's increased transfers from her husband did not prevent her from earning on her own account, and the second woman's lack of transfers from men did not keep her in poverty.

There is a similar lack of clarity at the other end of the scale. The women with little disposable cash include the young and old, married and unmarried. With respect to cash income, married and unmarried women are distributed equally around the mean.

One particular case, however, suggests what may be a new process of interdependent budgeting between husband and wife. A married woman with six dependent children received no transfers from her husband, even though his cocoa income was not significantly different from that of other members of the cooperative. She sold little produce because she needed most of her crops to feed her large family. Her own income earning was restricted to petty work that earned low returns, such as baking doughnuts and cracking palm kernels. Her low expenditure record was confirmed by the family's low level of meat and fish consumption.

This woman's poverty is closely associated with her husband's expenses on behalf of one of their children whose education costs were high. This family's case suggests that the new exigencies of school fees may be forcing a greater cooperation between parents, who now have to make trade-offs between education and routine consumption. In the recent past the "female" expenditures on consumption retained a certain degree of protection from requisition to meet "male" demands, but the rising cost of children could be changing this.*

In the short run children of single women may be no more vulnerable than children of married women. However, their mothers' relatively inferior access to male resources may compromise their chances of getting a higher education and impede their access to land—the only resources that count. The number of such children has been increasing as the marriage rate has fallen since the late 1950's. Rising school fees may be the primary force binding married couples into single budgetary units and at the same time feeding into processes of differentiation.† The processes of interaction within families intersect in this way with the historical conditions determining both the marriage rate and the costs of and returns to education.‡

To get a stronger indication of this one needs a kind of documentation different from the classic budget study, namely, data about the longer-term dimensions of income management represented by the rotating credit associations and the financing of the major intermittent expenditures of life.

Historical Trends in Domestic Budgeting

The problem of understanding changes in large-scale expenditure and its implications for the routines of domestic budgeting has to be put aside

*The subordination of routine needs to major expenses is familiar to urban populations. It is particularly well described for an African case by Buchi Emecheta in her novel, *The Joys of Motherhood.*

†Emecheta's novel reminds us that buying into the family strategy of education for children may not actually raise the status or level of living of the parental generation, even in the long run. Stratification is too long a process to be captured in the differentiation among the members of a single generation.

‡During the time of the study, rural parents paid school fees only at the secondary level and above, and even here different schools had different fee scales. Although Eton school-age children have a very high enrollment rate, fees in the mid-1970's seemed a less important budgetary concern there than in other areas of Africa.

for the moment. But there are some changes in routine budgeting that can be reconstructed historically.

The share of total rural income accounted for by the sale of food crops to the urban market has undoubtedly increased since the first major budget study done in 1954. At that time Binet found that sales of food crops produced only 2 percent of family income, so little that the information was difficult to collect (Binet 1956). By 1964 cocoa prices had declined and food sales had increased (and possibly the enumeration techniques were more accurate). As a result, the value of food sold was up to one-fourth of the value of cocoa income (Winter 1970: 167). But the proportion of the family budget spent on purchased food has also increased. In 1954 Binet's study showed 15 percent of family expenses going for food and minor household needs; in the 1964 study it was 30 percent.

I would argue that any attempt to explain how the two changes are related has to include attention to intradomestic dynamics. An increased proportion of expenditure for food cannot be understood as a simple function of declining incomes in line with Engel's Law, because the Beti population can retreat to almost total self-provisioning if necessary. Neither is it due to inflation in food prices; this developed later in the 1960's. Alternatively, one could argue that the growth in the food sector since 1960 puts a higher proportion of total income in the hands of women, who devote it to routine food and household needs. Women have generated their own income, and under the stress of low cocoa prices they have taken over and expanded certain routine costs that transfers from men had covered during the peak cocoa years. Only 15 percent of household food and supplies could have been financed from money earned from the food sector in 1954. By the 1960's and 1970's at least two-thirds of these expenditures could have been covered by women's incomes. The shift in domestic cash control since the 1950's must be seen as a factor in the shift in expenditure patterns.

Male and female incomes come from different sources and are used for different purposes. If a couple's budget can be regarded as a single fund, it is not through the literal pooling of cash, but through the ongoing process of bargaining about the organization of interpersonal transfers and responsibilities under shifting conditions.

Conclusions

It is clear that such concepts as autonomy, complementarity, and incorporation are too static and not contextual enough to describe and analyze the ways in which resources are mobilized. The interaction of men's and women's budgeting has to be looked at in different contexts: different domestic situations, different seasons, phases in developmental cycles, fluctuations in the rural economy as a whole, and long-term trends. The implications of domestic organization and wider social change for one another can be addressed systematically only by doing this kind of disaggregation.

There are two main methodological conclusions to be drawn: the importance of documentation by individual and that of tracing interactions over time. It is as important to document individual expenditure patterns as it is to document individual incomes because the allocation of responsibilities is as important a family process as the allocation of resources. Management of different responsibilities, with their different timing, has tended to be gender-specific in societies with a pronounced division into male and female spheres. But the specialization is never complete; it oscillates according to each sex's ability to cope with its own sphere, and its ability either to tap into the other or to shift the responsibilities.

All this is not just a question of demonstrating trends in "women's contributions," but also of approaching an understanding of major social processes relating to rural differentiation and the commoditization of food. The application of a unitary household model renders women invisible (see Edholm, Harris, and Young 1977). It also renders invisible the structural, cyclical, and historical processes determining rural consumption, investment, and long-term change.

Income Allocation and Marriage Options in Urban Zambia

MONICA MUNACHONGA

In precolonial Zambia, all marriages were according to tradition and rural men's and women's roles were defined clearly. Husbands and wives farmed together and the crops were under their joint control. Spouses had equal control of crops stored in their respective granaries (Colson 1958). This arrangement minimized the wife's problems in performing her role as provider of food. Any surplus crops produced were bartered for those foodstuffs and other essential items the household did not produce for itself (Fielder 1973). Money itself was unknown, or an innovation associated with colonialism; barter was the predominant system of exchange. Personal status, power, and prestige within the household therefore were not based on the power to spend and allocate but rather on access to and control of other types of resources.

In 1905, the colonial administration demanded hut-tax payments in the form of cash instead of labor as a means of supporting the government (Gelfand 1961); this had the effect of forcing peasants to leave their villages and work for wages in the modern sector. Life has changed rapidly since then. In modern Zambia, nearly half (43 percent) of the population resides in urban areas, in an almost entirely monetized economy. Yet urban women are still expected to fulfill the traditional obligations of housekeeping and purchasing and preparing the family's food. Husbands are expected to provide money for food and other critical purchases, but their allocations are often inadequate and not realistic in view of market prices. In urban households, conflict has begun to arise over the question of control over discretionary income. As I shall show in this paper, couples have come up with a variety of strategies for dealing with income, depending on whether the wife also works, and whether the marriage contract is customary or "ordinance" (under new legal codes).*

The majority of wives in the lower-income urban groups engage in petty trading as a means of supplementing their husband's low income— or insufficient contribution to the household pool (see Bardouille 1982;

* The research on which this paper is based was funded by the University of Zambia's Special Research Fellowship program. I am grateful for their support.

Hansen 1975, 1980). Many income-generating activities performed by women in the informal sector—beer brewing, selling items at bus stops or along the streets—are illegal. Traders are subject to police raids, arrest, and fines. Urban housewives seeking to earn are in a vulnerable position.

In the transition from traditional to modern life, men's and women's perceptions of the appropriate use of conjugal earnings have diverged. For instance, one woman complained in a newspaper: "Men think that because a wife is working then she should be left to run the house without his assistance. *Most of them regard wives as passports to pleasure*" (emphasis added). By contrast, a man is quoted in the same article: "Women should realize that a man should not be the sole provider. It is obvious that when a wife goes to work, then a lot of things are missing in the home. The children are not properly looked after and the house is not well attended to. *In view of this, the wife must bring home what she earns*. It is when she does not want to contribute that conflicts are bound to occur" (*Zambia Daily Mail* 1976b; emphasis added).

Clearly, men and women have different expectations about financial responsibilities and the consequences of a wife's employment. Wives who earn money increasingly want to control their own earnings as a way of "expressing explicitly the possessiveness their husbands express implicitly" (Hunt 1980:569). Husbands often respond by preventing (or threatening to prevent) their wives from working for pay. Wives' employment and earnings have been blamed for the increasing rate of divorce:

Industrialization or urbanization is completely threatening to destroy Zambia's traditional life. The most threatened are marriages, which are breaking down in the thousands. Sociologists have attributed this hitherto unknown problem to heavy drinking and sheer negligence by husbands. But the country's independence has posed a new danger to Zambian marriages, this time not from drunken husbands, but from the working woman. Obviously, the wife who feeds the family including her husband (i.e., if he is not earning) feels she is on top of the world. She often humiliates her husband by reminding him that as breadwinner, she is in charge of the house. Which husband can take this kind of insult? Even though a man may be a loafer . . . [his] dominant role as traditional head of the family should be respected. Zambian girls, women, and wives, this is good advice which you should not ignore. . . . Take it up! (*Zambia Daily Mail* 1982)

Ambivalence exists about women's role and status. A wife's employment is perceived as having financial advantages for the husband, because it relieves his economic burdens and enables him to keep more of his own earnings for personal use. At the same time, the wife's access to independent income is considered to have a negative effect on marriage and family stability. Thus, it is generally felt that a wife should give up her job if it inconveniences her husband, which implies that her insistence on continued employment can lead to major conflicts and even divorce.

Marriage in Traditional Zambian Society

In traditional Zambian society, ethnic groups tended to be endogamous and to observe one system of marriage law and custom. The choice of a marriage partner was the concern of the whole family, which arranged and sponsored marriages. Women were regarded as minors under customary law regardless of their previous marital status (McLain 1970), but in some cases they were given the opportunity to express their preferences (Colson 1958; Richards 1940). Conjugal duties and obligations in rural society were dictated by custom, clearly defined and known to everyone in the community. This system ensured that conjugal behavior and the responsibilities of kin groups to widows and orphans were highly predictable.

The relative positions of spouses were determined by a number of factors. One was the form of social organization (patrilineal or matrilineal) of the groups involved, which also determined the location of the children in a kinship group. The majority of the ethnic groups in Zambia (Brelsford 1965) are matrilineal, except for the Ngoni and the Mambwe, who are patrilineal, and the Lozi, who are bilateral. Thus, among the majority of the groups, women had a relatively strong claim to their children. Another factor involved rules of residence. For example, among the matrilineal Bemba, uxorilocal marriage enhanced a woman's position vis-à-vis her husband. A Bemba man lived and worked with his wife's family as a form of marriage payment. He tended to have less influence in family decision making, for his father-in-law was head of the family. Moreover, his food was prepared in his mother-in-law's kitchen, since married daughters had no kitchens of their own but prepared meals under their mother's supervision.

Even where marriage payments were made in the form of goods, the husband's power was not absolute, partly because payments were the responsibility of his whole family and did not represent an exchange of women for goods (see also Cutrufelli 1983). The main exchange was for the children anticipated from the woman. Further, the payments were made in installments closely linked to the various stages of a marriage since marriage was regarded as a process rather than a state of being resulting from a single act or ceremony (see also Vellenga 1983). The payments were widely distributed among a woman's paternal and maternal relatives, which implied dispersion of power and authority over women rather than their concentration in the hands of the husband.

Broadly speaking, the social and public lives of husband and wife were separate (Gluckman 1950); this did not necessarily imply women's inferiority (see Little 1973; Paulme 1963). The economic activities of spouses were complementary: husband and wife worked their fields as a team, although each generally was responsible for particular tasks and for growing certain crops (for example, groundnuts were grown by women). In general, however, husband and wife were economic partners in the production of crops for subsistence, and they had equal control of crops stored in their respective granaries.

Existing Systems of Marriage and Their Effect on Asset Distribution

At the time of independence in 1964, Zambia inherited a dual system of marriage and recognized unions under customary law and under statute as equally valid. In the colonial period, the law had discriminated against Africans; they were not permitted to marry under the colonial marriage ordinance (Hastings 1973). This policy continued until late 1963, when the ordinance was amended to allow Africans to contract civil marriages. Immediately after independence the Marriage Act was introduced, and with some modifications it allowed more Zambians to marry under it (Ndulo 1979). As I will show below, the ordinance form of marriage has received support from government policy, which suggests a movement toward the nuclearization of the family within the law.

Customary Marriage

Marriage is validated by fulfillment of customary rites and obligations; the consent of the woman's family and marriage payments by the man's family are particularly important. Marriage payments give a husband rights to his wife's labor and the fruits of her labor (Colson 1958). In urban society, the amount demanded for marriage payments tends to be calculated on the basis of the commercial value of a woman's education, which suggests that a husband also acquires rights to dispose of his wife's income.* Since customary marriage is polygynous, however, a woman does not have exclusive rights to be economically supported by her husband.

The system of marriage payments, an important feature of customary marriage, is incompatible with an ideology of wives' ownership of their

---

*The tendency for payments to rise has been supported by press reports (see, for example, *Times of Zambia*, December 4, 1975; *Sunday Times of Zambia*, September 19, 1982). The attitude that the wife's earnings belong to her husband has also been reported in a study in South Africa (Brandel 1958).

income. Technically, a husband who has paid *lobola* (marriage payments) is regarded as the owner of his wife's income, and he has the right to prevent his wife from working. Thus, in case of marital conflict about a wife's employment, courts are likely to rule in favor of the husband. This also implies that a woman who works against her husband's wishes risks divorce, for she is not fulfilling her obligation to obey him. In general, the persistence of the requirement that a husband make marriage payments places women in an unfavorable economic position.

The second important feature of customary marriage is that it does not alter a person's rights to inheritance in the natal kinship group; spouses do not expect to inherit property from each other. The disadvantaged partner in this case is the wife, since in addition she may be denied rights to household property. This is generally assumed to belong to the husband, the owner of the matrimonial home (see Epstein 1981). In the event of divorce, the sharing of household property accumulated during marriage is at the discretion of the husband (this was confirmed by the Local Courts Advisor at the High Court of Zambia, whom I interviewed). Customary wives who have contributed their earnings either directly or indirectly to the purchase of inheritable household items are not generally viewed as joint owners; this property too belongs to the husband.

The fact that a widow has no rights to inherit property from her husband has led to a new social problem in urban areas: the dispossession of widows and orphans. This did not occur in traditional rural societies because the husband's heir also "inherited" the widow and assumed responsibility for the children; the problem of the widow's inheritance from her deceased husband was not pressing because she was expected to marry one of her husband's heirs. But this does not necessarily apply in modern urban society, and there widows' economic circumstances have declined (see McClain 1970). Although the government has made efforts to introduce legislation on succession that would protect the interests of women, the proposed system of distributing a man's property has not received popular support, particularly among men (including some in influential positions, such as members of Parliament).* Moreover, the idea of widow inheritance is incompatible with the Western notion of free choice of marriage partners, an aspect of marriage that is favored by both men and

---

*The proposed system of distributing a man's property is 50 percent to his children, 25 percent to his widow, and 25 percent to his dependent relatives. Opponents have argued that this would actually mean that 75 percent of a man's property will go to the wife since children are likely to stay with her, and thus the property will pass to strangers (her relatives and her new husband if she remarries). For details on the background of these proposals and the fears that men hold about the introduction of legislation on succession, see Law Development Commission (1976, 1982). See also *Sunday Times of Zambia* (October 10, 1982, and October 24, 1982) and Zambia Information Services (1983).

women in present-day Zambia, particularly those who have been exposed to Western education.

Not only do these women lack property rights in their husbands' groups if they become widowed, they also have no rights to maintenance in the event of divorce. A divorced woman's kinship group is expected to assume responsibility for her support (interview with Local Courts Advisor, High Court, March 1983). In the urban socioeconomic system, divorce under customary law has highly adverse consequences for women, particularly for less-educated women, who are in the majority. Thus, women with no alternative means of support are likely to remain in unsatisfactory marriages.

Ordinance Marriage

Ordinance marriage, grounded in the English concept of marriage, is strictly monogamous. It stresses freedom from extended kin with regard to choice of partner and marriage rites and obligations. It is validated not by the consent of a woman's parents and by marriage payments, but by compulsory registration and other civil procedures as stipulated by the Marriage Act (Zambia, *Marriage*). In the case of a minor, a high court judge may give consent to a marriage if, for example, it is considered that parents have unnecessarily withheld their consent (*ibid.*, Section 19).

The ordinance form of marriage not only gives the wife security as the only legal wife, it provides for her maintenance in the event of divorce.* Under the Marriage Act, a couple is expected to share household property accumulated jointly during the marriage. This new form of marriage seeks to enhance women's economic position. However, my study revealed that although it is an improvement on customary marriage, it has serious limitations. For example, if a husband dies, the customary law of succession applies to his widow. The social problem popularly referred to as the "plight of widows" affects all women irrespective of the system of marriage considered. Marriage under the act is automatically ended at the death of either spouse. Unlike customary law, which emphasizes the continuance of women's conjugal obligations (Colson 1950), ordinance marriage permits widows to remarry anyone they choose.

---

*However, interviews with an Assistant Registrar at the High Court of Zambia revealed that maintenance is not automatic. The person granted it has to ensure that she actually receives it, through appeals to the court if the person ordered to pay fails to do so. The Assistant Registrar defended husbands who failed to pay, saying that this was due to the fact that in Zambia salaries are generally low. In addition, educated women often do not apply for maintenance in their petitions for divorce. Three such women I interviewed stressed that this was because they wanted to be completely free from their ex-husbands, which would not be the case if the men continued to support them.

In general, government policy appears to give priority to ordinance marriage. For instance, couples married according to customary law are permitted to remarry under the Marriage Act, but not vice versa. The Office of the Registrar-General is responsible for the registration only of statutory marriages, and it has prepared a detailed handbook to guide officers responsible for registration. Since independence, more marriage districts that coincide with administrative districts have been created to enable more Zambians to contract ordinance marriages. The High Court of Zambia handles divorce cases under the Marriage Act, which has universal principles; local courts are responsible for divorces under customary law, which varies according to the ethnic groups involved.

This official emphasis on the Western type of marriage has created more opportunities for conjugal financial cooperation. This raises the question of whether and how men and women have actually responded to the state's organization of marriage and the associated inheritance laws.

Choice of Marriage Form

Women tend to favor the ordinance form for egalitarian reasons; see Table 1. In general, they see the complicated and expensive divorce procedures, compulsory registration, and other new provisions—including penalties for bigamy and provisions for alimony—as sources of security within marriage. By contrast, men (who are generally more educated than women and so understand better the new form of marriage) tend to oppose ordinance marriage essentially for the same reasons that women favor it. In particular, men are not in favor of alimony. Some men also argue that this form of marriage encourages women to be arrogant to their husbands because it gives a wife the right to sue her husband for divorce on the grounds of adultery. Nevertheless, my study discussed later in the chapter reveals a close relationship between the ordinance form of marriage and university education for men as well as women; see Table 2.

TABLE I

Husbands' and Wives' Reasons for Marrying Under the Ordinance

Reasons for marrying	Total (N = 28)	Husbands (N = 14)	Wives (N = 14)
Long-term commitment/security	8	5	3
Spouse insisted/preferred it	3	3	–
Advised by others	2	–	2
Thought appropriate to own status	3	2	1
Monogamy	4	4	–
Equal rights	8	–	8

TABLE 2

Educational Levels of Couples by Form of Marriage

Educational level	Total	Customary		Ordinance	
		Male	Female	Male	Female
University	23	3	–	11	9
Form 6	1	–	–	1	–
Form 5	45	30	10	1	4
Form 2	43	13	28	1	1
Primary	67	32	35	–	–
None	21	8	13	–	–
Total	200	86	86	14	14

Educated men tend to favor the free choice of a marriage partner but to oppose joint ownership of property. For example, men tend to have ambivalent attitudes toward a widow's inheriting from her deceased husband. In many cases, husbands give qualified approval to a widow's inheriting: it is all right if she has children and if she does not remarry (if she did, the property would pass to a stranger). In other words, men approve of a man's property passing to his own children, but not necessarily to his wife. This means that children can provide an indirect source of long-term financial security for women.

In general, the ordinance form of marriage is not widely understood in Zambia, partly because it is relatively new and partly because of the general opposition to it on the part of most men. For these reasons, only a small number of Zambian marriages comply with the Marriage Act.* In addition, whereas the two forms of marriage are easily distinguished as legal forms, this cannot be done in practice. Although the new form is associated with white weddings, expensive receptions, and compulsory registration, the main elements that validate the customary form of marriage procedures, particularly the consent of a woman's family and the payment of *lobola* by a man's family, are also included in the ordinance form. (In my study—discussed later—of marriages of university graduates, only one, in which the wife held a master's degree, indicated that they had not fulfilled customary obligations at marriage.) This makes it much harder to define the economic status of an ordinance wife, for instance at divorce; she may be perceived as a customary wife since customary marriage is better understood than ordinance marriage. Moreover, the majority of Western-educated Zambians are of the first generation to be educated, which means that their parents are unlikely to understand the

*For example, between 1967 and 1975, only 2,356 out of 6,367 civil marriages contracted were by Africans. See Central Statistical Office (1975:2).

principles of the new system and are therefore probably opposed to the idea of a man maintaining his wife after divorce. Further, in actual practice there may not be much difference in income-handling patterns between customary and ordinance households.

Many legal matters relating to personal status, property rights, and succession are closely connected with marriage. The general economic position of women in the wider society, however, must be taken into consideration when examining conjugal financial relationships. It has been confirmed elsewhere that societal inequalities tend to be translated into inequalities within marriage (Pahl 1983).

The next section considers the general economic position of Zambian women. It brings together data and information on women's status, conjugal relationships, and financial relationships in contemporary urban Zambian society.

Trends of Socioeconomic Development and Their Impact on Women

Most accounts of economic development emphasize the fact that Northern Rhodesia's (now Zambia's) wealth was founded on copper mining, whose full-scale operations began in the mid-1920's. The copper-mining industry depended on cheap African labor. The workers left their villages to earn tax money; later, they used their earnings to buy manufactured goods. The imposition of taxes on adult males and, initially, on each wife except the first (Gann 1964) was a subtle means of coercing men to work for cash (Gugler 1968) and to have only one wife.

During the early period of industrialization, workers were rarely allowed to take their families with them (see Chauncey 1981; Heisler 1974; Parpart 1983). The colonial administration preferred women to remain in villages, where they were expected to continue subsistence agricultural production for maintenance of themselves and their children. This was seen to aid the government's general policy of "industrialization without urbanization," as Heisler reports: "It was also realized that if women accompanied peasant men to work in factories this would preclude any urge on the part of these men to return to women in peasant systems" (1974:64). Later, women were allowed to live in colonial towns, but only as wives of workers. Single women found living illegally in African compounds were repatriated to their villages.

Women at this time seemed to be caught between conflicting interests. The mining companies saw the domestic services of women as functional to their industry; the colonial administration wanted to reduce costs of social services by leaving responsibility for women and children to kinship groups in villages; and the traditional rulers and heads of kinship groups used their control of women—by organizing and sponsoring marriages—to control the labor of young men.

Many accounts show that even when women were allowed to live in towns, they did not join the industrial labor force. In the urban economy, the colonial labor policy generally reserved most jobs, even those that are defined as women's in industrialized countries (such as typist, sales assistant, and domestic servant) for males (Hansen 1980; Simons 1979). Thus, the colonial industrial policy led to a decline in women's economic power. They began to depend financially on their husbands, something they had not done in the traditional rural subsistence economy. Although a very small number of women were eventually employed in the civil service and in social welfare jobs in the mines (Parpart 1983), in 1956 women constituted only 2.1 percent and in 1961 only 2.8 percent of the labor force (Heisler 1974:66). Moreover, Heisler explains, these figures included non-Zambian African women.

Discrimination against women in wage employment was reinforced by discrimination against them in the area of education. Northern Rhodesians generally received less education than people in other colonies in the region, and Rhodesian women received less education than men (Elliott 1971; Hall 1965; Hansen 1975; Mwanakatwe 1968; Sanyal et al. 1976; Snelson 1974). At the time of independence in 1964, only 77 women, compared to 884 men, had completed secondary school (Zambia 1964). Parents tended to give preference to the education of sons (Little 1973: 29–32; Powdermaker 1962:199). As late as 1958, girls had to go outside the country for their secondary-school education; and in that year, only three girls from Northern Rhodesia were enrolled at Goromonzi Secondary School in Southern Rhodesia (now Zimbabwe) (Snelson 1974). Even when places in school for girls were increased, the curriculum emphasized the domestic arts (Sanyal et al. 1976:88), implying that the primary role girls were expected to play in adult life was that of housewife and mother.

Although the postcolonial government has expanded educational and training programs based on free education and created more opportunities for wage employment for both men and women, the position of women has not been radically improved. Girls' rate of participation in education was only half that of boys between 1970 and 1974; at the university level, women's rate of participation was only 17 percent that of men. From 1968 to 1973 only 141 out of 860 graduates from the University of Zambia were women (Sanyal et al. 1976). Similarly, in the field of technical education and vocational training, the scales weighed heavily against women (see Table 3), and women tended to be concentrated in secretarial courses.

There has been an increase in the number of women employees in all

TABLE 3
Graduates in Technical Education and Vocational Training by Program,
1976 and 1980

Program	1976			1980		
	Total	Males	Females	Total	Males	Females
Trades or crafts	581	576	5	463	463	–
Industrial technologist	329	327	2	177	177	–
Engineering technologist	74	73	1	52	52	–
Science and para-medical	89	74	15	65	54	11
Business studies	74	74	–	62	55	7
Secretarial	261	6	255	310	–	310
Air services	120	118	2	93	86	7
Applied arts	75	67	8	59	56	3
Teacher training	63	61	2	222	185	37
Academic (English as a foreign language)	12	12	–	28	25	3
Totals	1,678	1,388	290	1,531	1,153	378

SOURCE: Ministry of Education, *Educational Statistics*, 1976 and 1980. See also Women's League of Zambia, *Zambia's Report to the World Conference of the UN Decade for Women*, 1985, Appendices.

industries since independence, from 7,000 out of a total of 225,000 African employees in 1963 (Cutrufelli 1983; Central Statistical Office 1964) to 25,670 out of a total of 348,290 Zambian employees (Central Statistical Office 1982). The increase in number is impressive, but almost all these working women are in the lowest-paying and lowest-status jobs. For example, in 1977 only 5.3 percent of industrial employees were women (Zambia 1977). Women lag behind men because of their relative lack of education and industrial skills and because of the sociocultural factors that operate against them, in particular their unique domestic and familial responsibilities (Bardouille 1982; Hansen 1975, 1980).

Inequalities between the sexes exist in salary even when women have the same educational qualifications as men. Sanyal et al. state: "The mean salary of male university graduates was Kwacha 60 per month higher than that of female graduates" (1976:199).* In the category of professional and technical occupations, for example, the mean salary for males was ZMK 263.3, that for females ZMK 210.1, giving a mean difference of ZMK 53.2 (or 20.8 percent) in favor of males (see Sanyal et al. 1976:356). Therefore, although it is generally assumed that level of education determines salary, in fact sex appears to be an intervening variable.

* After July 1976, the exchange rate was ZMK (Zambian Kwacha) 1 = $1.25 U.S. However, the value of the Kwacha has continued to fall since then; on December 20, 1986, the rate was ZMK 12.50 = $1.00 U.S.

Although government policies concerning education and employment since independence have favored equality of opportunity for men and women (Hansen 1975; Pettman 1974), the data indicate that these egalitarian policies have not been effectively implemented (Zambia 1969:34). Women still do not enjoy equal access to and control of the valued resources on which personal status and power are based in modern urban society. As Hansen has pointed out, social and economic emancipation has affected only a small number of young and highly educated Zambian women. For the majority, status and security are still derived from marriage.

There is evidence that the United Nations' focus on women's developmental problems, reflected in the declaration of the United Nations Decade for Women (1975–85), has promoted awareness of women's issues on the part of governmental and nongovernmental agencies in the country. Increasingly, projects for women have been introduced and workshops concerning women organized. In addition, the post of National Coordinator of Women's Projects has been created at the National Commission for Development Planning. This appointment is said to have played an influential role in the decision to include a chapter on women in the Fourth National Development Plan. By contrast, both the first (1966–70) and the second (1972–76) plans made no mention of women's problems, while the third plan (1979–83) included a small section on women's clubs (Zambia Association for Research and Development 1985).

Inequalities between men and women's access to cash income make husbands the chief earners for their families in the majority of urban households, a factor that is likely to strengthen their position as allocators and controllers of money. A few cases have been reported where the wife controls the family income (Epstein 1981; Hansen 1975). But in general, the sexual division of labor that sends men to work and keeps women at home is radically different from the subsistence economic system in which husband and wife worked the fields as a team and their economic activities were complementary (Colson 1958; Richards 1939, 1940). In that type of society, both spouses enjoyed equal access to and control of economic resources.

An often-neglected influence on the allocation and control of earnings involves the demands of the extended family, which in Zambia, as in other developing countries, is still the main source of economic and social security for the majority of the population. Lack of financial cooperation may arise out of the conflict between a husband and wife's loyalties to each other on the one hand, and to their respective extended kin on the other. Women especially suffer from this conflict of loyalties, for a number of reasons. First, the majority of urban women are dependent on their husbands for economic support. Second, the predominance of the extended family system appears to influence attitudes against legislation on succession, in favor of men. Third, certain sociocultural factors undermine the wife's influence, such as the requirement that the wife defer to her husband in major family decisions, including those relating to the use of family economic resources. Finally, the traditional obligation of *lobola* has in urban conditions come to be interpreted in such a way that the husband "owns" his wife's earnings (Brandel 1958). The wife who earns money is expected to seek her husband's consent before disbursing some of her earnings to her extended family.

Employment Status and Form of Marriage

The survey data on which this paper is based were collected in 1982 and 1983 from 100 married couples in different socioeconomic categories and in different forms of marriage in Lusaka. Broadly speaking, the study was concerned with examining changing patterns in the distribution of power between husbands and wives in urban Zambia, assessing these in terms of financial relationships, family decision making, and division of labor within the home. Husbands and wives were interviewed separately for the purpose of assessing their perceptions about changing conjugal relationships.

The majority of the couples in the customary form of marriage reported wives' participation in informal trading. Nearly half of wives in customary marriages and none in ordinance marriages were unemployed (that is, not engaged in an income-generating activity in either the formal or the informal sector of the economy).

Only 21 of the 86 wives in customary marriages were formally employed. Their group included one manager, four Zambia Enrolled Nurses (Z.E.N.), four primary school teachers, two secretaries, two bank clerks, three machine operators, three typists, and two cleaners. Of the remaining 65 wives, 23 were self-employed in the informal sector, mainly selling foodstuffs (cooked or fresh) in or near their homes or in local markets where rental stalls are provided by the Lusaka District Council. Most of what these women earned was spent on food and other essentials for their families (Bardouille 1982, Hansen 1975). Forty-two wives earned no income at all.

All 14 wives in ordinance marriages were formally employed. Two were professionals in positions requiring postgraduate education, nine were senior administrators (seven with university degrees), one was a personal secretary, and two were typists. The majority of these women were in high-income groups because of their high levels of education, which suggests that their absolute financial contributions toward family maintenance were higher than those of the majority of income-generating customary wives.

A comparison between the sexes in terms of access to wage employment indicates that education does not automatically provide a means to wage employment for women. As Table 4 shows, although no husband with a Form 2 secondary-school education was unemployed, 17 wives with this level of schooling were unemployed. Indeed, marriage and the domestic and familial responsibilities associated with it may sometimes be obstacles to a woman's access to wage employment. For instance, 11 (or 26.2 percent) of the 42 unemployed wives stated that they were not working because their husbands would not allow them to do so, and a number suggested that their husbands disapproved of a wife working. Many respondents, particularly men in the customary form of marriage (who were also predominantly less educated), thought that working wives were difficult to control and that a wife's employment encouraged her to be unfaithful. One such husband (an administrator with a standard 6 education) said: "The idea of a wife working does not appeal to me. I would not like my wife to work." His views and attitude were confirmed by his wife (who had left school after grade 7) during a separate interview.*

Many respondents, mostly in customary marriages and particularly husbands, held the view that a wife should earn less money than her husband in order for him to be able to control her. Only two ordinance wives, both university graduates, agreed (one of them added, "reluctantly") that this would accord with the status of head of the family that society assigns to the husband. More men than women also agreed with the statement that a husband should have more education than his wife. It is generally believed that educated wives are arrogant to husbands (see also Powdermaker 1962:201).

A wife's income was regarded as supplementary to her husband's. Income tax policy treats a wife as economically dependent on or supported by her husband. This assumes that a wife's take-home pay is much lower than that of her husband. Unlike single working women, a working wife is not entitled to deduct a personal allowance before tax is calculated. The husband is not only entitled to a personal allowance, he also receives a family allowance. This policy helps weaken a wife's bargaining position in domestic budgeting for needs.

*Standard 6 represented the last primary school year during the colonial period. It was from this level that one qualified to go into the first year of junior secondary schooling, Form 1. The postindependence equivalent of standard 6 is grade 7, after which one qualifies to go into first year of junior secondary schooling, grade 8.

TABLE 4

Employment Status of Couples by Education Level

(Combined Sample)

Educational level	Total	Husbands				Wives			
		E	SEF	SEI	UNE	E	SEF	SEI	UNE
University	23	12	2	–	–	9	–	–	–
Form 6	1	1	–	–	–	–	–	–	–
Form 5	45	31	–	–	–	14	–	–	–
Form 2	43	12	–	2	–	10	–	2	17
Primary	67	30	–	1	1[a]	2	–	14	19
None	21	5	–	3	–	–	–	7	6
Total	200	91	2	6	1	35	–	23	42

NOTE: E = Employed; SEF = Self-employed (formal); SEI = Self-employed (informal); UNE = Unemployed.
[a] Retired.

Income Allocation

Four overall allocational systems were reported: doling out, allowance, separate spending, and pooling; see Table 5.* Husbands' answers to questions about allocation sometimes conflicted with those of their wives, as Table 5 indicates. However, some correspondence between allocation system and wives' income-earning is apparent.

Under the doling-out system, the husband keeps and controls all the money. He gives his wife small amounts that she requests for specific purchases. The wife has no personal spending money or access to the family income. Her movements outside the home, either to go shopping or to visit friends or relatives (where transportation has to be paid for) are thus strictly controlled by the husband through his control of the family purse. Husbands tend to argue that this arrangement is necessary because their wives are careless with money. For instance, one husband, a university graduate and senior civil servant, explained: "I keep all the money myself and give my wife when necessary. If you entrust money to a wife, you invite trouble." His wife, who had a Form 2 secondary-school education but was unemployed, indicated that she was unhappy with this arrangement. According to her, there was no proper arrangement in their household. These conflicting views suggest that this couple had a conjugal conflict that extended beyond income handling and control.

*My study did not obtain data on exact amounts of wives' contributions toward the family budget or relating to housekeeping allocations, because the majority of the study couples are unwilling to discuss the details of their financial arrangements. For more details see Munachonga 1986, Chapter 3.

TABLE 5

*Income Allocation System by Employment Status
of Couples*

Allocation system	Total couples	Wife unemployed	Wife employed
Doling out	11	10	1
Doling/Allowance[a]	8	8	–
Allowance	67	47	20[b]
Separate spending	5	–	5[c]
Separate/Allowance[a]	7	–	7[d]
Pooling	2	–	2[e]
Total	100	65	35

[a] Couple's answers conflicted.   [b] 3 ordinance couples.   [c] 4 ordinance couples.   [d] 5 ordinance couples.   [e] Both ordinance couples.

Many wives appear to be unhappy about their husbands' strict control of the finances. One unemployed wife who had a primary school education complained: "He keeps all the money and makes the budget every month." Wives appear to be unable to alter the arrangement. Table 5 suggests that husbands who were particularly authoritarian not only stopped their wives from going to work, but also exercised strict control of family income. In other words, authoritarianism of husbands tends to be associated with the doling-out system.

Under the allowance system, the husband gives his wife a fixed amount of money every month when he gets paid. He controls the remainder of the money. The wife, particularly if she is unemployed, has enough only for household expenditures, not for her personal use. Broadly speaking, each partner also has certain responsibilities regarding the spending of the main family income: the wife takes care of food purchases and the husband is in charge of major household needs such as furniture. For self-employed wives, most of their earnings go to supplement the fixed allowance.

As Table 5 indicates, this was the most common system. However, it was reported in only three of the 14 ordinance households. Wives generally complained that the fixed allowance was often inadequate. They also tended to be ignorant about how much money their husbands actually earned.* Some explained that they had a rough idea of how much their husbands earned, but that the husbands did not usually tell them when they received raises.

A comparison between working and nonworking wives indicates that

*This situation has been reported elsewhere in developed countries (such as Great Britain). See Young and Willmott (1957); Whitehead (1981).

the latter have particular problems stretching the allowance over the month. They also receive greater blame from their husbands if the money runs out before the next allowance. By contrast, working wives can supplement the allowance from their own earnings, and this is likely to reduce conflict over money. Yet they express more open dissatisfaction than nonworking wives about inadequate housekeeping allowances. One explanation might be that they receive reduced allowances. Another reason might be that an employed wife does not acquiesce to a husband's notion that it is not her business to know how much he actually earns or to complain about inadequate sums. Even wives in senior administrative positions complained about inadequate allowances. Two such wives, one a manager with a Form 5 secondary-school education, the other a university graduate and a senior administrator, indicated that their husbands would not give them extra money when the allowance ran out. These husbands might have expected their wives to contribute toward common needs since they were also in a higher-income group. A husband's decision to leave certain financial responsibilities to his wife may also be explained by the fact that in both customary and ordinance marriages his wife's income is technically his, if he has made the marriage payments to his wife's family (see also Brandel 1958).

Under the separate spending system, neither spouse has exclusive access to the family income. Husband and wife spend their respective earnings independently, sharing financial responsibility for certain items. This arrangement is more common among couples in ordinance marriages. It tends to be associated with high income levels, particularly for the wives.

In theory, separate spending seems to give a working wife, especially one in the higher-income group, a measure of economic independence. However, this depends partly on how much each partner earns, which favors men (Sanyal et al. 1976: 119), and partly on how financial responsibilities are shared. The sharing tends to be clearly defined in certain areas. A working wife buys her own clothes, and the husband, as owner of the matrimonial house, pays rent and electricity bills. The husband's traditional status is reinforced by urban housing policy that provides family accommodation through the husband's job; rent is deducted from his monthly salary and electricity bills are usually sent to him as the official occupant. (Under present housing policy, a wife can receive accommodation only if she is able to provide documentation proving that she is legally separated from her husband, or that her husband is unemployed.)

Separate spending tends to be characterized by suspicion and conflict between husband and wife, which is heightened by ignorance, particularly on the part of the wife, about actual earnings (income tax policy requires the husband to complete annual tax returns for both himself and his wife).

Shortages of essential commodities cause many people to buy items whenever they are available; duplication of items is thus another problem. In
one case involving university graduates, the wife indicated that they sometimes quarreled because of storage problems, particularly of fresh foodstuffs. Duplication may also suggest inadequate communication between
husband and wife.

Under the pooling system, husband and wife combine their earnings
into a common pool, usually a joint bank account. Both have responsibility
for managing the bank account and making withdrawals. Each thus has
access to and control over the other's earnings, although the extent of
control may be affected by the relative status of the sexes within marriage
and the patterns of authority within the home.

According to tradition, the husband is assigned more authority within
the home than the wife. In the two pooling households, both ordinance
marriages, the data indicate that the husband still has more power to make
major financial decisions. Thus, among the couples studied, pooling of
earnings did not necessarily imply equality of power in financial decision
making. Nonetheless, the responses indicate that this system gives wives
more satisfaction as partners, since they are involved in all cash transactions. Moreover, joint banking enables them to know how much money
their husbands earn.

Pooling seems to be the least advantageous system for the husband,
given the general emphasis on male control of money. However, pooling
may be motivated not only by the desire for access to a highly-educated
wife's income, which is likely to be substantial, but also by political considerations. Combining earnings may be perceived by a husband as a means
of ensuring control of an educated and potentially independent wife, since
it enables him to monitor her withdrawals of money. By contrast, wives
who controlled their earnings were in a better position to reserve some of
their earnings for relatives, as one working customary wife revealed during an interview. Positive reasons for pooling conjugal earnings were also
mentioned by both wives. For example, the pooling system made budgeting for immediate needs and planning major investments easy, and it also
made them feel united with their husbands.

Under the pooling system, couples indicated that they did shopping
jointly, but under the other systems financial responsibility for buying
food and children's clothing is not clearly defined. If the wife is employed,
most of her earnings are likely to be spent on these items, since they are
closely connected with her traditional role (see also Bardouille 1982;
Whitehead 1981). The traditional assignment of conjugal duties within
the home may thus provide an excuse for husbands of working wives not
to spend more than the normally accepted fixed allowance on these items.
This was suggested in the case of one working couple (both university

TABLE 6
Financial Contributions Toward Family Support by Form of Marriage

Item	Level of support	Customary (N = 172)		Ordinance (N = 28)	
		Husband	Wife	Husband	Wife
Wife's clothes	None	52	43	–	–
	Partial	33	39	9	9
	Full	–	4	5	5
Children's clothes	None	57	54	–	–
	Partial	28	28	14	12
	Full	–	4	–	2
Food	None	59	50	1	–
	Partial	24	30	13	13
	Full	3	6	–	1
Servants	None	18	22	2	2
	Partial	7	5	7	9
	Full	6	4	5	3
Transportation	None	64	57	2	3
	Partial	19	24	12	10
	Full	2	5	–	1
Electrical bills	None	67	72	8	9
	Partial	2	–	5	4
	Full	–	1	1	1
Rent	None	67	72	9	10
	Partial	2	–	4	3
	Full	–	1	1	1

NOTE: Not all items are applicable to every couple.

graduates, the wife holding a senior administrative position), where the wife complained that although her husband earned more than she did, he was reluctant to allocate extra money from his pay for food even when her usual allowance ran out. This, she claimed, forced her to spend more of her own earnings than the sum agreed upon as her monthly contribution toward the common budget. Financial conflicts in this household were highlighted when the wife explained that on a previous occasion she had refused to make her usual monthly contribution until her husband had made his, which, she said, he had not made during a month that she had been away from home. She made her contribution only after her husband had settled his "arrears." The general picture of financial contributions to household budgets is presented in Table 6.

Summary of Budgeting Arrangements

The existence of different systems of income allocation allows wives to be placed on a continuum representing degrees of male control of money

TABLE 7

*Types of Bank Accounts by Employment Status
of Couples*

(Combined Sample)

Type of account	Husband employed	Wife self-employed	Both employed
None	19	–	–
Separate	23[a]	23[b]	33[c]
Joint	–	–	2
Total	42	23	35

[a] Only husband held account.   [b] Only one self-employed wife (dressmaker)
also held account.   [c] 12 ordinance couples.

within the home. The wife's position depends on her own employment
status and level of income, the amount she receives for housekeeping, and
the way financial responsibilities are shared between husband and wife.
Doling out represents the most extreme form of male financial control; it
is often associated with the wife's unemployment and complete economic
dependence. These women had no information about men's income. By
contrast, pooling represents the most egalitarian form of financial management and control; it gives the wife the opportunity to participate in all
financial decision making. However, it is also the least common system. In
the majority of the income allocation systems, husbands control the family purse.

The data suggest that the wife's financial position relative to her husband does not improve radically when she is working. Her take-home pay
is reduced by the income tax system that does not give her a personal
allowance because it regards her as a dependent. The most frequent
allocation systems tend to operate in favor of the husband. The husband's
earnings also tend to be spent on major family projects (such as building a
house or buying a car) to which the wife has no rights in the event of her
husband's death.

The working wives in this study considered joint financial relationships
with their husbands to be ideal. In practice, however, they tended to argue
for separation of earnings. This was true despite the fact that the proportion of family income the wives actually controlled was less than that
controlled by their husbands. The common reason given for preferring
separation was the desire to avoid conflict between husband and wife, as
well as between the wife and her husband's extended kin, who also have
rights to the husband's economic support (see also Oppong 1974; Abu
1983).

In general, a wife's extended kin expect to receive financial help from her if she is working. Some husbands recognize their wives' obligations to extended kin. However, although a wife requires her husband's approval to give money to her relatives, a husband can help his kin without consulting his wife. Financial help to the husband's kin tends to be a major area of marital conflict. In the case of one ordinance couple (both university graduates), the wife indicated that she had decided not to interfere in her husband's dealings with his kin because he had "spoiled" his relatives by giving them the impression that they had a right to his money. It was argued, particularly by wives, that separate bank accounts (often used by separate-spending couples; see Table 7) give a woman a measure of security against her husband's relatives, who are widely reported to "grab" all of a man's money and household property after his death.*

Some husbands also have a favorable attitude toward separate bank accounts for the purpose of safeguarding their wives' financial interests. In one ordinance marriage of university graduates, the husband explained their solution: "We save separately so that my wife can always feel secure with her own money in case of my death, and to avoid the possibility of one feeling that the other partner is using his or her money, that is, that he or she is being exploited by the partner." His wife held a similar view. In the case of another ordinance couple, also university graduates, the husband emphasized: "I prefer my wife to have complete control of her own money. We once had problems running a joint bank account." Here the main reason was avoidance of conjugal conflict, although the wife added (in a separate interview) that she also wanted to avoid conflict with her husband's relatives, who did not like her.

In one customary couple (the husband a senior civil servant, the wife a bank clerk, both with Form 5 secondary-school educations), the husband explained that he and his wife had agreed to manage and save their earnings separately in the interest of the wife. Moreover, he added that each time either spouse bought a major household item, the couple called in relatives from both sides of the family in order to explain who had bought and therefore owned the item. Other husbands, however, appear to have been forced into this arrangement by their wives.

The practice of separation of earnings that is found especially among separate spending system couples contrasts with the ideal of the majority of couples, who favor joint property and joint savings accounts. Among the predominantly university-educated ordinance couples, 10 men and 11

---

*The "grabbing" of property by relatives has been strongly condemned by the president of the Republic of Zambia, Dr. K. D. Kaunda, for its adverse effects on the development of the nation as a whole. He has spearheaded the campaign for introducing legislation on succession. See *Zambia Information Services* (1983); *Sunday Times of Zambia* (October 24, 1982).

women approved of the idea of joint accounts and property, whereas only four men and three women disapproved. It seems that lack of legislation to protect a widow's rights as well as asset distribution to kin at a husband's death prevent the financial cooperation that urban Zambian men and women seem to desire.

Conclusion

The study's findings indicate links between gender inequalities in the wider society and inequalities within marriage. These tend to reinforce each other. For example, social and economic policies tend to be based on the assumption that an urban Zambian family is composed of a breadwinner husband and a dependent wife. Public attitudes toward domestic financial arrangements support the idea of male control of money, reflected in the predominance of the housekeeping allowance system of financial transfers.

The data also indicate a general tendency toward separate financial control in couples where the wife works, even when the couples concerned favor the idea of joint control. Separateness is explained partly by the predominant extended family ideology, which is buttressed by the national customary law regarding succession, and partly by the new ideology relating to ownership of wages, which favors the individual earner. The principles of the existing law of succession carry a wife's disadvantaged position during her husband's lifetime into the period after his death.

It is misleading to assume that these contemporary Zambian households, whatever their income-handling strategies, constitute single units in which husband and wife are in the same position structurally. My findings and those of previous researchers indicate that income is not equitably shared between spouses; generally speaking, the husband has support from the socioeconomic system at large while the wife does not. This also applies to rural households where women contribute most of the labor but do not benefit as much as their husbands from the marketing of agricultural surpluses (Colson 1958; ZARD 1985 : 113).* Money represents an important resource through which different forms of gender inequalities prevalent in the larger society are reinforced within marriage.

*ZARD is the Zambia Association for Research and Development. It is a nongovernmental organization concerned with furthering action-oriented research on women's issues.

The Constraints on and Release of Female Labor Power: Dominican Migration to the United States

PATRICIA R. PESSAR

Studies of migration have commonly focused on one of two extremes: macro-level trends in the political economies of host and recipient societies that stimulate migration (Portes 1978: Sassen-Koob 1980), and micro-level processes whereby individuals decide to relocate (Beijer 1969; Taylor 1969). In recent writings on migration, however, several authors have recommended the inclusion of the household as a basic unit of analysis, since it contributes to and mediates processes generated at the macro and micro levels (Wood 1981, 1982; Dinerman 1978; Bach and Schraml 1982; Pessar 1982a, 1982b). This paper on Dominican emigration to the United States adopts this expanded mode of analysis. It also aims, however, to correct those deficiencies in the household approach that threaten to contain and diminish its potential for increasing our understanding of migration.

In the social sciences generally there has been a tendency to channel investigations of the transformative role of history away from the household and toward larger sets of social relations, such as class or the world capitalist system. This orientation has left its mark on the study of migrant households; the act of migration is viewed as a collective strategy adjusting the unit to external changes in the productive system (Wood 1981, 1982; Roberts 1984). As in the larger body of literature on the household, the migrant household is portrayed as a "black box," with its structure and strategies purportedly determined by the maximization principles of supply and demand rooted in the larger capitalist economy.*

---

*Wallerstein and his colleagues (1979: 1) conceive of households as income-pooling units and believe that the function and morphology of these groups are determined by forces totally external to the household. These are alleged to be the maximization principles of supply and demand, rooted in the larger capitalist economy: "We are arguing that there are systematic pressures (from employers, state authorities, and other institutions) to create specific kinds of income-pooling households, in order to maximize the availablity on the one hand of a low-cost labor force and on the other hand of the continuing, relatively high short-run demand for commodities."

Meillasoux (1981) locates the origin of semiproletarian households in the economic exigencies of peripheral capital, which is able to extract surplus from its reserve army of labor by ensuring that some members remain in the rural peripheries. They engage in

To breathe life and observed experience into the analysis of migrant households, we must reintroduce the complexity of activities and social relations, which are guided by norms of gender and seniority. In doing so we may provide one important corrective to both migration and household analyses. The prevailing neoclassical conception of the household as a social group acting *collectively* to sponsor a member's migration may then be modulated through an exploration of the struggles and contradictions within the household—and, more specifically, between certain of its members and the larger political economy—that lead to the release of *selected* household members. Furthermore, by investigating evolving social relations within the household we are better posed to reexamine neofunctionalist assumptions and conclusions concerning the alleged "systems maintenance function" of domestic group action (Wood 1981; Meillassoux 1981; Coulson, Magas, and Wainwright 1975; Fox 1980). In particular, this paper analyzes the origins of Dominican immigrant women's resistance to patriarchal domestic relations. This paper also considers how the conflict and negotiation at the household level lead to a new domestic organization that less adequately fulfills the needs of capital.*

The Household

The household is the primary and basic unit oriented to the daily maintenance and reproduction of the members of a society. The activities in which it specializes are reproduction, production, distribution, consumption, and socialization. Contrary to the neoclassical view of the con-

noncapitalist relations of production to subsidize the low wages paid to proletarianized members, as well as socially reproduce a new generation that must periodically sell its labor. Social scientists who seek to explain the persistence of the working-class household in advanced industrial societies, and the resistance of this class to the proletarianization of women and children, also point to the needs of capital. They emphasize the changing requirements of advanced industrial capital for quality labor, the lack of substitutes for use-values produced in the home, and the association between the continued support of traditional family structures and political stability (Coulson, Magas, and Wainwright 1975; Fox 1980).

*The data and analysis found in this paper are by-products of three years of ethnographic fieldwork (1980–83) conducted in rural sending communities in the Cibao region of the Dominican Republic, in returned migrant neighborhoods in the city of Santiago, and in Dominican neighborhoods in the New York metropolitan area. The study was funded by the National Institutes of Health, the National Science Foundation, and New York University's New York Research program in Inter-American Affairs. Many of the data were collected by my research assistants, Catherine Benamou, Nancy Clark, Anneris Goris, and Julia Tavares. I would like to thank them for their help, and to acknowledge as well the continuing intellectual and personal support I have received from my research collaborator, Sherri Grasmuck, and from the staff and visiting scholars at New York University's Center for Latin American and Caribbean Studies.

sensual household, or its rendering as a "black box," we find that it is an arena of social relations organized along generational, gender, and kinship lines. These relations generate and are reinforced by a structure of power, ideological meanings, and sentiment (Schneider 1980; Rapp 1978; Ross and Rapp 1981). They contribute, as well, to hierarchy and inequity within the domestic unit (Hartmann 1981; Barrett 1980). Out of this may emerge conflict and struggle among members to control and change the lines and terms of power and authority over decision making, the division of labor, and household resources.

While the household maintains its own internal system of social relations and legitimating ideology, it also contains mechanisms for linkage with the outside ecological and political-economic systems. Minor alterations in productive strategies and patterns of distribution and consumption take place during changes in the agricultural cycle (Chayanov 1966; Deere and de Janvry 1979) or at times of recession and high unemployment (Jelin 1982). Major transitions such as those accompanying a modification in the dominant mode of production necessitate more radical changes on the part of households (Tilly and Scott 1978; Sacks 1979; Young 1978). Finally, the exchange between the household and the larger system may in turn activate large-scale transformations in the internal relationships of the household.

How these extra- and intrahousehold processes lead to and are affected by migration are the subject of this paper. I first explore why and how Dominican middle-class women, who with the advent of capitalism were often removed from productive activities, have championed labor migration to the United States. I then examine the struggle of these immigrant women to modify the terms of household authority. They have endeavored to substitute more egalitarian domestic relations for traditional, patriarchal ones, and have developed strategies to prolong the household's stay in the United States to sustain these gains. Long-term settlement in the United States, as we shall see, often conflicts with the interests of the woman's husband and employer. Before proceeding with this analysis, I will briefly describe the characteristics of the Dominican migrant stream.

The Dominican Migrant Stream

According to the 1980 census, 169,100 persons of Dominican birth were residing in the United States, with 127,700 of them (76 percent) living in the New York metropolitan area. These figures are considered undercounts by the New York City and state officials who filed a suit in 1980 against the Bureau of the Census. The numbers also diverge widely from the figure of approximately 500,000 frequently cited in scholarly works (Bray 1984; Georges 1984; Pessar 1982a).

Contrary to conventional wisdom as well as to early ethnographic accounts of Dominican emigration (Hendricks 1974; González 1970, 1976), the immigrant population is neither predominantly rural nor from the ranks of the chronically unemployed or underemployed. According to the *Diagnos* national survey conducted in 1974 in the Dominican Republic (cf. Ugalde, Bean, and Cardenas 1979) and the Hispanic Settlement in New York City Survey conducted in 1981 among Dominicans in Queens and northern Manhattan (cf. Gurak and Kritz 1982), the migrant stream is predominantly urban and middle-class. The *Diagnos* survey found that about a quarter of the migrants were from rural areas, and more than half the urban migrants were middle-class. While this survey did not provide information on class differences among the rural population, research conducted in the Dominican Republic and the United States documents that most migrants from rural areas come from fairly prosperous households. These are large and middle-sized land owning households that engage in capitalist and petty commodity production (see Grasmuck 1982; Bray 1984; Pessar 1982a, 1982b).

The 1981 probability survey, based on interviews with 560 Dominicans in New York, gives data on other characteristics of the immigrants. It is worth describing the findings in some detail, for they provide a useful picture of the New York Dominican population. Women migrants outnumbered men, with females constituting 60.4 percent of the immigrant population surveyed. The average age at arrival for women was 22.2 years and the median level of education was 8.0 years. The majority of the women (53 percent) were married; 12 percent had never been married, and 35 percent were divorced or separated. While only 31 percent of the women had been employed prior to emigration, 91.5 percent had worked for pay at some time since moving to the United States. In fact, at the time of the survey, half were in the labor force (employed or seeking employment). The mean income in 1981 for female migrants was $6,884, compared to $9,430 for males.

As for men, the 1981 survey showed that their average age at arrival was 22, and the median level of education was 9.4 years; 65 percent were married, 23 percent had never been married, and 12 percent were divorced or separated. The majority of the men (64 percent) had been employed prior to migration; 91.3 percent had worked for wages at some time during their residence in the United States, and 87.6 percent were in the labor force when interviewed.

The median income for Dominican immigrant households surveyed in 1981 was $11,800. The nuclear household was the most common type (48 percent), but female-headed units accounted for 37 percent of the households. During 1980–81, 55.7 percent of the Dominican women were

TABLE 1

Employment Patterns of Dominicans in New York

Occupation	Males		Females	
	No.	Pct.	No.	Pct.
No occupation	33	14.8%	162	48.1%
Professional workers	11	4.9%	11	3.3%
Managers, proprietors, officials	14	6.3%	3	0.9%
Clerical workers	11	4.9%	15	4.5%
Sales workers	10	4.5%	4	1.2%
Domestic services	0		15	4.5%
Other service workers	39	17.5%	12	3.6%
Farmers, farm laborers, miners, etc.	0		1	0.3%
Skilled, blue-collar, or craft workers	14	6.3%	4	1.2%
Semi-skilled operatives	68	30.5%	81	24.0%
Unskilled non-farm laborers	23	10.3%	27	8.0%
Unknown	0		2	0.6%
Total	223		337	

SOURCE: The Hispanic Settlement in New York City Survey 1981.

TABLE 2

Last Job Held by Immigrants Prior To Migration

Occupation	Males		Females	
	No.	Pct.	No.	Pct.
No occupation	53	23.8%	198	58.8%
Professional workers	20	9.0%	29	8.6%
Managers, proprietors, officials	12	5.4%	8	2.4%
Clerical workers	24	10.8%	28	8.3%
Sales workers	12	5.4%	5	1.5%
Domestic services	0		9	2.7%
Other service workers	24	10.8%	5	1.5%
Farmers, farm laborers, miners, etc.	14	6.3%	0	
Skilled, blue-collar, or craft workers	17	7.6%	3	0.9%
Semiskilled operatives	30	13.5%	32	9.5%
Unskilled nonfarm laborers	5	2.2%	9	2.7%
Unknown	12	5.4%	11	3.3%
Total	223		337	

SOURCE: The Hispanic Settlement in New York City Survey, 1981.

receiving or had received some form of public assistance (Gurak and Kritz 1982).

Table 1 indicates that most Dominican men and women in the work force were semi-skilled operatives, service workers, and unskilled non-farm laborers. When we compare the occupational distribution of these Dominican men and women prior to emigration, shown in Table 2, we see that this population has experienced the downward mobility in occupational status that normally accompanies each new wave of large-scale immigration.* This status decline is differentially experienced and managed by men and women, however. These differences will be addressed later in the paper.

Household and Gender Approaches to Emigration

In his cogent critique of neoclassical theories of migration, Guy Standing (1981) argues that labor migration is not a "natural" condition that is freely available to the individual as one of an array of productive options. Rather, it emerges as an alternative after historical transformations have produced the conditions and demand for a "free" work force that is obliged to sell its labor power. The writings on migration have, however, stopped here. An additional step must be taken. We must examine how these historical transformations in the organization of production interact with the organization of domestic activities to release the labor power of some household members and to constrain or prohibit the productive activities of others.

Emigration from Agricultural Communities

Agricultural reform and development have never been given high priority in the Dominican Republic. This can be traced in part to the efforts of the largest landowners (*latifundistas*), who possess large quantities of land that are extremely unproductive. This traditional elite has encouraged a succession of governments to avoid agrarian reform and large-scale investment in agriculture (Cedeño 1975). Those groups that have sought agricultural development have also had to compete for favors and funds with representatives of the more dynamic sector of Dominican society, such as the commercial and industrial elite.

Extreme inequality in land distribution and low productivity characterize the agricultural sector. In 1971, 2.3 percent of all private landholdings occupied 57.2 percent of the nation's land surface. On the other hand,

---

*When comparing the pre- and post-migration employment of the majority of Dominican men and women in the United States (see Tables 1 and 2), we note an objective decline in professional, managerial, clerical, and skilled positions and a marked increase in unskilled jobs in the service and manufacturing sectors. For men and women employment in the former sectors declined by approximately 10 percent, from 32.8 percent to 22.4 percent in the case of men, and from 20 percent to 10.9 percent for women. While in the Dominican Republic only 10.8 percent of the men were classified as "other service workers," the numbers rose to 17.5 percent in the United States, and employment as semiskilled operatives increased from 13.5 percent to 30.5 percent. For women the comparable figures are 1.5 percent versus 3.6 percent and 9.5 percent versus 24.0 percent.

77.1 percent of the total landholdings were small parcels of five hectares or less, and they occupied only 13 percent of the cultivated land surface (Oficina Nacional de Estadistica 1971). Owing to the low level of capitalization and modernization, the agricultural sector contributed only 20.8 percent to the 1973 gross national product. The annual growth of the agricultural GNP during the period 1966–74 was 5.1 percent, compared to an 11.2 percent rate for the entire economy during that period (Dore y Cabral 1979: 19–20).

It is not, however, solely the unproductive nature of agriculture that has promoted emigration. The release of labor power from middle and upper petty commodity–producing households was predicated on earlier historical changes in agricultural communities that emerged with the development of commercial agriculture. Through mechanisms such as land surveys that converted communal land into private property, a landless and smallholding stratum emerged that was obliged to sell its labor power. The discharge of household labor for international migration may be traced to contradictions within landholding families, most particularly between the interests of the senior and junior generations. The former experienced a conflict between the traditional mode of distributing land to junior members on their marriage in exchange for continued access to their unremunerated labor, on the one hand, and the opportunities for capital accumulation if household lands remained undivided and exploited by wage labor, on the other. The sponsoring of junior members' migration to Dominican cities or to the United States was a way in which this contradiction was resolved.*

Another feature of the organization of domestic activities that promoted migration is the custom of dividing the family land among all legitimate heirs, regardless of gender. This inheritance practice has led to fragmentation and overexploitation of the land. In most cases, owners of middle-sized holdings did not have the capital to invest in fertilizers and technology to improve productivity. Many faced downward mobility should they be unable to afford agricultural laborers on a regular basis and thus be forced to rely solely on their own labor. Under these conditions they might even be reduced to occasionally selling their own or their children's labor to meet basic household expenses. Emigration was often viewed as a way to accumulate funds to improve the land and purchase additional holdings. Emigration was also pursued to maintain the family's status in the community. This was accomplished by maintaining the basic integrity of the family holding by ceding usufruct rights to the undivided land to the few siblings who remained behind.

*For further discussion of this phenomenon, see Pessar 1982a, 1982b.

The productive role of women shifted in response to these developments. In the economically secure households, women were often withdrawn from agricultural production. This was done both because their agricultural tasks could be assumed by men and women of poorer households who were obligated to sell their labor power, and because of the ideological value associated with having female members "freed" from agriculture.* But while the household as a social unit may have benefited in prestige from this reallocation of female labor, the relative autonomy of its female members was reduced and patriarchal relations were intensified. Moreover, as we shall see below, the value of focusing women's labor on nonagricultural household work was fleeting for many domestic units.

Prior to male emigration, the allocation of female labor to reproduction, socialization, and household maintenance did not adversely affect the unit's economic viability, and it did increase its prestige. However, once male household members began to emigrate, the practice of withdrawing women from agricultural production became problematic. With the migration of their most productive members to the United States (generally husbands and unmarried sons), many households with medium-sized holdings faced a household labor scarcity. While the replacement of household labor with salaried workers would have been one solution, it was often uneconomical because of its relatively high cost in relation to the low productivity of the land and the unreliability of the market. The sexual division of labor that discouraged women's participation in most phases of agricultural production, in combination with an ideological bias against wives and daughters of the economically secure strata working outside the home and particularly in the fields, aggravated the labor shortage.† In those cases in which cost was not a major concern, a factor inhibiting the hiring of labor was the absence of the male household head and his reluctance to leave full administrative responsibilities to his wife.

Rural migrant households thus gradually lost their capacity to produce use-values, and they contributed little cash to the total household income through the sale of agricultural products. In many cases the remaining household members were dependents rather than contributors to the total budget. Rather than augmenting the remittances sent by wage earners in

---

*In socioeconomically stratified societies where there are few material resources available to higher-status households with which to communicate publicly their differences from other domestic groups, the removal of women from spheres of income generation serves as a status marker (Smale 1980).

†The Dominican bourgeoisie attempted to emulate the Spanish aristocratic norm whereby "ladies did not soil their delicate fingers" (Tancer 1973:224).

the United States, women and children depleted the wage income.* The contradiction for household budgeting posed by the woman's removal from income-generating activities was often resolved with her recruitment to the United States by household members currently residing abroad. There she was asked "to capture her opportunity costs" more fully by shouldering the double burden of housework and work outside the home.†

Emigration from Urban Communities

The emigration of men and women from middle-class urban households must be examined in the context of how this social class has been thwarted in its attempts to sustain itself and prosper in the Dominican Republic. Two key development policies introduced in the 1960s—import substitution and export-led industrialization—have proved detrimental to the advancement of this group. Let us briefly review how these two strategies limited the options for the newly emerging and expanding Dominican middle class.

Import substitution wreaked havoc on the balance of payments while failing to create many new jobs and to diversify local manufacturing. Furthermore, this capital-intensive and redundant manufacturing growth generated little in the way of multiplier effects throughout the Dominican economy. Some middle-sector jobs were created in financial, supervisory, clerical, and sales positions. Nonetheless, the limitations of the internal market and lack of multiplier effects limited employment expansion for the majority of the middle sector (Bray 1984).

The second development policy, export-led strategies based on free trade zones, was conceived as an alternative means of industrialization to

---

*This description of the role of women in the rural Dominican migrant household is very different from the model of the semiproletarian migrant household Meillassoux (1981) has developed for African societies and others have applied indiscriminately to labor migration in general. In rural Dominican sending communities, a fully proletarianized household was often a consequence of the practice whereby the sexual division of labor came to symbolize the status of more prosperous households. That is, migrant households changed from units whose income was derived from multiple sources—profits realized from the sale of crops raised by wage or household labor, from rent of land which was paid in cash or in kind, and from the budgetary savings realized from the production of food crops for home consumption—to proletarian structures whose members purchased commodities with the remittances derived from migrant member's wages.

†In contrast to labor migration in Africa, female migration to the United States has been aided by the legal policy of family unification and by an economic demand for cheap, vulnerable, female labor in secondary-sector industries such as the garment and electronics industries.

overcome the limitations of a small internal market and to avoid the difficult issue of redistribution of income to expand the internal market. The three free trade zones provided no significant economic opportunities for the middle sectors. For example, they offered little in the way of managerial positions. Inasmuch as the zones provided low-paying, extremely insecure jobs, their work force had little extra income to employ legal, medical, and other services from middle-class professionals. As consumers in the informal economy, the work force also did not channel much income to middle-class merchants. As with import substitution, free trade zones provided little in the way of multiplier effects for the Dominican middle class (*ibid.*).

An additional factor must be added to this discussion. While the unemployed did not generally fill the ranks of the Dominican emigrants, their role in migration should not be underestimated. According to the International Labor Office (1975), over 1 in 3 of the active Dominican population was unemployed or underemployed in 1973. The expanding reserve army of unemployed represented a threat to the lower-middle class. For this most insecure segment of the middle class, this labor reserve exerted downward pressures on wages, discouraged collective action in the workplace, and represented an ever-present threat of replacement by cheaper, more docile workers.

Ethnographic research I have conducted in the Dominican Republic and the United States revealed that migration was stimulated by the real, yet circumscribed success of the newly emerged middle class. The goal of the emigrants was to amass savings in the United States. With these savings, the migrants hoped to return to the Dominican Republic and invest in a business that would buttress their middle-class standing.

The physical and symbolic relegation of middle-class women to the household made them special targets for the ideology of consumerism and upward mobility via education that was transmitted by radio and television.* However, in the late 1960's and throughout the 1970's, middle-class women were receiving and administering a household allowance that was increasingly inadequate to meet the unit's consumption needs at a time when consumerism and educational expectations for children greatly expanded. For example, the cost of living rose by 17.0 percent in 1973 and 1974 and by 21.3 percent in 1975 (Guiliano Cury 1980:250). Meanwhile, between 1969 and 1978, real wages dropped from $80 to $54 per month (NACLA 1982:9).

While the majority of previously unemployed immigrant women from

---

*In 1966 there were 36 Dominican radio stations and 2 television stations; in 1976 this number had increased to 105 and 5 respectively (Urena and Ferreiras 1980).

urban backgrounds whom I interviewed in the United States indicated a willingness and desire to work, they had had difficulty locating jobs in the Dominican Republic to augment the household budget. Almost 60 percent of the jobs potentially available to urban middle-class women would have been, in their words, "socially inappropriate." A 1978 survey of female labor-force participation in the cities of Santo Domingo and Santiago, for example, found that domestic servant was the most frequent job last held by women aged 25–30 (34.2 percent of the respondents). The service professions accounted for 11.3 percent of female employment, and 13.8 percent of the women worked as factory operatives (Gurak et al. 1980:13). Neither the urban middle-class women nor their husbands who eventually migrated would have entertained the loss of prestige associated with a wife's employment in such low-paying and low-status jobs. On the other hand, the survey showed that 6.7 percent of the female respondents were employed in the professional/managerial sector, 11.9 percent were educators, and 17.6 percent were clerical workers (*ibid.*). My interviews show that while many women would have liked to have been employed in these occupations, most did not have the necessary education and training. The average education for female immigrants, it will be remembered, is eight years, and this figure is inflated because a substantial number of women arrived as children and thus received most of their education in the United States.

Migration provided a working solution to the inability of middle-class women to find an appropriate means of contributing income to their households. Armed with the knowledge that there were well-paying jobs for women in the United States, women were sometimes the first to emigrate, leaving behind their employed husbands until they could arrange for the migration of other family members. In other cases, women were active agents in promoting a husband's or single adult child's emigration, the plan being that this person would assist the household with remittances and also sponsor other members' migration.

In both rural and urban middle-strata households, the relegation of women to reproduction and socialization activities and their removal from income generation proved detrimental to the household's ability to meet its consumption needs. There is, however, one important difference in the way this relative surplus in female labor was perceived and hence experienced by rural and urban households. In most urban households this awareness emerged before the emigration of male household members. The level of involvement of these two types of households in the wage economy is likely to account for this difference. It is my speculation that the universalistic values of a wage economy had sufficiently permeated middle-strata urban households to incline women to reflect on the consequences of their nonemployment for the domestic unit. Women from rural middle-strata households, on the other hand, remained less exposed to new ideas about the appropriateness of "modern women" working for wages and were more responsive to the traditional notions of male and female roles. This variation may be an important factor underlying the large number of female Dominican immigrants of urban origin currently residing in the United States. Urban women directly experienced their role as relative surplus labor. For rural women this recognition emerged more indirectly, through men's absence after migration. As such, the former were more likely to instigate action to ameliorate their situations, while the latter awaited the impetus and financial assistance from male emigrants.

Female and Male Migrants: Contrasting Experiences and Strategies in Migrant Households

A consideration of household and gender relations is not only frequently absent from studies of emigration; it is also lacking in analyses of the migration settlement process. This shortcoming is evidenced in Michael Piore's important and influential thesis (1979) concerning the socioeconomic incorporation of immigrants into advanced industrial societies. As we shall see, Piore's gender-free model of immigrant settlement is inadequate to account for the contrasting orientations of men and women to return migration.

Piore's model of migration is based on a two-step process in which neither household nor gender plays a role. He raises two central questions: Why is the migrant at first so well suited to the role he or she is assigned in the economy of the receiving society? And why does the migrant population begin to lose its "special" status and adopt orientations toward work that are congruent with the native-born working class?

According to Piore, the answer to the first question is based on the fact that the migrant arrives as a pure economic maximizer. He or she is willing to accept any job, no matter how demeaning, because the temporary character of the immigrant's stay creates a sharp dichotomy between work and social identity. Social identity remains untouched by the work experience and is said to be rooted in the place of origin: "Work performed in the receiving society is purely instrumental: a means to gather income, income that can be taken back to his or her home community and used to fulfill or enhance his or her role within that social structure. From the perspective of the immigrant, work is essentially asocial" (1979:54).

His answer to the second query is that, because of the general instability of the jobs in which the migrant is employed, he or she is unable to accumulate sufficient savings to return after a short time, as initially intended. As the migrant's stay gets longer, social attachments develop and demands are made on the individual from within the migrant community. In keeping with this argument, Piore advises that in the second phase, "migration and settlement must be understood as processes relating to communities rather than individuals" (*ibid.* : 75).

Piore's heading for his discussion of the first stage of the migration process, "the migrant as economic man," takes more liberties than the generic *man* implies. The economist's central premise about the asocial nature of work may be applicable for many Dominican males; it is, however, totally inappropriate for Dominican women. It is my belief that for migrants from Latin America and the Caribbean, the stage of temporary orientation to work and settlement is much shorter-lived for women than for men. I base this contention on the fact that work for women in the United States is eminently social right from the beginning.

The assertion that temporary migrants dichotomize themselves into social beings on the one hand and workers on the other is contradicted by the very real negotiations over the sexual division of labor within the household and gender ideology, negotiations that are promoted because the home and the workplace are not dichotomized by Dominican women. These negotiations within immigrant households have resulted in a movement away from patriarchal relations and values toward greater egalitarianism. Changes have taken place in budgetary control, in beliefs about household authority, and in the allocation of housework (see Pessar 1985).*

*Data for the analysis of gender differences in the migration process come from fieldwork conducted in the United States and the Dominican Republic. The generalizations that are made about experiences in the United States are based on structured interviews and casual conversations with several hundred Dominican immigrants as well as participant observation in households, workplaces, and social gatherings. There are clearly problems inherent in generalizing about such a large population when people are not chosen on some sort of random basis to ensure a representative sample. Particularly in the New York phase of the study, a process of self-selection operated on the basis of people's willingness to participate over time in a series of visits and interviews, often in their homes.

Two principal groups form the basis for much of the data and analysis presented below: members of 55 households who provided information over a year's period (1981–82) on topics such as social networks, decision making, income generation, control over budgeting, and beliefs about sex roles; and 25 garment workers who were queried about their role as workers. These informants were obtained through various means. They include previous contact with the individual or family members and friends in the Dominican Republic, and introductions by community leaders in the United States, such as clergy, leaders of associations, and school officials. In the case of undocumented immigrants and people who were involved in illegal economic activities, sustained contact was possible when an assistant or myself was either personally known or had gained the deep trust of a close family member or friend. Finally, to explore the veracity and significance of patterns in beliefs and behavior that emerged in interviews and participant observation, key informants were relied on extensively.

Gender becomes an important variable in accounting for Piore's second phase of the migration process. Women's gains in the three areas mentioned above incline them to develop strategies that prolong the household's stay in the United States. Women realize that if they return to the Dominican Republic they will most likely lose the gains employment and residence in the United States have promoted. Women fear they will end up cloistered at home, since the sexual division of labor in the Dominican economy militates against productive employment for women of their training and class background.

Income Allocation and Generation

Three dominant modes of budgetary control characterize Dominican households. I term the first mode traditional or patriarchal; the second, household allowance; and the third, pooled income. The first occurs when members give all or part of their wages to a senior male member who is empowered to decide on income allocation and to oversee the payment of household expenditures. If there are savings, the account bears only the man's name. The household allowance mode operates when a senior woman is given funds and responsibility for basic expenditures such as food and clothing and the daily maintenance of the domestic group. Her authority over decision making and the management of income allocation exists only in this sphere. The senior male is the principal decision maker for long-term and costly expenditures, and he has greater freedom to direct household income to personal items of consumption, such as entertainment. In the pooled income mode, all income-generating members donate a specific amount of their wages or profits to fixed household expenses, such as food, rent, electricity, and gas. Meeting the daily needs of the unit becomes a collective task entailing more or less equivalent contributions and greater shared responsibility for activities such as shopping and paying bills.

There is a material underpinning for these three modes. The first two are associated with male ownership of the means of production or with unequal access to capitalist relations of production based on gender discrimination. For example, my own research, as well as other studies of rural communities, found a pairing of subsistence agriculture and petty commodity farming with the traditional patriarchal and household allowance forms of income control (Pessar 1982b; Brown 1972). Both productive forms commonly encompass virilocal residence with family members working under the authority of the male on land he has inherited or to which he has been granted usufruct rights.

A patriarchal ideology accompanies these productive relations. For example, in a study of 480 rural households representing nine communities located in different regions of the Dominican Republic, 90.4 percent of the women interviewed responded affirmatively to the question, "Do you consider having a husband to be advantageous?" The most frequent reason cited (42.2 percent) was to "have someone to maintain us" (Instituto Dominicano de Estudios Aplicados 1978:30). In cities, where employment is more readily available to women, the nature of the jobs for which they are recruited and the low wage structure similarly reinforce women's dependence on men. This is confirmed by a study of complaints filed between January 1978 and December 1980 by over one thousand women in the Office of Women and Minors of the Secretary of Labor. More than 70 percent of the claimants were paid below the minimum legal salary of 150 pesos per month, and of this group, approximately 78 percent earned less than 100 pesos (Coordinadora de Organizaciones Femeninas n.d.). What emerges is the norm that the man's income should sustain the household economically, while women's monetary contributions "help" the male breadwinner.

The pooled income mode is often a byproduct of restricted access to the means of production by all household members regardless of gender. The material base that permits men to establish and help maintain a nuclear family is lacking. Men often join mothers and sisters in contributing income, goods, and services to reproduce socially the members of their natal households. Men also direct resources to other domestic units to which they are allied through friendship, sexual relations, and paternity. The core of these income-pooling households is a mother-child dyad often linked intergenerationally to other such matrifocal pairs (Ferrán 1974; Brown 1972).

The material basis of income pooling among Dominican households in the United States is quite different and marks one of the profound changes associated with emigration. Rather than being associated with an insecure income base and a matrifocal household, the pooled income mode is found most frequently among nuclear units in which both partners work for wages. The causes and consequences of this transition, which is shown in Table 3, are described below.

TABLE 3

Dominant Mode of Budgetary Control in Dominican Households Before and After Emigration

Mode of budgetary control	Before emigration	After emigration
Traditional patriarchal	10	2
Household allowance	28	15
Pooled income	17	38

Of the 17 pooled-income households prior to migration, 15 were matrifocal. In 16 of the 38 households where men controlled the household
revenue, women, either as wives or as daughters, contributed income on a
regular or semiregular basis. Among the units characterized by the household allowance mode, women's income was most commonly directed
toward household, rather than personal, items of consumption. Women
tended to specialize in luxury items rather than staples. Both objectively
and symbolically, the direction of women's savings to nonessential prestige
items reinforced the image of the man as the breadwinner and the woman,
at best, as the bestower of modern status goods, and at worst, as the
purchaser of *tonterias* (frivolities).

As the figures indicate, there was a profound change in budgetary
allocation for Dominican households after migration to the United States.
Of the 38 households that pooled their income, 20 were nuclear and 18
were female-headed (owing either to the absence of a senior male or to his
irregular and limited financial contributions as measured against those of
the senior woman).

The predominance of income pooling within nuclear households
brings women advantages unknown in the three premigration patterns.
First, responsibility for meeting the basic reproduction costs of the domestic group are distributed among members regardless of gender, thus miti-
gating the invidious comparisons between "essential" male contributions
and "supplementary" female inputs. Second, according to informants,
men's greater participation in decision making and strategies for stretching the household budget and managing irregularities in income flow has
led them to appreciate more fully the experience and skills women bring
to this task.

How have women managed to gain greater respect for and control over
the fruits of their labor? Conversations with women, as well as observations of conflict between partners, reveal that the elevation of equity in
budgetary control to a right evolved within the symbolic and behavioral
domain of the household head.

For most Dominicans the status of household head is equated with the
concept of defending the household. This defense is conceived of in largely
material terms. As women demonstrate their capacity to share material
responsibility with men on more or less equal terms, they begin to expect
to be copartners in heading the household. Thus, in response to my
questions, Who is the household head now? and, Who was the head
previous to your emigration?, many echoed the words of this woman:
"We both are the heads. If both husband and wife are earning salaries then
they should equally rule in the household. In the Dominican Republic it is
always the husband who gives the orders in the household [*manda lo de la*

casa]. But here when the two are working, the woman feels herself the equal of the man in ruling the home [*se siente capacitada de mandar igual al hombre*]." Interviews revealed that when problems emerge in general, over joint access to the status of household head and more particularly over household budgeting, they reflect the traditional gender hierarchy that emphasizes the man's role as the provider and the relegation of the woman to the "nonproductive" domestic sphere. Of the 55 women in my household sample, 18 were divorced or separated while in the United States. Fourteen cited the struggle over domestic authority as a primary factor leading to the dissolution of the union. Three scenarios proved particulary disruptive. What unites them is a male perception (and in the first two instances, subsequent action reinforcing this belief) that the woman has entered alone into domains of income allocation that should be the sole responsibility of men, or at least should be shared.

In several cases difficulties arose when the woman lived and worked in the United States before sponsoring her mate's migration. The man was apparently unsettled by what he viewed as an inversion of gender roles. Informants described instances in which the husband attempted to take advantage of his wife's initially more secure economic position by insisting that she contribute disproportionately to the major fixed expenses, such as food and housing. The breaking point for several women came when the man behaved as if the patriarchal or household allowance mode was operative. That is, he monopolized his salary for personal expenses, such as entertainment. One woman expressed her frustration with an acknowledgement of the distortions in gender roles that her husband's behavior provoked: "How can I express how strange it all was? Sure, I suspected that he was spending *our* money on other women. This happened before in the Dominican Republic, and there I was angry but accepted it as 'men will be men.' However, here it was different. How can I put it? . . . I felt like I was a man being cuckolded, as well as a woman being shamed. . . . We fought all the time . . . finally I put his things outside the door, and it was over."

In two cases marital difficulties leading ultimately to divorce arose when the women received welfare payments while living with their partners. According to several Dominican informants and community workers who counsel such couples, the man often feels that his principal role as provider has been usurped by the woman and a more powerful patron, the state. The perception that the woman has somehow compromised his responsibility as household head may cause the man to redefine altogether his relationship to the domestic unit. As one informant expressed it: "Instead of viewing their expenses as joint expenses and their income as a common fund, the man will see the welfare money as belonging to the woman alone, and he will insist that she apply it to rent, food, etc. On the other hand, he will hoard his own salary and this causes marital problems, sometimes leading to separation and divorce."

A frequent source of discord between spouses that sometimes ends in separation and divorce is the woman's insistence that part of the pooled household income be used to purchase expensive durable goods, such as new appliances and home furnishings, rather than deposited in a joint savings account. The origin of this conflict can be attributed in part to the woman's greater identification with the household and her desire to have it graphically represent the struggles of all members to acquire a middle-class life-style. There is, however, another fundamental issue operating, and it is captured in the man's often-repeated refrain, "Five dollars wasted today means five more years of postponement of the return to the Dominican Republic." This quotation embodies, in my opinion, the most significant unintended outcome of female migration and wage work. Most employed, married women I interviewed sought to postpone the family's return to the Dominican Republic. A common strategy is to spend more money to root the family securely and comfortably in the United States and to deplete the collective fund needed to relocate. The woman fears that she will lose her newly acquired gains as wife, mother, and wage worker when she returns to the more traditional Dominican society, where "suitable" employment for middle-class women of limited education is scarce.

Households' Orientations to Return Migration and Implications of Prolonged Settlement

In order to determine the conditions that promote permanent or semi-permanent settlement, it is necessary to explore again household composition and organization. Two major household forms exist in the Dominican migrant community: the nuclear and the female-headed household. As noted earlier, the Hispanic Settlement Survey found that 48 percent of the Dominican households were nuclear, and 37 percent were female-headed. The nuclear form can be subdivided into those units in which the wife engages in both wage work and housework, and those in which she works solely in the home or in a family business. The female-headed household can be divided into units where the majority of income comes from wages, and units that subsist mainly on public assistance payments.

My research in return migrant neighborhoods in the Dominican Republic and in migrant communities in the United States indicates that nuclear households of the second type are those most likely to return to the

Dominican Republic. Several factors contribute to this outcome. Of the 34 return migrant households in which interviews were conducted, 20 owned their own business in the United States, and of these 80 percent of the wives were unemployed or worked in the family business at least one year prior to the return. These households combined sufficient savings to establish a business and middle-class life-style in the Dominican Republic with the wife's positive orientation toward relocating. The renegotiation of women's influence in the household—a change that informants who worked up until their departure cited as one of the most feared aspects of readjustment—was already being confronted and managed by these immigrant women while in the United States. They had accepted the traditional bourgeois model in which the removal of the wife from the labor market symbolizes the household's material and social achievements. In most cases the wife's decision to return was motivated by her desire to employ a domestic to relieve her of many housekeeping chores, to increase her social contacts, and to provide the children with a healthier (*más sana*) social environment.

In cases of dual wage-earning households in which couples relocated to the Dominican Republic, all of the women expressed reservations about the return. In most cases the decision was the husband's, who had convinced the wife that they had accumulated sufficient property and savings to replicate or improve their standard of living in the Dominican Republic. The second, and often more powerful, inducement from the wife's perspective was the husband's claim that the children would receive a better upbringing in the Dominican Republic. Reflected in women's acquiescence to these arguments is the strain that many women experience between their roles as wage-earner and as mother. The critical question is whether they are most effectively meeting their children's needs by working to acquire "necessary" commodities and savings for a good education, or whether they are gambling with their children's futures by not remaining at home to oversee their socialization. When the wife's income is needed merely to sustain the household in the United States, this role conflict must be relegated to a secondary concern. However, if the savings realized from the couple's combined income do ultimately result in the wife not being obligated to work, she is often prodded by the husband to weigh the personal gains derived from her work and salary against her responsibilities as a mother. When the children actively oppose the return, this fortifies the woman's belief that she is being a good mother by working. In these instances the weight of the wife-mother-child coalition diminishes the husband-father's ability to insist on relocation.

In the three other variants of migrant households I found a positive orientation on the part of women to postpone the family's return to the

Dominican Republic. In the case of nuclear households in which both wife and husband are employed, many women begin to use their income to create a household type that resembles in several features the domestic form that Tilly and Scott (1978) termed "the family consumer economy." This refers to a change for working families from a state of acquiring sufficient income to subsist, to a condition in which members toil to meet new and increasing family consumption needs that are often defined and managed by the wife.

The refrain "Five dollars wasted today means five more years of post-ponement of the return to the Dominican Republic" indicates that a man often does not share his wife's change in orientation. In the United States, men are for the most part laborers in menial, low-paying jobs. By re-turning to the Dominican Republic, men intend to re-establish or elevate themselves to the status of direct producer or owner of a business. From the husband's perspective, the wife's diversion of income threatens to prolong his inferior status as well as to delay his aspirations for an im-proved socioeconomic position in the Dominican Republic.

Female heads of households were much more adamant in their inter-views than were married women about the unlikelihood of their return to the Dominican Republic. One explanation is that female household heads do not have to contend with a husband's desire to return. There is, how-ever, a second issue at play that reinforces women's desires to remain in the United States. It will be recalled that most emigrants came to the United States with the intention of accumulating savings to ensure a secure middle-class standard of living back in the Dominican Republic. For female-headed households, the original plan to save money and return to the Dominican Republic is rendered highly problematic by the fact that they are women. The average Dominican woman earns approximately $2,500 less per year than a man. Furthermore, women are engaged in segments of the economy, such as the garment industry, that experience tremendous instability in employment and sometimes engage in illegal practices. Thus women may not have access to unemployment insurance when they are laid off, and must turn to their small savings to sustain themselves and their families. When these funds are dissipated, women may be forced to obtain welfare. The meager benefits they receive are insufficient to permit them to return to the Dominican Republic with savings to sustain the quality of life associated with a successful migratory experience.

What are the consequences of the prolongation of a household's stay in the United States? The work histories collected for the 55 women immi-grants show their tendency over time to seek and secure jobs that afford higher pay, more security, better working conditions, and some career mobility. These women became socialized by other workers and accumulated knowledge through their experiences in different workplaces. These changes in orientation to work rendered them less vulnerable to the illegal practices of some employers and less willing to remain in low-paying, dead-end jobs.*

Conclusion

This paper has emphasized the necessity of including the household in general, and gender-associated oppositions within this unit in particular, in the analysis of labor migration. To this end I have examined how historical transformations in the organization of production in the Dominican Republic have interacted with the organization of domestic activities to release the income-generating power of some household members and to constrain or prohibit this power in others. Prior to emigration, the organization of domestic activities and the supply of jobs excluded middle-sector women from production, while at the same time household members found it increasingly difficult to earn sufficient income to meet their consumption needs. The willingness of middle-stratum households to release female labor for employment in the United States has been traced to this contradiction.

Migration did not necessarily resolve the contradiction between the household and the larger Dominican economy. As my ethnographic data on the lives of immigrants in the United States demonstrate, many women attempted to prolong their stay in the United States, contrary to the wishes of their men. Not infrequently, migration led to new contradictions along gender lines within the household and between this unit and a sector of the capitalist class that seeks a cheap, docile, and mobile labor force.

*It must be stressed that there are gender-based structural and ideological factors that work interdependently to constrain women's progress. They are restricted by a gender ideology that makes both Dominican men and women feel "safe" in allocating women to "protected" work spaces, such as garment shops, and by the sexual division of labor in the garment industry and larger economy that assigns women to positions with lower salaries and fewer opportunities for mobility. This larger sexual division of labor is "legitimized" by sexist, bourgeois assumptions whereby all women are conveniently stereotyped as workers subsidized by men who are considered to be the primary wage-earners. These findings reveal a paradox. While women are usually the active agents in prolonging a household's stay, and while this action makes them and their household members less desirable workers for that sector of capital that depends on migrant labor, as women they are less likely than their male counterparts to reap the rewards of a more permanent work force.

The Impact of Agrarian Reform on Men's and Women's Incomes in Rural Honduras

CONSTANTINA SAFILIOS-ROTHSCHILD

Honduras is an appropriate milieu for studying the gender dynamics of income as they occur under the pressures of poverty and socioeconomic change.* Honduras is the second poorest country in the Western hemisphere, after Haiti (*Economic Survey for Latin America*, 1979, 1981). The average yearly per capita income is $50–63 (100–126 Lempiras). Forty-seven percent of the rural population are landless (*Agricultural Sector Assessment for Honduras, Annexes*, 1978); about half of these earn some income from microfarms of less than one hectare, as well as from occasional paid labor. An additional 35 percent are small farmers practicing traditional agriculture on plots of from 1 to 35 hectares, earning an average annual per capita income of $135 (L.270). Nine percent are medium-sized and large commercial farmers, and the remaining 9 percent earn $106–450 (L.212–900) per year, depending on the extent to which government has made agricultural information, inputs, and credit available. Since few *asentamientos* (communities created through agrarian reform) receive credit and technical assistance, 90 percent of the participants in agrarian reform fall below the rural poverty line of $220 (L.400) per capita set in 1978 by USAID (*Honduras: Country Development Strategy Statement* 1980).†

Agrarian reform has been a key development in Honduras, a country in which over 70 percent of the population is rural and where unequal land distribution is one of the fundamental causes of widespread poverty. Although the first agrarian reform law (Decree Law No. 2 of 1962) was passed 23 years ago, it was only as a result of the application of Decree No. 8 from January 1973 to January 1975 that the pace of agrarian reform quickened. This decree allowed peasants to occupy public land and to

*This paper is part of the larger research project, "The Impact of Agrarian Reform in Honduras on Different Members of the Family," supported by grant No. AID/OTR–g–1841 to The Population Council.

†According to USAID estimates, in 1981 about L.500/year represented an important cutoff point for household income. Therefore, it can be assumed that any household earning above this level escaped *dire* poverty.

lease for two years underutilized private land under very favorable rent conditions (Maldonado 1981).

The twin goals of agrarian reform in Honduras are to increase agricultural productivity and to diminish rural poverty by bringing about structural changes that will help decrease inequalities in land ownership, increase access to credit, and modernize agricultural inputs. More specifically, the stated goal is to grant an average landholding of five hectares to more than 120,00 peasant families. The preferred recipients were intended to be landless agricultural workers and tenant farmers, as well as those interested in undertaking collective farming.

Despite these ambitious goals, only 26,000 families had been settled in asentamientos by the end of 1977. After 1977, the implementation of agrarian reform slowed even more as greater efforts were made to provide credit and technical assistance to existing asentamientos than to create new ones (Agricultural Sector Assessment for Honduras, 1978).

Also a survey of 32 asentamientos throughout the country showed that members in half of them had obtained less than the average of five hectares mandated by the 1975 Agrarian Reform law. The survey also showed that a community's choice of an individual or collective style of land cultivation is a crucial determinant of the extent to which an asentamiento has access to credit and technical assistance. Asentamientos without collective farming are not organized into cooperatives or precooperatives and tend, therefore, to remain outside ongoing rural development efforts, which are critically oriented toward cooperatives and precooperatives. This trend has also had an impact on women's organizational behavior. In asentamientos in which an individual farming system is combined with adverse soil or climatic conditions, it was found that women have formed groups in an effort to help their families survive (Safilios-Rothschild 1983a).

Agrarian reform in Honduras provides an excellent example of a pervasive and powerful sex-stratification system within a liberalizing reformist context. Despite the fact that the law gives landless female-headed households rights to land equal to those of landless, male-headed households, the sex-stratification system and prevailing sex-role stereotypes in fact limit the access of female-headed households. While approximately 27 percent of all rural households are de jure or de facto female-headed, in 20 of the 32 asentamientos surveyed, there were no female-headed households, and in another seven, there were only one or two female-headed households as regular members (Safilios-Rothschild 1983a).

Furthermore, the operative sex-stratification system puts additional constraints on women in asentamientos. Opportunities for paid agricultural work for women are sometimes curtailed through the operation of sex-role stereotypes about their ability to perform such work; and women may often have limited access to opportunities for agricultural and co-operative training. Also, a variety of mechanisms operating at the inter-personal level help maintain the image of male superiority even when women are important breadwinners.

It seems, therefore, that agrarian reform law in Honduras—as has been found to be true for all types of development programs—is having a differential impact on men's and women's options and income. Studies undertaken in a substantial number of developing countries have docu-mented that women's income constitutes a more important part of total household income available for food than does men's income in low-income households (Cain 1979; *Women in Food-for-Work* 1979; Delaya 1978; Safilios-Rothschild 1980). Rural Honduras is, therefore, an appro-priate social and cultural milieu in which to examine the effects of differ-ent levels of women's income on family welfare and women's status in the household in villages and in asentamientos created by the agrarian reform. In addition, Honduras is an appropriate setting for an examination of the dynamics involved in women's ability to control their income and to translate income into decision-making power in a patriarchal society in which the majority of men are not able to function adequately as bread-winners. This paper will examine the differential impact of agrarian reform on rural men's and women's income and its consequences for intrahousehold dynamics.

Methodology

Data for this analysis were collected in 1981 in six rural communities in Honduras, two villages (El Peñon and El Tablon) and four asentamientos (Los Colorados, Zamora, El Tablon, and Nueva Choluteca). The villages were chosen because they represented communities that had some in-volvement with the agrarian reform movement. Some residents initially took part in agrarian reform but later became disillusioned and returned to the village; some never participated in it. The asentamientos, on the other hand, were chosen to represent such different key characteristics as type of farming system, management style, type of crops, and access to credit and other modernizing agricultural inputs. In addition, the asenta-mientos were chosen to include different degrees of womens' organization into income-generating groups.

In the smaller communities, Los Colorados and Nueva Choluteca, all households were interviewed. In the larger asentamientos, Zamora and El Tablon, and in the two villages, lists were made of all the residents and respondents were randomly selected. A total of 98 households were included in the study. In 75, a couple was present with or without children and other relatives; in the remaining 23, a man or a woman was living alone or with children or other relatives. Since analysis focuses on male-female dynamics, only data from the 75 households with couples living in nuclear or extended families are analyzed here.

The husband and wife were interviewed separately. The interviews were structured by specially prepared and extensively tested schedules consisting primarily of open-ended questions. On the average, each interview lasted about four hours, and sometimes had to be completed over two or three visits. The two interviewers, a man and a woman, lived in each asentamiento or village for three to four weeks. This enabled them to become acquainted with the life-style, prevailing work patterns, and nature of local institutions and management issues in each settlement, and to place an individual's answers within the larger community context. Their lengthy stay also allowed them to control the reliability of answers by checking and rechecking answers to key questions. Each interview contains a wealth of information, especially about the dimensions of poverty in different types of settlements and the intrahousehold dynamics between men and women.

Income is a key variable. For the purposes of this study, income is defined as the total amount of cash received for goods sold or services rendered as well as for wages for agricultural labor. In addition, when transactions were made in kind (particularly in the case of women's income), information obtained through discussions with the respondent and other local residents led to the assignment of a cash value. The lengthy testing of the interview schedule showed that the measurement of women's income can yield reliable information only in the context of an in-depth study in which interviewers have the opportunity to become acquainted with the different local sources of women's income and can check the reliability of answers at different times and interactions. As will be seen below, it would not be possible to collect reliable data through the usual type of survey study.

The Characteristics of Women's Income

Women in rural Honduras tend to earn small sums of money from different sources and at irregular times, and many sources of income are seasonal or available intermittently. Furthermore, they often use the small sums they earn as soon as they receive them to buy food for the family.

Thus, women usually do not have a well-delineated concept of the process of "earning an income," and they often underestimate the total amount they earn. In fact, when women were asked general questions about their monthly or yearly income, many had great difficulty answering the question, and some could not answer it at all. When, however, the total range of sources was identified, and women were asked to report the amounts of money earned from each source, they were able to provide better information. Because of this, women's income is hereafter measured on the basis of their answers regarding income from specific sources.

In half of the cases in which the women's income is below L.100, they report that they have no income. Another two women, one with an income of L.390 and one with L.260 per years, also report that they have no income. In addition, nine of the 28 women earning less than L.300 (32.1 percent) and three out of the 21 earning L.300–L.1,000 (14.3 percent) report that they spend everything on food and other household expenses so that no decisions have to be made about how to spend their earnings. Comments made during the interviews suggest that women often minimize their income in these ways in order not to threaten men.

The most important sources of women's income are the sale of chickens, eggs, pigs, and turkeys, and such foodstuffs as bread, tamales, and tortillas, which are sold on a retail basis (usually by sons) or through the regular provision of meals at home to boarders. Other income sources, such as making straw mats and the sale of small quantities of agricultural products, result in a very low return for very time-consuming work. An additional noteworthy source of income for women is their sons. While most sons help their fathers in the fields, in 71 percent of the households, sons give at least half of their income to their mothers.

Overall, women's income in all communities is low in comparison to men's income, as shown in Table 1. While only 18 percent of the men studied earn less than L.1,000 per year, practically all women (95 percent) are limited to such a low income. Of those who earn an income, 40 percent earn less than L.200 per year, and 34 percent earn L.200–500 per year.

Women in villages typically earn more than women living in asentamientos. Twelve percent of village women but 22 percent of asentamiento women earn less than L.100 per year. Furthermore, 72 percent of village women but only 58 percent of asentamiento women earn more than L.100 per year. Also, while 44 percent of village women earn L.300 per year, only 33 percent of the women living in asentamientos earn the same amount.

Men's income, on the other hand, is generally higher in asentamientos than in villages, with the exception of the asentamiento El Tablon, where their income level is comparable to that in the adjacent village El Tablon (Safilios-Rothschild 1983b). The agrarian reform programs and policies seem to have helped to create new income-generating opportunities for men. Land ownership and collective farming with a cooperative management structure provide cash earnings to male cooperative members in many asentamientos. Women's opportunities, however, have not uni-

TABLE I
Women's Income Arranged by Men's Income

Women's income	Men's income						Total
	Below L.1,000		L.1,000–1,999		Over L.2,000		
	No.	Pct.	No.	Pct.	No.	Pct.	
No income	3	21.4%	7	22.5%	5	17.2%	15
Below L.200	4	28.6%	10	32.3%	10	34.5%	24
L.200–500	6	42.9%	11	35.3%	6	20.7%	23
Over L.500	1	7.1%	3	9.7%	8	27.6%	12
Total	14		31		29		

formly expanded and, in fact, in some communities have been reduced. For some communities, little paid agricultural work is open to women owing to negative prevailing sex-role stereotypes about women's ability to do such work. Available paid agricultural work occasionally goes to young sons rather than to adult women (Safilios-Rothschild 1983b). Women's lesser ability to earn higher incomes also results from the fact that agrarian reform packages have included fewer training courses in directly productive skills (such as agricultural, bookkeeping, and cooperative skills) for women than for men. Thus, the knowledge gap between men and women has increased. While 93 percent of men in the asentamientos participated in directly productive courses, only 18 percent of women did the same (Safilios-Rothschild 1983a, 1983b). In only two asentamientos, Zamora and El Tablon, have women reported that agrarian reform has helped expand women's opportunities for paid employment. This is due to the fact that women in El Tablon have access to agricultural wages for sowing, hoeing, and harvesting, and women in Zamora can work in a fruit-packing plant.

The Visibility of Women's Income

Within the traditional cultural context of rural Honduras in which male superiority and dominance are highly valued, it can be expected that men whose low incomes do not allow them to adequately play the breadwinner role in the family might not feel secure in their dominant male position. Their insecurity might be felt more keenly when their wives earn incomes that are not markedly smaller then their own and that play an important role in the survival of the family (Safilios-Rothschild and Dijkers, 1978). They might, therefore, resort to mechanisms that allow them to minimize women's economic contributions in order to more comfortably maintain their superior position.

The data show that when men's and women's incomes are very low, that is at or lower than the poverty level (1,000 Lempiras), the disparities between men's and women's incomes are in 82 percent of the cases small (less than L.600). Furthermore, in 55 percent of the cases in which men have such a low income, women's income represents one-third to more than one-half of the total household income. In households in which wives' income represents a considerable percent of the total income and the income disparity between their and the men's income is small, men can be expected to feel their dominant position as breadwinners threatened. Indeed, we find that 75 percent of them underestimate the wife's income, thus minimizing women's critical economic role.*

The higher, on the other hand, is men's income, the larger are the disparities between men's and women's incomes because women's incomes remain low. Thus, in the 22 cases in which men's income is above L.2,000, the disparities range from L.2,000–5,500 because women's income is always below L.620.† In the majority (60 percent) of these households, women earn less than 10 percent and another 28 percent earn 10–16 percent of the total household income. Their economic contributions, therefore, are not threatening men's economic superiority. The data show that in fact only 28 percent of the men underestimate women's income. The majority of men (72 percent) report accurately their wives' income or even overestimate it (in 21 percent of the cases). In relatively better off households in which men are the sole breadwinners, women's small economic contributions are in no way threatening to men and are recognized and visible.

It seems, therefore, that the degree of visibility of women's income depends upon the size of their economic contributions and the relative importance of these contributions for the survival of the family. The more their contributions are essential, the more they represent a threat to men's social and economic dominance and the less visible they are.

Women's Ability to Control Income

Income pooling is not frequent in these rural households: in only 15 households of the 59 households (25 percent) in which men and women

---

*Tables presenting men's and women's level of income, income disparity, degree of underestimation of wife's income by the husband, wife's reported control of her income and of husband's income have been omitted from this paper because they are by necessity long and complex.

†The intermediate group in which men earn an income of L.1,000–2,000 has been left out because it is not possible to complete the analysis. This is due to the fact that in 65 percent of the cases there is no information about the husband's estimate of the wife's income and in 55 percent of the cases there is no information as to whether or not the wife controls her husband's income.

earn an income, their income is pooled.* In ten cases, the women control the pooled income; in four cases, the pooled income is jointly controlled by the couple; and in only one case it is controlled by the man.

In the remaining 34 households, men and women have separate incomes and in half of these cases, women report that they control their income. In total, therefore, women control their separate or pooled income in 46 percent of the households. In another 20 percent of the households, they report partial or joint control with their husband of their separate or pooled income; and in 24 percent that all their earnings are spent to buy food so that the issue of decision-making does not arise. Only in one household the woman reports not controlling her income.

Women's ability to control income is affected by gender-associated income disparities. When men's income is low (below L.1,000) and the discrepancy between men's and women's income is small, 60 percent of the women report controlling their income. In all these cases, men underestimate women's income level which in all cases represents 20 percent or more of the total household income. In the remaining cases, women report that there is no issue regarding control of income since they claim that they have no income or that they spend it all for food. One woman (the only one in the sample) whose income represents 53 percent of the total household income and whose husband does not underestimate her income, reports that he controls both his and her income. It is also noteworthy that only one woman reports that she controls her husband's income.

When, on the other side, men's income is relatively high (over L.2,000) and the discrepancies between men's and women's incomes are, as we have seen, large, 46 percent of the women report controlling their income as well as their husbands' income. Half of them control their husband's income because all household income is pooled and they control it: eight out of the ten households in which the pooled income is controlled by the wife belong to this group of relatively better off households. What is noteworthy is that women in this group are able to control their income *and his income* even when their income is visible. In only one case the husband underestimates his wife's income. In the remaining cases, her income is correctly reported (60 percent) or overestimated (30 percent). The remaining women either report having joint control with their husbands of all household income (14 percent) or report spending it all for food (27 percent).

Although fewer women are able to control their income in relatively

*Despite the fact that only women were asked whether or not they control men's income, I assume that the resulting picture of income pooling and control is not distorted. All data indicate that women respect the traditional patriarchal pattern of male dominance and would not, therefore, tend to exaggerate their ability to control men's income.

better off households than in poor households, they are able to do so when their income is visible and they are also able to control their husband's income. Women's income, therefore, in this case has a different meaning in terms of power than when it is only through underestimation and invisibility that women have access to control.

Since agrarian reform tends to lead to higher men's incomes in asentamientos (with the exception of El Tablon) and to higher disparities between men's and women's incomes, the visibility of women's economic contributions is greater in asentamientos than in villages. Women, however, play a less important economic role in asentamientos where men earn a considerable income than in villages where subsistence cannot be achieved without women's income. Thus, in the village El Peñon, in 43 percent of the cases in which the man earns less than L.1,000 per year and the woman earns an income that represents a sizeable percentage of the man's income, women play a crucial role in family subsistence. Despite this, women's economic role is not visible because, through a variety of mechanisms discussed earlier, men and women tend to minimize its importance.

It seems, therefore, that within the context of a patriarchal society, women's economic contributions are more often allowed to become visible and to lead to control of income when men have established their economic superiority over women. When, however, women's income is crucial to the survival of the household, women's economic contributions most often remain invisible because they are threatening to husbands. Even when they can control their income, they do so at the cost of lack of visibility and recognition of their contributions and their inability to translate this control into power.

Women's Decision-Making Power to Buy Food

The one area in which women can translate their income into decision-making power is in buying food for the household. In order for this to occur, it seems necessary that women have more than a negligible income as well as the ability to control this income. Thus, it is most often women who earn more than L.300 per year and can control their income (or their husband's income) who decide what food to buy. In Nueva Choluteca, for example, women who earn over L.300 per year and control their income make decisions about food, while women who earn less than L.300 per year and do not control their income do not make these decisions. (In the village El Peñon, on the other hand, no woman reports that she decides what food to buy because women there downplay the fact that they earn an income or that they control it.)

Men's income level determines the level of their contributions to food expenditures as well as whether or not they keep the decison-making power regarding food purchases. When men's incomes are high, men tend to relinquish control of food-buying regardless of women's income level. In Zamora and Los Colorados, where men's incomes are higher than in other communities, women make decisions about food regardless of the level of their income or their ability to control it. This is particularly true in Zamora, where men earn the highest incomes. Also men with incomes above subsistence levels do not want to bother with shopping. Only one-third of the men who earn over L.1,500 per year claim that they do the shopping themselves. Instead, they give money to their wives to buy food. It seems that men whose income allows them to adequately play the breadwinner role do not need to spend their time shopping in order to ensure their dominant role in the family. Most men, on the other hand, who earn less money prefer to maintain control of food purchasing in their hands. Thus, over half of the men earning less than L.1,500 per year report that they do the shopping and give very little or nothing to their wives for food (Table 2). In this way they do not have to confront their wives' displeasure with the small and inadequate amounts of money that they are able to spend on food and can maintain an image of dominance and control in the family. One-half, for example, of the husbands in the village of El Peñon who report spending less than L.400 per year—that is, less than the established minimum for survival—manage this small amount of money and do the shopping themselves.

Women report in 27.6 percent of the cases that the husband does the shopping, and in 37.9 percent of the cases that they both do the shopping. Men report in only 12.5 percent of the cases that both do the shopping. The discrepancy between men's and women's answers is even larger in households where men earn less than L.1,500 per year: 39.3 percent of the women report that they both shop for food, and 23.5 percent report that the husband shops, while none of the men report that both shop for food, and 52.9 percent report that they shop themselves. This gender difference in the responses probably results from men's unwillingness to recognize women's role in food procurement and family survival since according to prevailing cultural norms such recognition would signify their failure as breadwinners.

In half of the cases in which men do the food shopping themselves, they spend the minimum amount necessary for survival (L.400 per year) or less on food. Whether or not women also shop for food is, therefore, crucial to the family's nutritional status. The data show that in practically every case in which men do the shopping, women also report shopping for food (alone or with their children), and spend most of their income on food. In

TABLE 2
Weekly Money for Food Given to Wife, by Husband's Income (Husband's Answers)

Husband's income	L.5–9	L.10–19	L.20–29	L.30–50	Half of earnings	All earnings	Some	Little or nothing
Less than L.1,000	4 (33.4%)	4 (33.4%)	–	–	–	–	–	4 (33.4%)
L.1,000–1,999	7 (23.3%)	7 (23.3%)	1 (3.3%)	–	2 (6.7%)	1 (3.3%)	1 (3.3%)	11 (36.7%)
L.2,000–2,999	–	8 (53.3%)	1 (6.7%)	1 (6.7%)	–	2 (13.3%)	2 (13.3%)	1 (6.7%)
L.3,000–4,999	1 (10%)	3 (30%)	–	2 (20%)	–	1 (10%)	1 (10.0%)	2 (20%)
L.5,000 and over	–	–	2 (28.6%)	1 (14.3%)	–	1 (14.3%)	2 (28.6%)	1 (14.3%)
Total	12	22	4	4	2	5	6	13

TABLE 3

Who Pays for Weekly Expenditures

Wife's income	Husband; husband and sons; sons	Husband and wife; Husband, wife, and/or sons; Wife and sons and/or daughters
None	15 (100.0%)	–
Less than L.100	11 (73%)	4 (27%)
L.100–200	2 (22%)	7 (78%)
L.201–300[a]	5 (50%)	5 (50%)
L.301–500[a]	4 (50%)	4 (50%)
L.501–1,000	3 (37%)	8 (73%)
More than L.1,000	–	1 (100%)
Total	41 (55%)	29 (39%)

[a] In these two income categories, there are some cases of missing data regarding who pays for weekly expenditures.

fact in 39 percent of all households and in 52 percent of households in which the wife earns more than L.100 per year, the wife shares the breadwinner responsibility with the husband (Table 3). Husbands are the sole breadwinners only when the wife does not earn an income or her income is minimal. It is, therefore, clear that women's contributions, whether implicit or explicit, are crucial.

The Impact of Agrarian Reform on the Status of Women

Within a sex-stratification theoretical framework, the status of women can be measured by the extent to which they have access to valued resources such as income, as well as access to power—expressed, for example, through their ability to control income and to make decisions.* Therefore, women's status improves when their access to these resources increases and male-female disparities decrease.

Agrarian reform in Honduras has often tended to increase the disparities: men's income in asentamientos has risen, while in some cases, women's income has gone down. Agrarian reform programs have not paid attention to women's need for paid employment, and have not always created new income-generating activities for them. Furthermore, in three of the four asentamientos studied, these programs have not extended adequate technical and financial assistance to emerging women's groups

*Other valued resources are land and training in directly productive skills. The data collected in Honduras, and analyzed elsewhere, show that women have less access to both of these resources in asentamientos than in villages (Safilios-Rothschild 1983a).

that would allow them to become effective income-generating structures (Safilios-Rothschild 1983b).

With respect to ability to make visible economic contributions, to control income and to make decisions about buying food, women fare better in asentamientos than in villages. But this reflects men's increased adequacy as breadwinners, which allows them to relegate those decisions to women, rather than women's higher status or power.

Because agrarian reform depresses women's income and increases income inequalities, women in villages play more important economic roles than women in asentamientos. In villages in which men's income is close to subsistence, women's income often enables the family to survive. Because, however, men cannot adequately play the breadwinner role, women's crucial economic contributions are threatening and are either minimized or unrecognized altogether. This is facilitated by the characteristics of women's income that allow invisibility and underestimation. Thus, these contributions do not affect in any way the intrahousehold allocation of resources such as power; male superior position is not challenged or shared and the status of women remains low.

The above findings suggest that in low-income communities in which men's incomes are close to subsistence, there is a need for agricultural and rural development programs to bring about organizational changes that would allow increases in both men's and women's income. In most cases, these incomes are not pooled, and men and women spend money on different things. Increasing women's income is crucial for the nutritional status of the family and also for breaking women's economic dependence. However, women's projects that have succeeded in increasing rural women's income in the absence of programs helping to increase men's income were threatening to men's superior economic position and were usually taken over by the men (Safilios-Rothschild 1983c; McCormack, Walsh and Nelson 1986). Increasing men's income is, therefore, crucial not only for family welfare and agricultural investments, but also in order to safeguard women's ability to earn an income, to make visible economic contributions and to hold decision-making power.

Renegotiating the Marital Contract: Intrahousehold Patterns of Money Allocation and Women's Subordination Among Domestic Outworkers in Mexico City

MARTHA ROLDAN

Although feminist scholars have shown that family-based households are one of the primary sites of female subordination, comparatively little attention has been paid to the many concrete arrangements for money allocation that occur within working-class domestic groups. Since money constitutes an important base of power, the analysis of allocational forms should contribute substantially to our understanding of how gender hierarchies are imposed and reproduced within households as well as to the existence of points of resistance to such inequality. In particular, attention to inequities within the household should provide clues to why the "promised" liberating effects of women's incorporation into wage labor have not taken place as automatically as expected.

Similarly, such analysis may be useful in tracing the complex linkages and feedback between households and the wider society. Household members in their different gender-ascriptive roles (as husbands, wives, sons, and daughters) sell their labor power in exchange for wages or secure an independent income through self-employment. The extent to which differential access to income is reflected in the nature of intrahousehold exchanges and interaction must be explored. In particular, whether women's access to income reinforces or weakens preexisting gender asymmetries must be examined.

Studies on money allocation can especially help to eradicate a number of beliefs held by social and economic policy-makers on the nature of intrahousehold processes. These include the notion that all household members have a similar standard of living and that all income entering into households is equally or equitably distributed to all members according to their needs, irrespective of who brings it. Some recent studies (Pahl 1982) have shown that hidden poverty and inequality lurk behind the facade of family units. They also show—sometimes inadvertently—the inadequacy of nonfeminist theories of the family and the household, theories that define the family as a *unit,* an active social *agent,* or an *interest group* engaged in "survival strategies," and that assume that the family works to maximize its benefits to all, and each, of its members.

My research on these topics follows from different theoretical premises.

The family-based working-class household under capitalism is seen as an essentially contradictory institution, both vis-à-vis the overall socioeconomic structure and vis-à-vis its own members (see also Stolcke 1981). While it is a locus of gender and age hierarchies, it is also—and most often—a source of economic, psychological, and emotional/affective support (see also Sen 1980). As such, any analysis of distributional intra-household processes must be sensitive to the contradictory pressures exerted by the supportive and the oppressive elements involved in family interaction. Delineating the interplay of these elements is a first concern of this paper.

My second concern is explicating impacts, and I focus on the relationship between control of money flows within the household and the reinforcement or undermining of male domination. It is well documented in works on poverty, power, and class inequality that intergroup domination is closely related to differential control of utilitarian resources, such as money. Is it safe to assume that similar links will be found within working-class families? In other words, is the wife's autonomous access to a cash income directly translated into a position of power in the household? A direct extrapolation yields this relationship: the higher the income earned, the greater the power held. However, it may be argued that the relationship is not straightforward. Normative expectations concerning the interaction between husband and wife, and the preexisting power imbalance between the spouses, might (and in many cases do) mediate between the wife's access to an independent income and its later control and disposal.

Income distribution patterns represent only one type of exchange process taking place within the household. Members also exchange products and domestic and sexual services. Ideologies of marriage and gender, the emotions of love and hatred, and sentiments of affection and rejection, along with naked material economic needs, violence, and coercion, may qualify those exchanges. Since relations of domination/subordination between husband and wife are based on unequal access to and control of these diverse resources according to their position in class and gender hierarchies, patterns of money allocation cannot be studied in isolation. This paper examines how allocational processes articulate with other processes of conjugal interaction. My goal is to detect the dynamics of persistence versus change.

Domestic Outworkers: The Research Sample

The 140 domestic outworkers in Mexico City that Lourdes Beneria and I interviewed were engaged in a variety of industrial piecework, including assembling plastic flowers, toys, and paper boxes, cutting edges of plastic products, packing, and making coils for the electronics industry. All 140 women answered a first questionnaire dealing with general information about homework, conditions under which it is carried out, household information, occupational and class histories of the homeworkers and partial data on the same subject of their parents and husbands, unpaid housework, and women's perception of their own work and family situations.

Despite the variety of tasks and types of work performed, the women's work presents a number of common features. First, the work is industrial, not artisan, and results from the division of labor associated with the very fragmented labor process that typifies modern production. The tasks themselves represent a small step in the production of a final product for the market. Second, tools, raw materials, and components are provided by "jobbers" or subcontractors. Only the garment workers enjoy partial ownership of the means of production (sewing machines).

The work considered, therefore, is an intermediate form of production. Labor power, totally or partially "freed," is exchanged for piecework wages, while the laborer keeps partial control of the labor process, particularly the length and spacing of the work schedule and its intensity.

The work carries major disadvantages for the outworkers. In all cases it is highly labor-intensive, requiring a minimum of skills and quality control (except in the garment industry), and comprises specialized and monotonous tasks. Piecework wages fall below the legal minimum wage, and no fringe benefits are provided.

Domestic outwork is also hidden or clandestine, not because the work itself is outlawed in Mexico, but because it is done without minimum contractual requirements (workers are not registered, unionization is forbidden). Finally, work is not steady, and this uncertainty creates a high degree of dependence on jobbers as outworkers try to ensure a minimum of job security. Domestic outwork is linked to subcontracting chains connecting, at one end, enterprises of different sizes, including multinationals, which produce final goods for the market; factories producing similar goods or component parts; local workshops, intermediaries, and finally, domestic outwork. Hence, it may be considered an integral part of the total capitalist labor process. As the lowest echelon of the employment hierarchy—and as an almost exclusively female domain—domestic outwork typifies, in Beneria's words, "a case where the capitalist organization of production uses pre-existing gender relations for the purpose of reaching the cheapest labor possible."

This chapter reports on an in-depth study I carried out of a subsample of 53 women (of the 140), all of whom were currently married and

carrying on domestic outwork. Interviews with these women were generally taped. This phase dealt with domestic budgets, intrahousehold resource allocation, decision-making power, conjugal relations and motherhood, normative expectations and values concerning the working-class
"marriage contract," and women's situation as working wives and mothers. To carry out these interviews, we visited the homeworkers several
times and consulted them whenever doubts and problems of interpretation arose during fieldwork. It was in fact through the women's patience
in explaining why they thought the way they did that we could start a
process of unlearning our outsider's views and becoming attuned to their
visions of the world.

In all the households studied, money enters in the form of wages, or as a
dribble of profits in the case of the self-employed. It also leaves as cash,
paying for a whole range of household expenditures, with small amounts
put aside as savings in a few cases. I first describe the patterns of flow and
distribution between these entry and exit points, as well as the main
controls along this flow. Then I link these patterns with the normative
expectations that define the interactions of husbands and wives as well as
the other conjugal processes that qualify the exchange.

Allocational Patterns

Two allocational patterns were found. The first one is the *pool pattern
or common fund,* which was found in 62 percent (33 cases) of the subsample
of 53 households. The fund is used to cover basic household expenditures;
in other words, it becomes the basis of household reproduction. This
pattern was usually found in lower-income households, where the husband's wages either only just reached the minimum legal wage or fell
below it, or where his income was higher but his contributions to the
common fund did not meet basic household needs as defined by his wife.
Half the women in this subgroup also held one or two other jobs besides
outwork, the most common being laundering, ironing, or part-time paid
domestic service.

The second pattern is the *housekeeping allowance.* According to this
pattern, the husband fulfills the role of main economic provider or breadwinner. He hands over a portion of his earnings as an allowance to his wife
to cover basic housekeeping expenditures. The wife uses her earnings to
cover expenditures above and beyond the minimum standard of living.
This pattern, which occurred in 38 percent (20 cases) of the households
studied, was usually found in higher-income households in which husbands earned three or more times the minimum legal wage. In two
households displaying this pattern, husbands earned more than the mini-

mum wage but less than three times the minimum wage. A quarter of the wives (five) in this category held second jobs apart from outwork, selling clothes and household items or engaging in petty trade. A few combined outwork with laundering, sewing, ironing, or paid domestic service.

The Pool Pattern

Flows of money in both groups are subject to certain controls exercised by men at the entry stage. The first control point concerns the sharing or withholding of information about the real amount of the husband's earnings. Forty-five percent of the wives (15 women) in the pool group were not sure how much money their husbands earned per week. Moreover, when wives did know their husband's earnings, they knew his weekly wage, but not whatever extra amounts he received as overtime, bonuses, or tips.

Wives interpret this withholding of information as a means of control to keep them dependent, and they resent it accordingly: many of them express anxiety mixed with impotence, others express rage. They suspect that their husbands are not pooling all they can to meet collective expenditures.

Control over financial information is closely related to a second control point: the husband's decision-making power over the proportion of his earnings he keeps as personal spending money. It should be stressed that wives do not object to their husbands keeping a certain amount of pocket money. On the contrary, they consider it legitimate to do so to cover transportation to and from work, meals at work, and drinking with friends or *cuates* (buddies) after work. In certain cases the husband also uses pocket money to buy the clothes he needs for work or his social life. What comes under discussion between the sexes is the amount of this money, not the existence of it.

Disagreement over the amount of a husband's pocket money is the main cause of quarreling as well as verbal and physical abuse between spouses of the pool group. Despite these conjugal battles, which entail wives' manifest protest, 77 percent of the husbands (25 men) still have the final say on their personal expenditures. A joint decision is made in 14 percent of the cases (5 marriages), and 3 percent of wives (1 woman) report that they set the amount. In the last set of cases, the women calculated a minimum account that their men needed, and the husbands agreed without displaying much resistance. It is to be noted that the average amount kept as pocket money is sizable—close to a quarter of the husband's earnings.

A third control point refers to the form in which the allowance or contribution is given to the wife, whether as a lump sum or in installments.

Three main patterns were found. At one extreme is the "extended" allow-ance (14 cases), in which the weekly contribution is fixed and handed over in full. Together with the wife's contribution, this pool covers all the expenditures of the family: rent, normal food bills, gas, light, water, school, and clothes. The wife is then responsible for stretching the fund to cover all such expenditures without requesting further contributions ex-cept in emergencies. At the other end of the continuum (4 cases), a "re-stricted" allowance is provided, covering only normal food bills, gas, and daily school expenses. Finally, under an "intermediate" allowance (15 cases), the husband gives money to cover these last items, with the addition of clothing or rent.

The extended pattern was preferred by most wives interviewed, al-though it had a number of shortcomings. On the positive side, wives reported that an extended allowance freed them from the worries associ-ated with withholding on the part of the husband; the amount turned over by husbands to cover rent, electricity, or clothing could not then be spent on drinking, cards, horse races, or other women. An extended allowance also saved the wife from the daily or weekly humiliation of begging or quarreling to secure the promised amount. A wife who is not obliged to beg, quarrel, or engage in manipulative behavior on her own or through her children in order to persuade her husband to "deliver the goods" is in a less dependent position than the wife who must do so. On the negative side, such wives shoulder the entire responsibility of making ends meet. This requires a great deal of ingenuity and is itself a major cause of psychological stress. Indeed, it is the reported reason for two attempted suicides during the fieldwork period. With regard to restricted and inter-mediate allowances, the wives involved did not view these patterns as a form of shared division of labor and responsibilities between themselves and their husbands, but rather saw them as effective control mechanisms for keeping women uncertain, worried, and dependent until another rent payment was made.

In brief, 58 percent of the wives in the pool group must request addi-tional funds to meet expenses that are not covered by the original allow-ance. It is important to stress that the way the allowance is handed to the wife does not appear to be related to the level of the husband's earnings, but to his own preferences.

A fourth control point refers to wives' contribution to the common fund, which is 100 percent of their earnings in all pool-pattern cases. None of the women took the equivalent of male pocket money. Moreover, the decision whether to pool the woman's earnings or keep them apart for special expenditures is the wife's choice. In only three cases was a joint decision reported.

Although wives sound very proud when they declare that they alone, without their husbands' interference, decide what to do with their incomes, in fact they have little actual choice. Their incomes are very low, and the ideology of "maternal altruism" (Whitehead 1981) obliges them to devote their earnings to meet collective rather than individual consumption needs. Indeed, while wives pool their total earnings, their contributions to the common fund are practically always lower than their husband's (wives' contributions provide 40 percent of the common fund in the extended allowance pattern). Only when husbands earn less than the minimum legal wage do the outworkers' low incomes, which reach or even surpass their husband's share, become major contributions to the income pool. In only one case did the wife's contribution represent the major share of the weekly pool.

These figures illustrate how husbands' participation in better-paid and often more formalized jobs is translated into a commanding position within the family. It also pinpoints a major source of inferiority, insecurity, and dependence among women, who talk disparagingly about the level of their contributions to the common fund. Moreover, whatever wives spend on themselves must be saved out of the collective expenditures they have defined on their own. A feeling of guilt often accompanies and mars any pleasure a woman has on those rare occasions when she engages in personal consumption, for she feels that she is depriving her offspring of basic necessities.

The fact that wives' managerial role is fraught with problems and anxiety brings us to the fifth control point. Although a wife has a managerial role in handling a very limited money pool, her control is largely illusory, for she has no financial autonomy. The pool she manages must cover unavoidable expenditures. In addition, husbands do not withdraw from the scene after delivering their contribution; rather they exercise several mechanisms of control. Most important, and particularly in the case of restricted and intermediate allowances, a husband makes sure that "his" money is spent to cover basic family needs as well as his desired level of personal consumption. Indeed, when husbands are heavy drinkers or alcoholics (the majority of husbands fall within the former category), it is common for them to "borrow" money from the pool to cover drinking expenditures. This is particularly true if pocket money has already been spent by the middle of the week. Finally, husbands keep an ultimate veto power on types of expenditures. All decisions concerning major expenditures (buying a piece of land, an electrical appliance, or new furniture) are undertaken by husbands. While these are infrequent, they are important because they set the general style of life of the household. In only a few cases are they a matter of joint decision making.

A wife, then, has no actual control over the disposal of the pool. At most she can budget within the pool: that is, to decide whether to feed her family tortillas and beans or meat, whether to buy her daughter a dress or her son a piece of underwear. The budgeting nightmare that results is particularly acute at the end of the month when rents are collected. The wife who budgets on an extended allowance must save a bit at the end of each week to accumulate the rent by the end of the month. This goal is seldom attained: in the final week of the month most households show a marked decrease in food consumption, in both quality and quantity. Wives also try to borrow from relatives and neighbors.

Dona Sofia refers to the male-female interaction that underlies this dilemma in the following words:

He gives me the *gasto* [housekeeping allowance] all right, but I must see that everything is fine, that nothing is lacking, good food for him, yes, the best pieces are for him. I have to keep for him the best of what I get, if he wants beef, or whatever. He usually wants beer, or sometimes *pulque*. He says, "Vieja [old woman], is the *pulque* already here?" or "Bring me some beer, I'll pay you later," and he never does. On Thursday, I am without a cent, and I have to ask my *comadrita* [child's godmother] to complete the week. He collects his money on Saturday, and that day I get the *gasto,* and I start returning what I owe. You know, to manage the allowance is a difficult job. Prices are going up and we must buy food no matter what. And if something goes wrong, or he gets angry with me, he may even cut off the allowance for that week.

The Housekeeping Allowance Pattern

The essential control points in this pattern are similar to those in the pool pattern. Fifty-five percent of the wives (11 cases) do not know how much their husband earns. Husbands keep pocket money while wives do not. The allowance either is delivered as a lump sum (6 cases) or is restricted (13 cases), while in one case it is delivered daily. Wives contribute all their own earnings. They are also subject to similar restrictions concerning major or "important" expenditures.

Wives' reactions also follow the line reported in the pool group: the majority prefer an extended allowance. Because these households have higher incomes, however, women are engaged in fewer quarrels on strictly money matters.

The fundamental difference between the pool pattern and the housekeeping allowance pattern is that in the latter, earnings from husbands and wives are earmarked for different kinds of consumption. Basic needs (rent, food, clothing, schooling) are covered by the housekeeping allowance. So-called extras are paid for from wives' earnings. The latter expenditures are geared to improve the family's standard of living or may simply be treats (buying fruit or some special food, giving money for a Sunday outing to their children, helping poor relatives without having to ask a husband's permission). With reference to children, these expenditures include underwear, socks, pants, toys, soda, sweets, fruit, transportation to and from school, better-quality shoes or clothes, and items for special occasions, such as 15th-birthday parties or weddings. With reference to the household, expenditures include pots and pans, sheets, linens, curtains, mixers, sewing machines, kitchen furniture, and one typewriter. Wives' money can also be used for savings and medical emergencies. Wives' personal spending goes for clothes, shoes, and underwear.

These lists are significant for they identify an additional control point: husbands and wives have contrasting definitions of what is necessary, basic, and the minimum acceptable standard for children's clothing, schooling, and outings. It is only the male definition that relegates some of the items to the category of "extras." Husbands decide what is basic, depending on the quality that they define as the minimum, and their standards are seldom shared by their wives. Couples also do not seem to agree on the urgency of a given expenditure. Hence, husbands decide not only what is basic, but when it is needed. Da. Chela says in this connection: "I need this money [from outwork] to purchase shoes, or clothes for the children. He buys them when he feels like it, not at the time they are needed. For example, my daughter Lupita's shoes are so old, she has no dress to wear at her aunt's wedding. I told him Lupita has no shoes, no dress. He thinks they are not necessary. So I will buy them with my work."

The Renegotiation of Marital Contracts and Income Allocation

I have described the two overriding patterns of flows and allocation of money within the working-class households studied. Is there a relationship between the pool and the nonpool patterns, the form of wives' subordination, and the domination/subordination dynamic between spouses? How are these distributional processes arrived at and perceived, and are they negotiable? In order to answer these questions, and to understand the imposition and persistence of the two allocational configurations with their attendant conflicts and strains, it is necessary to consider the normative expectations regulating "legitimate" interaction and exchanges between husbands and wives, as well as the control mechanism used when ideology fails and compliance must be secured whatever the cost. I do not refer to the legal obligations involved in the formal marriage contract; rather, I examine the norms and expectations that women themselves hold concerning their unions.

As a starting point I suggest that there is no single static working-class marriage contract, but rather a process of continuous renegotiation of the terms of interaction and exchange between husbands and wives. In my sample this process correlates with the level of the husband's contribution to the pool; the importance of the wife's contribution to the common fund; the quality of the husband's behavior toward the wife; the husband's and wife's evaluation of the marriage situation; and their general life experience (whether the wife is a young, recently married woman, or older and more skeptical).

Initial Conjugal Expectations

At the beginning of their union, most couples' definitions of what their married life should and will be like differ from what actually transpires. This lays the foundation for the conflicts and open warfare that characterize the daily routines of most of the families interviewed. Economically and physically coercive mechanisms usually come to be utilized by men in an effort to resist or to impose a new definition of family interaction. Advances, withdrawals, and realignment of forces, usually with the collaboration of children, are common features of the marital struggle enacted by women.

The normative expectations that women most commonly hold at the onset of marriage are as follows:

- Husbands should provide a housekeeping allowance sufficient to support the family if possible, given the low or very low level of men's earnings. The housekeeping allowance should be as high as possible, and should cover most basic expenditures.
- Husbands have a right to their personal spending money (unanimous agreement).
- Men should help with some domestic chores, although women realize that this expectation is seldom, if ever, fulfilled (50 percent of the women agreed).
- The quality or nature of husbands' behavior is of major significance to women's contentment.

Regarding the last point, wives expect a measure of respect. They should not be physically or verbally abused, held in contempt or scorned because they are being supported, or humiliated by open unfaithfulness. Some delicacy of treatment (*delicadeza de trato*), sensitivity to personal feelings, and recognition of their contribution to the well-being of the household as wife and mother are asked. Only a few women, particularly younger and recently married ones, mention that they also expect companionship, affection, and love from their husbands. In exchange, wives believe that they should provide unpaid domestic service, child care, and sexual faithfulness.

Most women in the pool group say that they have always had to work for a living. Work is essential if they are to secure a better or even a basic standard of living or education for their children. They also want to work, however, to secure a minimum degree of autonomy or control over their lives. Wives in the nonpool group similarly defended their right to work, mainly for reasons of autonomy and self-esteem. It is important to stress that wives in both groups think that their behavior in the domestic and work spheres should never transgress the limits imposed by the respect owed to their "masters" (*mi señor*), respect being defined as obedience and deference. Only three women declared that their rightful domain was exclusively domestic and resented having to undertake paid employment.

From previous research, the main difference in husbands' and wives' expectations lies in the area of emotional interaction and respect. Men expect and usually get obedience and deference. But they generally do not feel obligated to attend to their wives' similar demands for respect, whether by recognizing and appreciating their contributions as house-wives and mothers or through companionship and affection. Nor do they usually abstain from physical violence, verbal abuse, or contemptuous behavior toward their wives.

Actual Marriage: Job-Holding and Women's Autonomy

Although all the women in the pool group sought a paid job because of economic need, a second consideration was mentioned in 29 of the cases (87 percent): these women work to secure an autonomous income as a means of diminishing or counteracting their husband's domestic power. These wives do not want to have to beg when the household allowance proves insufficient, nor do they want to be told, "You're good for nothing. I support you and this family."

Husbands opposed their wives' decision to look for a job in 13 pool-group cases, the opposition being particularly strong when work meant an outside job in a factory or as a domestic servant. In men's view, wives are unable to take proper care of the house, the children, and themselves if they work. In short, they are not able to behave as good wives should. Wives also reported that husbands did not want to lose face before rela-tives and friends who might criticize them for their breach of the marital contract as it is interpreted by males. The ideal is that husbands provide the family income while women do housework. A third explanation for husbands' reluctance to let a wife work is their feeling that "once women are allowed to work, they lose respect for their husbands."

Being a domestic outworker solves some of these problems, for it is invisible work. Few people notice the combination of paid and unpaid work carried out on the domestic premises. Earnings are also low, and so men seldom lose their standing as the main breadwinners. Moreover, wives are home as before, always ready to attend to their husband's wishes. Still, three women reported that they had started outwork without their husbands' permission. Their husbands had then broken the toys or boxes that they were assembling when they were caught working. They were not sure whether they could continue outwork in the face of such opposition.

Renegotiation

Wives' access to an independent income opens the possibility of renegotiating some of the more trying aspects of marital interaction. The efficacy of such renegotiation correlates closely with women's relative contribution to the household. Three patterns can be distinguished within the pool group; a fourth occurs among households with housekeeping allowances.

The first pattern includes wives who contribute less than 40 percent of the weekly pool but whose husbands fulfill their economic obligations toward the household. The 19 wives in this category are very conscious that their low earnings and unstable jobs prevent them from assuming a dominant economic role in the household. The decision to pool their incomes has typically been forced on them by economic necessity or a need to attain a modicum of domestic control and maintain self-esteem. Thus they have little leverage with regard to distributional processes. These women are generally unable to make their husbands disclose information about their earnings, influence the amount of their pocket money, affect the form of delivery of the housekeeping allowance (whether it is extended, restricted, or intermediate), or modify the narrow confines of their budgeting activities.

The low level of these women's power extends to other areas of potentially autonomous decision making. Husbands decide whether wives actually may work outside the home (in half the cases); whether wives may go out to visit relatives or friends (in half the cases); and whether and how the children should be disciplined (in 75 percent of the cases). By contrast, joint decisions seem to be prevalent in the area of wives' reproductive capacity, most important, how many children women have. Some other spheres of joint decision making concern children. Decisions are made jointly about the number of children; the wives' use of contraceptives; and whether children continue in school or start working. Husbands decide if and when to have sexual intercourse in 15 of the cases (80 percent); it is a joint decision in only four cases. This contrasts with wives' expressed sense of equity. Only two wives declared that it is their duty to provide sex under any circumstance.

This picture of relative powerlessness coincides with wives' definition of respect owed to economically reliable husbands; such respect extends to all occasions, whether in the private or public sphere. Wives define respect as obedience to their husbands' wishes or commands, and give the following overall rule: wives should not do anything without their husband's permission, whether going out, visiting relatives, talking to neighbors, or engaging in any behavior of which husbands do not approve. Respect also means getting up in the middle of the night to provide food if the husband comes home hungry, serving his friends if they are visiting (usually this is accomplished by using the allowance to buy drinks), waiting for him until he comes home, speaking to him with deference, never resorting to foul language, never answering back in a loud voice, being ready to respond to his whims, paying the bills, going to borrow from neighbors.

Several factors combine to ensure the continuation of these asymmetrical exchanges. Señora C. mentions two of them: "If he gives me my allowance, if he is supporting me, I must do whatever he wants me to do. This way, he will continue supporting me and the children. What I earn is too little to maintain them myself, to send them to school."

Normative expectations, threats of withdrawal of economic support, and physical and verbal violence emerge as effective mechanisms for keeping uppity wives in their place and teaching them a lesson in marital respect. Even when wives live up to these expectations, however, they do not refrain from complaining and quarreling, especially when husbands interfere with their legitimate spheres of action, such as child care and housekeeping. Foremost among the spheres that exhibit tension is the level of housekeeping allowance.

In the second pattern, wives contribute more than 40 percent of the weekly pool but their husbands fulfill their economic obligations toward the household. The 11 women in this category are important economic providers. Like women in the other groups, they pool their earnings because family subsistence cannot be maintained with the husband's contribution alone. Wives also seek to be less restricted in their budgeting of the weekly fund, and to escape their husband's strict control over the handling of his contribution to compulsory expenditures.

The importance of this group's contribution to the fund does not seem to affect the dynamics of the distributional processes already discussed (the amount of the husband's pocket money, the form of delivery of the allowance). However, these wives are more likely than wives contributing a small proportion to the common pool to attain joint or sole decision-making power in other areas of family interaction. In particular, they have a slightly greater (but not predominant) say about whether they may work outside the home (wives decide in 33 percent of the cases); whether they may go to visit relatives of friends (wives decide in 33 percent of the cases); and children's discipline (couples decide together in about 33 percent of the cases). In the area of biological reproduction, half the wives decide alone about their use of contraceptives and the total number of children. Child-rearing also becomes a woman's domain. No differences are found, however, in the area of decisions over children's schooling or their future work. Husbands still decide if and when to have sex in eight cases (70 percent of this group), but only one wife noted that it is a woman's duty to have sex at any time.

The emergent picture is one of slow renegotiation toward joint decision making in what used to be exclusively male spheres, such as those that concern women's physical and social mobility (Beneria and Roldan 1987). The pressure of economic necessity, coupled with loss of actual control over a woman's whereabouts when she goes out to wash, iron, or perform paid domestic work, contributes to this effect. Wives' behavior still falls within the range of respect due to husbands, who still fulfill the breadwinner role, even though it is now actually shared with wives. There has, however, been a change in role definition since many women have come to realize how fundamental their contribution has been to the pool and the family's survival.

Most women in this group report that although they continue to respect their husband, they have the right to answer back, not to accept his directives submissively, and to make their views known. Four women report that they no longer seek out their husband's opinions about visiting parents or other relatives. Not surprisingly, bitter quarreling over wives' trespassing the older boundaries of respect is commonly reported. This is how Doña B. describes the new pattern:

Now that I get my own money I feel better, less short of money, because now I know how much money I have for the week. Before I used to ask him for everything [he gave her a daily allowance]. I obey and respect him, but I feel I also have some rights. Before he used to shout at me if he thought I was spending too much on the children, or did not give him the food he wanted. Now I tell him, "With all the small salary you earn you go and spend it on drinking with your friends. Look at me, I am also earning, and I do not buy anything for me, but all I get I put in the house." It is not fair. Once or twice he slapped me in the face. He said I had shouted at him [le habia alzodo la voz]. I didn't feel I was better than he is, but I feel I have the right to tell him, "Look, why do you do this or that, like drinking, spending too much on cards, or the races." I am helping him, so somehow I have the right to expect him to change [exigirle una conducta distinta].

Of course, if husbands disagree with the new limits wives seek to impose, threats of withdrawing economic support, as well as actual or threatened violence, are always at hand to keep respect at an acceptable level.

In the third pattern, wives contribute more than 40 percent of the weekly pool and their husbands no longer contribute or contribute sporadically. The three wives in this group have openly "lost respect" for their husbands in action and thought. They report going out without permission; they do not wash, iron, or cook for him as before; they manage rather than budget the common fund; they take jobs without their husband's consent or against his will, and they resort to foul language if they feel like it. They now even strike their husband back if he tries to beat them. This changed pattern of interaction seems to have been brought about by the husband's "disobligation": he does not deliver a housekeeping allowance for weeks, or the amount has been reduced to an insignificant sum. In one case, the husband was supporting another household with a younger, common-law wife; in the second case, the husband seemed to be using his earnings for cards, drinking, and women; the third case involved an elderly, sick man who was once a family tyrant but was now too weak to prevent his wife's disrespectful behavior. Several factors—wives' substantial and steady contribution to the common fund, loss of the husbands' role as breadwinner, and low respect for wives' feelings, evidenced by violence, abusive language, and open unfaithfulness—combined to structure the context of a new pattern of marital interaction.

The fourth pattern refers to the housekeeping allowance group. The 20 women in this group seek out paid jobs in order to purchase items that they and their husbands define as extras. They also work in order to avoid begging for each and every item they feel the household needs, and to prevent humiliation and loss of self-esteem. They expect to have autonomous control over their earnings.

Husbands in this group offer great resistance to their wives' attempts at control. Getting permission to work is a protracted process, and these higher-income earners do not easily accept their wives' right to work. They fear losing face before their families and friends, losing control over their wives' activities, forfeiting their due share of domestic respect, and losing their own proud self-image and self-esteem as unique breadwinners. When husbands reluctantly do agree, it is after being reassured that customary housekeeping standards will not be neglected—wives will continue to serve them with old-time devotion and respect. Domestic outwork, rather then factory work, offers fewer risks within this context.

Wives face special problems in trying to devise a new style of family interaction. The distributional pattern, which earmarks the male's housekeeping allowance for necessary or important expenditures and the female's earnings for extras, acts as a powerful material and ideological mechanism for reproducing gender asymmetries within the household. As husbands' breadwinner role has not been diminished but rather strengthened via the pattern of money allocation, wives are justified neither in male eyes nor in their own if they engage in disrespectful behavior. They are still supported; they must obey and refrain from "showing off" their earnings, lest this display be interpreted as a sign of their intention to humiliate or demean their husbands' status. When ideological pressures are found wanting, wives' compliance is ensured through more direct means such as withdrawal of financial support and violence against them.

Wives' decision-making prerogatives are similar to those displayed in the other three patterns, with reference both to money allocation and to decision making in nonfinancial spheres. The one exception concerns the amount of housekeeping allowance. Eight wives out of 20 report sole or shared decision-making power in this area. This can be attributed to these husbands' much higher incomes compared to those of the pool group. Several threads of this pattern are exemplified by Señora S.:

I obey him as usual. My husband has always been the head of this house. I think this is good. But I could command more [*mandar mas*] and I do not want to; it is a form of showing him respect. My income is not important; it is additional money to manage; he gives me what is needed for the house. My money would show more if wages were higher, but all the same I feel fine having it. I buy the things I want. I do not have to beg him. I do not feel worry if I know that I do not need to touch his allowance. If I work I can buy things in installments and I know I can pay them. I feel less worried, more secure [*mas segura*], but I do not feel superior to him, because I owe him respect.

The preceding discussion points out the limits of change in marital interaction as it is associated with wives' access to an autonomous income. But it should not lead to the conclusion that these changes are trivial or insignificant to the women themselves. Changes in the definition of husbands' and wives' roles, in expectations, and in levels of consciousness cannot lead automatically to a new life-style. Husbands resist attepts at encroachment on their ancient prerogatives, and the capitalist-sexist society considered here places a whole array of individual and social control mechanisms at their disposal—among them economic coercion, physical abuse, and ideological manipulation—which work on women's fears and insecurities as they are derived from the internationalization of a subordinate self-image.

Women counteract with the weapons of the oppressed. They try to create a sense of guilt through selfless devotion to home and husband, and through the manipulation of other family members. Sometimes they pretend to be frigid; sometimes they use open contempt.

Family interaction is fraught with friction. Forty of the 53 wives studied reported very frequent discussions and quarrels over shortages of money, wives' "faulty" administration (as husbands put it), children's discipline, and husbands' drinking, unfaithfulness, and jealousy. Violence was frequent, and not surprisingly, 32 of the wives thought their marriage was a failure. Half of the 53 had separated at one point or another in their married lives. Why did they return to their husbands? They mention several needs: economic protection for themselves and their children, social protection in a sexist society, and a father's discipline to keep children straight. Some women also mentioned a need for companionship, affection, and love.

How do women's autonomous earnings relate to this overall fabric of gender subordination? Access to an independent income, even if it is small and is used to meet family rather than personal consumption needs, restores or strengthens these women's self-image and self-esteem. Women of both the pool and housekeeping allowance groups gave similar answers to questions about the importance of paid work in their lives. They all said that work was important not only to enlarge the common fund but particularly to secure a measure of control over their own lives. In the words of Señora S.:

Of course it is important because if you earn your own money you yourself distribute it and you do not have to beg for it. You buy food, or a dress for your daughter, the socks for your son. He used to tell me, "You just wait, because I do not have enough this month; I will buy it next month." But he would never do it, neither today nor tomorrow. Now if I want to buy it, I buy it. If he gives me the money, fine. If not, I buy it myself. And one feels fine [*se siente bonito*] and useful with one's own money. Also, in case of an emergency, an accident, if I have my own money I can fetch a taxi and take the child to the hospital. And it is money well spent because I earned it myself. Otherwise he would tell me, why did you not take a bus, why did you spend on a taxi?

This measure of autonomous control and self-esteem has been achieved through struggle, and women express their intention to defend it in the future. When I asked whether they would continue working even if their husbands increased the housekeeping allowance, 95 percent of them said that they certainly would. They know from experience that money is always handed over with strings attached, and that husbands would use an increased allowance as a means of further control.

Conclusion

From the point of view of the demand for labor power, women's hidden proletarianization as domestic outworkers represents the lowest rank in an employment hierarchy that links, via subcontracting chains, the domestic sphere to new national and international divisions of labor. As an integral part of the total capitalist labor scene, its fate depends on the character of the accumulation processes taking place inside and outside the

Mexican social formation. Recent reports indicate that subcontracting chains and the provision of domestic outwork seem to be on the increase, at least in certain branches of industrial production. To the extent that this trend is true, we can count on a continuous demand for female labor power to be provided through wage earning under the conditions described above.

Domestic outwork does not compare favorably in terms of wages, stability, fringe benefits, or the possibility of unionization with other processes of female proletarianization outside the household (such as factory work or rural wage work). Low wages and instability conspire to limit outwork income to a supplement to the male's earnings and share in the family pool. In this sense outwork contributes to the reproduction of gender hierarchies within the household. It also contributes to the fragmentation of the working class. The isolation, dispersion, and secrecy inherent in domestic outwork, coupled with women's knowledge that there exists a reserve of wives and mothers ready to take their place if they fall into disgrace with an intermediary, make collective organization extremely difficult and usually impossible. It also explains the absence of "trade-union" or "working-class" consciousness among the workers interviewed. They perceive the unfairness of their labor situation but do not know how to transcend it. Instead, they compete among themselves to get a higher quota of weekly outwork.

When we turn to the household context and consider patterns of marital interaction and women's own interpretation and assessment of outwork, the picture is different and contradictory. On the one hand, domestic outwork represents an extreme case of subordinate proletarianization to the extent that it can be conciliated with the traditional demands on mothers and wives more easily than factory work. In other words, the contradictions between the work role and the maternal and wifely roles are minimal in the domestic outwork context. By stretching the total amount of hours devoted to domestic work (both paid and unpaid), the outworker's daily domestic routine (housework, child care, attention to husband) continues more or less as normal. Indeed, this is one of the main reasons that married women with young children prefer domestic outwork to better-paid employment outside the household. To them, if not always to the observer, domestic outwork presents advantages in this respect.

With reference to patterns of allocation of money, particularly in the pool group, access to an independent income facilitates the renegotiation of the terms of marital interaction. It is associated with greater decision-making power in some areas, and with women's redefinition of their husband's rights and their own. This possibility is enhanced when husbands lose their role as breadwinners. In the case of the housekeeping allowance group, allocational patterns reinforce gender hierarchies, and autonomous decision making is curtailed. But no matter what allocational category a woman belongs to, her small yet independent income constitutes a lever to secure a measure of autonomous control and ameliorates the damage to her self-esteem done by economic dependence. Because of this increased or restored self-esteem and the small but meaningful control obtained by women, becoming an outworker is by far preferable to having no paid job at all.

This brings us back to the issue of collective organization for the purposes of improving female outworkers' labor situation, securing a legal minimum salary, and obtaining fringe benefits. Women like those interviewed are not against the principle of unionization, although only 40 percent of them have heard of trade unions. Rather, they are afraid that any attempts to constitute a common front will be unsuccessful owing to work-force competition, their lack of acquaintance with coworkers, and repression from the employer. They also fear that they will lose the chance of earning much-needed support money. During the course of this research Doña T. tried to organize ten outworkers, who were also her neighbors, to demand higher piecework wages. Half the women deserted at the last minute. The remaining five approached the intermediary; they were insulted, expelled from the premises, and lost their jobs. To teach that "rebellious" neighborhood a lesson, the man occupying the position in the subcontracting chain just above the intermediary moved part of the outwork to another area of Mexico City. Doña T. faced a difficult time with her co-workers, who blamed her for their having been deprived of their jobs.

Domestic outwork presents a complex and challenging example of women's incorporation into wage labor. On the one hand is the need to encourage collective organization to prevent the most extreme elements of exploitation that grow out of its clandestine nature. On the other hand is the danger that collective action poses to women's position and to their use of their wage as a lever for domestic control. It remains to be seen how female outworkers weigh these benefits and costs: whether they opt to organize collectively or whether the risks are adjudged to outweigh intra-household benefits.

The Black Four of Hearts:
Toward a New Paradigm of
Household Economics

NANCY FOLBRE

Years ago, in a classic experiment in the psychology of perception, Gestalt psychologists Jerome Bruner and Leo Postman asked subjects to identify individual playing cards that were flashed before them. The psychologists slipped a few anomalous cards, such as a black four of hearts, into the deck. Until the exposure time was considerably lengthened, the subjects almost always confidently identified these anomalous cards as normal (Bruner and Postman 1949). Thomas Kuhn uses this example, among others, to argue that scientists, as well as experimental subjects, are prone to see what they expect to see (1967).

Households, like decks of cards, have suits and hierarchies; their members are almost always differentiated by gender and by age. Although most social scientists live in households, or perhaps because they do, scientific views of the household are based on little more than glimpses of a deck that is constantly being shuffled. What is it, exactly, that we economists, in particular, expect to see? What combination of hearts and spades? And how do we ascertain the extent to which our respective expectations are fulfilled?

The major paradigms of economics, neoclassical theory and Marxian theory, have diametrically opposed theories of the firm, but remarkably similar theories of the household. Economists of both persuasions tend to treat the household as though it were an almost wholly cooperative unit. As the essays in this volume show, however, economists today are confronted by certain "anomalies," empirical evidence of economic conflict and inequality within the household. Most choose to ignore these anomalies; many seek ways of reconciling them with conventional assumptions. But some economists in both camps have begun to explore the possibility that economic self-interest operates within the home as well as within the market.

This exploration could benefit from more systematic methodological self-reflection. In this essay, I explain why the feminist critique of intrafamilial inequalities poses a serious challenge to conventional economic theories. But I insist that far more attention should be devoted to the development of an alternative theory that draws from both neoclassical and Marxian contributions. Furthermore, I argue the need for an inter-disciplinary effort to move beyond the traditional economic assumption that individuals always act in their own self-interest, narrowly defined.

The first section of this paper interprets the similarities and differences between neoclassical and Marxian economic theories from a feminist standpoint. The second section discusses new theoretical approaches to conflict within the family, arguing for a synthesis of microeconomic and structural approaches. The third section raises some questions about how altruistic behavior is socially defined and socially reproduced, questions that deserve far more serious consideration from economists than they have yet received.

Comparing Assumptions

Contemporary philosophy of science has had remarkably little impact on the theory or practice of economics. A simplistic and outdated brand of positivism has insulated the basic assumptions of neoclassical economic theory from critical scrutiny. Yet neoclassical theory, no less than Marxian theory, is largely structured by its basic assumptions. Thomas Kuhn argues that distinct "paradigms" are characterized by distinct, virtually incommensurable sets of assumptions (1967). Whatever their other differences, however, both neoclassical and Marxian economic theory seem to be wedded to a rosy picture of the household as home, sweet home.

Economists often pride themselves on practicing the most scientific of the social sciences. Yet as contemporary philosophers of science emphasize, the borderline between science and other intellectual pursuits is difficult to draw (Kuhn 1967; Feyerabend 1975, 1978). Even the most "scientific" theories are based on untestable or circular assumptions. They are seldom if ever validated in any conclusive way by empirical research. Even more important, normal scientific research agendas are often limited to questions that can be answered simply by means of technical ingenuity. As Kuhn writes, "Normal science does not aim at novelties of fact or theory, and, when successful, finds none" (Kuhn 1967:53).

Both neoclassical and Marxian theory take somewhat circular assumptions as their starting points. The principle of utility maximization is "impregnable" because utility can be defined as whatever is being maximized (Meek 1962). The principle serves primarily to generate very general predictions regarding the effects of changes in relative prices and incomes on individual behavior. The labor theory of value also holds true by definition. It merely asserts that value can be defined as the amount of socially necessary labor time embodied in a good, and that value bears a determinate mathematical relationship to prices (Steedman 1977). Individual utility functions are unobservable, and because revealed preferences can be ranked only in ordinal terms, they cannot be aggregated or compared (Arrow 1963). By the same token, socially necessary labor time (which includes infinite generations of indirect labor inputs) cannot be directly calculated, in part because it requires the aggregation of heterogeneous forms of labor (Bowles and Gintis 1977).

To take another pair of examples, neoclassical theorists assume that individuals (or households that behave as though they were individuals) and firms are the primary actors in an economy, and they interact almost exclusively through competitive markets in which no single individual or firm can affect supply and demand. They cling to methodologies based on this assumption despite considerable evidence that few if any markets are perfectly competitive (Friedman 1953). Marxian theorists tend to use classes as their unit of analysis, defining classes in terms of the relationship to the means of production and control over the labor process. They pursue the methodology of class analysis despite the evidence of more diverse and complicated forms of social stratification (Poulantzas 1975; Wright 1979).

Such assumptions, however unrealistic, seem to be an indispensable means of structuring research. Acknowledging this unpleasant fact, positivists argue that assumptions themselves merit little scrutiny, that theories should be judged solely by their success at generating and satisfying empirical predictions. Milton Friedman's classic statement of this view in "The Methodology of Positive Economics" continues to be widely quoted by economists, who tend to respond to criticisms of their assumptions simply by reiterating their empirical results. This response is not particularly convincing when the same empirical results may be consistent with more than one theoretical construction (Kuhn 1967:76).

The lack of realism inherent in most theoretical assumptions does not, however, render comparisons between them inconsequential or unnecessary. Among the criteria that are often used to compare alternative sets of theoretical assumptions are internal logic, consistency, and parsimony. Marxian economists, largely excluded from the dominant paradigm, often reject positivist or empiricist views; some have tended to the opposite extreme. Barry Hindess and Paul Hirst, for instance, question the relevance of historical "facts" and elevate the role of deductive logic (1975). Steven Resnick and Richard Wolff argue that neither assumptions nor facts provide adequate criteria for choosing between theories (1982). Different theories merely represent different "points of entry," chosen for somewhat arbitrary reasons.

Between these two extremes of epistemological self-confidence and epistemological skepticism lies a more appealing middle ground. On this terrain, both theoretical assumptions and empirical results deserve careful scrutiny, and the impossibility of specifying any absolute criteria for success or failure does not obviate the need for constant evaluation. As E. P. Thompson writes, the evidence "is there, in its primary form, not to disclose its own meaning, but to be interrogated by minds trained in a discipline of attentive disbelief" (1978 : 28). Such attentive disbelief can be enhanced by efforts to compare contending theories and "translate" them into commensurable terms. Such an analysis must go well beyond a comparison of competing hypotheses. As Foucault observes, the silences within theories often speak more loudly than the claims (1973).

Why are both the neoclassical and the Marxian paradigms so silent on the issue of inequality within the home? Neoclassical theory offers a well-developed theory of nonmarket production but remains largely unconcerned with any form of inequality. Marxian theory, characterized by an emphasis on conflict, remains largely unconcerned with issues of household production. The limitations of both theories are deeply embedded in their intellectual and political history.

As historians of economic thought have noted, neoclassical theory offers a "universal" theory of economic behavior that presumes the existence of markets but is independent of any other institutional context (Hunt 1979). Because neoclassical theory focuses on markets and markets are by definition sites of free and voluntary exchange, neoclassical theory does not provide explanations of conflict or inequality. In a neoclassical world, exploitation, in the economic sense, cannot exist; unless both parties benefit from a transaction it will not take place. The equality or inequality of any given exchange cannot be ascertained because interpersonal comparisons of utility cannot be made.

The plausibility of the "New Home Economics" rests on an analogy between the household and the firm, where individuals within the household operate in an implicit rather than explicit market. Gary Becker theorizes, for instance, that new households are formed by means of a marriage market (1976). Once established, households deploy labor in response to differences in marginal productivity between home and market (Gronau 1973). They choose between home-produced and market-produced goods on the basis of price, although some goods, like their own children, can only be produced at home. Decisions about family size are influenced by changes in the price of children owing to increases in production costs such as education (sometimes termed improvement in child quality) or the increased opportunity cost of time devoted to child care (Schultz 1981).

This analogy is, in some respects, an outgrowth of the changes in family behavior of the last two decades. Just as the neoclassical theory of consumer choice developed at a time when an emergent middle class was beginning to enjoy significant amounts of discretionary consumption, the new home economics emerged during a period in which conscious choice exercised a particularly visible influence on households. Between about 1960, when Gary Becker first systematically developed the concept of human capital, and 1981, when his authoritative *Treatise on the Family* was published, fertility rates in the United States declined sharply while divorce rates soared.

But however important the role of personal choice, the crucial analogy between the household and the firm is somewhat strained. Many different types of exchange take place within and between households, but these exchanges do not conform closely to sales and purchases in a competitive market. Individuals seeking mates are usually not satisfied with an "undifferentiated" product. In household production, unlike commodity production, demanders and suppliers are often one and the same. The cost of home-produced goods like children is not exogenously determined. Parents choose, to some extent, how much time and how many resources to devote to children. And children affect their own price when, as adults, they make certain choices concerning their economic commitments to aging parents (Parsons 1984).

Last, and perhaps most important, the neoclassical household does not have an objective function that is as clear-cut as that of the neoclassical firm. It does not maximize profits. It presumably maximizes the "joint utility" of its members. But the specification of a joint utility function poses a serious problem for neoclassical theory because it requires the aggregation of individual tastes and preferences, a task that is intrinsically problematic (Arrow 1963). One way of solving this aggregation problem is to assume that altruism prevails within the family (Samuelson 1956). But it is entirely inconsistent to argue that individuals who are wholly selfish in the market (where there are no interdependent utilities) are wholly selfless within the family, where they pursue the interests of the collectivity. The vision of pure altruism within the family resembles nothing so much as the Marxian vision of utopian socialism.

There is a delicious political paradox in the juxtaposition of naked self-interest, which presumably motivates efficient allocation of resources through the market, with a fully clothed altruism that presumably motivates efficient allocation of resources within the family. Lest Gary Becker unfairly be assigned responsibility for this paradox, note its distinguished roots in the history of the discipline. One of the most widely quoted passages of Adam Smith's *Wealth of Nations* observes, "It is not from the benevolence of the butcher, the brewer, or the baker that we expect our dinner, but from their regard to their self-interest (1776 : 14). But as Smith made clear in his somewhat neglected *Theory of Moral Sentiments* (1759), he was not particularly skeptical of the benevolence of fathers and husbands.

Becker seeks to provide a scientific basis for his modern explanation of "moral sentiments," drawing from the literature of sociobiology to argue that sharing in the family represents true altruism (rather than mere reciprocity) (1976, 1981). But the threat of selfishness dogs his analysis. In trying to explain why individual family members don't freeload on the benevolence of others, Becker resorts to the concept of a benevolent dictator. How else to describe heads of households who use their economic power to ensure that every family member acts in the interests of the family as a whole? In Becker's words, "parents may use contingent transfers of wealth to provide children with a long-run incentive to consider the interests of the whole family" (1981:188). This explanation of the joint utility function assumes that the only power holders in the family are altruists and the only rotten family members are those who wield no effective power. In other words, Becker allows for rotten kids, but not for rotten parents, rotten husbands, or rotten wives. Selfishness in the family is kept strictly in bounds.

One might expect to find Marxian economists less idealistic. The Marxian tradition has always emphasized the importance of conflict, inequality, and exploitation. Yet conflict is typically defined along the axes of the class position of families, rather than individuals (Ferguson 1979). Furthermore, much of Marxian theory is specific to capitalism as a dominant mode of production. Nonmarket institutions such as private property, the family, and the state are explained primarily in terms of their implications for class relations. Differences between men, women, and children in the same economic class remain largely unexplored (Hartmann 1981).

The Marxian preoccupation with capitalism as a mode of production has shaped the application of Marxian theory to the household. Like neoclassical theory, Marxian theory assumes that firms maximize profits. Unlike neoclassical theory, Marxian theory makes no explicit assumptions about the economic objectives of individuals, but aggregates them within economic classes. Workers' primary goal is to survive, to subsist, to struggle to claim the product of their labor. Household production, described as production for use motivated by basic needs, is often counterposed to production for exchange, motivated by an insatiable desire for gain. As a result, production for use is often placed outside the realm of economic analysis.

Conventional Marxian conceptualizations of relations within the household avoid the term *altruism*. Implicitly, however, they assume that altruism rules, particularly within the working-class family. To give only a few examples: Jane Humphries' essay on the working-class family in

Britain suggests that women choose to relinquish the economic independence that wage work might afford them in order to enhance their families' welfare (1979). Deere and De Janvry (1979) and Deere (1983) focus on
the extraction of surplus from the peasant household as a whole and bypass
the opportunity to explore material inequality within the peasant household. Mamdani's Marxian analysis of fertility decisions explains desired
family size by reference to externally imposed economic constraints (1981).
And finally, Arizpe's work, like many Marxian analyses of migration,
stresses the "survival strategies" of the household as an undifferentiated
unit (1982).

Interestingly, many Marxists concede or even emphasize the role of
domination and alienation in the household even as they proscribe the
possibility of exploitation there (Bowles and Gintis 1981; Vogel 1983).
While there is a growing interest in explaining gender inequality as a
manifestation of a noncapitalist mode of production (Resnick and Wolfe
1982), economic analyses of inequalities within the household have been
conducted primarily by those who heavily credit the influence of feminism
on their theoretical perspective (McCrate 1985; Folbre 1982; Hartmann
1981).

In short, the conventional neoclassical and Marxian paradigms present
a view of the household that is shaped by expectations of equality and
harmony within the family. Conventional neoclassical theory arbitrarily
aggregates individual tastes and preferences within a joint utility function.
Conventional Marxian theory arbitrarily aggregates men, women, and
children into classes consisting of undifferentiated households. Neoclassical economists typically expect their theory of markets to provide a
theory of household production, while Marxian economists typically expect their critical analysis of capitalism to suffice. These respective expectations have predisposed both theories against any empirical exploration of
inequalities within the family.

Accommodating Conflict

To call a spade a spade is to acknowledge an unpleasant reality; hearts
are emblematic of romantic affection. To return to the metaphor of the
psychology experiment described above, observers of the household tend
to see hearts instead of spades. The essays in this volume, representative of
a growing body of research informed by feminist concerns, document
inequalities that seem anomalous from the point of view of conventional
Marxian and neoclassical theories of the household. None of these essays,
however, offers a very systematic alternative theoretical approach.

We might forward the development of such an alternative by sum-
marizing the empirical evidence of inequality within families and explor-

ing three successively more difficult questions pertaining to it. Is this inequality related to systematic differences in the economic bargaining power of family members? What are the components and determinants of economic bargaining power within the family? And finally, how are both relative bargaining power and inequality affected by the process of capitalist development? Recent "revisionist" applications of both neoclassical and Marxian theory offer some important, if incomplete, answers to these questions.

The introductory essay to this volume admirably summarizes the case for more widespread recognition of economic inequalities within the family. Even where women devote a far larger share of their income to the household than men, they seldom have an equivalent claim on leisure time. Gender-based differences in the allocation of household resources are manifest in continuing gender differentials in nutritional and educational levels. And female-headed households in many developing countries seem particularly vulnerable to poverty.

Gender-based inequalities are inextricably linked to intergenerational income flows, as Caldwell and others have emphasized (1981). Economic incentives to rearing children reinforce economic incentives for control over women's productive and reproductive activities (Folbre 1983). In some countries women are so economically disadvantaged that raising sons becomes an indispensable survival strategy (Cain, this volume). In some countries, parents may demand and receive more economic assistance from daughters than from sons, limiting their daughters' future economic opportunities (Greenhalgh, this volume).

Evidence of such inequalities is by no means limited to the developing world. Intergenerational income flows in the developed countries do not currently reward those who have large numbers of children, but there is considerable historical evidence of economic incentives to high fertility in earlier periods (Berkner 1973; Folbre 1985). One might expect to find less evidence of economic inequality between men and women in the more developed countries than in the developing world, but time-budget studies reveal significant inequalities in leisure time between men and women in economies as different as the United States and the Soviet Union (Hartmann 1981; Lapidus 1978). The term *feminization of poverty* was coined to describe the worsening economic position of female-headed households within the United States.

Such findings cast considerable suspicion on assumptions of joint utility and unchanging solidarity within the family. But they are by no means irreconcilable with these assumptions. Inequalities of any sort can be explained by a "cultural bias" or a "taste" for voluntary sacrifice "for the good of the family." Neoclassical theorists have traditionally explained inequalities in the labor market in terms of a "taste for discrimination"

(Becker 1976). Rosenzweig and Schultz provide a similar explanation of inequality between boys and girls within Indian families when they suggest that parents are merely responding to differential wage rates partly determined by "exogenously given" bias against women (1982). Similarly, Behrman and Kenan use the term *promale bias* to explain allocational inequality that cannot be attributed to differential returns on nutrient investment (1984).

As long as differences in the tastes and preferences of men and women are exogenously given, they can be subsumed under the neoclassical economist's traditional assumption of ceteris paribus (other things being equal). The assertion that inequalities within the family are noneconomic in origin protects traditional neoclassical theory from the implications of documented inequalities. But the possibility that inequalities are partly a function of economic factors wreaks havoc with the traditional approach. The development of an alternative approach hinges on the answer to the first question: Is inequality in the family related to differences in economic bargaining power?

Some empirical research on households in developing countries suggests the answer may be yes. Roldan's case studies of Mexican women lead her to conclude that "husbands' participation in better-paid and often more formalized jobs is translated into a commanding position within the family" (p. 235), and access to an independent income facilitates the renegotiation of the terms of marital interaction. Similarly, Acharya's and Bennett's research on Nepalese families shows that women's employment outside the village significantly increases their domestic decision-making role (1982:37).

The need for additional empirical research on such topics is widely recognized. Safilios-Rothschild, in particular, calls for more studies of the relationship between structural indicators of women's status and their influence on household decisions at the microeconomic level (1982). Such empirical research could benefit from the development of a more explicit microeconomic foundation for the bargaining power approach. Some recent efforts to develop such a foundation draw from the formalist tradition of neoclassical theory.

Manser and Brown (1981) and McElroy and Horney (1981) specify a model in which individuals maximize the product of their utility gain from marriage and their partner's utility gain from marriage. Individuals' respective economic positions outside marriage serve as a threat-point in a Nash-bargaining game. Parsons (1984) provides several different specifications of a log linear Stone-Geary utility function in which both own utility and the utility of the younger or older generation enter as arguments. Here again, initial assets may be used as threat points in a Nash-bargaining game.

Pollak, diverging even more from the traditional neoclassical approach, develops a transactions cost analysis that treats the family as a governance structure (1985). This approach rejects the simplicity of the Nash-bargaining model, emphasizes the ways culture and tradition mediate the relationship between assets and threat points, and calls for the formulation of multiperiod bargaining models. Although Pollak seems distressed that he cannot offer a more formal, econometrically tractable framework, he provides a useful guide for historical and interpretive research.

Unlike a microeconomics of the family premised on a joint utility function, a microeconomics of bargaining power invites political economic analysis of structures of inequality. The more formalistic Nash-bargaining models simply treat differences in threat points as "exogenously given." They nonetheless raise the issue of how relative threat points are determined. And this question in turn raises the possibility that bargaining power cannot be defined purely as access to individual assets, because it is significantly affected simply by the cultural and political implications of membership in certain demographic groups.

It is no accident that a certain amount of Marxian terminology, such as "control over the means of production," occasionally suffuses the bargaining power literature (Mosk 1983; Caldwell 1981). In virtually all pre-capitalist and many capitalist societies, legal and political institutions, as well as property ownership, lend elder males considerable power within their families. The parallels between the sex stratification system, as Safilios-Rothschild and Greenhalgh describe it in this volume, and class stratification systems have been explored by scholars influenced by the Marxian tradition. A growing literature conceptualizes structural inequalities between the genders and the generations in terms of the logic of a patriarchal system, a family mode of production or a patriarchal mode of production (Hartmann 1981; Henn 1982).

All these conceptualizations share an emphasis on structural factors that place women and children in different social and economic (rather than merely biological) positions from adult men. Gender and age inequalities become analogous, though by no means identical, to class differences. The analogy between class and gender is an important step toward a consideration of their somewhat contradictory interaction. In this context, Marxian theory can and does make an important contribution to the analysis of household economics.

Recent innovations in the Marxian literature provide a good example of the potential complementarity between microeconomic and structural analyses of bargaining. Bowles (1985) and Schor and Bowles (1984) use a structural analysis of the changing tenor of class relationships to explain changes within individual firms. Similar models could be applied to the household. McCrate provides an excellent theoretical and empirical analysis of the relationship between changes in women's relative economic independence and rates of marriage within the United States (1985).

Marxian theory also offers some important insights into the third question, the relationship between the process of capitalist development and changes in women's position. Those who analyze patriarchy as a system but overlook or ignore the logic of capitalism as a system tend to be extremely optimistic about the positive effects of development on women. Caldwell (1981), Parsons (1984), and Mosk (1983) all treat the weakening of patriarchal power as though it were merely an inevitable byproduct of the process of capitalist development. Ironically, this assumption echoes the traditional Marxian argument, first articulated by Engels (1884) and rejected by most modern Marxian scholars, that capitalism would automatically bring about the liberation of women. This assumption ignores over fifteen years of research on women and development that has built on the early work of Ester Boserup (1970).

Boserup was among the first to argue that economic development could worsen the relative position of women, an argument recently restated by Rogers (1979). Although this issue is by no means settled, there is a growing consensus that the emergence of capitalist relations of production transforms rather than merely weakens preexisting patriarchal systems (Beneria and Sen 1981). Opportunities for wage labor eventually attentuate patriarchal control over the younger generation, curtail the economic incentives to have large numbers of children, and diminish the incentives for certain forms of patriarchal control over women. But elder men are able to control the ways in which women participate in wage labor, limiting their access to all but the lowest-paying jobs. Employers, as well as men, benefit from low-cost female labor, and both occupational segregation and the sexual wage differential reproduce traditional patriarchal inequalities within modern capitalist systems (Folbre 1983; Hartmann 1979; Rubery 1978).

There are other complementarities between patriarchy and capitalism that may help explain why women's relative bargaining power within the home does not increase more in the course of economic development. For instance, state policies toward the family may shift the burden of child-rearing expenses increasingly onto individual, often single, mothers (Folbre 1985). Until recently, relatively few historical studies traced the influence of employer's choices, trade union actions, or state policy on women as a group. But a growing historical and comparative literature provides a rich basis for more careful consideration of structural influences on women's role in economic development. Pyle's recent dissertation analyzing changes in female labor force participation in Ireland shows that state policies can effectively prevent the rapid incorporation of women into paid employment (1985). And Papanek's essay in this volume employs a comparative methodology to show how differences in preexisting patriarchal traditions affect the course of women's incorporation into the labor force.

Even when posed in purely descriptive, rather than theoretical, terms, the evidence of structural inequalities based on gender and age casts considerable doubt on approaches that treat the household as a purely altruistic unit. The suggestion that women and female children "voluntarily" relinquish leisure, education, and food would be somewhat more persuasive if they were in a position to demand their fair share. It is the juxtaposition of women's lack of economic power with the unequal allocation of household resources that lends the new approach to household economics much of its persuasive appeal.

But new approaches to household economics must grow out of a vivid awareness of the intellectual traditions of economic theory and a self-conscious consideration of methodological issues. Whether or not proponents of a bargaining power approach to the household accept the analogy with bargaining power within the capitalist firm, they have something in common with, and perhaps something to learn from, contemporary Marxian methodology. Likewise, conventional Marxists who have yet to apply their new game-theoretic models to the household have something to learn from revisionist neoclassical theorists. Last, and perhaps most important, all economists have something to learn from the peculiar economic puzzle of the concept of love.

Looking for Love

Is home never a sweet place, after all? Could it be that all the cards we thought were hearts were just different-colored spades? This view seems as unrealistic as its converse. But economists who reject the conventional neoclassical view that altruism resides in the family and the traditional Marxian view that it can thrive anywhere except under capitalism are left with the need for an alternative theory of altruism. If there are limits on the pursuit of economic self-interest, narrowly defined, how and why do these limits emerge?

The household remains one of the most interesting arenas for asking this question because altruism is more visible there than elsewhere. Parents may respond to changes in the costs and benefits of children, but they continue to raise children even when the economic costs are very high. Likewise, children may often resist a formal economic obligation to their parents, but they nonetheless remain an important source of security and support. The partial altruism that is one of the defining characteristics of family life cannot be attributed to a sociobiological imperative to maximize genetic fitness. It may be partially explained as a complicated form of reciprocity. The economics of the family highlights the importance of a theoretical understanding of how and why reciprocity occasionally prevails in economic life.

Altruism denotes, in Webster's words, "unselfish concern for the welfare of others." In neoclassical terms it denotes interdependent utility functions, the possibility that one might derive more pleasure from another's pleasure than from one's own. This is the pleasure that Adam Smith's butcher and baker could not be relied on to experience. This is the pleasure that, from Wilson's sociobiological point of view, represents an evolutionary dead end. Individuals who sacrifice a share of their resources for others (without guaranteed reciprocity) diminish their own chances of survival and, in the long run, are likely to be eliminated through natural selection (Wilson 1975).

The one exception, in Wilson's view, is kin-based altruism. Individuals who sacrifice for the sake of others who share their genes (brothers, sisters, or offspring) may diminish their own chances of survival, but they enhance the viability of their genes, and thereby improve their own "reproductive fitness." Becker's emphasis on altruism within the family and his frequent references to Wilson imply that he accepts this "reproductive fitness" argument. However, Becker diverges considerably from Wilson's view when he argues that altruists can garner important economic benefits in the form of reciprocity. Where there is considerable physical and social interaction, he argues, reciprocal altruism can benefit everyone (1976:294).

Of course, Becker never extols the merits of reciprocal altruism outside the family. If he did so he would come dangerously close to an endorsement of the possible merits of collective ownership and the possible virtues of democratic economic planning. Neoclassical economists have traditionally been skeptical of any cooperative behavior because of its associated "free-rider" problems (Olsen 1975). On the other hand, Marxian theorists have often assumed that the elimination of class differences would be a sufficient condition for effective economic cooperation. Both approaches are simplistic.

Recently, economists from both schools of thought have begun to examine the issues of reciprocity and cooperation more systematically. On the neoclassical side, Maital and Maital (1984) argue that appropriate socialization or enforcement mechanisms can make cooperation an effective long-run strategy for optimization. Andrew Schotter, among others, suggests that customs and habits may represent a more "efficient" solution to certain coordination problems than the market (1981). On the Marxian side, Roemer's argument that exploitation can take place within socialist economies illustrates the point that there are no simple or obvious guarantees of economic reciprocity (1982).

Even within the family, as the preceding sections have argued, reciprocity may break down. Still, more reciprocity and sharing seems to take place within families than elsewhere in the economy. Why is reciprocity relatively successful there? Becker seems confident that social and physical proximity are a sufficient guarantee, but this "small is beautiful" argument is a priori unconvincing.

One could make a much stronger case for the effects of the socialization of reciprocity. Virtually all the social sciences except economics emphasize the ways families and other social institutions convey culture, tastes, and preferences to children, in both conscious and unconscious ways. These acts of conveying help define individuals' concepts of themselves and their definitions of "selfish" behavior. Altruism as action may be, in some sense, produced, or at the very least reinforced, by altruism as ideal.

Stated in slightly more formal terms, shared ideals are one of the mechanisms of cooperation that help solve free-rider problems (North 1981). And the ideals of family life may help explain why families enjoy at least somewhat more reciprocity than other groups. Sharing within the family is viewed, not only by parents, but also by economists, as something resembling a responsibility. Sharing outside the family is typically viewed, at best, as charity. Parents seldom endorse the pursuit of individual self-interest as a means of achieving an optimal growth path within the home. Economists, however, eagerly reinforce the very self-interested behavior that they take as a heuristic starting point in explaining the magic of the market.

Perhaps women's position in and commitment to the ideals of family life help explain why women often seem less motivated by "economic" concerns than men. Recent feminist scholarship emphasizes the ways socialization in family and schools reinforces existing gender inequalities partly by encouraging women to be better altruists than men (Gilligan 1982). Wives and mothers are expected to be more selfless than other family members, to put other's needs before their own (Polatnick 1984). As women begin to spend less time working in the home and more time in the capitalist marketplace, and as their bargaining power increases, will their traditional altruism diminish?

The Marxian theory of historical materialism asserts that human nature, such as it is, is shaped by its material surroundings, its social context. Hence the implication that the pursuit of economic self-interest applies only to the capitalist context. However naive this implication, it does seem that capitalist culture sanctions and encourages the pursuit of economic self-interest more than most previous cultures have (Sahlins 1972). It is sometimes said that the invisible hand, wielding the ideology of laissez-faire, swept the medieval concept of a moral economy aside (Polanyi 1944).

It might better be said that the invisible hand swept the moral economy into the home, where an imaginary world of perfect altruism could counterbalance the imaginary world of perfect self-interest in the market. The bulk of economic theory either takes altruism as a given or rules it out of order. Neither of these alternatives is very convincing, and both legitimate the social institutions that structure economic life within the family and without. They also seriously handicap the development of any general theory of cooperation and conflict.

Cooperation and conflict in the family, in particular, raise questions that cut across the traditional boundaries of neoclassical and Marxian theory, revealing not only a common methodological bias, but also a common agenda for research: Under what conditions can economic reciprocity prevail? In pursuing this agenda, we should remember that our perceptions will be affected by what we hope for as well as what we expect to see. Household economics teaches us that it is all too easy to confuse hearts and spades. But it also teaches us that at least some of the cards we play with are the ones we deal ourselves.

REFERENCES CITED

References Cited

BRUCE AND DWYER: Introduction

Abdullah, A., and S. Zeidenstein. 1981. *Village Women of Bangladesh: Prospects for Change*. London.

Acharya, Meena, and Lynn Bennett. 1983. "Women and the Subsistence Sector: Economic Participation in Household Decisionmaking in Nepal." Washington, D.C.: World Bank.

Agarwal, Bina. 1981. *Agricultural Modernization and Third World Women: Pointers from the Literature and an Empirical Analysis*. Geneva.

Ahmad, Zubeida M., and Martha F. Loufti. 1982. *Women Workers in Rural Development*. Geneva.

Becker, Gary S. 1981. *A Treatise on the Family*. Cambridge, Mass.

Beneria, Lourdes, ed. 1982. *Women and Development: The Sexual Division of Labor in Rural Societies*. New York.

Benson, Janet E., and Jan Paul Emmert. 1987. "The Accelerated Mahaweli Program, Sri Lanka: A Women-in-Development Assessment." In Alice Carloni, ed., "Women in Development: AID's Experience, 1973–85." Unpublished synthesis paper. Vol. 1.

Blumberg, Rae Lesser. 1986. "A Women-in-Development Natural Environment in Guatemala: The Alcosa Agribusiness Project in 1980 and 1985." Aug. Mimeo.

————. 1988. "Income Under Female vs. Male Control: Differential Spending Patterns and the Consequences When Women Lose Control of Returns to Labor." Draft report prepared for the World Bank.

Boserup, Ester. 1970. *Women's Role in Economic Development*. London.

Buvinic, Mayra, Margaret A. Lycette, and William Paul McGreevey, eds. 1983. *Women and Poverty in the Third World*. Baltimore, Md.

Buvinic, Mayra, Nadia H. Youssef, and Barbara Von Elm. 1978. "Women-Headed Households: The Ignored Factor in Development Planning." AID report. Washington, D.C.

Cain, Mead. 1978. *The Household Life Cycle and Economic Mobility in Rural Bangladesh*. The Population Council, Center for Policy Studies, Working Paper no. 28. New York.

Cain, Mead, Syeda Rokeya Khanam, and Shamsun Nahar. 1979. "Class, Patriarchy, and Women's Work in Bangladesh," *Population and Development Review*, 5, no. 3:405–38.

Carloni, Alice, ed., 1987. "Women in Development: AID's Experience, 1973–1985." Unpublished synthesis paper. Vol. 1.

Chaney, Elsa, Emmy Simmons, and Kathleen Staudt. 1979. "Women in Development." Washington, D.C.

Chen, Martha. 1984. "The Working Women's Forum: Organizing for Credit and Change," *SEEDS*.

Conti, Anna. 1979. "Capitalistic Organization and Production Through Non-Capitalistic Relations: Women's Role in a Pilot Resettlement in Upper Volta," *Review of African Political Economy*, no. 15/16:75–91.

Dey, Jennie. 1983. "Gambian Women: Unequal Partners in Rice Development Projects?," *Journal of Development Studies*, 17, no. 1 (May): 109–22.

Dixon, Ruth B. 1978. *Rural Women at Work: Strategies for Development in South Asia*. Baltimore, Md.

———. 1982. "Women in Agriculture: Counting the Labor Force in Developing Countries," *Population and Development Review*, 8, no. 3:539–66.

Dwyer, Daisy H. 1983. "Women and Income in the Third World: Implications for Policy." The Population Council, International Working Paper no. 18. June.

Engle, Patricia. 1986. "The Intersecting Needs of Working Women and Their Young Children: 1980 to 1985." Jan. 24. Mimeo.

Engle, Patricia, and Mary Pederson. N.d. "Maternal Work for Earnings and Children's Nutritional Status Within Urban Guatemala." Mimeo.

Falbo, Tony, and Letticia Ann Peplau. 1980. "Power Strategies in Intimate Relationships," *Journal of Personality and Social Psychology*, 38, no. 4:618–28.

Hanger, Jane, and Jon Moris. 1973. "Women in the Household Economy." In Robert Chambers and Jon Moris, eds., *MWEA: An Irrigated Rice Settlement Scheme in Kenya*. Munich: Weltforum Verlag.

Hill, Russell C., and F. P. Stafford. 1980. "Paternal Care of Children: Time Dire Estimates of Quantity, Predictability, and Variety," *Journal of Human Resources*, 15:219–31. Quoted in Robinson, Warren C. 1987. "Time Cost of Children and Other Household Production," *Population Studies*, 41, no. 2:313–23.

Horton, Susan, and Barbara Diane Miller. N.d. "The Effect of Gender of Household Head on Expenditure: Evidence from Low-Income Households in Jamaica."

Jain, Devaki. 1974. *From Disassociation to Rehabilitation: A Report and Experiment to Promote Self-Employment in an Urban Area*. New Delhi: Allied Publishers.

Jain, Devaki, ed. 1985. *The Tyranny of the Household*. New Delhi.

Joekes, Susan P. 1987. "Evaluation of Research and Policies of Female Employment in Developing Countries." Prepared for OEC Development Centre, Conference on Evaluation of Urban Employment Research and Policies in Developing Countries, Paris, Nov. 2–4.

King, Elizabeth, and Robert E. Evenson. 1983. "Time Allocation and Home Production in Philippine Rural Households." In Mayra Buvinic, Margaret A. Lycette, and William Paul McGreevey, eds., *Women and Poverty in the Third World*. Baltimore, Md.: Johns Hopkins University Press.

Knudsen, Barbara, and Barbara A. Yates. 1981. *The Economic Role of Women in Small-Scale Agriculture in the Eastern Caribbean—St. Lucia.* Barbados: University of the West Indies Women-in-Development Unit.

Kossoudji, Sherrie, and Eva Mueller. 1983. "The Economic and Demographic Status of Female-Headed Households in Rural Botswana," *Economic Development and Cultural Change,* 31, no. 4 (July): 831–59.

Krishna, Raj. N.d. "Women and Development Planning (with special reference to Asia and the Pacific)." Mimeo prepared for the Asian and Pacific Women's Center.

Kumar, Shubh. 1977. "Composition of Economic Constraints in Child Nutrition: Impact from Maternal Incomes and Employment in Low Income Households." Ph.D. diss., Cornell Univ.

Leacock, Eleanore Burke, ed. 1984. *Women's Work.* South Hadley.

Leslie, Joanne. 1987. "Women's Work and Child Nutrition in the Third World." International Center for Research on Women. Mimeo.

Maher, Vanessa. 1981. "Work, Consumption, and Authority Within the Household: A Moroccan Case." In Kate Young, Carol Wolkowitz, and Roslyn McCullagh, eds., *Of Marriage and the Market: Women's Subordination in International Perspective.* London.

Manser, Marilyn, and Murray Brown. 1979. "Bargaining Analyses of Intra Household Decisions." In Cynthia Lloyd, Emily S. Andrews, and Curtis L. Gilroy, eds., *Women in the Labor Market.* New York.

Mason, Karen Oppenheim, and Anju Malhotra Taj. 1987. "Gender Differences and Reproductive Goals in Developing Countries." Paper commissioned by the Population Sciences Division of the Rockefeller Foundation. Feb. 27.

Massiah, Jocelin. 1980. "Family Structure and the Status of Women in the Caribbean, with particular reference to 'Women Who Head Households.'" Paper presented at the meeting of Experts on Research on the Status of Women, Development, and Population Trends: Evaluation and Prospects. Paris, Nov. 25–28.

Mukerjee, Moni. 1985. "Contributions to a Use of Social Product by Women." In Devaki Jain, ed., *The Tyranny of the Household.* New Delhi.

Nash, John. 1953. "Two Person Cooperative Games," *Econometrica,* 21: 128–35.

Nelson, Nici, ed. 1981. *African Women in the Development Process.* London: Frank Cass.

Pahl, Jan. 1983. "The Allocation of Money and the Structuring of Inequalities within Marriage," *The Sociological Review,* 31, no. 2 (May): 237–62.

Recchini de Lattes et al. 1981. *Women in the Bench of the Accused.* Mexico City.

Rogers, Beatrice Lorge. 1983. "The Internal Dynamics of Households: A Critical Factor in Development Policy." Tufts University School of Nutrition, Medford, Mass. Paper developed in fulfillment of an AID contract for AID/PPC/PDPR/HR. Oct. 1983.

Safilios-Rothschild, Constantina. 1982. "Female Power, Autonomy, and Demographic Change in the Third World." In Richard Anker et al., eds., *Women's Roles and Demographic Change.* Geneva: International Labour Organization.

Sanday, Peggy R. 1974. "Female Status in the Public Domain." In Michelle

Rosaldo and Louise Lamphere, eds., *Women, Culture and Society.* Stanford, Calif.: Stanford University Press.

Schmink, Marianne. 1984. "Household Economic Strategies." *Latin American Research Review,* 19, no. 3:87–101.

Sen, Amartya. 1985. "Women, Technology, and Sexual Divisions." UNCTAD/ TT/79.

SEWA (Self-Employed Women's Association). 1975. Annual and Project Reports. Ahmedabad, India.

Signs. 1979. Special Editions. "The Labor of Women: Work and Family." (Summer). "Women in Latin America." (Autumn).

Sivard, Ruth Leger. 1985. *Women: A World Survey.* Washington, D.C.

Smith, Peter C. 1981. "Migration, Sex, and Occupations in Urban Indonesia and Thailand." East-West Population Institute. Working Paper no. 21. Honolulu. Oct.

Tripp, Robert B. 1981. "Farmers and Traders: Some Economic Determinants of Nutritional Status in Northern Ghana," *Journal of Tropical Pediatrics,* 27:15–22.

Whitehead, Ann. 1981. "'I'm Hungry, Mum': The Politics of Domestic Budgeting." In Kate Young, Carol Wolkowitz, and Roslyn McCullagh, eds., *Of Marriage and the Market: Women's Subordination in International Perspective.* London.

Wilson, A. B. 1981. "Longitudinal Analyses of Diet, Physical Growth, Verbal Development, and Performance." In J. B. Balderston, A. B. Wilson, M. Freire, and M. Simonen, eds., *Malnourished Children of the Rural Poor.* Boston.

Young, Kate. 1987. "Enhancing Gender Awareness: Household Resource Management. A Training Module for Trainers—Pilot Project." The Institute of Development Studies, Sussex, England. Mimeo, May.

CAIN: Reproductive Failure in Rural South Asia

Abdul-Rauf, Muhammad. 1977. *The Islamic View of Women and the Family.* New York.

Cain, Mead. 1978. "The Household Life Cycle and Economic Mobility in Rural Bangladesh," *Population and Development Review,* 4, no. 3:421–38.

———. 1981. "Risk and Insurance: Perspectives on Fertility and Agrarian Change in India and Bangladesh," *Population and Development Review,* 7, no. 3:435–74.

———. 1982. "Perspectives on Family and Fertility in Developing Countries," *Population Studies,* 36, no. 2:159–75.

———. 1983. "Fertility as an Adjustment to Risk," *Population and Development Review,* 9, no. 3:688–702.

———. 1985. "The Fate of the Elderly in South Asia: Implications for Fertility." In *IUSSP International Population Conference, Florence 1985,* vol. 4, pp. 279–91. Liège.

Cain, Mead, S. R. Khanam, and S. Nahar. 1979. "Class, Patriarchy, and Women's Work in Bangladesh," *Population and Development Review,* 5, no. 3:405–38.

Datta, S. K., and J. B. Nugent. 1984. "Are Old Age Security and Utility of Children in Rural India Really Unimportant?," *Population Studies,* 38, no. 4:507–9.

Hajnal, John. 1982. "Two Kinds of Preindustrial Household Formation System," *Population and Development Review,* 8, no. 3:449–94.

Nugent, Jeffrey B. 1985. "The Old-Age Security Motive for Fertility," *Population and Development Review,* 11, no. 1:75–97.

Vlassoff, M., and C. Vlassoff. 1980. "Old Age Security and the Utility of Children in Rural India," *Population Studies,* 34, no. 3:487–99.

GREENHALGH: Sexual Stratification in Taiwan

Arrigo, Linda Gail. 1980. "The Industrial Work Force of Young Women in Taiwan," *Bulletin of Concerned Asian Scholars,* 12, no. 2:25–38.

Becker, Gary S. 1981. *A Treatise on the Family.* Cambridge, Mass.

Ben-Porath, Yoram. 1980. "The F-connection: Families, Friends, and Firms and the Organization of Exchange," *Population and Development Review,* 6, no. 1:1–30.

Boserup, Ester. 1970. *Woman's Role in Economic Development.* New York.

Burgess, John Stewart. 1928. *The Guilds of Peking.* New York.

Census Office, Executive Yuan. 1976. *General Report, the 1975 Sample Census of Population and Housing, Taiwan-Fukien Area, Republic of China.* Taipei.

Chow Yung-teh. 1966. *Social Mobility in China: Status Careers Among the Gentry in a Chinese Community.* New York.

Chuang Ying-chang. 1983. "Statuses and Roles of Women in the Changing Chinese Family: A Case from Taiwan." Paper presented at the Eleventh International Congress of Anthropological and Ethnological Sciences, Canada.

Cohen, Myron L. 1976. *House United, House Divided: The Chinese Family in Taiwan.* New York.

Council for Economic Planning and Development. 1982. *Taiwan Statistical Data Book.* Taipei.

Croll, Elisabeth. 1981. *The Politics of Marriage in Contemporary China.* Cambridge, Eng.

———. 1984. *Chinese Women Since Mao.* Armonk, N.Y.

Diamond, Norma. 1969. *K'un Shen: A Taiwan Village.* New York.

———. 1979. "Women and Industry in Taiwan," *Modern China,* 5, no. 3: 317–40.

Directorate-General of Budget, Accounting, and Statistics (DGBAS). 1977. *Statistical Yearbook of the Republic of China, 1977.* Taipei.

———. 1982. *Monthly Bulletin of Labor Statistics, Republic of China, December.* Taipei.

Ebrey, Patricia Buckley, trans. 1984. *Family and Property in Sung China: Yuan Ts'ai's Precepts for Social Life.* Princeton, N.J.

Eisenstein, Zillah R., ed. 1979. *Capitalist Patriarchy and the Case for Socialist Feminism.* New York.

Etienne, Mona, and Eleanor Leacock, eds. 1980. *Women and Colonization: Anthropological Perspectives.* New York.

Fei Hsiao-tung. 1939. *Peasant Life in China.* London.

Fei Hsiao-tung and Chih-i Chang. 1945. *Earthbound China: A Study of Rural Economy in Yunnan*. Chicago.

Free China Journal (Taipei). 1984a. "80,000 New Jobs Forecast." June 24.

———. 1984b. "Female Grads Find Many Job Openings." July 8.

Freedman, Maurice. 1979. *The Study of Chinese Society: Essays by Maurice Freedman*, ed. G. William Skinner. Stanford, Calif.

Galenson, Walter. 1979. "The Labor Force, Wages, and Living Standards." In W. Galenson, ed., *Economic Growth and Structural Change in Taiwan*. Ithaca, N.Y.

Galenson, Walter, ed. 1979. *Economic Growth and Structural Change in Taiwan: The Postwar Experience of the Republic of China*. Ithaca, N.Y.

Gallin, Bernard. 1966. *Hsin Hsing, Taiwan: A Chinese Village in Change*. Berkeley, Calif.

Gallin, Bernard, and Rita S. Gallin. 1982. "Socioeconomic Life in Rural Taiwan: Twenty Years of Development and Change," *Modern China*, 8, no. 2:205–46.

Gallin, Rita S. 1984. "The Entry of Chinese Women into the Rural Labor Force: A Case Study from Taiwan," *Signs: Journal of Women in Culture and Society*, 9, no. 3:383–98.

Green, Susan S. 1983. "Silicon Valley's Women Workers: A Theoretical Analysis of Sex-Segregation in the Electronics Industry Labor Market." In J. Nash and M. P. Fernandez-Kelly, eds., *Women, Men, and the International Division of Labor*. Albany, N.Y.

Greenhalgh, Susan. 1982. "Income Units: The Ethnographic Alternative to Standardization." In Yoram Ben-Porath, ed., *Income Distribution and the Family*. (Supplement to *Population and Development Review*, 8.)

Hartmann, Heidi. 1976. "Capitalism, Patriarchy, and Job Segregation by Sex." In Martha Blaxall and Barbara Reagan, eds., *Women and the Workplace: The Implications of Occupational Segregation*. Chicago.

Ho Ping-ti. 1962. *The Ladder of Success in Imperial China: Aspects of Social Mobility, 1368–1911*. New York.

Ho, Samuel P. S. 1978. *Economic Development of Taiwan, 1860–1970*. New Haven, Conn.

Hu Tai-li. 1983. "My Mother-in-Law's Village: Rural Industrialization and Change in Taiwan." Ph.D. diss., Dept. of Anthropology, City University of New York.

Huang, Nora Chiang. 1984. "The Migration of Rural Women to Taipei." In James T. Fawcett, Siew-Ean Khoo, and Peter C. Smith, eds., *Women in the Cities of Asia: Migration and Urban Adaptation*. Boulder, Colo.

Kung, Lydia. 1983. *Factory Women in Taiwan*. Ann Arbor, Mich.

Levy, Marion J., Jr. 1971. *The Family Revolution in Modern China*. New York. Orig. ed. 1949.

Lim, Linda Y. C. 1983. "Capitalism, Imperialism, and Patriarchy: The Dilemma of Third-World Women Workers in Multinational Factories." In J. Nash and M. P. Fernandez-Kelly, eds., *Women, Men, and the International Division of Labor*. Albany, N.Y.

Lin Ching-yuan. 1973. *Industrialization in Taiwan, 1946–72: Trade and Import-Substitution Policies for Developing Countries*. New York.

Liu, Paul K. C. 1983. "Trends in Female Labor Force Participation in Taiwan: The Transition Toward Higher Technology Activities," *Academia Economic Papers*, 11, no. 1 : 293–323.

Meskill, Johanna Menzel. 1979. *A Chinese Pioneer Family: The Lins of Wu-feng, Taiwan, 1729–1895*. Princeton, N.J.

Ministry of Education. 1983. *Education Statistics of the Republic of China, 1983*. Taipei.

Ministry of Interior. 1983. *1982 Taiwan-Fukien Demographic Fact Book, Republic of China*. Taipei.

Nash, June, and Maria Patricia Fernandez-Kelly, eds. 1983. *Women, Men, and the International Division of Labor*. Albany, N.Y.

Ozawa, Terutomo. 1979. *Multinationalism, Japanese Style: The Political Economy of Outward Dependency*. Princeton, N.J.

Robins, Lisa Dale, and Carol Cheng. 1977. "Women's Perception of Their Roles in Taiwan," *Area Studies* (June): 79–99.

Sahlins, Marshall. 1972. *Stone Age Economics*. Chicago.

Salaff, Janet W. 1981. *Working Daughters of Hong Kong: Filial Piety or Power in the Family?* Cambridge, Eng.

Smith, Arthur H. 1970. *Village Life in China*. Boston.

Sung Lung-sheng. 1975. "Inheritance and Kinship in North Taiwan." Ph.D. diss., Dept. of Anthropology, Stanford University.

Taiwan Provincial Labor Force Survey and Research Institute. Various years. *Quarterly Report on the Labor Force Survey in Taiwan*. Taichung.

Wen Ch'ung-i and Hsiao-ch'un Chang. 1979. "Occupational Status and Occupational Usefulness to Society" [in Chinese]. In Institute of Economics, Academia Sinica, *Conference on Human Resources in Taiwan, December 21–23, 1979*, vol. 2. Taipei.

Winckler, Edwin A., and Susan Greenhalgh, eds. 1988. *Contending Approaches to the Political Economy of Taiwan*. Armonk, N.Y.: M. E. Sharpe.

Wolf, Arthur P., and Chieh-shan Huang. 1980. *Marriage and Adoption in China, 1845–1945*. Stanford, Calif.

Wolf, Margery. 1972. *Women and the Family in Rural Taiwan*. Stanford, Calif.

Wu Rong-i. 1976. "Urbanization and Industrialization in Taiwan: A Study of the Specific Pattern of Labor Utilization." In Institute of Economics, Academia Sinica, *Conference on Population and Economic Development in Taiwan, 29 December 1975–2 January 1976*. Taipei.

Yang, Martin C. 1945. *A Chinese Village: Taitou, Shantung Province*. New York.

Young, Kate, Carol Wolkowitz, and Roslyn McCullagh, eds. 1984. *Of Marriage and the Market: Women's Subordination Internationally and Its Lessons* (2d ed.). London.

PAPANEK AND SCHWEDE: Women are Good with Money

Ahmed, K. S., and R. H. Chaudhury. 1981. "Nuptiality." In United Nations, Economic and Social Commission for Asia and the Pacific, *Population of Bangladesh*. Country Monograph Series no. 8. New York.

Alam, Iqbal, and Muhtab S. Karim. 1986. "Marriage Patterns, Marital Dissolution and Remarriage." In Nasra M. Shah, ed., *Pakistani Women*. Honolulu: East-West Center Population Institute.

Alamgir, M. 1981. "Economic Activity of the Population." In United Nations, Economic and Social Commission for Asia and the Pacific, *Population of Bangladesh*. Country Monograph Series no. 8. New York.

Bertocci, Peter J. 1970. "Elusive Villages: Social Structure and Community Organization in Rural East Pakistan." Ph.D. diss., Michigan State University.

Biro Pusat Statistik. 1982a. *Statistik Indonesia: Statistical Yearbook of Indonesia*. Jakarta.

———. 1982b. *Population of Indonesia 1980*, Series S, no. 1. Jakarta.

Cain, Mead T. 1980. "The Economic Activities of Children in a Village in Bangladesh." In Hans P. Binswanger et al., *Rural Household Studies in Asia*. Singapore: Singapore Univ. Press.

Chapman, Barbara Anne. 1984. "Preliminary Summary of Street Food Vending in Bogor." Paper presented at a Seminar on Micro-food Vending and Processing in Bogor. Photocopy.

Dewey, Alice G. 1962. *Peasant Marketing in Java*. Glencoe, Ill.: Free Press.

Geertz, Clifford. 1962. "The Rotating Credit Association: A 'Middle Rung' in Development," *Economic Development and Cultural Change*, 10, no. 3 : 241–63.

Geertz, Hildred. 1961. *The Javanese Family: A Study of Kinship and Socialization*. Glencoe, Ill.: Free Press.

Hart, Gillian. 1978. "Labor Allocation Strategies in Rural Javanese Households," Ph.D. diss., Cornell University.

———. 1986. *Power, Labor, and Livelihood: Processes of Change in Rural Java*. Berkeley: Univ. of Calif. Press.

Hull, Terence H., and Valerie Hull. 1977. "The Relations of Economic Class and Fertility: An Analysis of Some Indonesian Data," *Population Studies*, 31, no. 1.

Islam, Shamima, ed. 1982. *Exploring the Other Half: Field Research with Rural Women in Bangladesh*. Dhaka: Women for Women.

Jay, Robert R. 1969. *Javanese Villagers: Social Relations in Rural Modjokuto*. Cambridge, Mass.: MIT Press.

Jellinek, Lea. 1976. "The Life of a Jakarta Street Trader." Working Paper no. 9, Centre of Southeast Asian Studies, Monash University, Melbourne, Australia, Mimeo.

———. 1978. "The Life of a Jakarta Street Trader." Working Paper no. 13. Centre of Southeast Asian Studies, Monash University, Melbourne, Australia. Mimeo.

Kusuma, Ny. Sutarsih Mulia. 1976. *Berbagai Aspek Perbedaan Pola Perkawinan di Indonesia Dewasa Ini* [Various aspects of differences in marriage patterns in present-day Indonesia]. Survey Fertilitas-Mortalitas Indonesia 1973 Monografi Seri no. 2. Jakarta.

Lev, Daniel S. 1972. *Islamic Courts in Indonesia: A Study in the Political Bases of Legal Institutions*. Berkeley: Univ. of Calif. Press.

Manderson, Lenore, ed. 1983. *Women's Work and Women's Roles: Economics and Everyday Life in Indonesia, Malaysia and Singapore*. Canberra: ANU Press.

March, Kathryn S., and Rachelle Taqqu. 1982. *Women's Informal Associations and the Organizational Capacity for Development*. Ithaca, N.Y.: Rural Development Committee, Center for Int'l Studies, Monograph Series.

Nakamura, Hisako. 1983. *Divorce in Java*. Yogyakarta: Gadjah Mada Univ. Press.

Oey, Mayling. 1979. "Rising Expectations but Limited Opportunities for Women in Indonesia." In Rounaq Jahan and Hanna Papanek, eds., *Women and Development: Perspectives from South and Southeast Asia*. Dhaka: Bangladesh Inst. of Law and Development.

―――. 1984. "Changing Work Patterns of Women in Indonesia During the 1970's: Causes and Consequences." Paper prepared for the APDC/SAREC Regional Conferences on Identification of Priority Research Issues on Women in Asia and the Pacific, Kuala Lumpur, Feb. 27–Mar. 2.

―――. 1985. "The Role of Manufacturing in Labor Absorption: Indonesia During the 1970s." In Philip M. Hauser, ed., *Urbanization and Migration in Asian Development*. Honolulu: Univ. of Hawaii Press.

Panjaitan, Kartini. 1977. "Kegiatan Dagang Inang-Inang" [Activities of women traders], *Masyarakat Indonesia*, 4, no. 1:111–24.

Papanek, Hanna. 1979a. "Implications of Development for Women in Indonesia: Selected Research and Policy Issues." Center for Asian Development Studies, Discussion Paper no. 8, Boston University.

―――. 1979b. "Research on Women by Women: Interviewer Selection and Training," *Studies in Family Planning*, 10, no. 11–12:412–15.

―――. 1979c. "Family Status Production: The 'Work' and 'Non-Work' of Women," *Signs*, 4, no. 4:775–81.

―――. 1983. "Implications of Development for Women in Indonesia: Research and Policy Issues." In Kathleen Staudt and Jane Jaquette, eds., *Women in Developing Countries: A Policy Focus*. New York.

―――. 1985. "Class and Gender in Education-Employment Linkages," *Comparative Education Review*, 29, no. 3:317–46.

Papanek, Hanna, T. Omas Ihromi, and Yulfita Rahardjo. 1974. "Changes in the Status of Women and Their Significance in the Process of Social Change: Indonesian Case Studies." Paper presented at the Sixth International Conference on Asian History, International Association of Historians of Asia. Yogyakarta.

Papanek, Hanna, et al. 1976. *Women in Jakarta: Family Life and Family Planning*. Report to the Interdisciplinary Communications Program. Washington, D.C.

Rahardjo, Yulfita, et al. 1980. *Wanita Kota Jakarta: Kehidupan Keluarga dan Keluarga Berencana*. Yogyakarta: Gadjah Mada Univ. Press. (Trans. of Papanek et al. 1976.)

Sajogyo, Pudjiwati. 1983. "Impact of New Farming Technology on Women's Employment." Paper presented at the Conference on Women in Rice Farming Systems, IRRI, Los Banos, Philippines, 26–30 Sept.

Schwede, Laurel. Forthcoming. "Family Strategies of Labor Allocation and Decision Making in a Matrilineal, Islamic Society: The Minangkabau of West Sumatra, Indonesia." Ph.D. diss., Dept. of Anthropology, Cornell University.

Soewondo, Nani. 1984. *Kedudukan Wanita Indonesia Dalam Hukum dan Mas-*

yarakat [The position of Indonesian women in law and society] (4th rev. ed.). Jakarta: Ghalia Publ.

Stoler, Ann. 1975. "Some Socioeconomic Aspects of Rice Harvesting in a Javanese Village," *Masyarakat Indonesia*, 2, no. 1.

Sullivan, Norma. 1983. "Indonesian Women in Development: State Theory and Urban Kampung Practice." In Lenore Manderson, ed., *Women's Work and Women's Roles*. Canberra: ANU Press.

UI/FELD. 1973. *Indonesian Fertility-Mortality Survey 1973*. Jakarta: Universitas Indonesia Fakultas Ekonomi Lembaga Demografi.

United Nations Development Program. 1980. *Rural Women's Participation in Development*. Evaluation Study no. 3. New York.

World Development Report 1984. New York: Oxford Univ. Press.

MENCHER: Women's Work and Poverty

Bardhan, Pranab. 1974. "On Life and Death Questions," *Economic and Political Weekly*, 11:1293–1304.

Boserup, Ester. 1970. *Women's Role in Economic Development*. New York.

Gulati, Leela. 1981. *Profiles in Female Poverty*. New Delhi: Hindustan Publ. Co.

Mencher, Joan P. 1974. "The Caste System Upside Down: or the Not So Mysterious East," *Current Anthropology*, 15, no. 4:469–94.

————. 1978a. *Agriculture and Social Structure in Tamil Nadu: Past Origins, Present Transformations, and Future Prospects*. New Delhi: Allied Publs.

————. 1978b. "Agrarian Relations in Two Rice Regions of Kerala," *Economic and Political Weekly*, 13:349–66.

————. 1980. "The Lessons and Non-Lessons of Kerala: Agricultural Laborers and Poverty," *Economic and Political Weekly*, 15, nos. 1–2:41–43, 1781–1802.

————. 1982. "Agricultural Labourers and Poverty," *Economic and Political Weekly*, 17, nos. 1–2:38–43.

————. 1984. "What Constitutes Hard Work? Women as Laborers and as Managers in the Traditional Rice Regions of Kerala and Tamil Nadu." Paper presented at the American Anthropological Association Meeting in Denver, Nov. 14–18.

————. 1985a. "Landless Women Agricultural Labourers in India." In L. J. Unnevehr, ed., *Women in Rice Farming Systems*. Brookfield, Vt.: Gower Publ. Co.

————. 1985b. "Women Agricultural Labourers and Land Owners in Kerala and Tamilnadu: Some Questions About Gender and Autonomy in the Household." Paper presented at a Conference on Women and the Household in Asia, New Delhi, Jan. 27–31.

————. 1985c. "Women and Agricultural Labour: The Need for More Work." Photocopy.

————. 1986. "Women and Agriculture." In C. Mann and B. Huddelstan, eds., *Food Policy: Frameworks for Analysis and Action*. Bloomington: Indiana Univ. Press.

Mencher, Joan P., and D. D'Amico. 1986. "Kerala Women as Labourers and

Supervisors: Implications for Women and Development," in Leela Dube, Eleanor Leacock, and Shirley Ardener, eds., *Visibility and Power: Essays on Women in Society and Development*. New Delhi: Oxford Univ. Press.

Mencher, Joan P., and K. Saradamoni. 1982. "Muddy Feet, Dirty Hands: Rice Production and Female Agricultural Labour," *Economic and Political Weekly*, 17, no. 52: A149–67.

Mencher, Joan P., K. Saradamoni, and J. Panicker. 1979. "Women in Rice Cultivation: Some Research Tools," *Studies in Family Planning*, 10, no. 11: 408–11.

Miller, Barbara D. 1981. *The Endangered Sex: Neglect of Female Children in Rural North India*. Ithaca, N.Y.: Cornell Univ. Press.

Panikar, P. G. K. 1983. "Adoption of High Yielding Varieties of Rice in Kerala: A Study of Selected Villages in Palghat and Kuttanad." Paper, Centre for Development Studies, Trivandrum, India.

Rosenszweig, Mark R. and T. Paul Schultz. 1982. "Market Opportunities, Genetic Endowments, and Intrafamily Resource Distribution: Child Survival in Rural India," *American Economic Review*, 72, no. 4: 803–15.

Sen, Gita. 1983. "Paddy Production, Processing, and Women Workers in India— The South Versus the Northeast." In *Women in Rice Farming: Proceeding of a Conference on Rice Farming Systems*. Brookfield, Vt.: Gower Publ. Co.

Voluntary Health Association of India. 1980. *Arm Circumference Measuring Tape*. New Delhi. (Simplified cards for measuring the nutritional status of individuals and communities.)

Whitehead, Ann. 1981. "'I'm Hungry, Mum': The Politics of Domestic Budgeting." In Kate Young, Carol Wolkowitz, and Roslyn McCullagh, eds., *Of Marriage and the Market: Women's Subordination in International Perspective*. London: CSE Books.

Wijewardene, Ray. 1980. "'No-Till': A Tropical Revolution," *Mazingira*, 4, no. 1: 60–63.

HOODFAR: Household Budgeting in a Cairo Neighborhood

Bahr, J. 1974. "Effects of Power and Division of Labour Within the Family." In L. N. Hoffman and F. I. Nye, eds., *Working Mothers*. San Francisco: Jossey-Bass.

Brown, J. K. 1970a. "The Economic Organization and the Position of Women Among Iraqinois," *Ethnohistory*, 17: 151–67.

———. 1970b. "A Note on the Division of Labor by Sex," *American Anthropologist*, 72: 1073–78.

Dwyer, D. H. 1983. "Women and Income in the Third World: Implications for Policy." Population Council Working Paper no. 18. New York.

Engels, F. 1972. *The Origins of the Family and Private Property and the State*. Ed. E. B. Leacock. New York.

Gonzales Dela Rocha, M. 1984. "Domestic Organization and Reproduction of the Low Income Households: The Case of Guadalajara, Mexico." Ph.D. diss., Manchester University.

Gorer, G. 1971. *Sex and Marriage in England Today*. London.

Hammam, Mona. 1979. "Egypt's Working Women: Textile Workers of Chubra el-Kheima." In *Middle East Research and Information Project*, no. 82.

Hoodfar, H. 1986. "Impact of International Male Migration on Families Left Behind and the Position of Women: The Case of Lower Income Households in Cairo, Egypt." Unpublished paper.

Leacock, E. 1978. "Women's Status in an Egalitarian Society: Implications for Social Evolution," *Current Anthropologist*, 19, no. 2:247–75.

Macleod, A. E. 1984. Private communication in reference to her research on women and work in Cairo, 1983–84.

Maher, V. 1981. "Work, Consumption, and Authority Within the Household." In K. Young, C. Wolkowitz, and R. McCullagh, eds., *Of Marriage and the Market*. London.

Malinowski, B. 1963. *The Family Among the Australian Aborigines*. New York. Orig. ed. 1913.

McDonald, G. W. 1980. "Family Power: The Assessment of a Decade of Theory and Research, 1970–1979," *Journal of Marriage and the Family* (Nov.): 841–55.

Oakley, A. 1974. *Housewife: High Value, Low Cost*. New York.

Oppong, C. 1981. *Middle Class African Marriage*. London.

Pahl, J. 1980. "Pattern of Management Within Marriage," *Journal of Social Policy*, 9, no. 3.

————. 1982. *The Allocation of Money and the Structuring of Inequality Within Marriage*. Canterbury, Eng.: Health Center Research Unit, Univ. of Kent.

Roldan, M. 1982. "Intrahousehold Patterns of Money Allocation and Women's Subordination." Paper presented at the Conference on Women and Income Control in the Third World, Columbia University.

Sanday, P. R. 1974. "Female Status in the Public Domain." In M. Z. Rosaldo and L. Lamphere, eds., *Woman, Culture, and Society*. Stanford, Calif.

Shorter, E. 1978. "Women's Work: What Difference Does Capitalism Make?," *Theory and Society*, 3, no. 4:513–27.

Whitehead, A. 1981. "'I'm Hungry, Mum': The Politics of Domestic Budgeting." In K. Young, C. Wolkowitz, and R. McCullagh, eds., *Of Marriage and the Market*. London.

FAPOHUNDA: The Nonpooling Household

Adamu, S. O. 1970. "Some Aspects of Expenditure Patterns in Nigeria," *Nigerian Journal of Economics and Social Studies*, 12 (Nov.): 265–88.

Adejumobi, Elizabeth O. 1970. "Household Expenditure in Ibadan: A Statistical Analysis of Family Budget," *Nigerian Journal of Economics and Social Studies*, 12 (Nov.): 289–302.

Becker, Gary S. 1976. *The Economic Approach to Human Behavior*. Chicago.

————. 1981. *A Treatise on the Family*. Cambridge, Mass.

Boland, Lawrence A. 1979. "A Critique of Friedman's Critics," *Journal of Economic Literature*, 17 (June): 503–22.

Fapohunda, Eleanor R. 1988. "Urban Women's Occupational Roles and Nigerian

Government Strategies." In Christine Oppong, ed., *Sex Roles and West African Households*. London: James Currey.

Ferber, Robert. 1966. "Research on Household Behavior." In *Surveys of Economic Theory*, prepared for the American Economic Association and the Royal Economic Society. London.

Gupta, K. L. 1974. "A Model of Household Savings Behavior with an Application to the Indian Economy," *Journal of Development Studies*, 11 (Oct.): 91–97.

Guyer, Jane I. 1979. "Household Budgets and Women's Income." Boston University African Studies Center, Working Paper no. 28.

Jones, Christine. 1982. "Women's Labor Allocation and Irrigated Rice Production in Northern Cameroon." Paper prepared for the Conference of the International Association of Agricultural Economists, Jakarta, Aug. 30.

Karanja-Diejomaoh, W. M. 1978. "Disposition of Incomes by Husbands and Wives: An Exploratory Study of Families in Lagos." In C. Oppong et al., eds., *Marriage, Fertility, and Parenthood in West Africa*. Canberra.

———. 1980. "Women and Work: A Study of Female and Male Attitudes in the Modern Sector of an African Metropolis." In Fred Omu et al., eds., *Proceedings of the National Conference on Integrated Rural Development and Women in Development*. University of Benin, Center for Social, Cultural and Environmental Research.

Kelley, Allen C., and J. G. Williamson. 1968. "Household Savings Behavior in the Developing Economies: The Indonesian Case," *Economic Development and Cultural Change*, 16 (Apr.): 385–403.

Kuhn, Thomas S. 1962. *The Structure of Scientific Revolutions*. Chicago.

Lewis, Barbara C. 1977. "Economic Activity and Marriage Among Ivorian Urban Women." In Alice Schlegel, ed., *Sexual Stratification: A Cross-Cultural View*. New York.

Manser, Marilyn, and Murray Brown. N.d. "Bargaining Analyses of Household Decisions." Mimeo., Dept. of Economics, SUNY at Buffalo.

Oppong, Christine. 1981. *Middle-Class African Marriage*. London.

Philippine Economic Journal. 1978, Vol. 17.

Rosenszweig, Mark R., and Robert E. Evenson. 1977. "Fertility, Schooling, and the Economic Contribution of Children in Rural India," *Econometrica*, 45 (Sept.): 1065–80.

Strober, Myra H. 1977. "Wives' Labor Force Behavior and Family Consumption Patterns," *American Economic Papers and Proceedings*, 67 (Feb.): 410–17.

Strober, Myra H., and Charles B. Weinberg. 1977. "Working Wives and Major Family Expenditures," *Journal of Consumer Research*, 4 (Dec.): 141–47.

GUYER: Dynamic Approaches to Domestic Budgeting

Becker, Gary S. 1981. *A Treatise on the Family*. Cambridge, Mass.

Binet, Jacques. 1956. *Budgets familiaux des planteurs de cacao au Cameroun*. Paris.

Booth, Charles. 1889. *Labour and Life of the People*. London.

Boserup, Ester. 1970. *Woman's Role in Economic Development*. New York.

Deane, Phyllis. 1949. "Problems of Surveying Village Economies," *Rhodes-Livingstone Journal*, 8:42–49.

Dutta Roy, D. K., and S. J. Mabey. 1968. *Household Budget Survey in Ghana*. University of Ghana, Institute of Statistics, Technical Publication Series no. 2. Legon.

Edholm, F., O. Harris, and K. Young. 1977. "Conceptualizing Women," *Critique of Anthropology*, 3, no. 9–10:101–30.

Emecheta, Buchi. 1979. *The Joys of Motherhood*. New York.

Fortes, M., R. W. Steel, and P. Ady. 1948. "Ashanti Survey 1945–46: An Experiment in Social Research," *Geographical Journal*, 110, no. 4–6: 149–79.

Galletti, R., K. D. S. Baldwin, and I. O. Dina. 1956. *Nigerian Cocoa Farmers*. London.

Gold Coast. 1957. *Accra Survey of Household Budgets*. Feb. 1953. Office of the Government Statistician.

Golding, P. T. F. 1962. "An Enquiry into Household Expenditure and Consumption and Sale of Household Produce in Ghana," *Bulletin of the Economic Society of Ghana*, 6, no. 4:11–33.

Goody, Jack. 1976. *Production and Reproduction: A Comparative Study of the Domestic Domain*. Cambridge, Eng.

Guyer, Jane I. 1981. "Household and Community in African Studies," *African Studies Review*, 24, no. 2–3:87–137.

———. 1984. *Family and Farm in Southern Cameroon*. Boston University African Studies Center, Africa Research Studies no. 15.

Hill, Polly. 1972. *Rural Hausa: A Village and a Setting*. Cambridge, Eng.

———. 1975. "The West African Farming Household." In J. Goody, ed., *Changing Social Structure in Ghana*. London: Int'l African Institute.

Houthakker, H. S. 1957. "An International Comparison of Household Expenditure Patterns, Commemorating the Centenary of Engel's Law," *Econometrica*, 25:532–51.

Kaberry, Phyllis. 1952. *Women of the Grassfields*. London.

Kenya Colony and Protectorate. 1951. "The Pattern of Income, Expenditure, and Consumption of African Labourers in Nairobi, Oct.–Nov. 1950." Nairobi: East African Statistical Dept.

Laburthe-Tolra, Philippe. 1981. *Les Seigneurs de la forêt*. Paris.

Lawson, Rowena. 1962. "Engel's Law and Its Application to Ghana," *Bulletin of the Economic Society of Ghana*, 6, no. 4:34–46.

———. 1972. *The Changing Economy of the Lower Volta, 1954–1967*. London.

McCall, Daniel. 1961. "Trade and the Role of Wife in a Modern West African Town." In A. Southall, ed., *Social Change in Modern Africa*. London.

Medawar, P. B. 1967. *The Art of the Soluble*. London.

Meillassoux, Claude. 1981. *Maidens, Meal and Money*. Cambridge, Eng.

Muntemba, Maud. 1980. "Regional and Social Differentiation in Broken Hill Rural District, Northern Rhodesia, 1930–1964." In M. Klein, ed., *Peasants in Africa*. Beverly Hills, Calif.: Sage.

Netting, Robert McC. 1981. *Balancing on an Alp*. Cambridge, Eng.

Raynaut, Claude. 1977. "Aspects Socio-économiques de la préparation et de la circulation de la nourriture dans un village Hausa (Niger)," *Cahiers d'études Africaines*, 17, no. 4:569–97.

Rowntree, D. S. 1902. *Poverty*. London.

Sanjek, Roger. 1982. "The Organization of Households in Adabraka: Toward a Wider Comparative Perspective," *Comparative Studies in Society and History*, 24, no. 1:57–103.

Société d'Etudes pour le Développement Economique et Sociale. 1964–65. *Le Niveau de vie des populations de la Zone Cacaoyère du Centre Cameroun*. Yaoundé: Direction de la Statistique.

Williams, Gavin. 1981. "Inequalities in Rural Nigeria." University of East Anglia Occasional Paper no. 16. Norwich.

Winter, G. 1970. *Méthodologie des Enquêtes "niveau de vie" en milieu rural africain*. Paris.

Yanagisako, Sylvia. 1979. "Family and Household: The Analysis of Domestic Groups," *Annual Review of Anthropology*, 8:16–205.

MUNACHONGA: Marriage Options in Urban Zambia

Abu, K. 1983. "The Separateness of Spouses: Conjugal Resources in an Ashanti Town." In C. Oppong, ed., *Female and Male in West Africa*. London.

Bardouille, R. 1982. "Men and Women's Work Opportunities in the Informal Sector," *Manpower Research Report*, no. 10. Lusaka: Inst. for African Studies, Univ. of Zambia.

Brandel, M. 1958. "Urban Lobolo Attitudes: A Preliminary Report," *African Studies*, 17, no. 1:34–50.

Brelsford, W. V., ed. 1965. *The Tribes of Zambia* (2d ed.). Lusaka.

Central Statistical Office of Zambia. 1964. *Monthly Digest of Statistics*, no. 2 (May). Lusaka.

———. 1975. *Registered Births, Marriages, and Deaths (Vital Statistics)* (Mar.). Lusaka.

———. 1982. *Monthly Digest of Statistics*. 183, nos. 4–6. Lusaka.

Chauncey, G. 1981. "The Locus of Reproduction: Women's Labour in the Zambian Copperbelt, 1927–1953," *Journal of Southern African Studies*, 7, no. 2: 135–64.

Colson, E. 1950. "Possible Repercussions of the Right to Make Wills Among the Plateau Tonga of Northern Rhodesia," *Journal of African Administration*, no. 2:24–34.

———. 1958. *Marriage and the Family Among the Plateau Tonga of Northern Rhodesia*. Manchester, Eng.

Cutrufelli, M. R. 1983. *Women of Africa: Roots of Oppression*. London: Zed Press.

Daniel, P. 1979. *Africanisation, Nationalisation and Inequality: Mining Labour and the Copperbelt in Zambian Development*. Cambridge, Eng.

Elliott, C., ed. 1971. *Constraints on the Economic Development of Zambia*. London.

Epstein, A. L. 1981. *Urbanisation and Kinship: The Domestic Domain on the Copperbelt of Zambia, 1950–1956*. London.

Fielder, R. 1973. "The Role of Cattle in the Ila Economy: A Conflict of Views on the Uses of Cattle by the Ila of Namwala," *African Social Research*, no. 15 (June): 327–61.

Forde, C. D., and A. P. Radcliffe-Brown, eds. 1950. *African Systems of Kinship and Marriage*. London.

Gann, L. H. 1958. *The Birth of a Plural Society: The Development of Northern Rhodesia Under the British South Africa Company, 1894–1914*. Manchester, Eng.

———. 1964. *A History of Northern Rhodesia: Early Days to 1953*. London.

Gelfand, M. 1961. *Northern Rhodesia in the Days of the Charter: A Medical and Social Study*. Oxford.

Gluckman, M. 1950. "Kinship and Marriage among the Lozi of Northern Rhodesia and the Zulu of Natal." In C. D. Forde and A. P. Radcliffe-Brown, eds., *African Systems of Kinship and Marriage*. London.

Gugler, J. 1968. "The Impact of Labour Migration on Society and Economy in Sub-Saharan Africa: Empirical Findings and Theoretical Considerations," *African Social Research*, 6:46–85.

Hall, R. 1965. *Zambia*. London: Pall Mall Press.

Hansen, K. T. 1975. "Married Women and Work: Explorations from an Urban Case Study," *African Social Research*, no. 20 (Dec.): 777–79.

———. 1980. "When Sex Becomes a Critical Variable: Married Women's Extra-Domestic Work in Lusaka, Zambia," *African Social Research*, no. 30:831–50.

Hastings, A. 1973. *Christian Marriage in Africa*. London.

Heisler, H. 1974. *Urbanisation and the Government of Migration: The Inter-Relation of Urban and Rural Life in Zambia*. London.

Hunt, P. 1980. "Cash Transaction and Household Tasks: Domestic Behaviour in Relation to Industrial Employment," *Sociological Review*, 26:555–71.

Law Development Commission of Zambia. 1976. *Working Paper on Customary Law of Succession*. Lusaka.

———. 1982. *Report on Law of Succession*. Lusaka.

Little, K. 1973. *African Women in Towns: An Aspect of Africa's Social Revolution*. London.

Mabeza, R. M. 1977. "The Changing Role of African Women in Development." M.A. thesis, Clark University.

McClain, W. T. 1970. "The Position of Women and Children Under Zambia's Customary Laws." In Mindolo Ecumenical Foundation, ed., *Women's Rights in Zambia: Report of a Consultation*. Kitwe, Zambia.

Munachonga, M. L. 1986. "Conjugal Relations in Urban Zambia: Aspects of Marriage Under the Marriage Ordinance." M. Phil. thesis. University of Sussex.

Mwanakatwe, J. M. 1968. *The Growth of Education in Zambia Since Independence*. Lusaka.

Ndulo, M. 1979. "Liability of a Paramour in Damages for Adultery in Customary Law," *African Social Research*, no. 28 (Dec.): 655–66.

Oppong, C. 1974. "Domestic Budgeting Among Some Salaried Urban Couples." In *Legon Family Research Papers*. Institute of African Studies, University of Ghana.

———. 1981. *Middle-Class African Marriage*. London.

Pahl, J. 1983. "The Allocation of Money and the Structuring of Inequality Within Marriage," *Sociological Review*, 31, no. 2: 237–62.

Parpart, J. L. 1983. "Class and Gender on the Copperbelt in Northern Rhodesian Copper Mines, 1926–1964." Boston University African Studies Center Working Paper no. 77.

Parsons, T. 1964. *Essays in Sociological Theory*. New York.

Paulme, D., ed. 1963. *Women of Tropical Africa*. London.

Pettman, J. 1974. *Zambia: Security and Conflict*. Blandford Hts., Eng.: Davison.

Powdermaker, H. 1962. *Copper Town: Changing Africa*. New York.

Richards, A. I. 1939. *Land, Labour and Diet in Northern Rhodesia*. London.

———. 1940. "Bemba Marriage and Modern Economic Conditions," *Rhodes-Livingstone Papers*, no. 4.

Sanyal, B. C., J. Case, P. S. Dow, and M. E. Jackman. 1976. *Higher Education and the Labour Market in Zambia: Expectations and Performance*. Lusaka: UNESCO, Univ. of Zambia.

Simons, H. J. 1979. "Zambia's Urban Situation." In B. Turok, ed., *Development in Zambia*. London: Zed Press.

Snelson, P. D. 1974. *Educational Development in Northern Rhodesia, 1883–1945*. Lusaka: NEDCOZ.

Sunday Times of Zambia. 1982. "Greedy Relatives Face Axe: News of Widows' Act Cheers Women." Oct. 10: 4.

———. 1982. "Kaunda Ticks off 'Vultures.'" Oct. 24: 7.

Times of Zambia. 1975. "Lobola—We Need to Educate People on Marriage Importance." Dec. 4: 6.

Vallenga, D. D. 1982. "Who Is a Wife? Legal Expressions of Heterosexual Conflict in Ghana." In C. Oppong, ed. *Female and Male in West Africa*. London.

Whitehead, A. 1981. "'I'm Hungry, Mum': The Politics of Domestic Budgeting." In K. Young, C. Wolkowitz, and R. McCullagh, eds., *Of Marriage and the Market*. London.

Young, M., and P. Willmott. 1957. *Family and Kinship in East London*. London.

Zambia. 1964. *UN/ECA/FAO Economic Survey Mission on the Economic Development of Zambia* (Seer's Report). Ndola, Zambia: Falcon Press.

———. 1969. *Zambian Manpower Report*. Office of the Vice-President. Lusaka.

———. 1977. *Final Report of the Zambian Managerial Manpower and Training Needs Survey of the Private and Parastatal Sectors: A Joint Project of the Government of Zambia, United Nations Development Programme and International Labour Organisation*. Office of the Prime Minister, Lusaka. Apr.

———. N.d. *Marriage*. Chapter 211 of *The Laws of Zambia*. Lusaka.

Zambia Association for Research and Development. 1985. *An Annotated Bibliography on Research on Zambian Women*. Lusaka.

Zambia Daily Mail. 1976. "Are Double Salaries the Cause of Conflicts in Marriage?" May 17: 3.

Zambia Information Services. 1983. "Changing Customary Law of Succession," *Z Magazine*, no. 121 (Jan.): 4–6.

PESSAR: Dominican Migration to the United States

Bach, Robert, and Lisa Schraml. 1982. "Migration, Crisis and Theoretical Conflict," *International Migration Review*, 16, no. 2 : 320–41.

Barret, Michele. 1980. *Women's Oppression Today*. London: Verso.

Beijer, G. 1969. "Modern Patterns of International Migratory Movements." In J. A. Jackson, ed., *Migration*. London.

Bray, David. 1982. "Rural/Urban and Class Determinants of International Labor Migration: The Case of the Dominican Republic." Paper presented at a meeting of the Northeastern Anthropological Association, Princeton, N.J.

———. 1984. "Economic Development: The Middle Class and International Migration in the Dominican Republic," *International Migration Review*, 18, no. 2 : 217–36.

Brown, Susan. 1972. "Coping with Poverty in the Dominican Republic: Women and Their Mates." Ph.D. diss., University of Michigan.

Cedeño, Victor Livio. 1975. *La cuestión agraria*. Santo Domingo.

Chayanov, A. V. 1966. *The Theory of Peasant Economy*. Homewood, Ill.

Coordinadora de Organizaciones Femeninas. N.d. *Jornada de Denuncia a la Violencia Contra La Mujer*. Santo Domingo.

Coulson, M., B. Magas, and H. Wainwright. 1975. "The Housewife and Her Labour Under Capitalism," *New Left Review*, 89 : 59–71.

Deere, Carmen Diana, and Alain de Janvry. 1979. "A Conceptual Framework for the Empirical Analysis of Peasants," *American Journal of Agricultural Economics*, 61 : 601–11.

Dinerman, Ina. 1978. "Patterns of Adaptation Among Households of U.S.-Bound Migrants from Michoacán, Mexico," *International Migration Review*, 12, no. 4 : 485–501.

Dore y Cabral, Carlos. 1979. *Problemas de la estructura agraria dominicana*. Santo Domingo: Taller.

Ferrán, Fernando. 1974. "La familia nuclear de la subcultura de la pobreza dominicana," *Estudios Sociales*, 27, no. 3 : 137–85.

Fox, Bonnie. 1980. *Hidden in the Household*. Toronto: The Women's Press.

Georges, Eugenia. 1984. "New Immigrants and the Political Process: Dominicans in New York." New York University Center for Latin American and Caribbean Studies, Occasional Paper no. 45.

González, Nancie. 1970. "Peasants' Progress: Dominicans in New York," *Caribbean Studies*, 10, no. 3 : 154–71.

———. 1976. "Multiple Migratory Experiences of Dominican Women," *Anthropological Quarterly*, 49, no. 1 : 36–43.

Grasmuck, Sherri. 1982. "The Impact of Emigration on National Development: Three Sending Communities in the Dominican Republic." New York University Center for Latin American and Caribbean Studies, Occasional Paper no. 33.

Guiliano Cury, Hugo. 1980. *Reflecciones acerca de la económia dominicana*. Santo Domingo: Editora Alfary Omega.

Gurak, Douglas, and Mary Kritz. 1982. "Settlement and Integration Processes of Dominicans and Colombians in New York City." Paper presented at the annual meeting of the American Sociological Association, San Francisco.

Gurak, Douglas, Mary Kritz, Manuel Ortega, and Brian Early. 1980. "Early Employment of Two Cohorts of Women in the Dominican Republic." Paper presented at the annual meeting of the American Sociological Association, New York.

Hartmann, Heidi. 1981. "The Family as a Locus of Gender, Class, and Political Struggle: The Example of Housework," *Signs*, 6, no. 3: 366–94.

Hendricks, Glenn. 1974. *The Dominican Diaspora: From the Dominican Republic to New York City—Villagers in Transition*. New York.

Instituto Dominicano de Estudios Aplicados. 1978. "La condición de la campesina dominicana y su participación en la económia." Secretaria de Estado de Agricultura.

International Labor Office. 1975. "Generación de empleo productivo y crecimiento económico: El caso de la República Dominicana." Geneva.

Jelin, Elizabeth. 1982. "A Micro-Social Indictment of Life-Style: The Organization of Expenditures Among Domestic Units of the Popular Sectors." Paper presented at a seminar on Demographic Research in Latin America, Mexico City.

Meillassoux, Claude. 1981. *Maidens, Meal and Money: Capitalism and the Domestic Community*. New York.

NACLA. 1982. "Dominican Republic—The Launching of Democracy," 16, no. 6: 1–35.

Oficina Nacional de Estadistica. 1971. *Censo nacional agropecuario*. Santo Domingo.

Pessar, Patricia. 1982a. "The Role of Households in International Migration," *International Migration Review*, 16, no. 2: 324–64.

———. 1982b. "Kinship Relations of Production in the Migration Process: The Case of Dominican Migration to the United States." New York University Center for Latin American and Caribbean Studies, Occasional Paper no. 32.

Piore, Michael. 1971. "The Dual Labor Market: Theory and Implication." In David Gordon, ed., *Problems in Political Economy: An Urban Perspective*. Lexington, Mass.

———. 1979. *Birds of Passage: Migrant Labor and Industrial Society*. Cambridge, Eng.

———. 1985. "The Role of Gender in Dominican Settlement in the United States." In June Nash and Helen Safa, eds., *Women and Change in Latin America*. South Hadley, Mass.: Bergin & Garvey.

Portes, Alejandro. 1978. "Migration and Underdevelopment," *Politics and Society*, 8: 1–48.

Rapp, Rayna. 1978. "Family and Class in Contemporary America: Notes Toward an Understanding of Ideology," *Science and Society*, 42, no. 3: 278–300.

Roberts, Kenneth. 1984. "Agricultural Development, Risk Diversification and Circular Migration in Rural Mexico." Manuscript.

Ross, Ellen, and Rayna Rapp. 1981. "Sex and Society: A Research Note from the Intersection of Social History and Cultural Anthropology," *Comparative Studies in Society and History*, 23, no. 2:51–72.

Sacks, Karen. 1979. *Sisters and Wives: The Past and Future of Sexual Equality.* Westport, Conn.: Greenwood.

Sassen-Koob, Saskia. 1980. "Immigrant and Minority Workers in the Organization of the Labor Process," *Journal of Ethnic Studies*, 8:1–34.

Schneider, David. 1980. *American Kinship: A Cultural Account.* Chicago.

Smale, Melinda. 1980. *Women in Mauritania: The Effects of Drought and Migration on Their Economic Status and Implications for Development Programs.* Washington, D.C.: AID.

Standing, Guy. 1981. "Migration Modes of Exploitation: Social Origins of Immobility and Mobility," *Journal of Peasant Studies*, 8, no. 2:173–211.

Tancer, Shoshona. 1973. "La Quesqueyana: The Dominican Women, 1940–1970." In Ann Pescatello, ed., *Female and Male in Latin America*. Pittsburgh, Pa.

Taylor, R. C. 1969. "Migration and Motivation: Study of Determination and Types." In J. A. Jackson, ed., *Migration*. London.

Tilly, Louise, and Joan Scott. 1978. *Women, Work, and Family*. New York.

Ugalde, Antonio, Frank Bean, and Gil Cardenas. 1979. "International Migration from the Dominican Republic: Findings from a National Survey," *International Migration Review*, 13, no. 2:235–54.

Urena, Ernesto Ezequiel, and Aracelis Ferreiras. 1980. "Modelo de dominación y sectores medios en la República Dominicana: 1966–1978." B.A. thesis, Universidad Autónoma de Santo Domingo.

Wallerstein, Immanuel, William Martin, and Tory Dickinson. 1979. "Household Structure and Process: Theoretical Concerns, Plus Data from Southern Africa and Nineteenth-Century United States." Paper presented at a colloquium on Production and Reproduction of the Labor Force, Fiore, Italy.

Wood, Charles. 1981. "Structural Change and Household Strategies: A Conceptual Framework for the Study of Rural Migration," *Human Organization*, 40, no. 4:338–43.

————. 1982. "Equilibrium and Historical-Structural Perspectives on Migration," *International Migration Review*, 16, no. 2:298–319.

Young, Kate. 1978. "Modes of Appropriation and the Sexual Division of Labour: A Case Study from Oaxaca, Mexico." In Annette Kuhn and Anne Marie Wolpe, eds., *Feminism and Materialism*. Boston.

SAFILIOS-ROTHSCHILD: Agrarian Reform in Rural Honduras

Agricultural Sector Assessment for Honduras. 1978. Tegucigalpa.

————. 1978. Annexes. Tegucigalpa: USAID Mission in Honduras.

Cain, Mead. 1979. "Class, Patriarchy, and Women's Work in Bangladesh," *Population and Development Review*, 5, no. 3:405–38.

Carr, Marilyn. 1979. "Women in Rural Senegal: Some Implications of Proposed Integrated Food and Nutrition Interventions." World Bank, Office of the Adviser on Women in Development. Washington, D.C. Mimeo.

Dalaya, C. K. 1978. "Report on a Socio-Economic Study of Unorganized Women Workers in the Slum Areas of Bombay City—A Pilot Project." Matunga, Bombay: Ramnarian Ruia College.

Dwyer, Daisy Hilse. 1983. "Women and Income in the Third World: Implications for Policy." The Population Council, International Programs Working Paper no. 18. New York.

Economic Survey of Latin America—1979. 1981. New York: UN Economic Commission for Latin America.

Engle, Patricia. 1982. "The Effect of Maternal Employment on Children's Welfare in Rural Guatemala." Manuscript.

Fapohunda, Eleanor. 1983. "The Non-Pooling Household: A Challenge to Theory." Paper presented at the Seminar on Women, Income, and Policy, New York, Mar. 15–16.

Honduras: Country Development Strategy Statement. 1980. Tegucigalpa: USAID Mission in Honduras.

Kumar, Shubh. 1978. "The Role of the Household Economy in Child Nutrition at Low Incomes: A Case Study in Kerala." Cornell University Occasional Paper no. 95.

Maldonado, Mario. 1981. "Agrarian Reform Efforts in Honduras." In *Conference on Land Tenure in Central America.* Washington, D.C.

McCormack, Jeanne, Martin Walsh, and Candace Nelson. 1986. *Women's Group Enterprises: A Study of the Structure of Opportunity on the Kenya Coast.* Boston: World Education.

Mencher, Joan. 1982. "Women's Work and Poverty: Their Contributions to Household Maintenance in Two Southern Indian Regions." Paper presented at the Conference on Women and Income Control in the Third World, Columbia University, Oct. 7–9.

———. 1983. "Women, Work, and Household Maintenance." Paper presented at the Seminar on Women, Income, and Policy, The Population Council, New York, Mar. 15–16.

Roldan, Martha. 1982. "Intrahousehold Patterns of Money Allocation and Women's Subordination." Paper presented at the Conference on Women and Income Control in the Third World, Columbia University, Oct. 7–9.

Safilios-Rothschild, Constantina. 1980. "The Role of the Family: A Neglected Aspect of Poverty." In Peter Knight, ed., *Implementing Programs of Human Development.* Washington, D.C.

———. 1981. "The Role of Women in Modernizing Agricultural Systems." Mimeo.

———. 1983a. "Women and the Agrarian Reform in Honduras," *Land Reform*, no. 1–2:115–24.

———. 1983b. *The Impact of Agrarian Reform on Men and Women in Honduras.* New York: The Population Council.

———. 1983c. *Women in Sheep and Goat Production and Marketing.* Rome: FAO.

Safilios-Rothschild, Constantina, and Marcellinus Dijkers. 1978. "Handling Unconventional Asymmetries." In Rhona and Robert N. Rappoport, eds., *Working Couples.* London.

Tinker, Irene. 1979. "New Technologies for Food Chain Activities: The Imperative of Equity for Women." Washington, D.C.: USAID. Mimeo.

Tripp, R. B. 1981. "Farmers and Traders: Some Economic Determinants of Nutritional Status in Northern Ghana," *Journal of Tropical Pediatrics and Environmental Child Health*, 27:15–22.

Wilson, A. B. 1981. "Longitudinal Analyses of Diet, Physical Growth, Verbal Development, and School Performance." In J. B. Balderston, A. B. Wilson, M. Freire, and M. Simonen, eds., *Malnourished Children of the Rural Poor*. Boston.

Women-in-Food-for-Work: The Bangladesh Experience. 1979. Rome: FAO.

FOLBRE: The Black Four of Hearts

Acharya, Meena, and Lynn Bennett. 1982. "Women and the Subsistence Sector: Economic Participation and Household Decision Making in Nepal." World Bank Staff Working Papers, no. 526.

Arizpe, Lourdes. 1982. "Relay Migration and the Survival of the Peasant Household." In Helen Safa, ed., *Towards a Political Economy of Urbanization in Third World Countries*. Delhi: Oxford Univ. Press.

Arrow, Kenneth. 1963. *Social Choice and Individual Values*. New Haven, Conn.

Becker, Gary. 1976. "A Theory of Marriage: The Economics of the Family," in his *The Economic Approach to Human Behavior*. Chicago.

———. 1981. *Treatise on the Family*. Cambridge, Mass.

Behrman, Jere, and William R. Kenan. 1984. "Intrahousehold Allocation of Nutrients in Rural India: Are Boys Favored? Do Parents Exhibit Inequality Aversion?" Manuscript, Dept. of Economics, Univ. of Pennsylvania.

Beneria, Lourdes. 1982. "Accounting for Women's Work." In *Women and Development: The Sexual Division of Labor in Rural Societies*. New York.

Beneria, Lourdes, and Gita Sen. 1981. "Accumulation, Reproduction, and Women's Role in Economic Development: Theoretical and Practical Implications," *Feminist Studies*, 8, no. 1:157–76.

Berkner, Lutz. 1973. "Recent Research on the History of the Family in Western Europe," *Journal of Marriage and the Family*, 35:395–405.

Boserup, Ester. 1970. *Women's Role in Economic Development*. London.

Bowles, Samuel. 1985. "The Production Process in a Competitive Economy: Walrasian, Neo-Hobbesian, and Marxian Models," *American Economic Review*, 75, no. 1:16–36.

Bowles, Samuel, and Herbert Gintis. 1970. "The Marxian Theory of Value and Heterogeneous Labour: A Critique and Reformulation," *Cambridge Journal of Economics*, 1, no. 2:173–92.

———. 1981. "Structure and Practice in the Labor Theory of Value," *Review of Radical Political Economics*, 12, no. 4:1–26.

Bruner, Jerome, and Leo Postman. 1949. "On the Perception of Incongruity: A Paradigm," *Journal of Personality*, 18:206–23.

Cain, Mead, S. R. A. Kahnam, and Shamour Nahar. 1979. "Class, Patriarchy, and the Structure of Women's Work in Rural Bangladesh," *Population and Development Review*, 5 (Sept.): 405–38.

Caldwell, John. 1981. *The Theory of Fertility Decline*. New York.

Chodorow, Nancy. 1978. *The Reproduction of Mothering*. Berkeley, Calif.

Deere, Carmen Diana. 1983. "The Allocation of Familial Labor and the Formation of Peasant Household Income in the Sierra." In Mayra Buvinic, Margaret A. Lycette, and William Paul McGreevey, eds., *Women and Poverty in the Third World*. Baltimore, Md.

Deere, Carmen Diana, and Alain de Janvry. 1979. "A Conceptual Framework for the Empirical Analysis of Peasants," *American Journal of Agricultural Economics*, 61, no. 4:601–11.

Engels, Friedrich. 1968. *The Origin of the Family, Private Property and the State*. Moscow. Orig. ed. 1884.

Ferguson, Ann. 1979. "Women as a New Revolutionary Class." In Pat Walker, ed., *Between Labor and Capital*. Boston: South End Books.

Feyerabend, Paul. 1975. *Against Method*. London.

———. 1978. *Science in a Free Society*. London.

Folbre, Nancy. 1982. "Exploitation Comes Home: A Critique of the Marxian Theory of Labour Power," *Cambridge Journal of Economics*, 6, no. 4:318–29.

———. 1983. "Of Patriarchy Born: The Political Economy of Fertility Decisions," *Feminist Studies*, 9, no. 2:261–84.

———. 1984. "The Feminization of Poverty and the Pauperization of Motherhood," *Review of Radical Political Economics*, 16, no. 4:72–88.

———. 1985. "The Wealth of Patriarchs: Deerfield, Massachusetts, 1760–1840," *Journal of Interdisciplinary History*, 16, no. 2:199–220.

Foucault, Michel. 1973. *The Order of Things: An Archaeology of the Human Sciences*. New York.

Friedman, Milton. 1953. "The Methodology of Positive Economics." In his *Essays in Positive Economics*. Chicago.

Gilligan, Carol. 1982. *In a Different Voice: Psychological Theory and Women's Development*. Cambridge, Mass.

Gronau, Reuben. 1973. "The Intrafamily Allocation of Time: The Value of Housewives' Time," *American Economic Review*, 63 (Sept.): 634–51.

Hartmann, Heidi. 1979. "Capitalism, Patriarchy, and Job Segregation by Sex." In Zillah R. Eisenstein, ed., *Capitalist Patriarchy and the Case for Socialist Feminism*. New York.

———. 1981. "The Family as a Locus of Gender, Class, and Political Struggle: The Example of Housework," *Signs*, 6:366–94.

Henn, Jeanne. 1982. "Towards a Materialist Analysis of Sexism." Manuscript, Dept. of Economics, Northeastern University.

Hindess, Barry, and Paul Hirst. 1975. *Precapitalist Modes of Production*. London.

Humphries, Jane. 1979. "Class Struggle and the Persistence of the Working Class Family," *Cambridge Journal of Economics*, 1, no. 3:241–58.

Hunt, E. K. 1979. *History of Economic Thought: A Critical Perspective*. Belmont, Calif.

Kuhn, Thomas. 1967. *The Structure of Scientific Revolutions. International Encyclopedia of Unified Science*, vol. 2, no. 2. Chicago.

Lapidus, Gail. 1978. *Women in Soviet Society*. Berkeley, Calif.

Maital, Shlomo, and Sharone Maital. 1984. *Economic Games People Play*. New York.

Mamdani, Mahmoud. 1981. "The Economics of Population." In Karen L. Michaelson, ed., *And the Poor Get Children: Radical Perspectives on Population Dynamics*. New York.

Manser, Marilyn, and Murray Brown. 1981. "Marriage and Household Decision Making: A Bargaining Analysis," *International Economic Review*, 22, no. 2: 333–49.

McCrate, Elaine. 1985. "The Rise of Nonmarriage in the U.S." Ph.D. diss., Dept. of Economics, University of Massachusetts.

McElroy, Marjorie, and Mary Jane Horney. 1981. "Nash Bargained Household Decisions: Toward a Generalization of the Theory of Demand," *International Economic Review*, June.

Meek, Ronald. 1962. "Economics and Ideology." In his *Economics and Ideology and Other Essays*. London.

Meillasoux, Claude. 1981. *Maidens, Meal and Money: Capitalism and the Domestic Community*. Cambridge, Eng.

Miller, Barbara. 1981. *The Endangered Sex: Neglect of Female Children in Rural North India*. Ithaca, N.Y.

Mosk, Carl. 1983. *Patriarchy and Fertility: Japan and Sweden, 1880–1960*. New York.

North, Douglas. 1981. *Structure and Change in Economic History*. New York.

Olsen, Mancur. 1975. *The Logic of Collective Action: Public Goods and the Theory of Groups*. Cambridge, Mass.

Parsons, Donald. 1984. "On the Economics of Intergenerational Control," *Population and Development Review*, 10, no. 1: 41–54.

Polanyi, Karl. 1944. *The Great Transformation*. New York.

Polatnick, M. Rivka. 1984., "Why Men Don't Rear Children: A Power Analysis." In Joyce Trebilcot, ed., *Mothering: Essays in Feminist Theory*. Totowa, N.J.

Pollak, Robert A. 1985. "A Transaction Cost Approach to Families and Households." *Journal of Economic Literature*, 23, no. 2: 581–608.

Poulantzas, Nicos. 1975. *Classes in Contemporary Capitalism*. London.

Pyle, Jeanne. 1985. "Female Employment in a Small Open Economy." Ph.D. diss., Dept. of Economics, University of Massachusetts.

Resnick, Steven, and Richard Wolff. 1982. "Classes in Marxian Theory," *Review of Radical Political Economy*, 13, no. 4: 1–18.

Roemer, John. 1982. *The General Theory of Exploitation*. Cambridge, Mass.

Rogers, Barbara. 1979. *The Domestication of Women: Discrimination in Developing Societies*. New York.

Rosenzweig, Mark, and T. Paul Schultz. 1982. "Market Opportunities, Genetic Endowments, and Intrafamily Resource Distribution," *American Economic Review*, 72 (Sept.): 803–15.

Rubery, Jill. 1978. "Structured Labor Markets, Worker Organization, and Low Pay," *Cambridge Journal of Economics*, 2: 17–36.

Safilios-Rothschild, Constantina. 1982. "Family Structure and Women's Reproductive and Productive Roles." In Richard Anker, Mayra Buvinic, and Nadia Youssef, eds., *Women's Roles and Population Trends in the Third World*. London.

Sahlins, Marshall. 1972. *Stone Age Economics*. Chicago.

Samuelson, Paul. 1956. "Social Indifference Curves," *Quarterly Journal of Economics*, 90 (Feb.): 1–22.

Schor, Juliet, and Samuel Bowles. 1984. "Conflict in the Employment Relation and the Cost of Job Loss." Discussion paper, Harvard Institute for Economic Research, Aug.

Schotter, Andrew. 1981. *An Economic Theory of Social Institutions*. London.

Schultz, T. Paul. 1981. *The Economics of Populations*. Reading, Mass.

Smith, Adam. 1937. *An Inquiry into the Nature and Causes of the Wealth of Nations*. New York. Orig. ed. 1776.

———. 1966. *The Theory of Moral Sentiments*. New York. Orig. ed. 1759.

Steedman, Ian. 1977. *Marx After Sraffa*. New York.

Thompson, E. P. 1978. *The Poverty of Theory and Other Essays*. New York.

Vogel, Lise. 1983. *Marxism and the Oppression of Women*. New Brunswick, N.J.

Wilson, E. O. 1975. *Sociobiology*. Cambridge, Mass.

Wright, Eric Olin. 1979. *Class Structure and Income Determination*. New York.

Library of Congress Cataloging-in-Publication Data

A Home divided : women and income in the Third World / Daisy
   Dwyer and Judith Bruce, editors.
      p.   cm.
      "A project of the Population Council"—Verso of t.p.
      Bibliography: p.
      ISBN 0-8047-1485-1 (alk. paper) :
      1. Women—Developing countries—Economic conditions.
2. Wages—Women—Developing countries.   3. Women—Employment—Developing countries.   I. Dwyer, Daisy Hilse.
II. Bruce, Judith.   III. Population Council.
HQ1870.9.H65 1988
305.4'3'091724—dc19   88-4938
                                                            CIP